UNIT 3
Problems Influencing Personal Growth

The concepts in bold italics are developed in the article. For further expansion, please refer to the Topic Guide and the Index.

D0217784

UNIT 4
Relating to Others

The concepts in bold italics are developed in the article. For further expansion, please refer to the Topic Guide and the Index.

UNIT 5
The Individual and Society

UNIT 6
Enhancing Human Adjustment: Learning to Cope Effectively

The concepts in bold italics are developed in the article. For further expansion, please refer to the Topic Guide and the Index.

The concepts in bold italics are developed in the article. For further expansion, please refer to the Topic Guide and the Index.

Topic Guide

This topic guide suggests how the selections in this book relate to the subjects covered in your course. You may want to use the topics listed on these pages to search the Web more easily.

On the following pages a number of Web sites have been gathered specifically for this book. They are arranged to reflect the units of this *Annual Edition.* You can link to these sites by going to the student online support site at *http://www.mhcls.com/online/.*

ALL THE ARTICLES THAT RELATE TO EACH TOPIC ARE LISTED BELOW THE BOLD-FACED TERM.

Adolescents
20. The Divided Self

Adulthood
15. The Biology of Aging
21. Staving Off Middle-Age Spread Requires Portion Control and Plenty of Exercise
22. Lost & Found

Aging
15. The Biology of Aging
21. Staving Off Middle-Age Spread Requires Portion Control and Plenty of Exercise
22. Lost & Found

Alzheimer's disease
22. Lost & Found

Ambition
12. Ambition: Why Some People Are Most Likely to Succeed

Behaviorism
3. Skepticism of Caricatures: B.F. Skinner Turns 100

Biological issues
5. Nature Versus Nurture: How Is Child Psychopathology Developed?
6. Empirical Science for the Spotless Mind
8. Genetic Influence on Human Psychological Traits
9. The Amazing Brain: Is Neuroscience the Key to What Makes Us Human?
10. His Brain, Her Brain
15. The Biology of Aging
22. Lost & Found
38. Brain Imaging Struggles for Psychiatric Respect

Brain
9. The Amazing Brain: Is Neuroscience the Key to What Makes Us Human?
10. His Brain, Her Brain
22. Lost & Found
38. Brain Imaging Struggles for Psychiatric Respect

Brain imaging
9. The Amazing Brain: Is Neuroscience the Key to What Makes Us Human?
38. Brain Imaging Struggles for Psychiatric Respect

Children
5. Nature Versus Nurture: How Is Child Psychopathology Developed?
17. The Importance of Resilience
18. Kaleidoscope of Parenting Cultures
19. What American Schools Can Learn from Hogwarts School of Witchcraft and Wizardry
20. The Divided Self
30. Nurturing Empathy

Communication
36. Life-Saving Communication

Computers
20. The Divided Self

Culture
11. Cultural Psychology: Studying the Exotic Other
18. Kaleidoscope of Parenting Cultures

Death
23. Good Life, Good Death

Disasters
36. Life-Saving Communication
37. Soldier Support

Education
18. Kaleidoscope of Parenting Cultures
19. What American Schools Can Learn from Hogwarts School of Witchcraft and Wizardry
33. 50th Anniversary: Brown v. Board of Education

Emotional intelligence
25. Feeling Smart: The Science of Emotional Intelligence
26. What's Your Emotional IQ?

Emotions
25. Feeling Smart: The Science of Emotional Intelligence
41. Body of Emotion
42. 20 Weeks to Happiness

Environment
5. Nature Versus Nurture: How Is Child Psychopathology Developed?
18. Kaleidoscope of Parenting Cultures
19. What American Schools Can Learn from Hogwarts School of Witchcraft and Wizardry
20. The Divided Self

Freud, Sigmund
2. Freud in Our Midst

Friends
28. Relationships, Human Behavior, and Psychological Science
29. Budding Friendships Fill Out the Family Tree

Gender
10. His Brain, Her Brain
32. The Emperor's New Woes

Genes
5. Nature Versus Nurture: How Is Child Psychopathology Developed?
6. Empirical Science for the Spotless Mind
7. Nature vs. Nurture: Two Brothers With Schizophrenia
8. Genetic Influence on Human Psychological Traits

Internet References

The following Internet sites have been carefully researched and selected to support the articles found in this reader. The easiest way to access these selected sites is to go to our student online support site at *http://www.mhcls.com/online/*.

AE: Personal Growth and Behavior 07/08

The following sites were available at the time of publication. Visit our Web site—we update our student online support site regularly to reflect any changes.

General Sources

Chicago Institute of Rehabilitation
http://lifecenter.rehabchicago.org/
A site sponsored by the Chicago Institute of Rehabilitation with a special section on wellness. The site provides downloadable articles, links to other sites related to mental health and wellness, as well as tip sheets and other valuable resources relevant to personal growth and adjustment.

National Institute of Child Health and Human Development (NICHD)
http://www.nichd.nih.gov
The NICHD conducts and supports research on the reproductive, neurobiologic, developmental, and behavioral processes that determine and maintain the health of children and adults.

National Institute of Mental Health
http://www.nimh.nih.gov/publicat/index.cfm
This site contains information from the National Institute of Mental Health, which is charged with the responsibility of researching mental disorders and educating the public.

Psychnet
http://www.apa.org/psychnet/
Get information on psychology from this Web site through the site map or by using the search engine. Access *APA Monitor,* the American Psychological Association newspaper; APA Books on a wide range of topics; PsychINFO, an electronic database of abstracts on over 1,350 scholarly journals; and HelpCenter for information on dealing with modern life problems.

UNIT 1: Becoming a Person: Foundations

Abraham A. Brill Library
http://plaza.interport.net/nypsan/service.html
The Abraham A. Brill Library, perhaps the largest psychoanalytic library in the world, contains data on over 40,000 books, periodicals, and reprints in psychoanalysis and related fields. Its holdings span the literature of psychoanalysis from its beginning to the present day.

JungWeb
http://www.cgjungboston.com/
Dedicated to the work of Carl Jung, this site is a comprehensive resource for Jungian psychology. Links to Jungian psychology, reference materials, graduate programs, dreams, multilingual sites, and related Jungian themes are available.

Sigmund Freud and the Freud Archives
http://plaza.interport.net/nypsan/freudarc.html
Internet resources related to Sigmund Freud can be accessed through this site. A collection of libraries, museums, and biographical materials, as well as the Brill Library archives, can be found here.

UNIT 2: Determinants of Behavior: Motivation, Environment, and Physiology

American Psychological Society (APS)
http://www.psychologicalscience.org
APS membership includes a diverse group of the world's foremost scientists and academics working to expand basic and applied psychological science knowledge. Links to teaching, research, and graduate studies resources are available.

Federation of Behavioral, Psychological, and Cognitive Science
http://www.thefederationonline.org/
At this site you can hotlink to the National Institutes of Health's medical database, government links to public information on mental health, a social psychology network, and the Project on the Decade of the Brain.

Max Planck Institute for Psychological Research
http://www.mpipf-muenchen.mpg.de/BCD/bcd_e.htm
Several behavioral and cognitive development research projects are available on this site.

The Opportunity of Adolescence
http://www.winternet.com/~webpage/adolescencepaper.html
This paper calls adolescence the turning point, after which the future is redirected and confirmed, and goes on to discuss the opportunities and problems of this period to the individual and society, using quotations from Erik Erikson, Jean Piaget, and others.

Psychology Research on the Net
http://psych.hanover.edu/Research/exponnet.html
Psychologically related experiments on the Internet can be found at this site. Biological psychology/neuropsychology, clinical psychology, cognition, developmental psychology, emotions, general issues, health psychology, personality, sensation/ perception, and social psychology are addressed.

Serendip
http://serendip.brynmawr.edu/serendip/
Organized into five subject areas (brain and behavior, complex systems, genes and behavior, science and culture, and science education), Serendip contains interactive exhibits, articles, links to other resources, and a forum area for comments and discussion.

UNIT 3: Problems Influencing Personal Growth

Adolescence: Changes and Continuity
http://www.oberlin.edu/faculty/ndarling/adolesce.htm
This site offers a discussion of puberty, sexuality, biological changes, cross-cultural differences, and nutrition for adolescents, including obesity and its effects on adolescent development.

Facts for Families
http://www.aacap.org/info_families/index.htm
The American Academy of Child and Adolescent Psychiatry provides concise, up-to-date information on issues that affect teenagers and their families. Fifty-six fact sheets include many teenager's issues.

Mental Health Infosource: Disorders

http://www.mhsource.com/disorders/

This no-nonsense page lists hotlinks to psychological disorder pages, including anxiety, panic, phobic disorders, schizophrenia, and violent/self-destructive behaviors.

Mental Health Risk Factors for Adolescents

http://education.indiana.edu/cas/adol/mental.html

This collection of Web resources is useful for parents, educators, researchers, health practitioners, and teens. It covers a great deal, including abuse, conduct disorders, and stress.

Suicide Awareness: Voices of Education

http://www.save.org

This is the most popular suicide site on the Internet. It is very thorough, with information on dealing with suicide (both before and after), along with material from the organization's many education sessions.

UNIT 4: Relating to Others

Emotional Intelligence Discovery

http://www.cwrl.utexas.edu/~bump/Hu305/3/3/3/

This site has been set up by students to talk about and expand on Daniel Goleman's book, *Emotional Intelligence*. There are links to many other EI sites.

The Personality Project

http://www.personality-project.org/personality.html

The Personality Project of William Revelle, director of the Graduate Program in Personality at Northwestern University, is meant to guide those interested in personality theory and research to the current personality research literature.

UNIT 5: The Individual and Society

AFF Cult Group Information

http://www.csj.org/index.html

Information about cults, cult groups, and psychological manipulation is available at this page sponsored by the secular, not-for-profit, tax-exempt research center and educational organization, American Family Foundation.

National Clearinghouse for Alcohol and Drug Information

http://www.health.org

This is an excellent general site for information on drug and alcohol facts that might relate to adolescence and the issues of peer pressure and youth culture. Resources, referrals, research and statistics, databases, and related Internet links are among the options available at this site.

UNIT 6: Enhancing Human Adjustment: Learning to Cope Effectively

John Suler's Teaching Clinical Psychology Site

http://www.rider.edu/users/suler/tcp.html

This page contains Internet resources for clinical and abnormal psychology, behavioral medicine, and mental health.

Health Information Resources

http://www.health.gov/nhic/Pubs/tollfree.htm

Here is a long list of toll-free numbers that provide health-related information. None offer diagnosis and treatment, but some do offer recorded information; others provide personalized counseling, referrals, and/or written materials.

Knowledge Exchange Network (KEN)

http://www.mentalhealth.org

The CMHS National Mental Health Services Exchange Network (KEN) provides information about mental health via toll-free telephone services, an electronic bulletin board, and publications. It is a one-stop source for information and resources on prevention, treatment, and rehabilitation services for mental illness, with many links to related sources.

Mental Health Net

http://www.mentalhealth.net

This comprehensive guide to mental health online features more than 6,300 individual resources. It covers information on mental disorders, professional resources in psychology, psychiatry, and social work, journals, and self-help magazines.

Mind Tools

http://www.mindtools.com/

Useful information on stress management can be found at this Web site.

NetPsychology

http://www.psychology.info/

This site explores the uses of the Internet to deliver mental health services. This is a basic cybertherapy resource site.

We highly recommend that you review our Web site for expanded information and our other product lines. We are continually updating and adding links to our Web site in order to offer you the most usable and useful information that will support and expand the value of your Annual Editions. You can reach us at: *http://www.mhcls.com/annualeditions/*.

UNIT 1

Becoming a Person: Foundations

Unit Selections

1. **Carl Rogers's Life and Work: An Assessment on the 100th Anniversary of His Birth**, Howard Kirschenbaum
2. **Freud in Our Midst**, Jerry Adler
3. **Skepticism of Caricatures: B.F. Skinner Turns 100**, Scott T. Gaynor
4. **Psychology of Safety: The "Big Five" and You: How Personality Traits Can Affect Behavior**, Scott Geller

Key Points to Consider

- What are the various theories of psychology? What do they say about human nature?

- Do you think any one theory is better than another? Why?

- Which theory of human nature best describes you? Why?

- Which theories promote the idea of personal growth?

- Which theories address the need for adjustment and coping?

- What role does culture play in shaping who we are?

Student Web Site

www.mhcls.com/online

Internet References

Further information regarding these Web sites may be found in this book's preface or online.

Abraham A. Brill Library
http://plaza.interport.net/nypsan/service.html

JungWeb
http://www.cgjungboston.com/

Sigmund Freud and the Freud Archives
http://plaza.interport.net/nypsan/freudarc.html

A baby sits in front of a mirror and looks at himself. A chimpanzee sorts through photographs while its trainer carefully watches its reactions. A college student answers a survey on how she feels about herself. What does each of these events share with the others? All are examples of techniques used to investigate self-concept.

That baby in front of the mirror has a red dot on his nose. Researchers watch to see if the baby reaches for the dot in the mirror or touches his own nose. Recognizing the fact that the image he sees in the mirror is his own, the baby touches his real nose, not the nose in the mirror.

The chimpanzee has been trained to sort photographs into two piles—human pictures or animal pictures. If the chimp has been raised with humans, the researcher wants to know into which pile (animal or human) the chimp will place its own picture. Is the chimp's concept of itself animal or human? Or does the chimp have no concept of self at all?

The college student taking the self-survey answers questions about her body image, whether or not she thinks she is fun to be with, whether or not she spends large amounts of time in fantasy, and what her feelings are about her personality and intellect.

These research projects are designed to investigate how self-concept develops and steers our behaviors and thoughts. Most psychologists believe that people develop a personal identity or a sense of self, which is a sense of who we are, our likes and

dislikes, our characteristic feelings and thoughts, and an understanding of why we behave as we do. Self-concept is our knowledge of our gender, race, and age, as well as our sense of self-worth and more. Strong positive or negative feelings are usually attached to this identity. Psychologists are studying how and when this sense of self develops. Most psychologists do not believe that infants are born with a sense of self but rather that children slowly develop self-concept as a consequence of their experiences.

This unit delineates some of the popular viewpoints regarding how sense of self, personality, and behavior develop. The knowledge of how self develops provides an important foundation for the rest of the units in this book. This unit explores major theories or forces in psychology: self or humanistic, behavioral, psychoanalytic, and trait theories.

The first article reviews an interesting question regarding personal growth and development. In "Carl Rogers' Life and Work: An Assessment on the 100th Anniversary of his Birth," author Howard Kirschenbaum reviews the work of the seminal humanistic psychologist and psychotherapist, Carl Rogers. Rogers postulated that the development of the self in childhood guides the rest of our journey through life. Specifically, Carl Rogers, with fellow humanistic psychologist Abraham Maslow, proposed that humans have an innate tendency to self-actualize or to optimize their potential over a lifetime unless that potential is damaged in childhood.

1

This unit examines small and therefore fairly intimate interpersonal relationships such those among friends and married couples. The next unit examines the effects of a much larger group, specifically, American society.

In the first article, "Mirror, Mirror: Seeing Yourself as Others See You," the author discusses how others perceive you. Accurately gauging how others judge you is important to traversing the social world *and* helping you establish your self-identity. Inaccurate perceptions can create a myriad of psychological and social problems for an individual.

In the next series of articles, various factors that enhance or inhibit our relationships with others are discussed. The next two articles review a fairly important concept—emotional intelligence or EQ. Emotional intelligence relates to our ability to get along with and be sensitive to other people's needs and emotions. It also enables us to interpret accurately our own feelings and needs. Emotional intelligence therefore is important to our success in interpersonal interactions.

A related ability is the capacity to discern the self from others. Some individuals, however, carry this tendency too far. In an extreme way, they grossly differentiate their *own group* from *other groups*, known respectively as the in-group and the out-group.

This tendency is particularly strong relative to racial or ethnic groups. In "Us vs. Them," Raphael Cushnir criticizes this propensity and suggests ways we can stop being so judgmental of others and the groups to which they belong.

Our self-concept and our ability to distinguish ourselves from others are important to interpersonal relationships. However, developing *healthy* relationships goes beyond simply knowing others and deciding whether they are similar or different from us. Two articles address this point. In "Relationships, Human Behavior, and Psychological Science," the authors review research that demonstrates all the positive ways interpersonal connectedness is good for us. A companion article on friendships, "Budding Friendships Fill Out the Family Tree," contends that close friendships are filling the void left by social mobility and the geographic move away from nuclear families. Good friends in faraway places offer the same social support and therefore positive health outcomes offered by good families.

In "Contagious Behavior," the author contends that certain behaviors, beyond yawns, are passed ("caught") from one person to another—often without anyone's awareness. Even psychogenic (loosely, imaginary) illnesses can be thusly contagious.

Carl Rogers's Life and Work

An Assessment on the 100th Anniversary of His Birth

HOWARD KIRSCHENBAUM

Carl Rogers (1902–2002) was America's most influential counselor and psychotherapist—and one of its most prominent psychologists. On the occasion of the 100th anniversary of his birth, it seems fitting to review his life, work, and professional contributions and to assess his historical and current influence on counseling and counseling psychology.

Early Years

Born in Oak Park, Illinois, a suburb of Chicago, Rogers was the third son in a family of five brothers and a sister. His parents, Walter and Julia Rogers, were conservative, Protestant Midwesterners who led family prayers daily and tried to keep their children free from society's corrupt influences. Hence, Carl had few real friends outside the family. He was a sensitive child, easily hurt by the family's teasing. The expression of feelings was not encouraged in the Rogers family, so Carl's emotions and imagination were often expressed in creative school papers and childhood games. (Biographical detail throughout is derived from Kirschenbaum, 1979, 1995; Rogers, 1967; and Rogers & Russell, 2002.)

Walter Rogers owned a successful construction company business, and when Carl was a teenager, his father purchased a working farm and manor house in Glen Ellen, Illinois, where he moved the family. Here Carl developed a love of nature and a serious working knowledge of scientific method, as he and his younger brothers conducted agricultural experiments on a plot they managed. As a result, Rogers decided to become a farmer.

He enrolled in the University of Wisconsin at Madison, following in his father and older siblings' footsteps. There he made his first close friends, and after a series of Christian revival meetings, he experienced the call to religious work, switching majors from agriculture to history as a better preparation for the ministry. In his junior year, he was selected as 1 of 10 American students to attend an international Christian youth conference in China—a trip that lasted 6 months and helped broaden his religious and social philosophy. Now motivated more by the "social gospel" than theological conviction, he applied to the liberal Union Theological Seminary in New York City. Upon college graduation, he married his childhood friend and college sweetheart, art student Helen Elliott—a union that would last 55 years.

New York City—Choosing a Profession

In addition to studying at the Seminary, Rogers also took psychology courses at the adjoining Teachers College of Columbia University. There his religious doubts combined with his fascination with psychology and progressive education. Influenced by instructors Leta Hollingworth, Goodwin Watson, and William Heard Kilpatrick, the leading interpreter of John Dewey's education philosophy, Rogers transferred to Teachers College to pursue a doctorate in clinical psychology.

At Columbia he was exposed to the testing and measurement movement of E. L. Thorndike, but this was balanced by his clinical fellowship at the Institute for Child Guidance, where he encountered Freudian thought, a lecture by Alfred Adler, Rorschach testing, and other psychoanalytic and psychiatric approaches. Seeking to integrate psychological measurement with clinical practice, Rogers came to appreciate the importance of understanding clients' inner world while also objectively assessing the outcomes of treatment.

Rogers's (1931a) doctoral dissertation, in which he created a test for measuring personality adjustment in children 9 to 13 years of age, combined both subjective and objective measures, from children's self-reports of their feelings to assessment by outside observers. On the basis of his dissertation, Rogers's (1931b) Personality Adjustment Inventory was published by the YMCA's press and sold a half million copies over a period of 50 years.

Rochester—Years of Experimentation

While working on his dissertation, Rogers needed to find a job to support himself, Helen, 2-year-old David, and Natalie, who was on the way. In 1928, however, jobs for clinical psychologists were not easy to come by, so he ended up taking a position in Rochester, New York, some 300 miles from New York City, where his academic colleagues predicted he would never be heard from again. There he spent the next 12 years—as director of the Child Study Department of the Rochester Society for the

Prevention of Cruelty to Children and then director of the new Rochester Guidance Center.

Rogers's years in Rochester provided a laboratory in which he worked with thousands of troubled children and adults and gradually developed his own ideas about counseling and psychotherapy. During this period, he was influenced by students of Otto Rank, especially Jessie Taft (1933) whose "relationship therapy" shifted emphasis from past content to a focus on the patient's self-insight and self-acceptance within the therapeutic relationship. Later, he often described three experiences in Rochester that gradually influenced his thinking (Rogers, 1961c, 1967).

In one therapeutic relationship, he was working with a young boy who had a compulsion to set fires. At the time, Rogers was impressed with the work of a noted psychotherapist whose theory was that juvenile delinquency could be traced to unresolved sexual conflicts. Over several sessions, Rogers used leading questions and skillful interpretations to help the boy see how his pyromania was the result of a sexual impulse regarding masturbation. Rogers thought the case was solved, but when the boy was released on probation, he continued to set fires. Rogers said this incident caused him to be more skeptical about expert theories and began to think that he might have a role in discovering new knowledge about helping people.

On another occasion, Rogers observed a renowned hypnotherapist work with a young bed wetter. The therapist gradually succeeded in inducing a trance state in the boy, but when he began making posthypnotic suggestions related to ceasing the bed-wetting, the boy became resistant to the point of no longer entering the trance state. Rogers was impressed at how strong the human will is and how patients will resist even the most skillful therapist interventions when it goes against their purposes or they have not chosen to change themselves.

In the most telling anecdote, Rogers had been working with the mother of a troubled boy. He explored with her, skillfully he thought, how her rejection of her son was causing much of the difficulty, but she continued to resist his interpretation. Finally, he acknowledged to her that they were not making any progress, and they agreed to end their sessions. On her way out the door, she turned to him and asked, "Do you ever take adults for counseling here?" Upon his affirmative reply, she returned to her chair, sat down, and began pouring her heart out about the troubles she was experiencing with her marriage and her sense of failure. As they explored these issues, over time, she began to make real progress with helping her son. This incident, Rogers (1961c) wrote,

> helped me to experience the fact—only fully realized later that it is the client who knows what hurts, what directions to go, what problems are crucial, what experiences have been deeply buried. It began to occur to me that unless I had a need to demonstrate my own cleverness and learning, I would do better to rely on the client for the direction of movement in the process. (p. 11)

In his last years in Rochester, Rogers (1939) wrote his first book, The Clinical Treatment of the Problem Child. It described the range of methods for working with young people—from in-

stitutional and foster home placement; to modifying their school program and using clubs, groups, and camps; to treatment interviews using education, persuasion, and release; and to deeper therapies. On the strength of the aforementioned book and his part-time teaching experience at the University of Rochester, he was offered and accepted a full-professorship at Ohio State University.

Ohio State University—The Nondirective Approach

At Ohio State, Rogers's students were not satisfied with his simply reviewing all the methods for helping children or counseling adults. They wanted to know what he believed was effective. And so Rogers began to articulate his own views on counseling and psychotherapy, which resulted in a second book of that same title, Counseling and Psychotherapy: Newer Concepts in Practice (Rogers, 1942). It was a book that challenged the field of psychotherapy to its core, and as most introductory counseling textbooks state, the book (and author) virtually founded the field of professional counseling (Capuzzi & Gross, 2001; Gibson & Mitchell, 1999; Gladding, 2000; Nugent, 2000). How could one book have such a profound influence?

First, although Rogers was not the first author to use the term client for the recipient of therapy, with Counseling and Psychotherapy, Rogers popularized it. More than a semantic distinction, the word connotes a departure from the medical model of illness, emphasizing that a person seeking help should be not treated as a dependent patient but as a responsible client and that those in psychological distress were not necessarily "sick," therefore requiring treatment by medical specialists. Rather, Rogers demonstrated that all people could be helped by the growth-producing process of counseling and that professionals from many fields could be trained to provide this help. Thus, counselors, social workers, clergy, medical workers, youth and family workers, and other helping professionals could use counseling methods.

Second, Rogers introduced his "nondirective" method. He credited others with working in this same direction, but his own statement of the position was the most extreme, and what he called "a newer psychotherapy" (Rogers, 1942, p. 27) became identified with him. His method was based on a core hypothesis about human growth and personality change, which he summarized a few years later:

> This hypothesis is that the client has within himself the capacity, latent if not evident, to understand those aspects of his life and of himself which are causing him pain, and the capacity and the tendency to reorganize himself and his relationship to life in the direction of self-actualization and maturity in such a way as to bring a greater degree of internal comfort. The function of the therapist is to create such a psychological atmosphere as will permit this capacity and this strength to become effective rather than latent or potential. (Rogers, 1950, p. 443)

Although other therapies might profess similar belief, Rogers's method of creating the therapeutic psychological atmosphere was radically different from other approaches commonly used. Rogers's initial "nondirective method" totally avoided questions, interpretation, suggestions, advice, or other directive techniques. Rather, it relied exclusively on a process of carefully listening to the client, accepting the client for who he or she is—no matter how confused or antisocial that might be at the moment—and skillfully reflecting back the client's feelings. The acceptance and reflection of feelings would create a level of safety for deeper exploration and a mirror in which to further understand and reflect on the client's own experience, which would lead the individual to further insight and positive action.

Not only was Rogers's "nondirective method" a more extreme statement of what he called the "newer direction" in psychotherapy, it blurred the boundary between counseling and psychotherapy. Before Rogers, it was assumed that "counseling" applied to mild problems of adjustment or career guidance, whereas "psychotherapy" was needed for more deep-seated psychological problems. Counseling and Psychotherapy suggested that the same nondirective method of helping could be applied to all problems along the adjustment continuum. Consider for example, the case of Loretta—a hospitalized woman with a diagnosis of schizophrenia whom Rogers was counseling. In the following recorded counseling session, Loretta was discussing with Rogers whether she was ready for a change in her work assignment in the hospital. The next 6 minutes of the session are given verbatim. The client speaks rapidly. Rogers, on the other hand, takes his time responding, letting the meaning of her words sink in as she tries to understand her experience.

L: I don't think I'm going to like working in the laundry—that I know. Cause I didn't like it either the other two times. And I don't think I care too much working in the food center over there either because I've worked there before, and I didn't care for it. Well, I didn't have anything, I, the first day I worked all right; the second day I worked. But a half an hour and I blacked out and I tried it three more days and I blacked out each day, so I just quit trying to work there then. There was too much electricity or something.

R: Uh-hum, uh-hum. You feel … something was wrong over there, too much electricity or something. It really had a bad effect on me when I was working …

L: It did! I blacked out completely. If I hadn't gone and sat down I would have fainted.

R: You feel really you were, you were in kind of a desperate way at those points.

L: No, I didn't feel desperate. I just, I didn't understand that I didn't know why I blacked out.

R: I see.

L: It did frighten me though. I just couldn't work so…

R: You felt something very odd was happening to you, more.

L: Cause I don't have epilepsy seizures or anything like that so I couldn't imagine what it was. And I don't, I'm not, I don't usually have fainting spells.

R: It made you feel real puzzled. What is happening to me?

L: What it was, yeah. I tried to work and I couldn't work and they wanted me to work, so…. Sometimes I think you get put back on treatment if you refuse to work.

R: Uh-huh. So maybe, maybe shock treatment is really something they may use for punishment if you don't do the things they want you to do…

L: Well, it would appear that way from what everybody says, but I don't think it was even—I don't know even why they even gave it to me in the first place. I was just beginning to come to enough to realize that I was in an institution, I think, and the next thing I knew they said, "You're outa here on treatment," and I said, "Why? I didn't do anything. I haven't had any fights or anything with anybody." And they said, "Well, doctor's orders," and I said, "Well, I haven't even talked to a doctor," because I hadn't talked to one, at least I didn't know it if I had…. And so…

R: So to you it seemed, Here I was just beginning to come to life a little bit, to really to know a little bit what was going on…

L: I was just beginning to realize I was in the hospital when they put me on it. And they put me to work the same day.

R: And then you feel that for no reason you could discern, zingo, you were right…

L: And I began talking very badly and everything and I still have forgotten some of the things they said.

R: It feels that as though that somehow sort of brought out the worst in you, is that what you mean?

L: If I had a worst part. Uh, uh, it was like it wasn't even me talking

R: Uh, huh. Almost seemed as though this was…

L: And then I went home weekends and I got in trouble there because I talked so much. Of course I was getting sodium amytol too, so it might have been the combination of the two—not just the one thing.

R: But there, too, I guess I get the feeling that you're wishing you could understand that part of yourself, why there's this something that was not you talking, or was it just the effect of the drugs or what was it that made you…

L: It was the combination, I think, of all…. As you notice my, I move my feet… as I…

R: Yes I did notice that.

L: said, my knees tickle.

R: Uh-hum.

L: And I don't know if it's the drugs I'm getting or what, but it's something I can't help. It isn't that I'm so terribly nervous that I can't sit still; that isn't it. I do that at group meetings or anything, and I can't control them. And it's rather embarrassing.

R: Uh, hum. And you would like me to understand that it isn't just tenseness or something.

L: No.

R: It's, uh, simply…

L: I can't control.

R: [An] uncontrollable tickling sensation.

L: In my knees and therefore, and my feet just move. If I'm sitting up there in the corner alone that isn't so much, but my knees still tickle.

R: Uh-hum.

L: But when I get in the group and that's my ... so I don't know, they just move.

R: It seems as though being in a group makes this worse.

L: Well, I have it when I'm alone sometimes, too. I think it's the medication I'm getting.

R: You feel probably it's just the drugs.

L: I think it's the green medication I'm getting. I don't even know what it is, cause I haven't asked. I inquired once but then I...

R: Uh-hum.

L: [After a long pause] ... I think these meetings are very enlightening.

R: Do you?

L: Well, if you can't think quite clear at the time, you can think about it later on.

R: Uh-hum. Uh-hum. And in that sense they, they're somewhat helpful in that you can...

L: I think I've been helped a lot, more by talking than I have by the pills and that.

R: Uh-hum, uh-hum.... It really seems as though getting things out to some degree in talk...

L: Seems to alleviate whatever the situation is.

R: Uh-hum

L: If it's a created situation, that seems to alleviate [it].... (Rogers, n.d.)

One reason that Rogers was able to demonstrate the propositions of nondirective therapy so cogently was that he was the first person ever to record and publish complete cases of psychotherapy. This fourth innovation of Counseling and Psychotherapy was illustrated in the last 170 pages of the book—"The Case of Herbert Bryan," which included, verbatim, every client statement and every counselor statement for the eight sessions of counseling. This was a remarkable achievement before the invention of tape recorders. It required a microphone in the counseling room connected to two alternating phonograph machines in an adjoining room, which cut grooves in blank record disks that had to be changed every 3 minutes. With graduate student Bernard Covner, Rogers and his team recorded thousands of disks involving scores of clients. These recordings became pivotal in the clinical training of psychotherapists, which, in the 1940s, Rogers may have been the first to offer in an American university setting.

The recordings and transcripts also allowed Rogers and his students to begin undertaking scientific research on the process of therapy—another important feature of Counseling and Psychotherapy. For example, Rogers could classify counselor responses as to degree of directiveness, count their frequency of occurrence, and correlate them with subsequent client statements of insight. He made many counselors uncomfortable by reporting how directive counselors used 6 times as many words as nondirective ones.

Chicago—The Client-Centered Approach and Research

Because he wanted to do much more research on the process and outcomes of counseling and psychotherapy, Rogers left Ohio State after only 4 years to move to the University of Chicago, where he developed and ran the internationally renowned Counseling Center and taught in the Psychology Department from 1945 to 1957.

But first he spent an interim year training United Service Organization (USO) workers to counsel returned servicemen who were having problems adjusting to civilian life (Rogers & Wallen, 1946). On the last evening of each of the weeklong workshops, there was a social event in which participants entertained and performed skits. Invariably there would be a skit satirizing Carl Rogers in his tenth floor office counseling a suicidal client (see Kirschenbaum, 1979):

"Dr. Rogers," the client would say, "I'm feeling suicidal."
"You're feeling suicidal?" Rogers would answer.
"Yes, I'm walking over to the window, Dr. Rogers."
"I see. You're walking over to the window," Rogers answers.
"Look, Dr. Rogers, I'm opening the window," the client says.
"You feel like opening the window?" Rogers reflects.
"Yes, I'm putting one foot out of the window, now."
"You're halfway out, is that it?"
"Yes, now I'm jumping Dr. Rogers"
"Uh, huh, uh, huh, you're jumping," says Rogers.

And, sure enough the client jumps, making a whooshing sound as he falls through the air before landing with a crash.

Thereupon Rogers walks over to the window, looks out and reflects, "Whooooosh ... Plop!"

As he continued at the University of Chicago to teach, write, and conduct research on what he soon was calling the "client-centered approach" to counseling and psychotherapy, Rogers soon came to recognize that the satire he endured so many times the previous year, and would endure all his life, had a serious point to make. Although he always remained primarily nondirective in his own practice, Rogers soon recognized that the counselor's attitudes were as important as his particular techniques. The techniques or methods were the way to implement the facilitative attitudes of accepting and understanding. Moreover, if these attitudes of the counselor were not genuine, all the reflecting of feelings in the world would not be of much help to the client.

Still later, Rogers clarified that it was the therapeutic relationship, which the attitudes helped create, that was most growth producing, and he continued to refine the three key "conditions" in the client-centered relationship that brought about positive change in clients. The first condition is to accept the client as he or she is, as a person of inherent worth possessing both positive and negative feelings and impulses. Rogers adopted a term from his student Standal (1954) and called this acceptance and prizing of the person "unconditional positive regard." Second is empathy—"the therapist's willingness and sensitive ability to understand the client's thoughts, feelings and struggles from the client's point of view ... to adopt his frame of reference" (Rogers, 1949, p. 84.). Third is congruence to be genuine, real, authentic, or congruent in the relationship. Rogers (1956) wrote, "It is only as [the therapist] is, in that relationship, a unified person, with his experienced feeling, his awareness of his feelings, and his expression of those feelings all congruent or similar, that he is most able to facilitate therapy" (pp. 199–206).

Rogers's appreciation of congruence was advanced by his own struggle in 1949–1951, when a difficult relationship with a schizophrenic client caused Rogers to become confused about his own sense of self. This led to a near breakdown, a "runaway trip" of several months with Helen, and a year or so of receiving counseling himself. The childhood teasing, suppression of feelings, and isolation from peers had left their mark. Through counseling, Rogers developed a newfound self-esteem, capacity to experience more of his feelings, and ability to be increasingly congruent in personal and professional relationships.

In one of his most important essays, Rogers (1957a) wrote that when a counselor communicates this congruence, unconditional positive regard, and empathic understanding so that the client perceives them at least to a minimal degree, then the "necessary and sufficient conditions for therapeutic personality change" (p. 95) are present. Rogers argued and demonstrated that the client has within himself the ability and tendency to understand his needs and problems, to gain insight, to reorganize his personality, and to take constructive action. What clients need, said Rogers, is not the judgment, interpretation, advice or direction of experts, but supportive counselors and therapists to help them rediscover and trust their "inner experiencing" (a concept borrowed from Gendlin, 1958), achieve their own insights, and set their own direction.

Rogers's (1951) next book, Client-Centered Therapy: Its Current Practice, Implications, and Theory, and subsequent articles described these principles of effective therapy and presented ample case studies from recorded sessions to illustrate his points. Beyond audio recording of therapy sessions, Rogers also was among the first to make cinematic recordings of counseling and psychotherapy. The American Academy of Psychotherapists became a leading distributor of training tapes and movies, with Rogers the most frequent therapist portrayed. A still widely distributed set of training films showed Rogers, gestalt therapist Frederick Peris, and rational-emotive therapist Albert Ellis each demonstrating his method with the same client.

The audiovisual recording of actual therapy sessions provided the data, and the Ford, Rockefeller, and other foundations provided the financial support (about $650,000, which was a small fortune in the 1940s and 1950s) with which Rogers and his colleagues conducted more scientific research on one therapeutic approach than had ever been undertaken before (e.g., Rogers & Dymond, 1954). Rogers and his team devised and used numerous instruments for measuring the variables of client-centered therapy and its outcomes, including measuring the therapist's acceptance, empathy, and congruence; the client's expression of feelings, insight, self-concept, self-acceptance, and self ideal; the client's positive actions, emotional maturity, and social adjustment; and numerous other variables. In 1956, the American Psychological Association (1957) awarded Rogers its first "Distinguished Scientific Contribution Award"

for developing an original method to objectify the description and analysis of the psychotherapeutic process, for formulating a testable theory of psychotherapy and its effects on personality and behavior, and for extensive systematic research to exhibit the value of the method and explore and test the implications of the theory. His imagination, persistence, and flexible adaptation of scientific method … have moved this area of psychological interest within the boundaries of scientific psychology. (p. 128)

As the award citation suggests, Rogers was interested in psychological theory and in the effects of therapy on personality as well as behavior. Building upon the Gestalt and phenomenological movements in psychology, and on the work of his students Victor Raimy (1943, 1948) and Donald Snygg and Arthur Combs (1949), he developed a "self-theory" of personality, which is still included in many psychology textbooks. The theory describes how an individual's concept of self emerges; how the process of socialization causes individuals to distrust their feelings and sense of self; how experiences that are inconsistent with the concept of self become denied and distorted causing personal distress and psychological problems; and how the therapeutic relationship can help the individual restructure the sense of self, allowing previously denied and distorted experience into awareness, leading to reduction in stress and openness to new experiencing.

Rogers's impact on psychology and the helping professions came about not only through research, teaching, and practice, but also through leadership in many professional associations. Earlier in his career he was active in the social work field—serving in national positions in the American Association of Social Workers and the American Association of Orthopsychiatry. In the 1940s and 1950s, he was president of the American Psychological Association, the American Association of Applied Psychology, and the American Academy of Psychotherapists, among other distinguished positions and honors.

Wisconsin—Research and Humanistic Psychology

Seemingly at the peak of his career, after 12 years at Chicago, Rogers surprised the profession by moving in 1957 to the University of Wisconsin. By now the children were grown. David had begun medical school, on his way to a distinguished career, including dean of medicine at Johns Hopkins and president of the Robert Wood Johnson Foundation. Natalie would go on to become an art therapist ("client-centered expressive therapist") and an author. Helen Rogers continued with her love of painting while taking primary responsibility for raising the family and running the household. When the children left home, she and Carl took long winter vacations in the Caribbean and traveled widely—on holidays, to visit their children and eventually six grandchildren, and in connection with professional activities.

In moving to Wisconsin, Rogers had joint appointments in the Departments of Psychology and Psychiatry. This would allow him to conduct further research on therapy with patients diagnosed with schizophrenia residing in the Mendota state psychiatric hospital, work that he hoped would have an impact on the psychiatric profession. The massive and well-funded research project went forward, and after years of delay because of complications involving authorship and the unethical behavior of one of the team members, it was eventually published (Rogers, Gendlin, Kiesler, & Truax, 1967). The results were important. The client-centered therapists achieved no better patient outcomes than therapists of other orientations; however, regardless of orientation, those therapists who demonstrated higher levels of unconditional positive regard, empathy, and congruence achieved better patient outcomes than therapists who provided lower levels of the three conditions. This was but one of several important findings.

While at Wisconsin, Rogers (1961a) wrote his most famous book, On Becoming a Person: A Therapist's View of Psychotherapy. Aimed at both a professional and lay audience, in a personal style, the collection of essays written over the past decade or more explored Rogers's learning about counseling and psychotherapy and its application to other helping professions and to the areas of creativity, philosophy, and the behavioral sciences. One reason the book was so popular, and remains widely read today, was a growing interest by the public in psychology in general and in what Abraham Maslow described as a "third force" in psychology, which became prominent in the latter half of the twentieth century.

"Humanistic psychology," as it came to be known, differed from psychoanalysis and behaviorism in at least three ways. First, this psychology gave more emphasis and credence to the individual's phenomenal field, for example, the client-centered therapist's empathizing with the client's frame of reference rather than evaluating or diagnosing from the outside, or the existential psychotherapist's helping the patient find "meaning" in life—meaning as perceived by the client. Second, this psychology focused not just on remediation of psychological problems but on psychological health, wellness, creativity, self-actualization, or what Rogers (1957b, 1961b) described as "the fully functioning person." The goal was more than "adjustment," but helping people experience their full human potential. Third, it was a psychology interested in what distinguishes human beings from other species. Choice, will, freedom, values, feelings, goals, and other humanistic concerns were all central subjects of study.

Because Rogers's career and that of leading behavioral psychologist B. F. Skinner were parallel—in timing, productivity, and influence—their views inevitably were contrasted. Meeting on several occasions, including a 6-hour debate-dialogue in 1962 (Rogers & Skinner, 1989), their earliest exchange on "Some Issues Concerning the Control of Human Behavior" (Rogers & Skinner, 1956) became one of the most reprinted articles in the behavioral sciences, and Rogers became a leading spokesperson for the humanistic psychology movement.

California—The Person-Centered Approach

As Rogers's professional interests and influence increasingly extended beyond the fields of counseling and psychotherapy,

and as his frustrations with the research project in Wisconsin continued, in 1963 the Rogers moved to La Jolla, California, where Rogers joined the staff of the Western Behavioral Sciences Institute. After 10 years, he and others then formed their own organization, Center for Studies of the Person, where Rogers remained for another 15 years.

In California, for a quarter century, Rogers continued to promulgate the client-centered approach and to apply his theory and method to other fields—education, parenting, group leadership, and the health professions, to name a few. In each instance, he demonstrated how the facilitative conditions of positive regard, empathy, and congruence could unleash growth, creativity, learning, and healing in children, students, group members, clients, and others. Drawing on earlier essays, he expanded his ideas into many new books that explored the implications of his thinking in diverse fields.

Applied to education, Rogers's work on "student-centered learning" illustrated how a teacher or, as he preferred, a "facilitator of learning" could provide the trust, understanding, and realness to free his or her students to pursue significant learning. Rogers's work coincided with and contributed to the "open education" movement in the United States, Great Britain, and elsewhere. His book Freedom to Learn: A View of What Education Might Become (Rogers, 1969) went through two new editions over the next 25 years (including posthumously, Rogers & Freiberg, 1994).

His book on marriage, Becoming Partners: Marriage and Its Alternatives (Rogers, 1972), used case studies of couples to explore new forms of relationships that young people were implementing in the 70s. He somewhat naively and somewhat accurately predicted the relegation of traditional marriage to only one of many alternatives for what he sometimes called "the person of tomorrow." Rogers and William Coulson's (1968) book on the behavior sciences, Man and the Science of Man, included proceedings and commentary from an international conference they organized on the philosophy of science, including major addresses by scientist, philosopher, and Nobel laureate Michael Polanyi; Jacob Brownowski; and Rogers.

But most of all, during the late 1960s and the 1970s, Rogers and his colleagues explored the applications of client-centered thinking to groups and group leadership. In the 1940s and 1950s, Rogers, Thomas Gordon (1951), and colleagues at the University of Chicago had experimented with "group-centered leadership," whereby the leader's acceptance, understanding, genuineness, and willingness to let the group set its own directions stimulated great energy, creativity, and productivity among group members. In the late 1950s and 1960s, Gordon, Richard Farson, Rogers, and associates extended this approach to what Rogers called the "basic encounter group"—an unstructured group experience in which so-called "normal" group members came to greater self-understanding, spontaneity, improved communication, and genuineness in relationships. Rogers led scores of encounter groups in professional, business, religious, medical, academic, personal growth, and organizational settings. Look magazine called Rogers an "elder statesman of encounter groups." Rogers's (1970) book, Carl Rogers on Encounter Groups, was a major seller, and Bill McGaw's (1968) filmed encounter group, Journey Into Self, featuring Rogers and Dick Farson as the group facilitators, won an Academy Award (an "Oscar") for best full-length feature documentary in 1968.

Recognizing the ever-widening applicability of the client-centered, student-centered, group-centered approach, Rogers and his colleagues at Center for Studies of the Person increasingly used a broader term—person-centered—to describe their work. (In the counseling literature, "person-centered" and "client-centered" are often used interchangeably today.)

International Conflict Resolution and Peace

In the 1970s and 1980s, Rogers experimented with a person-centered approach to resolving intergroup and international conflict. Through workshops and filmed encounter groups with multicultural populations, such as Catholics and Protestants from Northern Ireland and Blacks and Whites in South Africa, Rogers demonstrated how positive regard, empathy, and congruence—the same growth-promoting conditions useful in all helping relationships—can enhance communication and understanding among antagonistic groups. He and his colleagues led person-centered workshops for groups of 100 to 800 participants around the world, including Brazil, Mexico, South Africa, Hungary, Soviet Union (Rogers, 1987), and other newly emerging democracies. They organized a gathering of international leaders in Rust, Austria, about resolving tensions in Central America—an experience that vividly demonstrated the potential of the person-centered approach for resolving international conflict (Rogers, 1986).

Testimonials suggested that these efforts in professional development and citizen diplomacy helped foster peace and democratization in several countries. Of the Austria gathering, Rodrigo Carazo (2002), former President of Costa Rica and of the United Nations University for Peace, later wrote,

> Previous efforts for achieving peace in Central America, which were plenty, culminated in the Austria meeting…. Carl made it possible. There, for the first time, I repeat, representatives from all groups in conflict met and the first step in reaching peace in Central America was taken. This was the real beginning of many things toward peace. There is a picture of Carl Rogers in the central building of the University for Peace. Carl Rogers is in our memory and the master in our heart.

For Rogers's 85th birthday party, former U.S. President Jimmy Carter sent these words:

> To Carl Rogers—Congratulations and sincere best wishes on your 85th birthday celebration. It's wonderful that so many of your friends and supporters can be with you tonight. Your work as a peacemaker is internationally known and highly regarded. As you embark on still another mission, this time to South Africa, please know that you are in our thoughts. God speed your journey. The world can use more global citizens

like you. With warm regards, Jimmy Carter. (Kirschenbaum, 2003)

In acknowledgment of his efforts to bring about international understanding and conflict resolution, although he was not ultimately selected, Carl Rogers was nominated posthumously in 1987 for the Nobel Prize for Peace.

In his later years, personally, Rogers continued to pursue lifelong hobbies of photography, making mobiles, and gardening. When Helen became ill in her 70s, Carl cared for her until her death in 1979. Thereafter he remained involved in his work writing (e.g., Rogers, 1980), traveling the world, leading groups and workshops on the person-centered approach, and developing the Carl Rogers Peace Project. He had rich friendships with both men and women, and his daughter Natalie was a frequent colleague and companion. Rogers was active until his death at age 85, on February 4, 1987, from complications resulting from a fall and hip injury in his home in La Jolla.

Continuing Influence

Carl Rogers's career spanned six decades. For most of these, he presented a vivid role model of the person-centered approach, demonstrating his theories and methods through teaching, lecturing, live demonstrations, workshops, and audiovisual recordings. By all accounts, he embodied his theories by being an exceptional listener and communicator and a decent, honorable person. He wrote some 15 books and well over 200 professional articles, book chapters, and research studies. Millions of copies of his books have been printed, including over 60 foreign language editions. Two volumes of his major writings and dialogues with intellectual leaders of the twentieth century were published after his death (Kirschenbaum & Henderson, 1989a, 1989b), and a long-awaited, lengthy, oral history (Rogers & Russell, 2002) has recently been released.

In 1972, Rogers had received the American Psychological Association's Distinguished Professional Contribution Award, becoming the first psychologist ever to receive that organization's highest scientific honor and its highest professional honor. The citation read as follows:

> His commitment to the whole person has been an example which has guided the practice of psychology in the schools, in industry and throughout the community. By devising, practicing, evaluating and teaching a method of psychotherapy and counseling which reaches to the very roots of human potentiality and individuality, he has caused all psychotherapists to reexamine their procedures in a new light. Innovator in personality research, pioneer in the encounter movement, and respected gadfly of organized psychology, he has made a lasting impression on the profession of psychology. (APA, 1973, p. 71)

Not everyone agrees that Rogers's lasting impression is a positive one. As critic Christopher Lasch (1979) began his book review of the first English-language biography of Rogers (i.e., Kirschenbaum, 1979), "As a founding father of humanistic psychology, the human potential movement and the encounter group, Carl Rogers has a lot to answer for" (p. 30).

Critics of Rogers's work have argued that client-centered therapy is superficial (De Mott, 1979; Friedenberg, 1971), unworkable with some populations, and unmindful of multicultural and feminist issues (Usher, 1989; Waterhouse, 1993), the social context, and recent advances in behavioral, drug, and alternative therapies; that Rogers's views on human nature are unrealistically optimistic and underestimate human evil (May, 1982); that encounter groups and humanistic psychology have fostered widespread selfishness, narcissism, and moral permissiveness (Coulson, 1988, 1989; Lasch, 1979); and that Rogers's experiments with organizational change were naive (Kirschenbaum, 1979) and counterproductive (Coulson, 1988). Such criticisms have sometimes been fair; for Rogers, like any other individual, was a product of his times, with personal and historical limitations. Just as often, criticisms of Rogers and his work have been wanting, because the critic was unfamiliar with the full scope of Rogers's theories, research, and ever-widening practice.

Critics notwithstanding, Rogers more than anyone helped spread professional counseling and psychotherapy beyond psychiatry and psychoanalysis to psychology and other helping professions. Near the end of his career, surveys in the Journal of Counseling Psychology (Heesacker, Heppner, & Rogers [no relation], 1982) and American Psychologist (Smith, 1982) still ranked Carl Rogers as the most influential author and counselor/psychotherapist.

A generation later, the client-centered/person-centered approach continues to exert a significant influence on the world of counseling and psychotherapy. Although database searches show many more citations for cognitive and behavioral therapy than references to the client-centered/person-centered approach, attention to the person-centered approach remains strong, with more books, articles, and research studies appearing in the 15 years since Rogers's death than in the 40 years before (Kirschenbaum & Jourdan, in press).

Moreover, Rogers's work continues to serve as a foundation for the counseling profession (Capuzzi & Gross, 2001; Gibson & Mitchell, 1999; Gladding, 2000; Nugent, 2000). It also plays a major part in the practice of the vast number of counselors, clinical psychologists, and psychotherapists who describe their practice as "eclectic" or "integrative," including the client-centered approach as a major component in their repertoire (Aspy, Aspy, Russel, & Wedel, 2000; Bergin & Garfield, 1994; Shaft, 2000). And it continues to exert a significant influence on numerous helping professions from social work to pastoral counseling to the health professions.

It is interesting that, as meta-analyses of psychotherapy research continue to emerge (see summaries in Sexton, Whiston, Bleuer, & Walz, 1997; Wampold, 2001), the data increasingly suggest that the success of counseling and therapy is not due to any particular method, whether cognitive behavioral, psychodynamic, client-centered, or other. Rather, the research demonstrates that there are a number of "common factors" in the context of the therapy relationship that account for successful outcomes (e.g., Grencavage & Norcross, 1990; Lambert,

1992).What are these common factors? Many of them point back to the therapist's support, empathic understanding, and ability to form a therapeutic alliance with the client. Ironically, Rogers's core conditions for therapeutic change, decades later, are being validated by the latest generation of scientific research (e.g., Elliott, Greenberg, & Lietaer, 2003; Norcross, 2002). Although this research suggests that positive regard, empathy, and congruence may not be absolutely necessary in every case, nor sufficient for all counseling relationships, what the research does affirm is the following: first, Rogers's initial insights about the importance of the therapeutic relationship; second, the usefulness and practicality of the core conditions for forming the essential therapeutic alliance; and third, the definite or probable efficacy of empathy, positive regard/acceptance, and congruence for achieving positive counseling outcomes.

Since Rogers's death in 1987, perhaps the greatest new interest in his work has been outside the United States. In Europe, the person-centered approach has become one of the leading counseling and therapeutic approaches of the twenty-first century, with major organizations and centers for person-centered research and practice throughout Western and Central Europe. Equally significant, there has also been a great deal of interest in the person-centered approach in emerging democracies in Eastern Europe, Russia, and Latin America. As a Japanese counselor explained in the 1960s, Rogers helped "teach me … to be democratic and not authoritative." Rogers (1977) eventually recognized the political implications of his theories and methods and explored these in Carl Rogers on Personal Power: Inner Strength and Its Revolutionary Impact. His life's work demonstrated how supportive, growth-producing conditions can unleash healing, responsible self-direction, and creativity in individuals and groups in all walks of life. As countries around the world strive to resolve intergroup tensions and practice self-government and self-determination, many have recognized in Rogers's work not only useful methods for helping professionals, but also a positive, person-centered, empowering, democratic philosophy consistent with their national aspirations. At Rogers's memorial service (and earlier), Richard Farson (1975) described Carl Rogers as "a quiet revolutionary."

References

American Psychological Association. (1957). Distinguished Scientific Contribution Awards for 1956—Carl R. Rogers. The American Psychologist, 12, 125–133.

American Psychological Association. (1973). Distinguished professional contribution award for 1972. American Psychologist, 28, 71–74.

Aspy, D., Aspy, C., Russel, G., & Wedel, M. (2000). Carkhuff's human technology: A verification and extension of Kelly's (1997) suggestion to integrate the humanistic and technical components of counseling. Journal of Counseling & Development, 78, 29–37.

Bergin, A. E., & Garfield, S. L. (1994). Overview, trends, and future issues. In A. E. Bergin & S. L. Garfield (Eds.), Handbook of psychotherapy and behavior change (4th ed., pp. 821–830). New York: Wiley.

Capuzzi, D., & Gross, D. R. (2001). Introduction to the counseling profession (3rd ed.). Needham Heights, MA: Allyn & Bacon.

Carazo, R. (2002, June 24). Statement read to the general session at the Carl Rogers Symposium, San Diego, CA.

Coulson, W. (1988, April 23). Memorandum to Federal Drug Education Curriculum Panel.

Coulson, W. (1989, April). Founder of "value-free" education says he owes parents an apology. AFA Journal, 20–21.

De Mott, B. (1979, January). Mr. Rogers' neighborhood. Psychology Today, 90, 94, 95.

Elliott, R., Greenberg, L., & Lietaer, G. (2003). Research on experiential and person-centered therapies. In M. Lambert, A. Bergin, & S. Garfield (Eds.), Handbook of psychotherapy and behavior change (5th ed., pp. 493–539). New York: Wiley.

Farson, R. (1975). Carl Rogers, a quiet revolutionary. In R. I. Evans, Carl Rogers: The man and his ideas (pp. xxviii–xliii). New York: Dutton.

Friedenberg, E. Z. (1971). Review of C. R. Rogers' Freedom to Learn. Journal of Higher Education, 42, 239–242.

Gendlin, E. T. (1958). The function of experiencing in symbolization. Unpublished doctoral dissertation, University of Chicago.

Gibson, R. L., & Mitchell, M. H. (1999). Introduction to counseling and guidance (5th ed.). Upper Saddle River, NJ: Prentice Hall.

Gladding, S. T. (2000). Counseling: A comprehensive profession. Upper Saddle River, NJ: Merrill/Prentice Hall.

Gordon, T. (1951). Group-centered leadership and administration. In C. R. Rogers, Client-centered therapy: Its current practice, implications, and theory (pp. 320–383). Boston: Houghton Mifflin.

Grencavage, L. M., & Norcross, J. S. (1990). Where are the commonalities among the therapeutic common factors? Professional Psychology: Research and Practice, 21, 372–378.

Heesacker, M., Heppner, P., & Rogers, M. E. (1982). Classics and emerging classics in counseling psychology. Journal of Counseling Psychology, 29, 4.

Kirschenbaum, H. (1979). On becoming Carl Rogers. New York: Delacorte Press.

Kirschenbaum, H. (1995). Carl Rogers. In M. Suhd (Ed.), Carl Rogers and other notables he influenced (pp. 1–90). Palo Alto, CA: Science and Behavior Books.

Kirschenbaum, H. (Producer). (2003). Carl Rogers and the person-centered approach [Videotape]. Webster, NY: Values Associates.

Kirschenbaum, H., & Henderson, V. L. (Eds.). (1989a). Carl Rogers: Dialogues: Conversations with Martin Buber, Paul Tillich, B. F. Skinner, Gregory Bateson, Michael Polanyi, Rollo May, and others. Boston: Houghton Mifflin.

Kirschenbaum, H., & Henderson, V. L. (Eds.). (1989b). The Carl Rogers reader. Boston: Houghton Mifflin.

Kirschenbaum, H., & Jourdan, A. (in press). Carl Rogers' current influence. Journal of Humanistic Counseling, Education and Development.

Lambert, M. J. (1992). Psychotherapy outcome research: Implications for integrative and eclectic therapists. In J. C. Norcross & M. R. Goldfried (Eds.), Handbook of psychotherapy integration (pp. 94–129). New York: Basic Books.

Lasch, C. (1979, March 31). On becoming Carl Rogers by Howard Kirschenbaum [Review]. New Republic, 228(12), 30–31.

May, R. (1982, Summer). The problem of evil: An open letter to Carl Rogers. Journal of Humanistic Psychology, 22(3), 10–21.

McGaw, B. (Producer). (1968). Journey into self [Documentary]. United States: Western Behavioral Sciences Institute.

Norcross, J. (2002). Psychotherapy: Relationships that work. London: Oxford University Press.

Nugent, F. A. (2000). Introduction to the profession of counseling (3rd ed.). Upper Saddle River, NJ: Merrill.

Raimy, V. (1943). The self-concept as a factor in counseling and personality organization. Unpublished doctoral dissertation, Ohio State University, Columbus.

Raimy, V. (1948). Self-reference in counseling interviews. Journal of Consulting Psychology, 12, 153–163.

Rogers, C. R. (1931a). Measuring personality adjustment in children nine to thirteen years of age. New York: Teachers College, Columbia University.

Rogers, C. R. (1931b). A test of personality adjustment. New York: Association Press.

Rogers, C. R. (1939). The clinical treatment of the problem child. Boston: Houghton Mifflin.

Rogers, C. R. (1942). Counseling and psychotherapy: Newer concepts in practice. Boston: Houghton Mifflin.

Rogers, C. R. (1949). The attitude and orientation of the counselor in client-centered therapy. Journal of Consulting Psychology, 13, 82–94.

Rogers, C. R. (1950). A current formulation of client-centered therapy. Social Service Review, 24, 442–450.

Rogers, C. R. (1951). Client-centered therapy: Its current practice, implications, and theory. Boston: Houghton Mifflin.

Rogers, C. R. (1956). Client-centered therapy: A current view. In F. Fromm-Reichmann & J. L. Moreno (Eds.), Progress in psychotherapy (pp. 199–209). New York: Grune and Stratton.

Rogers, C. R. (1957a). The necessary and sufficient conditions of therapeutic personality change. Journal of Consulting Psychology, 21, 95–103.

Rogers, C. R. (1957b). A therapist's view of the good life. The Humanist, 17, 291–300.

Rogers, C. R. (1961a). On becoming a person: A therapist's view of psychotherapy. Boston: Houghton Mifflin.

Rogers, C. R. (1961b). A therapist's view of the good life: The fully functioning person In C. R. Rogers, On becoming a person: A therapist's view of psychotherapy (pp. 184–196). Boston: Houghton Mifflin

Rogers, C. R. (1961c). This is me. In C. R. Rogers, On becoming a person: A therapist's view of psychotherapy (pp. 3–27). Boston: Houghton Mifflin.

Rogers, C. R. (1967). Autobiography. In E. W. Boring & G. Lindzey (Eds.), A history of psychology in autobiography (Vol. 5, pp. 341–384). New York: Appleton-Century-Crofts.

Rogers, C. R. (1969). Freedom to learn: A view of what education might become. Columbus, OH: Merrill.

Rogers, C. R. (1970). Carl Rogers on encounter groups. New York: Harper and Row.

Rogers, C. R. (1972). Becoming partners: Marriage and its alternatives. New York: Delacorte Press.

Rogers, C. R. (1977). Carl Rogers on personal power: Inner strength and its revolutionary impact. New York: Delacorte Press.

Rogers, C. R. (1980). A way of being. Boston: Houghton-Mifflin

Rogers, C. R. (1986, Summer). The Rust workshop. Journal of Humanistic Psychology, 26(3), 23–45.

Rogers, C. R. (1987, Summer). Inside the world of the Soviet professional. Journal of Humanistic Psychology, 27(3), 277–304.

Rogers, C. R. (Speaker). (n.d.). Carl Rogers and Loretta [Audio recording]. Champaign, IL: American Academy of Psychotherapists.

Rogers, C. R., & Coulson, W. R. (1968). Man and the science of man. Columbus, OH: Merrill.

Rogers, C. R., & Dymond, R. F. (Eds.). (1954) Psychotherapy and personality change: Coordinated research studies in the client-centered approach. Chicago: University of Chicago Press.

Rogers, C. R., & Freiberg, H. J. (1994). Freedom to learn (3rd ed.). Columbus, OH: Merrill.

Rogers, C. R., Gendlin, E. T., Kiesler, D. J., & Truax, C. B. (Eds.). (1967). The therapeutic relationship and its impact: A study of psychotherapy with schizophrenics. Madison: University of Wisconsin Press.

Rogers, C. R., & Russell, D. (2002). Carl Rogers: The quiet revolutionary: An oral history. Roseville, CA: Penmarin Books.

Rogers, C. R., & Skinner, B. F. (1956). Some issues concerning the control of human behavior. Science, 124, 1057–1066.

Rogers, C. R., & Skinner, B. F. (1989). A dialogue on education and the control of human behavior. In H. Kirschenbaum & V. Henderson (Eds.), Carl Rogers: Dialogues: Conversations with Martin Buber, Paul Tillich, B. F. Skinner, Gregory Bateson, Michael Polanyi, Rollo May, and others (pp. 79–152). Boston: Houghton Mifflin.

Rogers, C. R., & Wallen, J. L. (1946). Counseling with returned servicemen. New York: McGraw-Hill.

Sexton, T., Whiston, S., Bleuer, J., & Walz, G. (1997). Integrating outcome research into counseling practice and training. Alexandria, VA: American Counseling Association.

Sharf, R. S. (2000). Comparison, critique, and integration. In R. S. Sharf, Theories of psychotherapy and counseling: Concepts and cases (2nd ed., pp. 599–645). Belmont, CA: Brooks/Cole.

Smith, D. (1982). Trends in counseling and psychology. American Psychologist, 37, 7.

Snygg, D., & Combs, A. W. (1949). Individual behavior. New York: Harper.

Standal, S. (1954). The need for positive regard: A contribution to client-centered theory. Unpublished doctoral dissertation, University of Chicago.

Taft, J. (1933). The dynamics of therapy in a controlled relationship. New York: Macmillan.

Usher, C. H. (1989). Recognizing cultural bias in counseling theory and practice: The case of Rogers. Journal of Multicultural Counseling and Development, 17, 62–71.

Wampold, B. (2001). The great psychotherapy debate: Models, methods, and findings. Mahwah, NJ: Erlbaum.

Waterhouse, R. L. (1993, February). Wild women don't have the blues: A feminist critique of "person-centred" counselling and therapy. Feminism & Psychology, 3(1), 55–71.

HOWARD KIRSCHENBAUM, Department of Counseling and Human Development, Warner Graduate School of Education and Human Development, University of Rochester. This article is based on a featured presentation given at the American Counseling Association's annual conference in New Orleans, LA, on March 26, 2002. Correspondence concerning this article should be addressed to Howard Kirschenbaum, Warner School, University of Rochester, Rochester, NY 14627 (e-mail: Howard.Kirschenbaum@rochester.edu).

From *Journal of Counseling and Development*, Winter 2004, pp. 116-124. Copyright © 2004 by American Counseling Association. Reprinted by permission. No further reproduction without permission from the American Counseling Association.

Freud in Our Midst

On his 150th birthday, the architect of therapeutic culture is an inescapable force. Why Freud—modern history's most debunked doctor—captivates us even now.

JERRY ADLER

We stand now at a critical moment in the history of our civilization, which is usually the case: beset by enemies who irrationally embrace their own destruction along with ours, our fate in the hands of leaders who make a virtue of avoiding reflection, our culture hijacked by charlatans who aren't nearly as depraved as they pretend in their best-selling memoirs. As we turn from the author sniveling on Oprah's couch, our gaze is caught by a familiar figure in the shadows, sardonic and grave, his brow furrowed in weariness. *So*, he seems to be saying, *you would like this to be easy. You want to stick your head in a machine, to swallow a pill, to confess on television and be cured before the last commercial. But you don't even know what your disease is.*

Yes, it's Sigmund Freud, still haunting us, a lifetime after he died in London in 1939, driven by the Nazis from his beloved Vienna. The theoretician who explored a vast new realm of the mind, the unconscious: a roiling dungeon of painful memories clamoring to be heard and now and then escaping into awareness by way of dreams, slips of the tongue and mental illness. The philosopher who identified childhood experience, not racial destiny or family fate, as the crucible of character. The therapist who invented a specific form of treatment, psychoanalysis, which advanced the revolutionary notion that actual diagnosable disease can be cured by a method that dates to the dawn of humanity: talk. Not by prayer, sacrifice or exorcism; not by drugs, surgery or change of diet, but by recollection and reflection in the presence of a sympathetic professional. It is an idea wholly at odds with our technological temperament, yet the mountains of Prozac prescribed every year have failed to bury it. Not many patients still seek a cure on a psychoanalyst's couch four days a week, but the vast proliferation of talk therapies—Jungian and Adlerian analyses, cognitive behavioral and psychodynamic therapy—testify to the enduring power of his idea.

And Freud: the great engine of an ongoing middlebrow bull session that has engaged our culture for a century. Without Freud, Woody Allen would be a schnook and Tony Soprano a thug; there would be an Oedipus but no Oedipus complex, and then how would people at dinner parties explain why the eldest son of George Bush was so intent on toppling Saddam? (This is a parlor game Freud himself pioneered in his analysis of Napoleon, who'd been dead for a century when Freud concluded that sibling rivalry with his eldest brother, Joseph, was the great drive in his life, accounting for both his infatuation with a woman named Josephine and his decision—following in the footsteps of the Biblical Joseph—to invade Egypt.) In America Freud is now more likely to be taken seriously as a literary figure than a scientific one, at least outside the 40 or so institutes that specifically train analysts. Just last year, in fact, NEWSWEEK lumped Freud with Karl Marx as a philosopher whose century had come and gone, in contrast to the continuing intellectual relevance of Darwin. In an act of expiation, therefore, and to stake out the high ground before the tsunami of lectures, seminars and publications scheduled for his 150th birthday on May 6, we ask ourselves: Is Freud still dead? And if not, what is keeping him alive?

That he retains any life at all is remarkable. To innocently type his name into a search engine is to unleash a torrent of denunciation that began the moment he began publishing his work in the 19th century. Merely being wrong—as even his partisans admit he probably was about a lot of things—seems inadequate to explain the calumny he has engendered, so Freudians invoke a Freudian explanation. "The unconscious is terribly threatening," says Dr. Glen O. Gabbard, professor of psychiatry at Baylor College of Medicine. "It suggests we are moved by forces we cannot see or control, and this is a severe wound to our narcissism." Resistance came early from a bourgeoisie appalled by one of Freud's central tenets, that young children have a sexual fantasy life—a theory that American adults rejected by a margin of 76 to 13 in a NEWSWEEK Poll. And it's not just Western culture that Freud scandalized; as recently as last month, in an interview with David Remnick of The New Yorker, Sheik

Nayef Rajoub of Hamas explained the necessity for Israel's destruction on the ground that "Freud, a Jew, was the one who destroyed morals."

And opposition came from feminists who would have you know that they don't envy any man his penis. It is now universally acknowledged that Freud's ideas about women's sexuality—in summary, that they were incomplete men—were so far wrong that, as his sympathetic biographer Peter Gay jokes, "If he were president of Harvard, he'd have to resign." The low point of Freud's reputation was probably the early 1990s, when women were filling the talk shows with accounts of childhood sexual abuse dredged from their unconscious. This was a no-win situation for Freud—who, admittedly, had staked out positions on both sides of this question, as he often did in his long career. Those who took the side of the accused parents and siblings blamed him for having planted the idea, in his early work, that the repressed memory of actual sexual abuse was a common cause of adult neurosis. Those who believed the accusers charged him with cravenly surrendering to community pressure when he ultimately decided that many of these recovered memories were actually childhood fantasies. "Sending a woman to a Freudian therapist," Gloria Steinem said at the time, "is not so far distant from sending a Jew to a Nazi."

His reputation has only barely begun to recover. In the wake of the repressed-memory wars, the vast Freud archive at the Library of Congress, much of which had been embargoed for decades into the future, has been opened to scholars. And Freud's debunkers are finding much to confirm what they've said all along, that his canonical "cures" were the product of wishful thinking and conscious fudging, and his theories founded on a sinkhole of circular logic. Efforts to validate Freudian psychology through rigorous testing or brain-imaging technology is still in its infancy. "I'm afraid he doesn't hold up very well at all," says Peter D. Kramer, a psychiatrist and author of "Listening to Prozac," who is working on a biography of Freud due to appear next year. "It almost feels like a personal betrayal to say that. But every particular is wrong: the universality of the Oedipus complex, penis envy, infantile sexuality."

How much debunking can Freud withstand? Jonathan Lear, a psychiatrist and philosopher at the University of Chicago, identifies a "core idea" on which Freud's reputation must rest, that human life is "essentially conflicted." And that the conflict is hidden from us, because it stems from wishes and instincts that are actively repressed—you don't have to believe that it involves a desire to have sex with one of your parents, if that idea strikes you as outlandish—because our conscious self cannot bear to acknowledge them. Identifying and resolving those conflicts as they emerge into awareness, deeply cloaked in symbolism, is the work of analysis.

Everything else is, ultimately, negotiable. Not even Freud's most orthodox adherents defend his entire body of work in all its details, but they do talk about the bigger picture. "He was wrong about so many things," says James Hansell, a University of Michigan psychologist. "But he was wrong in such interesting ways. He pioneered a whole new way of looking at things." Freud "helps us find deep meanings and motivations, and find meaning in love and work," says Dr. K. Lynne Moritz, a professor at St. Louis University School of Medicine and the incoming president of the American Psychoanalytic Association. Certainly he does, at least for some people, although that seems like a better recommendation for a poet than a scientist.

But then, deep meaning is just what some people want out of life, a fact that helps support the 3,400 members of Moritz's group (up, barely, from 3,200 in 1998) and 1,500 in a rival organization, the National Association for the Advancement of Psychoanalysis. That compares with 33,500 in the American Psychiatric Association. Psychiatrists are medical doctors trained to treat mental illness; they typically see patients referred to them specifically for drug therapy, or they work in hospitals or clinics with the seriously ill. The American Psychological Association, which represents psychotherapists without medical degrees, has 150,000 members. In the NEWSWEEK Poll, nearly 20 percent of American adults say they have had some form of therapy or counseling, and 4 percent are currently in therapy. The ability to tinker directly with the brain synapses, through drugs, holds the promise of making psychoanalysis redundant for some conditions. But patients respond differently, and for some a combination of drug and talk therapy seems to work best. Moritz maintains that for some conditions, such as adolescent borderline personality disorder, analysis remains the treatment of choice. As for Freud, he himself went through a brief phase in which he advocated drug therapy. Regrettably, the drug he advocated was cocaine. That remains the one salient fact that many Americans seem to have retained about him.

A major factor in the decline of psychoanalysis is the reluctance of insurance companies to foot the bill for an open-ended treatment at a cost of more than $2,000 a month. Back in the 1950s, analysis was a status symbol and a mark of sophistication, a role filled in society today by cosmetic surgery. But it is still a valued luxury good for those with the time and the means to live up to the Delphic injunction to "know thyself." "There are many people who don't respond to brief therapy or to medication," says Gabbard, "people who want the experience of being listened to and understood, to search for a truth about themselves that goes beyond symptom relief." Take one of Moritz's patients, a married woman in her 40s we'll call Doreen in honor of one of Freud's most famous cases, who was given the pseudonym Dora. Doreen is the model of many early Viennese patients, an educated upper-middle-class woman with an overtly tranquil and satisfying life. Like most patients today, her symptoms were vague and general. Neuroses no longer seem to manifest themselves in hysterical blindness or paralysis. "I decided I have a good life, but it could be better," she says. At work she was too eager to please, taking on more than she could handle; with her family she felt the need to stifle her playfulness and sense of humor. Probably many people wouldn't think it necessary to devote four hours a week for four years (and ongoing) to solving those problems, but to her it's been worth it, totally. "It makes you examine your life, retell your life, to understand where your attitudes, your beliefs and behaviors come from," she says. "I'm so much happier now. It's not something I could do alone. You have to confront the parts of yourself that are painful and shameful and difficult to face. Dr. Moritz asks the questions that cause me to dig deeper into myself."

That, of course, is the essence of Freud's technique. He was a man intoxicated with the voyage of inward discovery. You can see this clearly in his 1901 book "Psychopathology of Everyday Life." Here, Freud discusses an encounter with a young man who cannot recall the Latin word "aliquis" ("someone") in a passage from Virgil. To Freud, such moments are never without significance, and the very obscurity of the slip gave it added interest. Freud wouldn't waste couch time on a slip that was obvious to the person who uttered it. He employs his trademark technique of "free association" ("tell me the first thing that comes into your mind …") to uncover a link to "liquid," then to "blood," and through several other steps to the revelation that the young man was worried that a woman with whom he had been intimate had missed her period. What a tour de force for psychoanalysis!

Does it detract from our appreciation of his genius that the freelance historian Peter Swales has shown that there most probably was no such young man, that the memory lapse was probably committed by Freud himself and that the woman he was worried about was Minna Bernays, the sister of Freud's own wife?

Well, not to Lear. His reaction is, "I couldn't care less. I could imagine someone in Freud's position changing the story in that way. But it's just not very important [to our appreciation of his work]."

If Einstein had a romance with his sister-in-law, it wouldn't change what we thought about the speed of light. But this is Freud! His own thoughts and emotions were precisely the raw material from which he derived much of his theory. He is our postmodern Plato, our secular Saint Augustine. He fascinates us endlessly, even those who have made their reputations in part by denouncing him, like Frederick Crews, emeritus professor of English at UC Berkeley. Explaining Freud's enduring interest, he observes caustically, "Academic humanists find that by entering Freud's world of interlocking symbols and facile causal assertions they will never run out of shrewd-looking, counter-intuitive things to say in their essays and books." As if that were a bad thing! Don't we all need an excuse now and then to sound smart by referring to interpretation as "hermeneutics"? Kramer finds echoes of Freud in T. S. Eliot's dream-like symbolism, in the emotional transference (of boss to father to son) in Joyce's "Dubliners." ("Transference" refers to the displacement of emotion that a patient undergoes in therapy, making the therapist the object of feelings the patient has toward a parent. Mr. Soprano, take your hands off Dr. Melfi's throat, please.)

"We refer to Freud every day when we call someone 'passive-aggressive'," Kramer muses. "I don't know how people expressed that thought a hundred years ago." Not everyone is convinced by this argument, though: "Shakespeare managed to say an awful lot about human nature without the vo-cabulary provided by psychoanalysis," observes Patricia Churchland, of the University of California, San Diego, a leading philosopher of consciousness. She adds that in any case she finds that the language of analysis is being supplanted in popular culture by the jargon of neuroscience. People talk about getting their endorphins going. Someone acting rashly is said to be "frontal," referring to the part of the brain involved in impulse control.

Admittedly, hermeneutics isn't exactly where the action is in American society today. In the id-driven worlds of politics, athletics and business, Freud is the ultimate non-bottom-line guy; he pays off five years down the road in the non-negotiable currency of self-knowledge. When President George W. Bush told an interviewer in 2004 that he wouldn't "go on the couch" to rethink his decisions about the Iraq war, it so outraged Dr. Kerry J. Sulkowicz, a professor of psychiatry at NYU Medical School, that he wrote a letter to The New York Times pro-testing this slur on analysis, with the implication "that not understanding oneself is a matter of pride." Sulkowicz knows this attitude firsthand as a consultant to corporate CEOs and boards of directors, where he struggles daily to beat some introspection into his clients' heads. "There's so much emphasis on 'execution' and 'action' in the business world," he says. "I try to convey that action and reflection are not mutually exclusive." Freud's insights into the irrational and the unconscious find application in the corporation, where even high-level executives may bring transference issues into the office, seeking from their boss the approval they once craved from their parents. Freud's writings on group dynamics and sibling rivalry can serve the thoughtful CEO well, Sulkowicz adds. It helps, though, if the source is somewhat obscured. "I hardly ever talk about Freud by name," he says.

In the shadows, the tip of the cigar wiggles up and down in agitation. *Americans!* he seems to be thinking. *A money-grubbing mob; they made me fear for the future of civilization itself. I should have told them when I had the chance.*

Freud, rooted in the great civilizations of Europe, wrote little about America, which he visited briefly in 1909, but his attitude was clear from a few terse sentences in his dark classic, "Civilization and Its Discontents." Published in 1930, when Freud was already an old man, the book was a psychological meditation on the social contract: the surrender of mankind's natural instinct for aggression and sexual domination in exchange for the security and comfort of civilized society. But in Freud's view, that is not an easy bargain. Those instincts are powerful and their repression creates unconscious conflict—what Lear described as the "core idea" of Freudian thought. And that is the source of the disease that we cannot name, and that we can never really cure, because it is built into the human condition. It is no accident, says Lear, that Freud's reputation reached a low point in the early 1990s, which was not only the height of the recovered-memory hysteria, but also of the post-cold-war optimism that made a best seller of Francis Fukuyama's book "The End of History." Fukuyama predicted that the dissolution of the Soviet Union would pave the way for the triumph of liberal democracy around the world—an idea that came crashing to the ground one sunny morning in 2001. "We are always susceptible," Lear says, "to the illusion that these are not our problems. The end of history was a brave hope that the ongoing dynamic of human conflict was over." But what Freud has to say, which is worth hearing even if analysis never cures another patient, is that history will never end. Because it is made by human beings.

Skepticism of Caricatures: B.F. Skinner Turns 100

Juxtaposition of recent claims about B.F. Skinner in popular science books with actual quotations from Skinner's work reveals several enduring misinterpretations. Their promulgation is unnecessary and serves no beneficial purpose for the broader scientific community.

March 20 marks the 100th anniversary of B.F. Skinner's birth (March 20, 1904; he died August 18, 1990). Skinner championed psychology as a science of behavior, and in so doing, emphasized the study of behavior and the environmental events preceding and following instances of behavior. He was one of the most influential and controversial psychologists of the twentieth century. But despite his prominence, misinformation about Skinner's radical behaviorism remains widespread and is apparent in a variety of recent books. I will address three common and partially overlapping myths about Skinner, which I will refer to as the Blank Slate Myth, the Empty Organism Myth, and the Only Overt Behavior Myth.

The Blank Slate Myth

Skinner's emphasis on environment-behavior relations has led to inferences that he believed the organism was a virtual blank slate upon which the environment writes unfettered by genetics or biology. Unbelievably, this view still exists and for many, references to Locke, Watson, and Skinner appear to be interchangeable. For example, Pinker (2002, 169) describes Skinner as "a staunch blank-slater," while a recent book on child development suggests "Skinner's view was that children were the ultimate blank tablets, passively waiting to be inscribed by reinforcement schedules" (Gopnik et al.; 1999, 19). LeDoux (2002, 83) further suggests that according to Watson and Skinner "learning was a universal capacity that worked more or less the same regardless of which animal was doing the learning and what was being learned." These authors are overgeneralizing, failing to distinguish Skinner's approach from that of Locke and Watson, the latter being infamous for making what even he admitted was the exaggerated claim that he could train any infant to any specialty. Skinner took no such position, noting that Watson

> is probably responsible for the persistent myth of what has been called "behaviorism's counterfactual dogma." And it is a myth. No reputable student of animal

behavior has ever taken the position "that the animal comes into the laboratory as a virtual tabula rasa, that species differences are insignificant, and that all responses are about equally conditionable to all stimuli." (Skinner, 1966/1969, 173)

If Skinner was unwilling to postulate that a laboratory animal arrives as a blank slate it strains credulity to assume he thought otherwise of humans. Skinner (1959/1972, 558) went further, lamenting that Watson is remembered "for an extreme environmentalism, and for a coldly detached theory of child care, no one of which was a necessary part of his original program." Thus, it is even more regrettable and contrary to fact when Skinner is characterized similarly.

For Skinner, behavior was clearly seen as the product of the combination of genetics and environment: "The environment made its first great contribution during the evolution of the species, but it exerts a different kind of effect during the lifetime of the individual, and the combination of the two effects is the behavior we observe at any given time" (Skinner 1974, 17).

Thus, behavior is seen as the result of both genes and environment. Genes alone do not engage in behavior. Unified, whole organisms interacting in and with an environment behave. The influence is interactive and nonreducible. This point, while apparently obvious, is especially important when dealing with a fluid subject matter like behavior (or patterns of behavior), where environmental consequences for a particular class of behavior commingle with innate repertoires, quickly making them inseparable: "It would be hard to say how much of the strength of the behavior is due to each.... We may have an innate repertoire of aggressive behavior, but similar behavior is generated by many contingencies of reinforcement" (Skinner 1984, 220).

The Empty Organism Myth

A corollary of the Blank Slate Myth about Skinner is the Empty Organism Myth, which suggests that Skinner dismissed or ignored the role of the brain in learning. For example, according to Ridley (1996, 258) Skinner's "behaviorism held that animals' brains were black boxes which relied upon pure association to learn any task with equal ease." Similarly, Pinker (2002, 20) suggested that for Skinner "studying the brain was just another misguided quest to find the causes of behavior inside the organism rather than out in the world."

In Skinner's view, the contingencies of survival (i.e., evolution) give us not only a genetic heritage, but also a central nervous system that is modifiable by consequences (the first great contribution of the environment): "What evolves is an organism as a physical system, and it is such an organism that is modified by operant conditioning" (Skinner 1975, 120).

In other words, organisms have as an evolved feature a central nervous system that is capable of being altered by experience. We are born with a brain that is flexible, plastic, and incomplete. The flexible, adaptable brain can take full advantage of selection by consequences occurring during the lifetime of the organism (the second great contribution of the environment): "Just as genetic characteristics which arise as mutations are selected or discarded by their consequences, so novel forms of behavior are selected or discarded through reinforcement" (Skinner 1953, 430).

One unique aspect of humans is our protracted period of immaturity (i.e., childhood), which must have been evolutionarily selected for. Why this lengthy period of immaturity? One reasonable hypothesis is that it provides us time to learn about our specific environment (see also Gopnik et al., 1999): "A long infancy gives the ontogenic process greater scope, and its role in adapting to very unstable environments is a great advantage" (Skinner 1984, 220).

Thus, the development of the trillions of neural connections in the brain is shaped collaboratively by biological and environmental factors. Moreover, given a central nervous system that is modifiable by consequences, one can conclude that all variables that affect behavior inevitably also affect the neurobiological state of the organism. Moreover, changes in behavior derive from—and are correlated with—neurobiological changes. In Skinner's words:

> The physiologist of the future will tell us all that can be known about what is happening inside the behaving organism. His account will be an important advance over a behavior analysis, because the latter is necessarily "historical"—that is to say, it is confined to functional relations showing temporal gaps. Something is done today which affects the behavior of the organism tomorrow. No matter how clearly that fact can be established, a step is missing, and we must wait for the physiologist to supply it. He will be able to show how an organism is changed when exposed to contingencies of reinforcement and why the changed organism then behaves in a different way, possibly at a much later date. What he discovers cannot invalidate the laws of a science of behavior, but it will make the picture of human action more nearly complete. (Skinner 1974, 236–237)

The last sentence of the above quote may be a source of much of the confusion. While biological science is clearly seen as important and useful, a science of behavior is not dependent upon and need not wait around for biological advances. That is to say, psychology and neurology/physiology are different sciences, working at different levels of analysis. Neurological/physiological explanations are not necessary to legitimize psychological science. Neurology/physiology may provide explanations at that level of analysis, but that explanation cannot undo established environment-behavior relations at the psychological level of analysis. Moreover, when important neurological events are identified, "These events in turn will be found to be preceded by other neurological events, and these in turn by others. This series will lead us back to events outside the nervous system and, eventually; outside the organism" (Skinner 1953, 28).

This is not a rejection of biology, but rather a call for, and emphasis on, rigorous understanding of environment-behavior relationships in their own right. Indeed, "A comprehensive set of causal relations stated with the greatest possible precision is the best contribution which we, as students of behavior, can make in the cooperative venture of giving a full account of the organism as a biological system" (Skinner 1956/1972, 270).

An example might help to clarify here. It is well established that a tone that has preceded a shock comes to reliably produce a response (e.g., a lever press) that has terminated the tone and preempted the shock (escape/avoidance conditioning). Finding that damage to, or removal of, the amygdala influences this type of learning (LeDoux 2002) provides important additional information and was more readily achieved because it could build upon an already known environment-behavior relationship. Likewise, that effective psychosocial intervention for social phobia produces changes in amygdalar functioning (similar to effective pharmacotherapy, see Furmark et al., 2002) is fascinating, consistent with the view that changes in behavior are correlated with changes in neurology, and leads to a fuller account of the process of effective psychotherapy. However, it is also the case that identification of the biological changes was not required to establish the validity of the behavior changes observed: "By appealing only to environmental variables (while assuming a given set of genetic and organic variables), psychology may make this contribution entirely within its own field. That there are etiological factors lying beyond this field is doubtless true" (Skinner 1957/1972, 253).

The preceding should make clear that Skinner was not antagonistic to biology, recognized that brain changes are necessarily correlated with changes in behavior, and would concur that the most complete account involves understanding environment-gene-brain-behavior relationships. However, his level of analysis was environment-behavior relationships and these cannot be removed from the sequence. He writes, "The organism is, of course, not empty, and it cannot be adequately treated simply as a black box, but we must carefully distinguish between what is known about what is inside and what is merely inferred" (Skinner 1974, 233).

While Skinner clearly recognized the importance of genetics and biology, he was adamantly opposed to mentalism—that is, to invented, hypothetical, or metaphorical nervous systems that are in principle unobservable (i.e., nonphysical) and confuse psychology with physiology/neurology. I turn to Skinner's rejection of mentalism, but not covert events, next.

The Only Overt Behavior Myth

Even if we accept that Skinner recognized that humans are not biologically empty, clearly it is accurate that he saw the organism as cognitively empty, right? According to Seligman (2002, 31), Skinner "argued for half a century that all of mental life was mere epiphenomena...." Pinker (1997, 62) concurred that Skinner "held that beliefs and desires have nothing to do with behavior—indeed, that they are as unscientific as banshees and black magic." Not exactly. Skinner opposed mentalism but did not reject the role of private events.

> The distinction between public and private is by no means the same as that between physical and mental. That is why methodological behaviorism (which adopts the first) is very different from radical behaviorism (which lops off the latter term in the second). The result is that while the radical behaviorist may in some cases consider private events (inferentially, perhaps, but nonetheless meaningfully), the methodological operationist has maneuvered himself into a position where he cannot. (Skinner 1945/1972, 383)

Furthermore, Skinner writes that

> Mentalism kept attention away from the external antecedent events which might have explained behavior, by seeming to supply an alternative explanation. Methodological behaviorism did just the reverse: by dealing exclusively with external antecedent events it turned attention away from self-observation and self-knowledge. Radical behaviorism restores some kind of balance. It does not insist upon truth by agreement and can therefore consider events taking place in the private world within the skin. It does not call these events unobservable, and it does not dismiss them as subjective. (Skinner 1974, 18)

Behavior lies on a continuum: some is only privately observed (e.g., thinking, imagining), while some is publicly observed (e.g., movements), but all of it is in principle observable and hence amenable to scientific analysis. Private responses are not dismissed by Skinner (as in Warsonian, methodological, behaviorism) but are also accorded no special status and are not seen as different in kind from other behavior.

> Covert behavior is almost always acquired in overt form and no one has ever shown that the covert form achieves anything which is out of reach of the overt.... It [covert behavior] does not explain overt behavior: it is simply more behavior to be explained. (Skinner 1974, 115)

Consider, for example, the question "What is the tenth word of the National Anthem of the United States?" To solve this problem you might a) write out the words and then count them, b) rehearse the words silently while counting on your fingers, or c) rehearse and count silently. What happened here? In response to the external antecedent event—the problem—a sequence of overt and/or covert responses were then emitted, each of which changed the situation/environment and controlled subsequent responses that ultimately made emission of the correct response (i.e., light) more probable. Skinner's analysis recognizes the importance of the various overt and/or covert responses in the causal sequence but requires that the causal sequence be completed by extending it backwards to the external antecedent and forward to the consequences for correct or incorrect responses. Furthermore, note that there was no necessity that your sequence of overt and/or covert behavior led to a correct answer. Most obviously, if you lack exposure to the National Anthem of the United States (or your repertoire is deficient in basic counting skills), effective overt or covert adjustments are unlikely. The last point emphasizes again the importance of prior selection by consequences (i.e., the individual's learning history) in explaining current behavior (both overt and covert).

> Human beings attend to or disregard the world in which they live. They search for things in that world. They generalize from one thing to another. They discriminate. They respond to single features or special sets of features as "abstractions" or "concepts." They solve problems by assembling, classifying, arranging, and rearranging things. They describe things and respond to their descriptions, as well as to descriptions made by others. They analyze the contingencies of reinforcement in their world and extract plans and rules which enable them to respond appropriately without direct exposure to the contingencies. They discover and use rules for deriving new rules from old. In all this, and much more, they are simply behaving, and that is true even when they are behaving covertly. (Skinner 1974, 245–246)

This description is a far cry from considering human beings passive, empty, nonthinking black boxes.

The purpose of this article is not to recruit adherents or to convince anyone of the relative merits of Skinner's position, nor to denigrate or dismiss the theories of the contemporary authors cited. My goal was simply to use the occasion of the approaching 100th anniversary of Skinner's birth to clear away some mythical debris that remains about his approach to psychology as a science of behavior. The material presented does not constitute historical revisionism, but Skinner in his own words with some supporting text and examples. You may disagree with Skinner's actual positions, but it serves no purpose to disagree with myths or caricatures. Indeed contemporary behavior analysis does not sit still looking backwards, but continues forward from the tradition established by Skinner making important advances in a natural science approach to emotions and motivation (see Dougher and Hackbert 2000; Michael 2000), problem solving, cognition, and language (see Donahoe and Palmer 1994; Hayes, Barnes-Holmes, and Roche 2001). Skinner would have it no other way: "The study of human behavior is, of course, still in its infancy, and it would be rash to suppose that anyone can foresee the structure of a well-developed and successful science Certainly no current formulation will seem right fifty years hence" (Skinner 1956/1972, 260).

References

Donahoe, J.W., and D.C. Palmer. 1994. Learning and Complex Behavior. Needham Heights, Massachusetts: Allyn & Bacon.

Dougher, M.J., and L. Hackbert. 2000. Establishing operations, cognition, and emotion. Behavior Analyst 23(1): 11–24.

Furmark, T., M. Tillfors, I. Marteinsdottir, H. Fisher, A. Pissiota, B. Langstrom, and M. Fredrikson. 2002. Common changes in cerebral blood flow in patients with social phobia treated with citalopram or cognitive-behavioral therapy. Archives of General Psychiatry 59(5): 425–433.

Gopnik, A., A.N. Meltzoff, and E. K. Kuhl. 1999. The Scientist in the Crib: What Early Learning Tells Us About the Mind. New York: HarperCollins.

Hayes, S.C., D. Barnes-Holmes, and B. Roche. 2001. Relational Frame Theory: A Post-Skinnerian Account of Human Language and Cognition. New York: Kluwer Academic/ Plenum Publishers.

LeDoux, J. 2002. Synaptic Self. How Our Brains Become Who We Are. New York: Penguin.

Michael, J. 2000. Implications and refinements of the establishing operation concept. Journal of Applied Behavior Analysis 33(4): 401–410.

Pinker, S. 1997. How the Mind Works. New York: W.W Norton & Co.

———. 2002. The Blank Slate: The Modern Denial of Human Nature. New York: Penguin.

Ridley, M. 1996. The Origins of Virtue. New York: Penguin.

Seligman, M.P. 2002. Authentic Happiness: Using the New Positive Psychology to Realize Your Potential for Lasting Fulfillment. New York: Free Press.

Skinner, B.F. 1945. The operational analysis of psychological terms. Psychological Review 52: 270–77.

———. 1953. Science and Human Behavior. New York: Free Press.

———. 1956. What is psychotic behavior? In F. Gilda et al. (Eds.), Theory and Treatment of the Psychoses: Some Newer Aspects. St. Louis: Washington University Studies.

———. 1957. Psychology in the understanding of mental disease. In H. D. Kruse (Ed.), Integrating the Approaches to Mental Disease. New York: Hoeber-Harper.

———. 1959. John Broadus Watson, behaviorist. Science 129: 197–98.

———. 1966. The phylogeny and ontogeny of behavior. Science 153:1205–13.

———. 1969. Contingencies of Reinforcement: A Theoretical Analysis. New York: Appleton-Century-Crofts.

———. 1972. Cumulative Record: A Selection of Papers (3rd ed.). New York: Appleton-Century-Crofts.

———. 1974. About Behaviorism. New York: Knopf.

———. 1975. The shaping of phylogenetic behavior. Journal of the Experimental Analysis of Behavior 24(1): 117–120.

———. 1984. The evolution of behavior. Journal of the Experimental Analysis of Behavior 41(2): 217–221.

SCOTT T. GAYNOR is in the Department of Psychology, Western Michigan University, Kalamazoo, MI 49008-543R E-mail scott.gaynor@wmich.edu.

Psychology of Safety: The "Big Five" and You

How Personality Traits Can Affect Behavior

E. SCOTT GELLER, PH.D.

Faithful readers of this column may have noticed that most of my articles this year have addressed how personality factors relate to individual safety performance. But I believe there is much to be learned about the personality/behavior connection, and especially the implications for workplace health and safety.

My intent with this series of columns, is to stir the pot, to stimulate thinking and conversations among safety and health professionals and hopefully some breakthrough research on the role of personality traits and states in achieving an injury-free workplace. Clearly, there is much to be gained from a better understanding of how personality characteristics affect safety performance.

Increasing Risks

For instance, I believe, as I stated in my May column, that certain personality characteristics increase the chance that an individual will perform at-risk behaviors and experience an unintended injury. Other personality dimensions influence one's willingness to engage in injury preventive behaviors. In other words, there are personality factors that contribute to injury proneness, and other factors that lead to injury preventiveness.

Sometimes, a personality factor can work both ways. For example, one research study showed that people who scored high on a measure of personal control were more likely to take risks, making them more injury prone. But these individuals were also more likely to follow safety precautions, making them more injury preventive.

States & Traits

We can't get too far into a discussion of personality factors and safety performance without distinguishing between personality states and traits, which was the topic of my April column. I'm biased to the state perspective. This is the idea that personality is dramatically shaped by the environmental context. That is, personality characteristics are not etched in stone, but fluctuate according to the situation. For example, a person might be an optimistic success-seeker in recreational activities but be a pessimistic failure avoider when it comes to work.

This is what you find in most self-help books and audiotapes. Change conditions of your situation and follow certain self-management steps and you can improve your attitude, behavior and even career success. You can be whatever you want to be, proclaim some of these pop psychologists. It's a matter of changing your "state" of mind.

Limits of Change

Of course we simply cannot become any kind of person we'd like to become, even if all the relevant environmental variables are on our side. We do face physical limitations. And certain personality characteristics are indeed genetically determined and inherited, according to psychological research conducted in the past two decades.

For example, a systematic comparison of identical twins reared apart after only five months of age with twins raised together showed that those twin pairs raised in the same home were not more similar than those raised separately in respect to various personality traits.

This and similar research has led to the conclusion that genetics account for about 50 percent of individual differences in personality.

So recent psychological research has swung the pendulum back toward the nature side of the nature/nurture question. This doesn't diminish environmental factors as being inconsequential. Behavior is determined by an interaction of the context in which we perform with personality characteristics. Sometimes situations are the primary determinant of behavior, sometimes personality shapes behavior.

Primary factors

Now to take our discussion of personality further, let's examine personality types. Every research-based textbook among more

Table 1 The Big Five Personality Traits

Openness to Experience
Curious, broad interests, creative, original, imaginative, untraditional, flexible, sensitive, adventuresome

opposite characteristics
conventional, down-to-earth, narrow interests, rigid, inflexible, insensitive, crude

Conscientiousness
achievement-oriented, organized, reliable, hard-working, careful, self-disciplined, ambitious, persevering, responsible

opposite characteristics
aimless, unreliable, lazy, careless, lax, negligent, weak-willed, hedonistic, impulsive, disorganized

Extraversion
sociable, assertive, talkative, optimistic, people-oriented, outgoing, fun-loving, affectionate

opposite characteristics
reserved, sober, cautious, quiet, aloof, task-oriented, shy

Agreeableness
soft-hearted, trusting, good-natured, helpful, forgiving, caring, cooperative, gentle

opposite characteristics
cynical, rude, suspicious, irritable, manipulative, vengeful, uncooperative, ruthless, hostile, self-centered, headstrong

Neuroticism
worrisome, nervous, emotional, insecure, hypochondriachal, frequent distress, hypersensitive, excitable

opposite characteristics
calm, relaxed, unemotional, hardy, secure, self-satisfied, composed

than 20 I consulted that covered personality traits identified the same five primary person factors.

Table 1 identifies these traits as bipolar dimensions, referred to in the research literature as the "Big Five." Note that the order of the dimensions presented in Table 1 spell the word "ocean," making it easy to remember these critical personality characteristics.

These dimensions remain relatively stable over an individual's lifetime, and carry across (generalize) cultural lines, according to substantial research conducted in the 1990s. Plus, the "Big Five" personality traits have been found to be 40 percent to 60 percent inheritable.

Table 2 provides a few representative questions per each of the "Big Five" traits. Higher numbers reflect qualities of the particular trait, except for those items followed by an "R." These need to be reverse scored, meaning the number circled should be subtracted from "6" to make the score consistent with other items.

Please don't consider your totals on these select items to be a valid measure of the "Big Five." Rather, read them to improve your understanding of each trait, and use individual scores to trigger conversations about these constructs and their relation to safety-related behaviors. How do the "Big Five" affect safety performance?

We don't really know the answer to that—yet. Research to date has not studied specific connections between "Big Five" traits and injury proneness or injury preventiveness.

Table 2 Sample Questions Used to Assess the Big Five

	Never	Rarely	Sometimes	Often	Always
Openness to Experience					
I have a vivid imagination.	1	2	3	4	5
I have a rich vocabulary.	1	2	3	4	5
I am not interested in abstract ideas. (R)	1	2	3	4	5
Conscientiousness					
I am exacting in my work.	1	2	3	4	5
I neglect my duties. (R)	1	2	3	4	5
I like order.	1	2	3	4	5
I pay attention to details.	1	2	3	4	5
I am always prepared.	1	2	3	4	5
Extraversion					
I feel comfortable around people.	1	2	3	4	5
I start conversations.	1	2	3	4	5
I keep in the background. (R)	1	2	3	4	5
I don't like to draw attention to myself. (R)	1	2	3	4	5
I am quiet around strangers. (R)	1	2	3	4	5
Agreeableness					
I feel little concern for others. (R)	1	2	3	4	5
I make other people feel at ease.	1	2	3	4	5
I feel others' emotions.	1	2	3	4	5
I insult people. (R)	1	2	3	4	5
I take time out for others.	1	2	3	4	5
Neuroticism					
I change my mood a lot.	1	2	3	4	5
I get upset easily.	1	2	3	4	5
I worry about things.	1	2	3	4	5
I get stressed out easily.	1	2	3	4	5
I am relaxed most of the time (R).	1	2	3	4	5

But still, certain relations between these personality traits and safety-related behaviors seem reasonable and worth our serious consideration:

- For example, my April column made a case for a positive correlation between anxiety and proactive injury prevention, and the definition of anxiety I used is similar to the neuroticism dimension.
- Plus, it is likely that individuals scoring high on conscientiousness are more apt to partake in injury-prevention processes.
- I also predict that those scoring relatively high on openness to experience will be more likely to accept and participate in an innovative approach to preventing injuries.
- And common sense suggests that injury-prevention procedures requiring interpersonal conversation (such as behavioral observation and feedback) will be more accepted by those who score high on extroversion and agreeableness.
- It's also likely those with these personality traits will be more successful at implementing an interpersonal coaching process.

These hypotheses reflect only a few of the possible ways the "Big Five" could influence workplace safety. Clearly, we need systematic research in this area, especially given the pervasive behavioral influence of these five genetically determined dimensions of human personality. As I mentioned at the outset, we have much to learn about personality that could benefit our safety initiatives in the workplace.

E. SCOTT GELLER, Ph.D., is professor and director, Center for Applied Behavior Systems, Virginia Tech, and senior partner, Safety Performance Solutions.

From *Industrial Safety & Hygiene News*, Vol. 38, no. 17, July 2004, pp. 12+. Copyright © 2004 by BNP Media. Reprinted by permission of BNP Media via the Copyright Clearance Center

UNIT 2
Determinants of Behavior: Motivation, Environment, and Physiology

Unit Selections

Key Points to Consider

- What is meant by nature? What is meant by nurture?

- If a mental disorder is controlled by something genetic, does that mean that the disorder is untreatable?

- Why is it important for psychologists to study the human brain and nervous system?

- What is motivation and how is it important to personal growth and adjustment?

- How can people set better goals and then strive to meet them?

- How do ambition, perfectionism, and procrastination affect motivation?

Student Web Site
www.mhcls.com/online

Internet References
Further information regarding these Web sites may be found in this book's preface or online.

American Psychological Society (APS)
http://www.psychologicalscience.org

Federation of Behavioral, Psychological, and Cognitive Science
http://www.thefederationonline.org/

Max Planck Institute for Psychological Research
http://www.mpipf-muenchen.mpg.de/BCD/bcd_e.htm

The Opportunity of Adolescence
http://www.winternet.com/~webpage/adolescencepaper.html

Psychology Research on the Net
http://psych.hanover.edu/Research/exponnet.html

Serendip
http://serendip.brynmawr.edu/serendip/

On the front page of every newspaper, in practically every televised newscast, and on many magazine covers, the problems of human behavior such as substance abuse haunt us. Innocent children are killed by the crossfire of guns of drug lords or even of their own classmates. Prostitutes selling their bodies for drug money and spreading the deadly AIDS virus. The white-collar middle manager loses his job because he embezzled company money to support his lavish lifestyle. And more recently, the threat of terrorism has changed the way people in the Western world live.

Why do people do the things they do? For example, why do people turn to drugs? Why doesn't the publicity about the ruination of human lives diminish the drug problem? Why can some people consume two cocktails and stop, while others feel helpless against the inebriating seduction of alcohol? Why do some people crave heroin as their drug of choice, while others choose cigarettes or caffeine? Why are some people religious, even zealous, while others are not? Why do some religious groups kill others while other religious groups believe in peaceful coexistence of all religions?

The causes of individual behavior are the focus of this unit. If physiology—biochemistry, the nervous system or genes—is the determinant of our behavior, then solutions to such puzzles as alcoholism lie in the field of psychobiology, the study of behavior in relation to biological processes, or in human medicine. However, if learning as a function of our environment or experience creates personal growth and adjustment, then researchers must take a different tack and explore features of the environment responsible for certain behaviors. Yet a third explanation for growth and behavior suggests that ability to adjust to change is produced by some complex interplay between learning and biology. If such an interaction accounts for individual development and ability to cope, scientists then have a very complicated task ahead of them.

Conducting research designed to unravel the determinants of behavior is difficult. Scientists must call upon their best design skills to develop studies that will yield useful and replicable findings. A researcher hoping to examine the role of experience in personal growth and behavior needs to be able to isolate one or two stimuli or environmental features that seem to control a particular behavior. Imagine trying to delimit the complexity of the world sufficiently so that only one or two events stand out as the cause of an individual's substance abuse. Likewise, researchers interested in psychobiology also need refined, technical knowledge. Suppose a scientist hopes to show that a particular form of mental illness is inherited. She cannot merely examine family genetic histories, because family members can also learn maladaptive behaviors from one another. The researcher's ingenuity will be challenged; she must use intricate techniques such as comparing children to their adoptive as well as to their biological parents. Additionally, volunteer subjects may be difficult to find, and, added to that, the data may be hard to interpret.

The first article in this unit offers an introduction to the determinants of human behavior by examining the interplay of nature and nurture. The article, by Leslie Knowlton, explores the joint contributions of nature and nurture. The article discusses the contributions of genes as well as the relative influence of the environment on child psychopathology. The author provides a good, general overview of the nature/nurture controversy by trying to unravel the influence of child maltreatment *and* genetic predispositions on maladaptive behaviors of children.

We subsequently turn to the role of nature, in particular of genes, in shaping our behaviors. The next article, by Eric Jaffe, reviews the role of nature or biology in shaping who we are. A steady stream of research in psychology has aimed researchers more and more in the direction of genetics or heredity as the cause of many human behaviors. The research, however, has drawn the ire of opponents who fear that such scientific endeavors will unsettle the current, American social order.

In a companion essay, psychologist Thomas Bouchard contends that traits are not all equally influenced by genes. Stated another way, genetic influence varies for different traits. Bouchard provides evidence about the magnitude of genetic influence on several different human characteristics.

The nervous system is also an important contributor to personal qualities and human behaviors. In the next article, "The Amazing Brain: Is Neuroscience the Key to What Makes Us Human?", the author credits the brain for generating much of our behavior. Richard Restak, the author, proposes that understanding neural pathways is crucial to our understanding of human actions. Neuroscientific knowledge may one day be the key to understanding some baffling psychological syndromes.

As an example of how important the brain is, a companion article follows and is entitled "His Brain, Her Brain." Larry Cahill, writing in *Scientific American*, attributes sex differences to the hard wiring of the brain. He declares that males and females are different and that sex differences exist because of neurological differences between men and women and boys and girls. Cahill maintains that knowing more about these neurological differences may help researchers fashion sex-specific treatments for various brain disorders.

Culture is another extremely important determinant of who we are. In "Cultural Psychology: Studying the Exotic Other," the author reviews the work of cultural psychologists. Cultural psychologists do not assume that there are common or universal human behaviors. Rather, these psychologists search for important ways that behavior varies as a consequence of culture. Their work demonstrates the importance of the environment and of learning.

We next turn our attention to motivation, which involves specific goal-directed activity often stimulated by deprivation of some need. Have you ever noticed how some people seem to be very goal-oriented and ambitious? In "Ambition: Why Some People Are Most Likely to Succeed," Jeffrey Kluger, writing for *Time Magazine*, discusses ambition, something that interestingly does not characterize everyone. What it is, where it comes from, and who possesses it are investigated in this article.

"How to Keep Those New Year's Resolutions" is an article most of us need to read. A large number of people set resolutions each January 1st and then a month later allow the resolutions to fall victim to neglect. Because motivation is an important determinant of human behavior, this article, which reviews how better to set and meet goals, is included.

It is quite human to procrastinate or so says Maia Szalavitz in a companion article, "Stand and Deliver." Maintaining motivation is a problem common to many of us. What we need to do to overcome procrastination is discussed in this article.

In summary, this unit reviews factors that shape our behaviors and thoughts; in other words, factors that are moderated by genes, the nervous system, culture and the environment, motives, or some combination of all.

Nature Versus Nurture: How Is Child Psychopathology Developed?

LESLIE KNOWLTON

In an attempt to reframe the long-standing debate over the either-or impact of genetics versus environment on emotional makeup, a panel titled "Genes-Environment Interactions: Developmental and Psychotherapeutic Implications" convened at the American Psychoanalytic Association's Winter 2005 Meeting in New York City.

Glen O. Gabbard, M.D., Brown Foundation chair of psychoanalysis and professor of psychiatry at the Baylor College of Medicine in Houston, presented data on the gene-environment interaction in antisocial and borderline personality disorders, showing that DNA is both inherited and environmentally modifiable. Gabbard told Psychiatric Times that there is today, in the field of psychiatry, a simplistic thinking that wants everything reduced to the genome.

"Most people do not like complexity, so there's a seductiveness about genetic reductionism," he said. "But genes alone do not determine personality, and we have good data now showing that it is a matter of genes interacting with the environment in the expression of those genes, and the environment making actual changes in that expression."

At the meeting, Gabbard described a long-term, follow-up study of 1,037 children in Dunedin, New Zealand—a birth cohort assessed every two years up to age 26 (Caspi et al. 2002). Measures included degree of maltreatment, monoamine oxidase A (MAOA) gene activity and antisocial behavior. Results showed that males with low MAOA activity who were maltreated in childhood had elevated antisocial scores, whereas males with high MAOA activity did not have the elevated scores even when they had experienced maltreatment. Overall, 85% of the males with both the low MAOA activity genotype and severe maltreatment became antisocial.

"The authors concluded that a functional polymorphism in the MAOA gene moderates the impact of childhood maltreatment on development of antisocial behavior. The point here, against reductionism, is that neither the low-activity gene alone nor the environmental maltreatment alone is enough to create antisocial behavior," explained Gabbard.

Those findings were replicated in a study of 514 male twins (ages 8 to 17), which showed that low MAOA activity increased risk for conduct disorder only in the presence of an adverse

childhood environment (Foley et al., 2004). "Once again, the combination had to be present," Gabbard said.

In a study of the effects of differential parenting on antisocial behavior in 708 families with at least two same-sexed adolescent siblings, almost 60% of the variance in adolescent antisocial behavior and 37% of the variation in depressive symptoms were accounted for by conflictual and negative parental behavior directed specifically at the adolescent, not at the sibling (Reiss et al., 1995).

"So there's differential parenting and you can't assume that every kid in a family has the same parenting," said Gabbard. "Non-shared environmental influences appear to have the largest impact on normal versus pathological development."

Inherited traits can produce differential parenting responses that could ameliorate or exacerbate those traits.

"One implication that hasn't been studied in a sophisticated prospective design is that psychotherapeutic interventions with caregivers might actually alter genetic expression in genetically vulnerable children," said Gabbard.

Provocative data confirming this idea comes from a 15-year follow-up of a randomized, controlled trial of the impact of home visitation by a nurse on children's antisocial behavior (Olds et al., 1998). The study found that adolescents born to young, low-income women who received nurse visits indeed had significantly lower rates of antisocial behavior than controls. They also had lower rates of substance abuse and fewer lifetime sex partners.

"So this kind of intervention made quite a difference in what we might expect from these kids," Gabbard said. "So what I am saying so far is that genes and environment are inextricably connected in the pathogenesis of antisocial behavior; a strict dichotomy is specious. Psychotherapy of parents and caregivers may influence genetic vulnerability, and a neglected benefit of psychotherapy in the literature is its impact on offspring of the patient."

Shifting to a discussion of borderline personality disorder (BPD), Gabbard said there are much less genetic data regarding this condition. Some data come from neuroimaging studies that showed smaller hippocampus and amygdala volumes in patients with BPD versus controls (Driessen et al., 2000; Schmahl et al., 2003; Tebartz van Elst et al., 2003). "But the exact relationship between early trauma and decreased volumes in the amygdala is unclear, since 60% to 80% of patients with BPD have substantial childhood trauma," explained Gabbard.

A volumetric study of response to facial expressions found that patients with BPD showed significantly greater left amygdala activation to happy, sad and fearful expressions compared with normal controls, and attributed negative qualities to neutral faces (Donegan et al., 2003).

"A hyperactive amygdala may be involved in the predisposition to be hypervigilant and overreactive to relatively benign emotional expressions," said Gabbard. "Misreading neutral faces is clearly related to transference misreadings that occur in psychotherapy and the creation of bad object experiences linked with projective identification."

Another study found that individuals with one or two copies of the short allele of the serotonin transporter (5-HTT) promoter gene demonstrated greater amygdala neuronal activity in response to fearful stimuli compared to individuals homozygous for the long allele (Hariri et al., 2002).

"There may be a genetic vulnerability that predisposes one to amygdala hyperreactivity in response to trauma," Gabbard said. "We need more data to know that, but we do know from the Dunedin longitudinal study that the short allele moderated the influence of stressful life events on depression, and stressful life events predicted suicidal ideation or attempt among individuals carrying the short allele but not among those with the long variant [Caspi et al., 2003]."

In a study of how social support might moderate depression after mistreatment, 57 maltreated children were compared to 44 controls (Kaufman et al., 2004). "What was ideal here is that there were no differences in short versus long alleles of the serotonin transporter gene between maltreated [participants] and controls," said Gabbard. Results showed that maltreated children with the short allele and no social support had the highest depression ratings, but positive social supports reduced risk of depression associated with maltreated children and the short allele.

"So the environment can moderate the impact of the genetic constellation," said Gabbard. "This is a very provocative study showing that genetic vulnerability can be modified by intensive social support."

It may be more than the presence of trauma that makes the difference in outcome, according to Gabbard. The child's intrapsychic interpretation of the trauma may be highly relevant. Parents and caretakers can contextualize events so that the child can make sense of them in ways that are beneficial. These ideas also relate to the potential for psychoanalysis and other therapies to change the impact of those experiences, added Gabbard.

"Whether or not environmental factors trigger the expression of the gene may depend on the conscious or unconscious meaning attributed to these experiences," stated Gabbard.

The studies on the influence of genes and environment on human development are supported by studies of primates and rats. "The support from laboratories, where you can manipulate genes and environments in ways you can't do with human beings because of ethics, definitely shows that the environment alters genetic expression," explained Gabbard.

One example is a series of lab and field studies of monkeys done by Stephen Suomi, Ph.D., chief of the Laboratory of Comparative Ethology, and his team at the National Institute of Child Health and Development (see Suomi, 2003). Suomi presented data on a group of rhesus monkeys that showed the aggressive and highly impulsive characteristics of antisocial personalities. Such monkeys had deficits in serotonin, a highly heritable characteristic also associated with a tendency to drink an excessive amount of alcohol. But a series of studies showed that these highly heritable characteristics can be modified substantially by a nurturing environment.

Specifically, the studies looked at monkeys with short and long alleles of the serotonin transporter 5-IITT promoter gene, the short version being associated with low serotonin and the long version associated with normal serotonin levels. The two types of monkeys were separated into groups raised by peers and other groups raised by mothers. The mother-raised monkeys of both allele types showed normal 5-HIAA levels, while peer-raised monkeys with short alleles showed much lower levels than either group of normal monkeys. The same pattern was seen with aggression, with short-allele mother-raised monkeys showing the same low level of aggression as normal monkeys in either group, and peer-raised short-allele monkeys showing high levels of aggression. The peer-raised monkeys acted far more anxious, clingy and fearful, no matter what their allele type.

"So good mothering is very important and goes a long way toward protecting these [at-risk] monkeys," said Suomi.

Furthermore, there is a non-genetic transmission of mothering, as the attachment style of monkey mothers—whether foster or not—is usually copied by daughters. Rat studies also support evidence for the gene-environment interaction.

Regina Pally, M.D., assistant clinical professor at the University of California at Los Angeles Neuropsychiatric Institute and chair of the panel, reviewed rat projects conducted by Michael Meaney, Ph.D., and colleagues at McGill University (see Zhang et al., 2004.) She explained that in rats, maternal care runs across a spectrum from highly nurturing mothers to poorly nurturing mothers, and that offspring resemble their mothers as to behavior and emotional temperament.

To address the question of nature versus nurture with regard to these observations, Meaney used an experimental design called "cross-fostering," wherein rats who are inbred to share the same genes are developed into two strains, each at opposite ends of the nurturing spectrum. Right after birth, some of the pups of low-nurturing mothers are placed with high-nurturing mothers, and some of the pups of high-nurturing mothers are likewise switched. Therefore, each mother is rearing both biological and foster pups.

"The mothering environment shaped the genes. Every gene has a promoter region which turns it on or off, and the environment influences the promoter," explained Pally.

Results showed that in terms of emotion and behavior, pups resemble the mother that raised them more than their biological mother. The results were interpreted in terms of gene expression.

"It is in this way that over the course of development, the growth of the brain—in terms of neurons, neurotransmitters, and neurotransmitter receptors—will be affected and will be manifest as behaviors and emotions, such as how that individual responds to stress or how nurturing that individual is," concluded Pally.

References

Caspi A, McClay J, Moffitt TE et al. (2002), Role of genotype in the cycle of violence in maltreated children. Science 297(5582):851–854 [see comment].

Caspi A, Sugden K, Moffitt TE et al. (2003), Influence of life stress on depression: moderation by a polymorphism in the 5-HTT gene. Science 301(5631):386–389 [see comment].

Donegan NH, Sanislow CA, Blumberg HP et al. (2003), Amygdala hyperreactivity in borderline personality disorder: implications for emotional dysregulation. Biol Psychiatry 54(11):1284–1293.

Driessen M, Herrmann J, Stahl K et al. (2000), Magnetic resonance imaging volumes of the hippocampus and the amygdala in women with borderline personality disorder and early traumatization. Arch Gen Psychiatry 57(12):1115–1122.

Foley DL, Eaves LJ, Wormley B et al. (2004), Childhood adversity, monoamine oxidase A genotype, and risk for conduct disorder. Arch Gen Psychiatry 61(7):738–744.

Hariri AR, Mattay VS, Tessitore A et al. (2002), Serotonin transporter genetic variation and the response of the human amygdala. Science 297(5580):400–403 [see comment].

Kaufman J, Yang BZ, Douglas-Palumberi H et al. (2004), Social supports and serotonin transporter gene moderate depression in maltreated children. Proc Natl Acad Sci U S A 101(49):17316–17321 [see comment].

Olds D, Henderson CR Jr, Cole R et al. (1998), Long-term effects of nurse home visitation on children's criminal and antisocial behavior: 15-year follow-up of a randomized controlled trial. JAMA 280(14):1238–1244 [see comments].

Reiss D, Hetherington EM, Plomin R et al. (1995), Genetic questions for environmental studies. Differential parenting and psychopathology in adolescence. Arch Gen Psychiatry 52(11):925–936.

Schmahl CG, Vermetten E, Elzinga BM, Bremner DJ (2003), Magnetic resonance imaging of hippocampal and amygdala volume in women with childhood abuse and borderline personality disorder. Psychiatry Res 122(3):193–198.

Suomi SJ (2003), Gene-environment interactions and the neurobiology of social conflict. Ann N Y Acad Sci 1008:132–139.

Tebartz van Elst L, Hesslinger B, Thiel T et al. (2003), Frontolimbic brain abnormalities in patients with borderline personality disorder: a volumetric magnetic resonance imaging study. Biol Psychiatry 54(2):163–171.

Zhang TY, Parent C, Weaver I, Meaney MJ (2004), Maternal programming of individual differences in defensive responses in the rat. Ann N Y Acad Sci 1032:85–103.

Empirical Science for the Spotless Mind

Traditional theories of the mind as a blank slate are gradually being replaced by a scientific understanding of what aspects of behavior may be innate.

ERIC JAFFE

The blank slate, the dominant theory of human nature in modern intellectual life stating that humans are shaped entirely by their experiences and not by any preexisting biological mechanisms, is being challenged and soundly trounced by the cognitive, neural, and genetic sciences, said Steven Pinker, Harvard University, in his Keynote Address.

"Everyone has a theory of human nature," Pinker said. "Everyone has to anticipate the behavior of others, and that means all of us have theories, tacit or explicit, about what makes people tick."

For hundreds of years, three such theories—the blank slate, the noble savage, and the ghost in the machine—have provided the foundation for moral values and social conduct. Each of the theories, while flawed, is not without its appeal.

John Locke's tabula rasa, or blank slate, compares the mind to white paper inscribed gradually by experience. Such a proposal is attractive to egalitarian spirits, as it undermines aristocratic claims of innate, superior wisdom. Jean Jacques Rousseau's account of the noble savage holds that "nothing could be more gentle than [man] in his primitive state," providing philosophical hope for a utopian society in which armed governments and police forces are unnecessary. Rene Descartes' belief in the division of soul and body—the ghost and the machine—is welcomed by optimists seeking transcendent pursuits of love, worship, beauty, and knowledge, as well as a soul that can survive the death of the body.

What unsettles Pinker isn't that these theories hold sway but that they are accepted unconditionally despite increasing evidence against them. "There's something deeply wrong with all of this," he said, "beginning with the blank slate."

Challenges to the Blank Slate

As Pinker argued, this trilogy of theories becomes undone, repeatedly and irreparably, under the lenses of modern science—particularly, cognitive understanding, evolutionary psychology, and neurology. "There have to be some innate mechanisms to do the learning, to achieve the socializing, to create and transmit the culture" upon which experiences are based, Pinker said.

From a cognitive perspective, such mechanisms include a number sense; a sense of spatial representation; the ability to

grasp the thoughts of others; a language instinct; and decision rules that govern behavior. Other human drives can only be understood within the context of evolution. For example, our desire for sugar and fat, resources whose scarcity once made their rapid consumption vital, has not diminished, though we can now reproduce them at large.

Perhaps the most devastating argument against the blank slate comes from neuroscience, where research by APS William James Fellow Award winner Robert Plomin and others has shown that identical twins separated at birth share many astonishing similarities despite vastly different upbringings. Take the remarkable case of this pair: one twin raised as a Catholic in Nazi Germany, the other by his Jewish father in Trinidad. When they were reunited in their 40s at a Minnesota lab, both of them were wearing identical navy blue shirts with epaulets; rubber bands around their wrists; flushed the toilet before using it as well as after; and intentionally sneezed in crowded elevators to watch other people jump.

The noble savage theory has been subjected to equally rigorous attacks from the brain and behavioral sciences, Pinker said. Neuroscience has identified brain mechanisms associated with aggression, and the resulting data conflicts with Rousseau's theory; as ignoble as Western civilization may seem at times, it remains leaps and bounds ahead of savage existence. A study documenting warfare in various societies showed that in prestate, or relatively uncivilized, areas such as the New Guinea highlands and the Amazon rainforest, the percentage of male deaths due to warfare ranged from around 10 to 60 percent. The same statistic for the United States and Europe combined during the 20th century, including both World Wars, was infinitesimal by comparison.

In opposition to the ghost and the machine theory, cognitive science has shown that intelligence can be explained in mechanistic terms, Pinker said. Machines that display artificial intelligence can be built, such as Deep Blue, which defeated world chess champion Garry Kasparov in 1997. Surgery can demonstrably alter the functioning of the brain, most famously in APS President Michael Gazzaniga's studies of split brain patients, in which the corpus callosum is severed, "leaving two, largely autonomous consciousnesses co-residing in the same skull," Pinker said, "as if the soul could be bisected with a knife."

To Pinker, such findings hoist the blank canvas onto a finely engineered easel, creating a much more comprehensive view of human nature. "The challenges [to the blank slate] are seen to threaten sacred moral values, but in fact that doesn't follow," he said. "On the contrary, a better understanding of what makes us tick can clarify those values." But to others, the idea that thoughts, feelings, and experiences consist of physiological activity in the tissues of the brain leaves a much emptier picture.

Fearing the Science

Despite the abundance of scientific evidence, "there's a widespread fear and loathing of the sciences of human nature," Pinker argued. "Many people are sorry to lose God when they hear of these findings, or at least sorry to lose the values traditionally associated with God." Like the character in "The Truman Show," who believed his world was the beautiful, harmonious product of chance only to find it was a systematically organized series of set-ups, certain irrational fears drive a resistance to scientific discoveries of human nature.

Scientific fear and loathing can result in profound misunderstanding, as exemplified by House of Representatives majority leader Tom DeLay's remarks after Columbine. "Such outbursts of violence are inevitable," DeLay said, "because our school systems teach children that they are nothing but glorified apes evolutionized out of some primordial soup of mud."

DeLay's conclusion is a non-sequitur that arises, said Pinker, because the scientific ideas of human nature "are so unfamiliar in our larger, cultural framework." Pinker, who has done his part to mend this social rift with numerous books on the subject aimed at a general audience—two of which were finalists for the Pulitzer Prize—boiled scientific fear and loathing into four concerns: the fears of inequality, imperfectability, determinism, and nihilism.

The fear of inequality contends that if the mind possesses innate organization, then people could be biologically different, and that would condone discrimination and oppression. "This confuses the idea of fairness with idea of sameness," Pinker said. "Political equality does not require sameness but policies that treat people as individuals with rights."

A common fear of imperfectability is that if ignoble traits like violence, prejudice, and selfishness are inherent, attempts at social reform and human improvement would be futile. But even if we do house ignoble motives, argued Pinker, "they do not automatically lead to ignoble behavior, precisely because the human mind is a complex system of many parts, and some parts"—a moral sense, and the ability to learn lessons of history, for example— "can counteract others."

The fear of determinism cautions that if behavior is caused by a person's biology, he cannot be held responsible for his actions, exemplified in a *Wall Street Journal* headline that read: "Man's genes made him kill, his lawyers claim." However, the belief that certain people are born to commit crimes and cannot be stopped is misguided, since behavioral deterrents such as jail time can appeal "to parts of the brain that anticipate the consequences of behavior and can inhibit it accordingly," Pinker said.

As for the fear of nihilism, the fear that "biology strips life of meaning and purpose—that love, beauty, and morality are just figments of a brain pursuing selfish evolutionary strategies," Pinker admitted a sticky existential dilemma. After all, to pass on our genes is not always a satisfying answer to the question: Why am I here? Frequently, Pinker argued, people who are afraid that evolution implies nihilism are confusing two different timescales: human time, or what is meaningful to us now, and evolutionary time, or how we came to have these thoughts in the first place, as the result of millions of years of evolution.

Interestingly, Pinker's presentation betrayed an unannounced, almost atavistic proclivity toward tabula rasa. Each of his slides began as a white background upon which variegated text—often the borrowed words of philosophers, statesmen, and political satirists—was placed. "Meaning in life does not require that the processes that shape the brain have a purpose," Pinker said, "only that the brain itself have a purpose." As his slides withdrew into their original states—colorless, vacant, receptive—it could be said that having meaning in a presentation does not require that its arguments end all discussion, only that the arguments themselves leave a mark. Pinker's Keynote Address at the APS annual meeting did that and more, and in the process set the tone for two days of the most interesting and lively discussions about the science of human nature.

ERIC JAFFE is a freelance writer and graduate student in journalism at Columbia University.

Nature vs. Nurture: Two Brothers With Schizophrenia

NORMAN L. KELTNER; CHRISTOPHER A. JAMES; RANI J. DARLING; LISA S. FINDLEY; KELLI OLIVER

One of the great debates in 20th century psychiatry centered on etiology: Is upbringing (nurturing) or biology (nature) at the root of mental illness? In the late 19th century, Kraepelinian thinking, which postulated an organic causation, dominated psychiatric thought. As the new century dawned, however, this view quickly gave way to what Cohn (1974) called the Freudian revolution. By the time of Freud's death in 1939, psychoanalytic thought was well on its way to achieving all its goals. It was the application of these principles during World War II that firmly entrenched psychoanalysis, and by extension psychodynamic assumptions, into the heart and soul of our culture. "From the end of World War II until the mid-1970s, a broadly conceived psychosocial model, informed by psychoanalytic and sociological thinking, was the organizing model of American psychiatry" (Wilson, 1993, p. 400).

While the nurture advocates held sway for most of the century, clearly as the millennium closed the proponents of a biological view had won the day. These biologically oriented theorists, in contrast to their more dynamically inclined colleagues, dominated influential academic positions, controlled research direction and subsequent funding, and offered the public some reprieve from the family-blaming psychodynamic models.

The quintessential point in this circling back to a Kraepelinian-like viewpoint was the development of the third edition of the *Diagnostic and Statistical Manual (DSM-III)* (American Psychiatric Association [APA], 1980). Strauss, Yager, and Strauss (1984), summarizing psychiatrists' opinions, stated it was the most important psychiatric publication to appear during the 1970s. Wilson (1993) suggests this document led to the 'remedicalization" of psychiatry: "The history of the development of *DSM-III* is a story about the changing power base, as well as the changing knowledge base, within American psychiatry" (p. 408). With this background in mind, the authors present an interesting case review of two brothers with schizophrenia. Reasoning suggests a nature perspective (i.e., genetic causation), and that may well be the most fruitful model to embrace. Yet after working with these individuals, we are attracted to a more holistic framework that accounts for the significance of heredity-environment interactions. Andreasen

(1999) likens this approach to the model used to understand cancer: "schizophrenia probably occurs as a consequence of multiple 'hits' which include some combination of inherited genetic factors and external, nongenetic factors that affect the regulation and expression of genes governing brain function or that injure the brain directly" (p. 645).

Schizophrenia

Schizophrenia is one of the most common causes of psychosis, affecting about 1% of the adult population (Regier et al., 1993). It is a biological brain disorder typically emerging in late adolescence or early adulthood, is exacerbated by stress, and responds to dopamine receptor antagonists (Weinberger, 1987). It is a thought disorder; symptoms include hallucinations, delusions, withdrawal, poor rapport, and difficulties in communication (APA, 1994; Keltner, Folks, Palmer, & Powers, 1998). It affects men and women almost equally, but men have an earlier age of onset by approximately 4 to 6 years. Though schizophrenia most likely first occurs early in life, a significant minority of women have a first-time episode perimenopausally; this bimodal expression is thought to be estrogen related. Since schizophrenia is thought to be neurodevelopmental rather than neurodegenerative (there is no evidence of gliosis as found in degenerative disorders), influences that disrupt brain development at critical times have been postulated to cause downstream effects, many of which are not evident for years.

These effects include subtle cerebral abnormalities (e.g., enlarged lateral ventricles; enlarged third ventricle; reductions in cortical gray matter in frontal, thalamic, limbic, and hippocampal structures); disrupted neural circuitry (e.g., dopaminergic afferents to the dorsolateral prefrontal cortex); and altered neurotransmitter systems. Disruptive influences can be divided into three causative categories: genetic, shared environmental, and individual-specific environmental influences (Kendler, Myers, & Neale, 2000; Tsuang, 2000). When reviewing the cases of the brothers in this article, it will become evident that all three categories are potentially involved.

Genetic Considerations in Schizophrenia

Individuals with schizophrenia inherit a predisposition to this disorder, hence schizophrenia runs in families (Mortensen et al., 1999; Stall et al., 2000). Cardino and colleagues (1999) estimate 85% of the susceptibility to schizophrenia is genetic. Roberts, Leigh, and Weinberger (1993) outline the genetic risks for relatives of people with schizophrenia (Table 1).

As is clear from Table 1, individuals related to people with schizophrenia have a significantly higher likelihood of developing schizophrenia (2%–50%) than do members of the general population (1%). Twin studies are crucial to our understanding of the impact of heredity. Studies among monozygotic twin groups have repeatedly demonstrated high concordancy rates (50% per Table 1). While compelling indeed, a pure genetic causation would predict even higher concordancy rates among individuals who share the exact same genetic blueprint. The fact that there is not 100% concordancy suggests nongenetic variables influence schizophrenogenesis.

There are multiple nongenetic factors that influence the development of schizophrenia (Andreasen, 1999; McNeil, Cantor-Graae, & Weinberger, 2000; Nicolson et al., 1999; Rapoport, 2000; Sherman, 1999). For example, the following have been implicated in schizophrenia causation: birth during the winter, infection during pregnancy, famine (e.g., the Dutch Hunger Winter, 1944–45), exposure to toxins (e.g., alcohol) prenatally, obstetrical complications, exposure to radiation, and maternal exposure to great stress (e.g., natural disasters).

Of particular interest to this article is the high incidence of schizophrenia among individuals raised in homes in which one or both parents suffered from schizophrenia. This high incidence (15%–35%) may be partially accounted for by poor parenting (Rosen, 1978). In other words, in a home with (a) disabled parent(s), childrearing may be so inadequate that what might appear to be a clear-cut biological process is hopelessly confounded by nurturing issues. As will become evident, these brothers were raised by disabled parents.

Case Reviews

The following case reviews are presented because they are compelling, filled with pathos, and instructive. The destructive forces of poor parenting and mistreatment are the backdrop for boys with apparent genetic predisposition to severe mental illness. Within the context of a disordered biology interacting with a malicious environment, we attempt to reconstruct lives forever assigned to the periphery of "normal" society. We refer to these brothers as Al and Pete.

Al. Many of us think back to our childhood and remember birthday parties, hide and seek, baseball games, etc. Al thinks back to his past and remembers molestation, cruelty, and punishment. Al has been diagnosed with undifferentiated schizophrenia since the age of 20.

Al is the next to youngest of eight children. According to Al, more than half these siblings suffer from major mental illness.

Table 1. Genetic Risk for Schizophrenia

Familial Relationship	Risk Schizophrenia
* Identical twin affected	50%
* Fraternal twin affected	15%
* Sibling affected	10%
* One parent affected	15%
* Both parents affected	35%
* Second-degree relative affected	2%–3%
* No affected relative	1%
* General population	1%

Source: Roberts, Leigh, & Weinberger (1993)

Al stated, "My mama had schizophrenia for 10 years, then God saved her." When asked about his relationship with his mother now, Al states she left the rest of the family after "daddy" died. When questioned about his father, Al speaks of how his father used to beat his mother and the children. Al recalls seeing his father beat one brother so severely he thought the boy might die. Al further described a beating he received from his father that left him bleeding. When asked why he thought his father beat him, Al responded, "He got mad a lot. I forgot to get firewood like he asked me to." In discussing his illness, Al was asked to describe when he first started hearing voices. He replied, "When I was little, after those boys did that to me. I was out fixing my bicycle and I heard the devil talk to me over and over." Al reported numerous incidents of abuse during his life. At one point during the interview, Al stated his belief that his schizophrenia was God's punishment for what he had done.

Al's first documented psychiatric episode occurred in the early 1980s when he was in his early 20s. In the psychological evaluation emanating from this experience, the psychiatrist noted the presence of hallucinations and delusions; Al described spaceships, command hallucinations, and stated he had killed Christ. His condition deteriorated further and he was committed to a public hospital. During that hospitalization Al was diagnosed as having undifferentiated schizophrenia.

Today, Al lives in a residential group home and attends day treatment. He continues to manifest both auditory and visual hallucinations. Though prescribed two atypical antipsychotic drugs, symptom control varies from day to day.

Pete. Pete is older than Al and has a diagnosis of chronic undifferentiated schizophrenia. His psychiatric symptoms began after his father died suddenly. It was more than 10 years later before he was given a formal diagnosis. Presumably his family and the community were able to absorb his behaviors during those intervening years. He was self-supporting for a while, working in a country store, before being let go for out-of-control behavior.

Pete has a good memory, yet it is fairly selective in that there are certain life experiences he repeatedly shares with others. Some of the stories could be entirely true but are unverifiable, and one has the sense of delusional or grandiose embellishment.

He does not admit to hearing voices but frequently complains of seeing flashing lights of different colors.

Pete had a turbulent childhood as well, but a portion of his childhood was spent in the home of a relative. Though he also experienced his father's wrath, he was spared some of the more difficult years in the household. As noted, Pete's symptoms emerged after the death of his physically and emotionally abusive father. When asked about his childhood, Pete is less apt to remember the negative. He states that his dad "loved me with all his heart." He also remembers his mother as loving him.

Pete did not altogether escape the stranger trauma experienced by his brother. Pete reports being robbed at gunpoint when he was a resident of a psychiatric boarding home. The event, as would be expected, was very traumatic and left an indelible scar.

Pete does not maintain close contact with family members. At one time he tried to maintain contact but circumstances beyond his control led to his curtailing any future, meaningful contact. Pete states that he has "a spiritual mother who speaks to him through his soul."

Today, Pete lives in a residential group home and attends day treatment. The only relative he sees on a regular basis is his brother Al.

Commentary

This brief review of two brothers with schizophrenia provides support for what may be the most compelling model for explaining causative agents of schizophrenia: a multifactorial view (Andreasen, 1999). This model is perhaps best captured by Kendler et al. (2000) and Tsuang (2000) as they divide disruptive influences associated with schizophrenia into genetic, shared environmental, and individual-specific environmental causes. As evidenced by the histories of the brothers, their mental disabilities may be directly linked to all the aforementioned causative factors.

Although many calamitous situations and crises have been shared by these brothers, both have had life experiences that are psychologically traumatic in their own right. One was a victim of sexual abuse while the other was subject to robbery (i.e., individual-specific issues). Kendler et al. (2000) state that shared environmental factors affect family members "through several mechanisms that cluster in families, including parental monitoring, religious and cultural values, community organizations, and drug availability. Undoubtedly, these areas were absent while shared dysfunctional events occurred with regularity.

The individual stressors compounded by an abusive home life seem to be logical grounds from which to mount the nurture argument. The nature argument, however, is not to be ignored. From reviewing charts and performing interviews, it was revealed that at least one of the parents may have had a history of schizophrenia. A family with this many mentally dysfunctional people is of etiologic significance because epidemiological studies suggest a high concordancy rate when a parent or sibling suffers from schizophrenia. An increase beyond these "normal" morbidity rates could be expected when several members of one family are diagnosed with this condition.

In examining the cohesiveness among the above factors (i.e., genetics, shared and individual-specific environmental factors), one can see that each of these variables could have played an active role in the development of schizophrenia for these men. Using Kendler and associates' (2000) views, we are able to speculate on the synergistic effects with which these variables/stressors may have converged to predispose these men to this disability. Further, this view provokes these questions:

- If multifactorial causation is indeed the explanation for schizophrenia, could the severity of the brothers' illnesses have been diminished by removing one or more factors?
- Which factor must be removed?
- How many factors must be present before schizophrenia develops?

Each brother has developed differing severities in the pathology of the illness, along with differing symptoms and dates of onset. These variances are reminders of the unfortunate troth that there is much to learn regarding the disease process of schizophrenia and its causes.

Nursing Implications

These two case studies chronicle a modern American tragedy. The tragedy is experienced at both individual and family levels. First, as individuals, these men have suffered directly from their illness and have missed out on life experiences others take for granted (an indirect consequence). Second, this family has never experienced the "normal" family life. One can only imagine the degree of angst and misery generated in a family with this level of dysfunction. In response to such dysfunction (individual and familial) the nurse is called on to bolster strengths and minimize/prevent deterioration.

Nurses can play a pivotal role in applying prevention strategies across a variety of practice settings. Research links poor prenatal care, second-trimester viruses, and other intrauterine insults to the subsequent development of disorders including schizophrenia (Hultman & Ohman, 1998). Advanced practice psychiatric nurses can contribute to this level of prevention by consultation and collaboration with their colleagues in antepartal, obstetric, and pediatric nursing. Education and outreach services to pregnant women would be a primary prevention effort to decrease the prevalence rates of schizophrenia caused by prenatal risk factors.

Also pertinent to primary prevention efforts are the studies that implicate early childhood trauma in the later development of psychiatric illnesses such as depression, post-traumatic stress disorder, and even schizophrenia. This line of research addresses how experiences alter neurocircuitry, thereby increasing vulnerability to neurotransmitter malfunction (Yehuda, 2000). Child abuse detection, reporting, and prevention efforts are another area in which nurses can have a potential impact on the morbidity of schizophrenia.

A final primary prevention strategy that nurses can provide is in management of the schizophrenic patient's stress factors. Evidence to support the effects of stress on schizophrenia has been found in the life experiences of people with the disorder, who have been shown to experience a higher rate of environmental stressors prior to episodes of illness. Schizophrenia patients suffer from disturbances in emotional processing and in their reactions to stressful events (Walker & Diforio, 1997). Peplau (1952) wrote about the psychotherapeutic management of delusions and hallucinations through the use of the interpersonal problem-solving approach and management of anxiety. These techniques are well known and used by psychiatric nurses.

Secondary prevention strategies would address stabilization of illness and minimization of disability. It is speculated that the neuroanatomical abnormalities worsen over time in first-episode patients with schizophrenia, and that earlier, more intense interventions produce better outcomes (Larsen, Johannessen, & Opjordsmoen, 1998; Linszen, Lenior, De Haan, Dingemans, & Gersons, 1998). Nurses can facilitate patient recovery and improve outcomes by intervening in the early phases of illness. Engaging the patient in psychoeducational groups while closely supervising medication adherence and response also has proved effective (Castle, 1997; O'Connor, 1991). Given the high propensity for comorbid substance-abuse problems among patients with schizophrenia (Dixon, 1999; Kessler et al., 1997), education about the effects of substance use on illness course would be an important aspect of the psychoeducational program (Holland, Baguley, & Davies, 1999). Some of the most hopeful news in schizophrenia research is emerging in the field of psychosocial rehabilitation. Nurses are learning to incorporate these principles in working with schizophrenic patients to improve their hope for recovery and successful community living (Farrell & Deeds, 1997; Kirkpatrick et al., 1995).

While one's genetic heritage creates a predisposition toward schizophrenia, other factors such as the home environment, the prenatal environment, dietary factors, and others may determine whether the disease is manifested. The NIMH is providing funding for this area of research. There are a number of indicators that can be detected in children who have been associated with the later development of schizophrenia. Case finding and tracking of high-risk individuals across periods of vulnerability would permit the creation of a database for subsequent prevention strategies and/or research by nurses and other colleagues in mental health.

References

Acocella, J. (2000, May). The empty couch. *The New Yorker*, 8, 112–118.

American Psychiatric Association. (1980). *Diagnostic and statistical manual of mental disorders* (3rd ed.). Washington, DC: Author.

American Psychiatric Association. (1994). *Diagnostic and statistical manual of mental disorders* (4th ed.). Washington, DC: Author.

Andreasen, N.C. (1999). Understanding causes of schizophrenia. *New England Journal of Medicine*, 340, 645–647.

Cardino, A.G., Marshall, E.J., Coid, B., Gottesman, I., Farmer, A., McGuffin, P., Reveley, A., & Murray, R. (1999). Heritability estimates for psychotic disorders. *Archives of General Psychiatry, 56*, 162–168.

Castle, L. (1997). Beyond medication. What else does the patient with schizophrenia need to reintegrate into the community? *Journal of Psychosocial Nursing and Mental Health Services, 35*(9), 18–21.

Cohn, J.H. (1974). The decline of psychoanalysis: The end of an era, or here we go again. *JAMA*, 228, 711–712.

Dixon, L. (1999). Dual diagnosis of substance abuse in schizophrenia: Prevalence and impact on outcomes. *Schizophrenia Research, 35*(Suppl.), 93–100.

Farrell, S.P., & Deeds, E.S. (1997). The clubhouse model as exemplar: Merging psychiatric nursing and psychosocial rehabilitation. *Journal of Psychosocial Nursing and Mental Health Services, 35*(1), 27–34.

Holland, M., Baguley, I., & Davies, T. (1999). Hallucinations and delusions: A dual diagnosis case study. *British Journal of Nursing, 8*, 1095–1102.

Hultman, C.M., & Ohman, A. (1998). Perinatal characteristics and schizophrenia: Electrodermal activity as a mediating link in a vulnerability-stress perspective. *International Journal of Developmental Neuroscience, 16*, 307–316.

Keltner, N.L., Folks, D.G., Palmer, C.A., & Powers, R.E. (1998). *Psychobiological foundations of psychiatric care*. St. Louis: Mosby.

Kendler, K.S., Myers, J.M., & Neale, M.C. (2000). A multidimensional twin study of mental health in women. *American Journal of Psychiatry, 157*, 506–513.

Kessler R.C., Crum, R.M., Warner, L.A., Nelson, C.B., Schulenberg, J., & Anthony, J.C. (1997). Lifetime co-occurrence of DSM-III-R alcohol abuse and dependence with other psychiatric disorders in the National Comorbidity Survey. *Archives of General Psychiatry, 54*, 313–321.

Kirkpatrick, H., Landeen, J., Byrne, C., Woodside, H., Pawlick, J., & Bernardo, A. (1995). Hope and schizophrenia: Clinicians identify hope-instilling strategies. *Journal of Psychosocial Nursing and Mental Health Services, 33*(6), 15–19.

Larsen, T.K., Johannessen, J.O., & Opjordsmoen, S. (1998). First-episode schizophrenia with long duration of untreated psychosis. Pathways to care. *British Journal of Psychiatry, 33*(Suppl. 172), 45–52.

Linszen, D., Lenior, M., De Haan, L., Dingemans, P., & Gersons, B. (1998). Early intervention, untreated psychosis and the course of early schizophrenia. *British Journal of Psychiatry, 33*(Suppl. 172), 84–89.

McNeil, T.F., Cantor-Graae, E., & Weinberger, D.R. (2000). Relationship of obstetric complications and differences in size of brain structures in monozygotic twin pairs discordant for schizophrenia. *American Journal of Psychiatry, 157*, 203–212.

Mortensen, P., Pedersen, C., Westergaard, T., Wohlfahrt, J., Ewald, H., Mors, O., Andersen, P., & Melbye, M. (1999). Effects of family history and place and season of birth on the risk of schizophrenia. *New England Journal of Medicine, 340*, 603–608.

Nicolson, R., Malaspina, D., Giedd, J.N., Hamburger, S., Lenane, M., Bedwell, J., Fernandez, T., Berman, A., Susser, E., & Rapoport, J. (1999). Obstetrical complications and childhood-onset schizophrenia. *American Journal of Psychiatry, 156*, 1650–1652.

O'Connor, F. (1991). Symptom monitoring for relapse prevention in schizophrenia. *Archives of Psychiatric Nursing, 5*, 193–201.

Peplau, H. (1952). Interpersonal relations in nursing. New York: Putnam.

Rapoport, J.L. (2000). The development of neurodevelopmental psychiatry. *American Journal of Psychiatry, 157*, 159–161.

Regier, D.A., Narrow, W.E., Rae, D.S., Manderscheid, R.W., Locke, B., & Goodwin, F. (1993). The de facto US mental and addictive disorders service system: Epidemiologic catchment area prospective 1-year prevalence rates of disorders and services. *Archives of General Psychiatry, 50,* 85–94.

Roberts, G.W., Leigh, P.N., & Weinberger, D.R. (1993). *Neuropsychiatric disorders.* London: Mosby Europe.

Rosen, H. (1978). A guide to clinical psychiatry. Coral Gables, FL: Mnemosyne.

Sherman, C. (1999). Natural catastrophe linked to rise in schizophrenia rate. *Clinical Psychiatry News, 27*(9), 24.

Stall, W.G., Pol, H.E.H., Schnack, H.G., Hoogendoorn, M., Jellema, K., & Kahn, R. (2000). Structural brain abnormalities in patients with schizophrenia and their healthy siblings. *American Journal of Psychiatry, 157,* 416–420.

Strauss, D.G., Yager, J., & Strauss, G.E. (1984). The cutting edge in psychiatry. *American Journal of Psychiatry, 141,* 38–43.

Tsuang, M.T. (2000). Genes, environment, and mental health wellness. *American Journal of Psychiatry, 157,* 489–491.

Walker, E.F., & Diforio, D. (1997). Schizophrenia: A neural diathesis-stress model. *Psychological Review, 104,* 667–685.

Weinberger, D.R. (1987). Implications of normal brain development for the pathogenesis of schizophrenia. *Archives in General Psychiatry, 44,* 660–668.

Wilson, M. (1993). DSM-III and the transformation of American psychiatry: A history. *American Journal of Psychiatry, 150,* 399–410.

Yehuda, R. (2000). Biology of posttraumatic stress disorder. *Journal of Clinical Psychiatry, 61*(Suppl. 7), 14–21.

NORMAN L. KELTNER, EDD, RN, is Professor, University of Alabama School of Nursing, Birmingham, AL. **CHRISTOPHER A. JAMES, MED,** is Coordinator II, Chilton-Shelby Mental Health, Clanton, AL. **RANI J. DARLING, BSN, RN,** is currently attending school in Europe; **LISA S. FINDLEY, BSN, RN,** is Staff Nurse, University of Alabama Hospital; and **KELLI OLIVER, BSN, RN,** is Staff Nurse, East Alabama Medical Center, Opelika, AL.

Genetic Influence on Human Psychological Traits

A Survey

There is now a large body of evidence that supports the conclusion that individual differences in most, if not all, reliably measured psychological traits, normal and abnormal, are substantively influenced by genetic factors. This fact has important implications for research and theory building in psychology, as evidence of genetic influence unleashes a cascade of questions regarding the sources of variance in such traits. A brief list of those questions is provided, and representative findings regarding genetic and environmental influences are presented for the domains of personality, intelligence, psychological interests, psychiatric illnesses, and social attitudes. These findings are consistent with those reported for the traits of other species and for many human physical traits, suggesting that they may represent a general biological phenomenon.

THOMAS J. BOUCHARD, JR.

Among knowledgeable researchers, discussions regarding genetic influences on psychological traits are not about whether there is genetic influence, but rather about how much influence there is, and how genes work to shape the mind. As Rutter (2002) noted, "Any dispassionate reading of the evidence leads to the inescapable conclusion that genetic factors play a substantial role in the origins of individual differences with respect to all psychological traits, both normal and abnormal" (p. 2). Put concisely, all psychological traits are heritable. Heritability (h^2) is a descriptive statistic that indexes the degree of population variation in a trait that is due to genetic differences. The complement of heritability ($1 - h^2$) indexes variation contributed by the environment (plus error of measurement) to population variation in the trait. Studies of human twins and adoptees, often called behavior genetic studies, allow us to estimate the heritability of various traits. The name behavior genetic studies is an unfortunate misnomer, however, as such studies are neutral regarding both environmental and genetic influences. That they repeatedly and reliably reveal significant heritability for psychological traits is an empirical fact and one not unique to humans. Lynch and Walsh (1998) pointed out that genetic influence on most traits, as indexed by estimates of heritability, is found for all species and observed that "the interesting questions remaining are, How does the magnitude of h^2" differ among characters and species and why?" (p. 175).

Why Study Genetic Influences On Human Behavioral Traits?

A simple answer to the question of why scientists study genetic influences on human behavior is that they want a better understanding of how things work, that is, better theories. Not too many years ago, Meehl (1978) argued that "most so-called 'theories' in the soft areas of psychology (clinical, counseling, social, personality, community, and school psychology) are scientifically unimpressive and technologically worthless" (p. 806). He listed 20 fundamental difficulties faced by researchers in the social sciences. Two are relevant to the current discussion: heritability and nuisance variables. The two are closely related. Nuisance variables are variables assumed to be causes of group or individual differences irrelevant to the theory of an investigator. Investigators seldom provide a full theoretical rationale in support of their choice of nuisance variables to control. As Meehl pointed out, removing the influence of parental socioeconomic status (SES; i.e., treating it as a nuisance variable) on children's IQ, when studying the causes of individual differences in IQ, makes the assumption that parental SES is exclusively a source of environmental variance, as opposed to being confounded with genetic influence. Meehl argued that this example "is perhaps the most dramatic one but other less emotion-laden examples can be found on all sides in the behavioral sciences" (p. 810). His point was that knowledge of how genetic factors influence any given measure (e.g., SES) or trait (e.g., IQ) will allow scientists to develop more scientifically impressive and worthwhile theories about the sources of individual differences in psychological traits.

Evidence of genetic influence on a psychological trait raises a series of new questions regarding the sources of population variance for that trait. All the questions addressed in quantitative genetics (Lynch & Walsh, 1998) and genetic epidemiology (Khoury, 1998) become relevant. What kind of gene action is involved? Is it a simple additive influence, with the effects of genes simply adding up so that more genes cause greater expression of the trait, or is the mode of action more complex? Are the effects of genes for a particular trait more pronounced in men or women? Are there interactions between genes and the environment? For example, it has been known for a long time that stressful life events lead to depression in some people but not others. There is now evidence for an interaction. Individuals who carry a specific genetic variant are more susceptible to depression when exposed to stressful life events than individuals who do not carry the genetic variant (Caspi et al., 2003). Are there gene-environment correlations? That is, do individuals with certain genetic constitutions seek out specific environments? People who score high on measures of sensation seeking certainly, on average, tend to find themselves in more dangerous environments than people who score low for this trait. McGue and I have provided an extended list of such questions (Bouchard & McGue, 2003).

Estimates Of the Magnitude Of Genetic Influence On Psychological Traits

Table 1 reports typical behavior genetic findings drawn from studies of broad and relatively representative samples from affluent Western societies. In most, but not all, of these studies, estimates of genetic and environmental influences were obtained from studies of twins. Because the studies probably undersampled people who live in the most deprived segment of Western societies, the findings should not be considered as generalizable to such populations. (Documentation for most of the findings can be found in Bouchard & McGue, 2003.)

Personality

Psychologists have developed two major schemes for organizing specific personality traits into a higher-order structure, the Big Five and the Big Three. As Table 1 shows, the findings using the two schemes are much the same. Genetic influence is in the range of 40 to 50%, and heritability is approximately the same for different traits. There is evidence of nonadditive genetic variance. That is, genes for personality, in addition to simply adding or subtracting from the expression of a trait, work in a more complex manner, the expression of a relevant gene depending to some extent on the gene with which it is paired on a chromosome or on genes located on other chromosomes. Research has yielded little evidence for significant

shared environmental influence, that is, similarity due to having trait-relevant environmental influences in common. Some large studies have investigated whether the genes that influence personality traits differ in the two sexes (sex limitation). The answer is no. However, sometimes there are sex differences in heritability.

Mental Ability

Early in life, shared environmental factors are the dominant influence on IQ, but gradually genetic influence increases, with the effects of shared environment dropping to near zero (see the twin studies in Table 1). Although not reported here, adoption studies of (a) unrelated individuals reared together and (b) adoptive parents and their adopted offspring have reported similar results—increasing genetic influence on IQ with age and decreasing shared environmental influence. Results from two twin studies of IQ in old age (over 75) are reported in Table 1. Both studies found a substantial level of genetic influence and little shared environmental influence. The results do, however, suggest some decline in heritability when compared with results for earlier ages. There is no evidence for sex differences in heritability for IQ at any age.

Psychological Interests

Heritabilities for psychological interests, also called vocational or occupational interests, are also reported in Table 1. These heritabilities were estimated using data gathered in a single large study that made use of a variety of samples (twins, siblings, parents and their children, etc.) gathered over many years. All respondents completed one form or another of a standard vocational interest questionnaire. There is little variation in heritability for the six scales, with an average of .36. As with personality traits, there is evidence for nonadditive genetic influence. Unlike personality, psychological interests show evidence for shared environmental influence, although this influence is modest, about 10% for each trait.

Psychiatric Illnesses

Schizophrenia is the most extensively studied psychiatric illness, and the findings consistently suggest a very high degree of genetic influence (heritability of about .80), mostly additive genetic influence, with no shared environmental influence. There do not appear to be gender differences in the heritability of schizophrenia. Major depression is less heritable (about .40) than schizophrenia. Men and women share most, but not all, genetic influences for depression. Panic disorder, generalized anxiety disorder, and phobias are moderately heritable, and the effect is largely additive, with few if any sex differences. The heritability of alcoholism is in the range of .50 to .60. mostly because of additive genetic effects. Findings regarding the possibility of sex differences in the heritability of alcoholism are mixed.

Antisocial behavior has long been thought to be more heritable in adulthood than childhood. The results of a recent analysis do not support that conclusion. The genetic influence is additive

TABLE 1

Estimates of Broad Heritability and Shared Environmental Influence and Indications of Nonadditive Genetic Effects and Sex Differences in Heritability for Representative Psychological Traits

Trait	Heritability	Nonadditive genetic effect	Shared environmental effect	Sex differences in heritabilily
Personality (adult samples)				
Big Five				
Extraversion	.54	Yes	No	Perhaps
Agreeableness (aggression)	.42	Yes	No	Probably not
Conscientiousness	.49	Yes	No	Probably not
Neuroticism	.48	Yes	No	No
Openness	.57	Yes	No	Probably not
Big Three				
Positive emotionality	.50	Yes	No	No
Negative emotionality	.44	Yes	No	No
Constraint	.52	Yes	No	No
Intelligence				
By age in Dutch cross-sectional twin data				
Age 5	.22	No	.54	No
Age 7	.40	No	.29	No
Age 10	.54	No	.26	No
Age 12	.85	No	No	No
Age 16	.62	No	No	No
Age 18	.82	No	No	No
Age 26	.88	No	No	No
Age 50	.85	No	No	No
In old age (> 75 years old)	.54-.62	Not tested	No	No
Psychological interests				
Realistic	.36	Yes	.12	NA
Investigative	.36	Yes	.10	NA
Artistic	.39	Yes	.12	NA
Social	.37	Yes	.08	NA
Enterprising	.31	Yes	.11	NA
Conventional	.38	Yes	.11	NA
Psychiatric illnesses (liability estimates)				
Schizophrenia	.80	No	No	No
Major depression	.37	No	No	Mixed findings
Panic disorder	.30-.40	No	No	No
Generalized anxiety disorder	.30	No	Small female only	No
Phobias	.20-.40	No	No	No
Alcoholism	.50-.60	No	Yes	Mixed findings
Antisocial behavior				
Children	.46	No	.20	No
Adolescents	.43	No	.16	No
Adults	.41	No	.09	No
Social attitudes				
Conservatism				
Under age 20 years	.00	NR	Yes	NR
Over age 20 years	.45-.65	Yes	Yes in females	Yes
Right-wing authoritarianism (adults)	.50-.64	No	.00-.16	NA
Religiousness				
16-year-olds	.11-.22	No	.45-.60	Yes
Adults	.30-.45	No	.20-.40	Not clear
Specific religion	Near zero	NR	NA	NR

Note. NA = not available: NR = not relevant.

and in the range of .41 to .46. Shared environmental influences decrease from childhood to adulthood, but do not entirely disappear in adulthood. There are no sex differences in heritability.

Social Attitudes

Twin studies reveal only environmental influence on conservatism up to age 19; only after this age do genetic influences manifest themselves. A large study (30,000 adults, including twins and most of their first-degree relatives) yielded heritabilities of .65 for males and .45 for females. Some of the genetic influence on conservatism is nonadditive. Recent work with twins reared apart has independently replicated these heritability findings. Conservatism correlates highly, about .72, with right-wing authoritarianism, and that trait is also moderately heritable.

Religiousness is only slightly heritable in 16-year-olds (.11 for girls and .22 for boys in a large Finnish twin study) and strongly influenced by shared environment (.60 in girls and .45 in boys). Religiousness is moderately heritable in adults (.30 to .45) and also shows some shared environmental influence. Good data on sex differences in heritability of religiousness in adults are not available. Membership in a specific religious denomination is largely due to environmental factors.

A Note on Multivariate Genetic Analysis

In this review, I have addressed only the behavior genetic analysis of traits taken one at a time (univariate analysis). It is important to recognize that it is possible to carry out complex genetic analyses of the correlations among traits and compute genetic correlations. These correlations tell us the degree to which genetic effects on one score (trait measure) are correlated with genetic effects on a second score, at one or at many points in time. The genetic correlation between two traits can be quite high regardless of whether the heritability of either trait is high or low, or whether the correlation between the traits is high or low. Consider the well-known positive correlation between tests of mental ability, the evidentiary base for the general intelligence factor. This value is typically about .30. The genetic correlation between such tests is, however, much higher, typically closer to .80. Co-occurrence of two disorders, a common finding in psychiatric research, is often due to common genes. The genetic correlation between anxiety and depression, for example, is estimated to be very high. Multivariate genetic analysis of behavioral traits is a very active domain of research.

Concluding Remarks

One unspoken assumption among early behavior geneticists, an assumption that was shared by most for many years, was that some psychological traits were likely to be significantly influenced by genetic factors, whereas others were likely to be primarily influenced by shared environmental influences. Most behavior geneticists assumed that social attitudes, for example, were influenced entirely by shared environmental influences, and so social attitudes remained largely unstudied until relatively recently. The evidence now shows how wrong these assumptions were. Nearly every reliably measured psychological phenotype (normal and abnormal) is significantly influenced by genetic factors. Heritabilities also differ far less from trait to trait than anyone initially imagined. Shared environmental influences are often, but not always, of less importance than genetic factors, and often decrease to near zero after adolescence. Genetic influence on psychological traits is ubiquitous, and psychological researchers must incorporate this fact into their research programs else their theories will be "scientifically unimpressive and technologically worthless," to quote Meehl again.

At a fundamental level, a scientifically impressive theory must describe the specific molecular mechanism that explicates how genes transact with the environment to produce behavior. The rudiments of such theories are in place. Circadian behavior in humans is under genetic influence (Hur, Bouchard, & Lykken, 1998), and some of the molecular mechanisms in mammals are now being revealed (Lowrey & Takahashi, 2000). Riclley (2003) and Marcus (2004) have provided additional examples of molecular mechanisms that help shape behavior. Nevertheless, the examples are few, the details are sparse, and major mysteries remain. For example, many behavioral traits are influenced by nonadditive genetic processes. These processes remain a puzzle for geneticists and evolutionists, as well as psychologists, because simple additive effects are thought to be the norm (Wolf, Brodie, & Wade, 2000). We also do not understand why most psychological traits are moderately heritable, rather than, as some psychologists expected, variable in heritability, with some traits being highly heritable and others being largely under the influence of the environment. It seems reasonable to suspect that moderate heritability may be a general biological phenomenon rather than one specific to human psychological traits, as the profile of genetic and environmental influences on psychological traits is not that different from the profile of these influences on similarly complex physical traits (Boomsma, Busjahn, & Peltonen, 2002) and similar findings apply to most organisms.

Recommended Reading

Bouchard, T.J., Jr., & McGue. M. (2003). (See References)

Carey, G. (2003). *Human genetics for the social sciences.* Thousand Oaks, CA: Sage.

Plomin, R., DeFries, J.C.. Craig, I.W., & McGuffin, P. (Eds.). (2003). *Behavioral genetics in the post genomic era.* Washington, DC: American Psychological Association.

Rutter, M., Pickels, A., Murray, R., & Eaves, L.J. (2001). Testing hypotheses on specific environmental causal effects on behavior. *Psychological bulletin, 127,* 291-324.

Note

1. See Evans (2004, Fig. 1) for a recent commission of this error.

References

Boomsma, D. I., Busjahn, A., & Peltonen, L. (2002). Classical twin studies and beyond. *Nature Reviews: Genetics, 3,* 872–882.

Bouchard, T. J., Jr., & McGue, M. (2003). Genetic and environmental influences on human psychological differences. *Journal of Neurobiology, 54,* 4–45.

Caspi, A., Sugden, K., Moffitt, T. E., Taylor. A., Craig, I. W., Harrington, H., McClay, J., Mill, J., Martin, J., Braiwaite. A., & Poulton, R. (2003). Influence of life stress on depression: Moderation by a polymorphism in the 5-HTT gene. *Science, 301,* 386–389.

Evans, G. W. (2004). The environment of childhood poverty. *American Psychologist, 59,* 77–92.

Hur, Y.- M., Bouchard, T. J., Jr., & Lykken. D. T. (1998). Genetic and environmental influence on morningness-eveningness. *Personality and Individual Differences, 25,* 917–925.

Khoury, M. J. (1998). Genetic epidemiology. In K. J. Rothman & S. Greenland (Eds.), *Modem epidemiology* (pp. 609–622). Philadelphia: Lippincott-Raven.

Lowrey, P. L., & Takahashi, J. S. (2000). Genetics of the mammalian circadian system: Photic entrainment, circadian pacemaker mechanisms, and postranslational regulation. *Annual Review of Genetics, 34,* 533–562.

Lynch, M., & Walsh, B. (1998). *Genetics and analysis of quantitative traits.* Sunderland. MA: Sinauer.

Marcus, G. (2004). *The birth of the mind: How a tiny number of genes creates the complexities of human thought.* New York: Basic Books.

Meehl, P. E. (1978). Theoretical risks and tabular asterisks: Sir Karl, Sir Ronald, and the slow progress of soft psychology. *Journal of Consulting and Clinical Psychology, 46,* 806–834.

Ridley, M. (2003). *Nature via nurture: Genes, experience and what makes us human.* New York: HarperCollins.

Rutter, M. (2002). Nature, nurture, and development: From evangelism through science toward policy and practice. *Child Development, 73,* 1–21.

Wolf, J. B., Brodie. E. D. I., & Wade. M. J. (Eds.), (2000). *Epistasis and the evolutionary process.* New York: Oxford University Press.

From *Current Directions in Psychological Science,* August 2004 13:04, pp. 148-151. Copyright © 2004 by the Association for Psychological Science. Reprinted by permission of Blackwell Publishing, Ltd.

The Amazing Brain

Is Neuroscience the Key to What Makes Us Human?

Richard Restak

While in medical school, V. S. Ramachandran, director of the Center for Brain and Cognition at the University of California at San Diego, encountered a patient given to episodes of alternately weeping and laughing uncontrollably. This display of emotional mercuriality struck Ramachandran as a replay of the human condition. "Were these just mirthless joy and crocodile tears, I wondered? Or was he actually feeling alternately happy and sad, the same way a manic-depressive might, but on a compressed scale?"

During his professional career as a neurologist and researcher, Ramachandran has retained his curiosity and formulated about his patients the "kinds of very simple questions that a schoolboy might ask but are embarrassingly hard for experts to answer."

For example, "Why does this patient display these curious symptoms? What do the symptoms tell us about the working of the normal brain?" In the process, Ramachandran has learned that many patients with damage in a localized part of the brain often suffer a highly selective loss of one specific function with other functions remaining unaffected—an indication that the damaged area is normally involved somehow in mediating the impaired function. Further, some of these selective impairments can be both fascinating and informative.

Consider David, a patient of Ramachandran's who emerged from a coma mentally intact, with the exception of the bizarre delusion that his mother had been replaced by an impostor.

Further evaluation revealed an important distinction: Although David couldn't recognize his mother when encountering her face to face, he had no trouble identifying her when talking to her on the telephone. What could account for such an anomaly?

It turns out that separate pathways lead from the auditory and visual regions of the brain to the amygdala, an important component of the brain's emotional circuitry. In David's case, the fibers connecting the visual center to the amygdala were no longer functioning normally. As a result, whenever he looked at his mother he no longer got that warm feeling of recognition that normally accompanies seeing one's parent. He therefore accused her of being an impostor.

The auditory fibers in David's brain, in contrast, retained their normal connections with the amygdala. Consequently, the emotional linkage of voice and person remained intact and David recognized his mother's voice.

"This is a lovely example... of neuroscience in action; of how you can take a bizarre, seemingly incomprehensible neurological syndrome ... and then come up with a simple explanation in terms of the known neural pathways in the brain," writes Ramachandran.

Other bizarre but informative disorders taken up in this wide-ranging book include phantom limb (the sensation that an amputated arm or leg is still present); synesthesia (a condition in which the senses are mingled so that the affected person tastes a shape, or sees a color in a sound or a number); and achromotopsia (seeing the world in shades of gray, like a black-and-white film).

"By studying neurological syndromes which have been largely ignored as curiosities or mere anomalies, we can sometimes acquire novel insights into the functions of the normal brain," the author writes. Moreover, he suggests, "the study of patients with neurological disorders has implications for the humanities, for philosophy, maybe even for aesthetics and art."

While all this sounds reasonable, Ramachandran sometimes comes across like the proverbial carpenter who approaches all issues as resolvable via the use of hammer and nail. Specifically, he claims that neuroscience can answer (or soon will) "some lofty questions that have preoccupied philosophers since the dawn of history: What is free will? What is body image? What is art? What is the self? Who am I?"

At times, his reductionism pushes the envelope a bit: "We recognize that life is a word loosely applied to a collection of processes—DNA replication and transcription, Krebs cycle, Lactic acid cycle, etc., etc." At another point, after naming several brain structures he asserts, "Know how they perform their individual operations, how they interact, and you will know what it means to be a conscious human being."

Despite such extravagant and hubristic statements, no one so far has been able to perform the alchemical conversion whereby "To be or not to be" can be understood in terms of neurotransmitters and brain structures. Nor is such a conversion ever likely since, as philosopher Gilbert Ryle pointed out, it would invoke the category mistake: intermingling separate and distinct orders of discourse.

For example (Ryle's own example, incidentally), the university that I attended cannot be equated except associatively with the buildings comprising it. True, the buildings when considered together may loosely be referred to as "the university"; but the entity defined by that word is far more nuanced than just real estate.

Likewise, can the mind be explained totally in terms of the brain? Ramachandran thinks so and while, on the whole, I tend to agree with him, I also have to admit to a trace of agnosticism on the question.

Not surprisingly, when discussing mental illness, Ramachandran is strictly in the neuropsychiatric camp: Neurology and psychiatry are so interpenetrated that future treatments and cures can only come about via increased knowledge about the brain. As a neurologist and neuropsychiatrist myself, I certainly don't disagree with that claim. Many psychiatrists, however, may find Ramachandran's phrasing of the matter a bit off-putting ("it is only a matter of time before psychiatry becomes just another branch of neurology").

But his heart is in the right place. Freudianism and other guru-driven "isms" are dead, replaced by an emphasis on the brain. Indeed, so much has been learned about mental illness in the past two decades as a result of brain research that it's difficult to imagine any alternative approach.

My principal criticism of this book concerns its odd arrangement: 112 pages of text accompanied by 44 pages of endnotes. As he mentions in his introduction, Ramachandran holds a rather quirky notion about endnotes ("the real book is in the endnotes"). Perhaps that's true, but the delegation of large parts of the narrative to the endnotes presents several difficulties.

For one, this text-endnote dichotomy makes it too easy for both author and editor to forsake their most important duty: organizing the material into a free-flowing narrative. Second, on occasion—such as his description of the more exotic forms of synesthesia—the endnotes prove even more interesting than the main text.

Finally, material in the text is sometimes repeated in the endnotes, such as Ramachandran's explanation of the origin of the ear. And given this emphasis on the endnotes, why are the notes corresponding to the last two citations in the final chapter missing?

Admittedly, these are minor quibbles that detract not at all from a perfectly marvelous book. Overall, reading Ramachandran in *A Brief Tour of Human Consciousness* is like listening to a John Coltrane solo: The man is here, there, and everywhere; he's inventive, inspired, wildly speculative, and yet disciplined by the demands of his craft. Give him a fact about the brain and he'll link it with a quote from Shakespeare; a nanosecond later he'll suggest an experiment that you can carry out in your living room to learn more about the fact.

To Ramachandran, the brain is more than an enchanted loom, and wider than the sky; it's an endless source for manic excitement, intriguing questions, profound reflections and a zany humor ("our brains ... if raised in a culture-free environment like Texas would barely be human"). And like Coltrane, Ramachandran leaves you marveling at how he does it; wondering how he's learned all that he knows; and spinning like a top from the effort of trying to absorb all the wonderful things that he's telling you.

A Brief Tour of Human Consciousness is well worth the effort. You'll be entertained, provoked, amused and—most important of all—eager to learn more.

RICHARD RESTAK, a neurologist and neuropsychiatrist, is the author of *Poe's Heart and the Mountain Climber: Exploring the Effects of Anxiety on Our Brains and Our Culture,* 2004.

His Brain, Her Brain

It turns out that male and female brains differ quite a bit in architecture and activity. Research into these variations could lead to sex-specific treatments for disorders such as depression and schizophrenia

LARRY CAHILL, PH.D.

On a gray day in mid-January, Lawrence Summers, the president of Harvard University, suggested that innate differences in the build of the male and female brain might be one factor underlying the relative scarcity of women in science. His remarks reignited a debate that has been smoldering for a century, ever since some scientists sizing up the brains of both sexes began using their main finding—that female brains tend to be smaller—to bolster the view that women are intellectually inferior to men.

To date, no one has uncovered any evidence that anatomical disparities might render women incapable of achieving academic distinction in math, physics or engineering. And the brains of men and women have been shown to be quite clearly similar in many ways. Nevertheless, over the past decade investigators have documented an astonishing array of structural, chemical and functional variations in the brains of males and females.

These inequities are not just interesting idiosyncrasies that might explain why more men than women enjoy the Three Stooges. They raise the possibility that we might need to develop sex-specific treatments for a host of conditions, including depression, addiction, schizophrenia and post-traumatic stress disorder (PTSD). Furthermore, the differences imply that researchers exploring the structure and function of the brain must take into account the sex of their subjects when analyzing their data—and include both women and men in future studies or risk obtaining misleading results.

Sculpting the Brain

Not so long ago neuroscientists believed that sex differences in the brain were limited mainly to those regions responsible for mating behavior. In a 1966 Scientific American article entitled "Sex Differences in the Brain," Seymour Levine of Stanford University described how sex hormones help to direct divergent reproductive behaviors in rats—with males engaging in mounting and females arching their backs and raising their rumps to attract suitors. Levine mentioned only one brain region in his review: the hypothalamus, a small structure at the base of the brain that is involved in regulating hormone production and controlling basic behaviors such as eating, drinking and sex. A generation of neuroscientists came to maturity believing that "sex differences in the brain" referred primarily to mating behaviors, sex hormones and the hypothalamus.

That view, however, has now been knocked aside by a surge of findings that highlight the influence of sex on many areas of cognition and behavior, including memory, emotion, vision, hearing, the processing of faces and the brain's response to stress hormones. This progress has been accelerated in the past five to 10 years by the growing use of sophisticated noninvasive imaging techniques such as positron-emission tomography (PET) and functional magnetic resonance imaging (fMRI), which can peer into the brains of living subjects.

These imaging experiments reveal that anatomical variations occur in an assortment of regions throughout the brain. Jill M. Goldstein of Harvard Medical School and her colleagues, for example, used MRI to measure the sizes of many cortical and subcortical areas. Among other things, these investigators found that parts of the frontal cortex, the seat of many higher cognitive functions, are bulkier in women than in men, as are parts of the limbic cortex, which is involved in emotional responses. In men, on the other hand, parts of the parietal cortex, which is involved in space perception, are bigger than in women, as is the amygdala, an almond-shaped structure that responds to emotionally arousing information—to anything that gets the heart pumping and the adrenaline flowing. These size differences, as well as others mentioned throughout the article, are relative: they refer to the overall volume of the structure relative to the overall volume of the brain.

Differences in the size of brain structures are generally thought to reflect their relative importance to the animal. For example, primates rely more on vision than olfaction; for rats, the opposite is true. As a result, primate brains maintain proportionately larger regions devoted to vision, and rats devote more space to olfaction. So the existence of widespread anatomical disparities between men and women suggests that sex does influence the way the brain works.

Other investigations are finding anatomical sex differences at the cellular level. For example, Sandra Witelson and her colleagues at McMaster University discovered that women possess a greater density of neurons in parts of the temporal lobe cortex associated with language processing and comprehension. On counting the neurons in postmortem samples, the researchers found that of the six layers present in the cortex, two show more neurons per unit volume in females than in males. Similar findings were subsequently reported for the frontal lobe. With such information in hand, neuroscientists can now explore whether sex differences in neuron number correlate with differences in cognitive abilities—examining, for example, whether the boost in density in the female auditory cortex relates to women's enhanced performance on tests of verbal fluency.

Such anatomical diversity may be caused in large part by the activity of the sex hormones that bathe the fetal brain. These steroids help to direct the organization and wiring of the brain during development and influence the structure and neuronal density of various regions. Interestingly, the brain areas that Goldstein found to differ between men and women are ones that in animals contain the highest number of sex hormone receptors during development. This correlation between brain region size in adults and sex steroid action in utero suggests that at least some sex differences in cognitive function do not result from cultural influences or the hormonal changes associated with puberty—they are there from birth.

Inborn Inclinations

Several intriguing behavioral studies add to the evidence that some sex differences in the brain arise before a baby draws its first breath. Through the years, many researchers have demonstrated that when selecting toys, young boys and girls part ways. Boys tend to gravitate toward balls or toy cars, whereas girls more typically reach for a doll. But no one could really say whether those preferences are dictated by culture or by innate brain biology.

To address this question, Melissa Hines of City University London and Gerianne M. Alexander of Texas A&M University turned to monkeys, one of our closest animal cousins. The researchers presented a group of vervet monkeys with a selection of toys, including rag dolls, trucks and some gender-neutral items such as picture books. They found that male monkeys spent more time playing with the "masculine" toys than their female counterparts did, and female monkeys spent more time interacting with the playthings typically preferred by girls. Both sexes spent equal time monkeying with the picture books and other gender-neutral toys.

Because vervet monkeys are unlikely to be swayed by the social pressures of human culture; the results imply that toy preferences in children result at least in part from innate biological differences. This divergence, and indeed all the anatomical sex differences in the brain, presumably arose as a result of selective pressures during evolution. In the case of the toy study, males—both human and primate—prefer toys that can be propelled through space and that promote rough-and-tumble play. These qualities, it seems reasonable to speculate, might relate to the behaviors useful for hunting and for securing a mate. Similarly, one might also hypothesize that females, on the other hand, select toys that allow them to hone the skills they will one day need to nurture their young.

Simon Baron-Cohen and his associates at the University of Cambridge took a different but equally creative approach to addressing the influence of nature versus nurture regarding sex differences. Many researchers have described disparities in how "people-centered" male and female infants are. For example, Baron-Cohen and his student Svetlana Lutchmaya found that one-year-old girls spend more time looking at their mothers than boys of the same age do. And when these babies are presented with a choice of films to watch, the girls look longer at a film of a face, whereas boys lean toward a film featuring cars.

Of course, these preferences might be attributable to differences in the way adults handle or play with boys and girls. To eliminate this possibility, Baron-Cohen and his students went a step further. They took their video camera to a maternity ward to examine the preferences of babies that were only one day old. The infants saw either the friendly face of a live female student or a mobile that matched the color, size and shape of the student's face and included a scrambled mix of her facial features. To avoid any bias, the experimenters were unaware of each baby's sex during testing. When they watched the tapes, they found that the girls spent more time looking at the student, whereas the boys spent more time looking at the mechanical object. This difference in social interest was evident on day one of life—implying again that we come out of the womb with some cognitive sex differences built in.

Under Stress

In many cases, sex differences in the brain's chemistry and construction influence how males and females respond to the environment or react to, and remember, stressful events. Take, for example, the amygdala. Goldstein and others have reported that the amygdala is larger in men than in women. And in rats, the neurons in this region make more numerous interconnections in males than in females. These anatomical variations would be expected to produce differences in the way that males and females react to stress.

To assess whether male and female amygdalae in fact respond differently to stress, Katharina Braun and her coworkers at Otto von Guericke University in Magdeburg, Germany, briefly removed a litter of Degu pups from their mother. For these social South American rodents, which live in large colonies like prairie dogs do, even temporary separation can be quite upsetting. The researchers then measured the concentration of serotonin receptors in various brain regions. Serotonin is a neurotransmitter, or signal-carrying molecule, that is key for mediating emotional behavior. (Prozac, for example, acts by increasing serotonin function.)

The workers allowed the pups to hear their mother's call during the period of separation and found that this auditory input increased the serotonin receptor concentration in the males' amygdala, yet decreased the concentration of these same receptors in females. Although it is difficult to extrapolate from this sturdy to human behavior, the results hint that if something similar occurs in children, separation anxiety might differentially affect the emotional well-being of male and female infants. Experiments such as these are necessary if we are to understand why, for instance, anxiety disorders are far more prevalent in girls than in boys.

Another brain region now known to diverge in the sexes anatomically and in its response to stress is the hippocampus, a structure crucial for memory storage and for spatial mapping of the physical environment. Imaging consistently demonstrates that the hippocampus is larger in women than in men. These anatomical differences might well relate somehow to differences in the way males and females navigate. Many studies suggest that men are more likely to navigate by estimating distance in space and orientation ("dead reckoning"), whereas women are more likely to navigate by monitoring landmarks. Interestingly, a similar sex difference exists in rats. Male rats are more likely to navigate mazes using directional and positional information, whereas female rats are more likely to navigate the same mazes using available landmarks. (Investigators have yet to demonstrate, however, that male rats are less likely to ask for directions.)

Even the neurons in the hippocampus behave differently in males and females, at least in how they react to learning experiences. For example, Janice M. Juraska and her associates at the University of Illinois have shown that placing rats in an "enriched environment"—cages filled with toys and with fellow rodents to promote social interactions—produced dissimilar effects on the structure of hippocampal neurons in male and female rats. In females, the experience enhanced the "bushiness" of the branches in the cells' dendritic trees—the many-armed structures that receive signals from other nerve cells. This change presumably reflects an increase in neuronal connections, which in turn is thought to be involved with the laying down of memories. In males, however, the complex environment either had no effect on the dendritic trees or pruned them slightly.

But male rats sometimes learn better in the face of stress. Tracey J. Shors of Rutgers University and her collaborators have found that a brief exposure to a series of one-second tail shocks enhanced performance of a learned task and increased the density of dendritic connections to other neurons in male rats yet impaired performance and decreased connection density in female rats. Findings such as these have interesting social implications. The more we discover about how brain mechanisms of learning differ between the sexes, the more we may need to consider how optimal learning environments potentially differ for boys and girls.

Although the hippocampus of the female rat can show a decrement in response to acute stress, it appears to be more resilient than its male counterpart in the face of chronic stress. Cheryl D. Conrad and her co-workers at Arizona State University restrained rats in a mesh cage for six hours—a situation that the rodents find disturbing. The researchers then assessed how vulnerable their hippocampal neurons were to killing by a neurotoxin—a standard measure of the effect of stress on these cells. They noted that chronic restraint rendered the males' hippocampal cells more susceptible to the toxin but had no effect on the females' vulnerability. These findings, and others like them, suggest that in terms of brain damage, females may be better equipped to tolerate chronic stress than males are. Still unclear is what protects female hippocampal cells from the damaging effects of chronic stress, but sex hormones very likely play a role.

The Big Picture

Extending the work on how the brain handles and remembers stressful events, my colleagues and I have found contrasts in the way men and women lay down memories of emotionally arousing incidents—a process known from animal research to involve activation of the amygdala. In one of our first experiments with human subjects, we showed volunteers a series of graphically violent films while we measured their brain activity using PET. A few weeks later we gave them a quiz to see what they remembered.

We discovered that the number of disturbing films they could recall correlated with how active their amygdala had been during the viewing. Subsequent work from our laboratory and others confirmed this general finding. But then I noticed something strange. The amygdala activation in some studies involved only the right hemisphere, and in others it involved only the left hemisphere. It was then I realized that the experiments in which the right amygdala lit up involved only men; those in which the left amygdala was fired up involved women. Since then, three subsequent studies—two from our group and one from John Gabrieli and Turban Canli and their collaborators at Stanford—have confirmed this difference in how the brains of men and women handle emotional memories.

The realization that male and female brains were processing the same emotionally arousing material into memory differently led us to wonder what this disparity might mean. To address this question, we turned to a century-old theory stating that the right hemisphere is biased toward processing the central aspects of a situation, whereas the left hemisphere tends to process the finer details. If that conception is true, we reasoned, a drug that dampens the activity of the amygdala should impair a man's ability to recall the gist of an emotional story (by hampering the right amygdala) but should hinder a woman's ability to come up with the precise details (by hampering the left amygdala).

Propranolol is such a drug. This so-called beta blocker quiets the activity of adrenaline and its cousin noradrenaline and, in so doing, dampens the activation of the amygdala and weakens recall of emotionally arousing memories. We gave this drug to men and women before they viewed a short slide show about a young boy caught in a terrible accident while walking with his mother. One week later we tested their memory. The results showed that propranolol made it harder for men to remember the more holistic aspects, or gist, of the story—that the boy had been run over by a car, for example. In women, propranolol did the converse, impairing their memory for peripheral details—that the boy had been carrying a soccer ball.

In more recent investigations, we found that we can detect a hemispheric difference between the sexes in response to emotional material almost immediately. Volunteers shown emotionally unpleasant photographs react within 300 milliseconds—a response that shows up as a spike on a recording of the brain's electrical activity. With Antonella Gasbarri and others at the University of L'Aquila in Italy, we have found that in men, this quick spike, termed a P300 response, is more exaggerated when recorded over the right hemisphere; in women, it is larger when recorded over the left. Hence, sex-related hemispheric disparities in how the brain processes emotional images begin within 300 milliseconds-long before people have had much, if any, chance to consciously interpret what they have seen.

These discoveries might have ramifications for the treatment of PTSD. Previous research by Gustav Schelling and his associates at Ludwig Maximilian University in Germany had established that drugs such as propranolol diminish memory for traumatic situations when administered as part of the usual therapies in an intensive care unit. Prompted by our findings, they found that, at least in such units, beta blockers reduce memory for traumatic events in women but not in men. Even in intensive care, then, physicians may need to consider the sex of their patients when meting out their medications.

Sex and Mental Disorders

PTSD is not the only psychological disturbance that appears to play out differently in women and men. A PET study by Mirko Diksic and his colleagues at McGill University showed that serotonin production was a remarkable 52 percent higher on average in men than in women, which might help clarify why women are more prone to depression—a disorder commonly treated with drugs that boost the concentration of serotonin.

A similar situation might prevail in addiction. In this case, the neurotransmitter in question is dopamine—a chemical involved in the feelings of pleasure associated with drugs of abuse. Studying rats, Jill B. Becker and her fellow investigators at the University of Michigan at Ann Arbor discovered that in females, estrogen boosted the release of dopamine in brain regions important for regulating drug-seeking behavior. Furthermore, the hormone had long-lasting effects, making the female rats more likely to pursue cocaine weeks after last receiving the drug. Such differences in susceptibility—particularly to stimulants such as cocaine and amphetamine—could explain why women might be more vulnerable to the effects of these drugs and why they tend to progress more rapidly from initial use to dependence than men do.

Certain brain abnormalities underlying schizophrenia appear to differ in men and women as well. Ruben Gur, Raquel Gur and their colleagues at the University of Pennsylvania have spent years investigating sex-related differences in brain anatomy and function. In one project, they measured the size of the orbitofrontal cortex, a region involved in regulating emotions, and compared it with the size of the amygdala, implicated more in producing emotional reactions. The investigators found that women possess a significantly larger orbitofrontal-to-amygdala ratio (OAR) than men do. One can speculate from these findings that women might on average prove more capable of controlling their emotional reactions.

In additional experiments, the researchers discovered that this balance appears to be altered in schizophrenia, though not identically for men and women. Women with schizophrenia have a decreased OAR relative to their healthy peers, as might be expected. But men, oddly, have an increased OAR relative to healthy men. These findings remain puzzling, but, at the least, they imply that schizophrenia is a somewhat different disease in men and women and that treatment of the disorder might need to be tailored to the sex of the patient.

Sex Matters

In a comprehensive 2001 report on sex differences in human health, the prestigious National Academy of Sciences asserted that "sex matters. Sex, that is, being male or female, is an important basic human variable that should be considered when designing and analyzing studies in all areas and at all levels of biomedical and health related research."

Neuroscientists are still far from putting all the pieces together—identifying all the sex-related variations in the brain and pinpointing their influences on cognition and propensity for brain related disorders. Nevertheless, the research conducted to date certainly demonstrates that differences extend far beyond the hypothalamus and mating behavior. Researchers and clinicians are not always clear on the best way to go forward in deciphering the full influences of sex on the brain, behavior and responses to medications. But growing numbers now agree that going back to assuming we can evaluate one sex and learn equally about both is no longer an option.

Overview/Brains

- Neuroscientists are uncovering anatomical, chemical and functional differences between the brains of men and women.
- These variations occur throughout the brain, in regions involved in language, memory, emotion, vision, hearing and navigation.
- Researchers are working to determine how these sex-based variations relate to differences in male and female cognition and behavior. Their discoveries could point the way to sex-specific therapies for men and women with neurological conditions such as schizophrenia, depression, addiction and post-traumatic stress disorder.

LARRY CAHILL received his Ph.D. in neuroscience in 1990 from the University of California, Irvine. After spending two years in Germany using imaging techniques to explore learning and memory in gerbils, he returned to U.C. Irvine, where he is now an associate professor in the department of neurobiology and behavior and a Fellow of the Center for the Neurobiology of Learning and Memory.

From *Scientific American*, Vol. 292, Issue 5, May 2005, pp. 40-47. Copyright © 2005 by Scientific American, Inc. Reproduced with permission. All rights reserved. www.sciam.com

Cultural Psychology

Studying the Exotic Other

Alana Conner Snibbe

In psychology departments across the country, a growing number of psychologists are doing something called "cultural psychology." As they unpack their experiences and observations, unveil their theories and methods, and unfurl their often surprising results, an air of mystery collects around them. Who are these people? What is culture? What does it have to do with psychology? Why should I care? How can I join?

To address these questions, several cultural psychologists explained who they are, what they do, how they do it, why it's important, and what it takes to succeed.

What Is Cultural Psychology?

Cultural psychology is an interdisciplinary field that unites psychologists, anthropologists, linguists, and philosophers for a common pursuit: the study of how cultural meanings, practices, and institutions influence and reflect individual human psychologies. It is not a freestanding area within psychology, and most cultural psychologists would like to keep it that way. Rather than cordoning it off as its own subfield, cultural psychologists want to benefit from the breadth of expertise of its sundry practitioners, and to have a broader impact on all areas within psychology and across the social sciences.

Cultural psychology differs from other areas not only organizationally, but also philosophically. In contrast to psychologists who tend to assume that their findings and theories are universal until proven otherwise, cultural psychologists tend to assume that their findings and theories are culturally variable.

"This doesn't mean that cultural psychologists aren't interested in discovering psychological universals," explained APS Fellow Hazel Rose Markus, a social psychologist at Stanford University. "To the contrary. We suggest that the cultural patterning of psychological processes is precisely what is universal across humans. To discover these universals, however, we have to test our theories in other populations. We also have to explore the particulars we find and what they tell us about basic psychological processes."

Steven Heine, a social psychologist at the University of British Columbia, agreed that the road to basic psychological theory may be paved with cultural differences.

"Cultural differences can be informative to mainstream psychological theorizing in the same way that brain injuries are to neuroscience. That Phineas Gage lost his ability to plan for the future when he lost most of his medial prefrontal cortex was extremely informative for understanding how healthy minds are able to forecast future events. Likewise, knowing that certain groups do or do not show the same tendencies under different social and cultural conditions is very informative of how minds work."

So far, cultural psychologists' efforts have yielded a bevy of intriguing, often controversial cultural differences in psychological processes, including reasoning styles, motivation, perceptions of time, space, and color, relational styles, and emotional experience, regulation, and expression.

The Nature of Culture

The presence of cultural differences and of a field called cultural psychology encourages the questions: What is culture? And what does it have to do with you and your psyche?

Culture is much more than foods, festivals, and costumes. It's the set of ideas that coordinate the actions and construct the meanings of a group of people. More often than not, these ideas are implicit and automatic, guiding our practices, structuring our institutions, and generally infusing the everyday business of our lives. As people engage with a culture's practices, artifacts, and institutions, their thoughts, feelings, and behaviors come to reflect the culture's values and beliefs.

In contrast to psychologists who tend to assume that their findings and theories are universal until proven otherwise, cultural psychologists tend to assume that their findings and theories are culturally variable.

But that's only half the story. Culture shapes individual minds and behaviors as much as the minds and behaviors shape the culture. As a result, "People are active cultural agents, rather than passive recipients of cultural influences," said social psychologist Chi-Yue Chiu, University of Illinois. "They create, apply, reproduce, transform, and transmit their cultural routines in their daily social interactions."

One implication of the cyclical, transactional relationship between cultures and psyches is that culture is not an independent variable. Culture may predict, but it does not "cause." A second implication is that neither cultures nor psychologies exist independent of each other. Without human beings, cultures don't exist, and without cultures, human beings don't exist. Indeed, theorists increasingly argue that what separates humans from other species is our ability to produce and perpetuate cultures.

Mainstream psychological science's language and methods are primarily concerned with linear, causal relationships between separable entities. So cultural psychologists must create new terms and models to describe the processes by which cultures and psyches "make each other up." Current terms include mutual constitution, mutual influence, and mutual interdependence.

Developmental psychologist Joan Miller of New School University notes that neuroscientists face a similar challenge in describing the relationship between biology and mind. "Just as it is problematic to treat biological and psychological processes as discrete and separable, it is likewise problematic to understand mental events as occurring independently of cultural experiences," Miller said.

Yet since the cognitive revolution and the rise of neuroscientific methods, psychologists have increasingly considered biology the cause of behavior, and named the brain the seat of the mind. If we take seriously the proposition that human beings are both biological and cultural beings, though, it makes sense that the sources of mind may be found both in the head and in the world. Markus accordingly advocates that psychologists "scan the sociocultural environment for the sources of the structure of behavior, just as we currently scan the brain for those sources."

The Exotic Other

One good reason to care about cultural psychology is the empirical evidence that many psychological processes once deemed universal seem instead to be culturally variable. Another is the mounting empirical evidence for the role of culture in human evolution and development.

A third reason is simply that the world is getting smaller.

"Rates of globalization are skyrocketing," observed cultural anthropologist Rick Shweder, University of Chicago. "As the world globalizes, we will have to negotiate the ground rules for the production and distribution of cultural practices and beliefs. There will be a huge niche for cultural psychologists who understand what culture is and what it does."

A fourth reason is that, just as the world outside our labs is becoming smaller, the worlds within our lecture halls are becoming larger. Fifty years ago, diversity in higher education ran the gamut from tweed to gabardine. As immigration laws have changed and access to higher education has increased, the student bodies to which psychologists offer their science have changed from lily white to varicolored. Increasingly, the psychology that European American researchers produce does not resonate with the experiences of these multicultural consumers.

The good news for psychologists who want to do cultural psychology is this: You're already doing it.

"Mainstream psychology is really cultural psychology, dealing with a very particular cultural context," said social psychologist Virginia Kwan, Princeton University. That particular cultural context is the middle-class, college-educated, predominantly Protestant European-American milieu from which the vast majority of psychological researchers and research participants hail.

Jeffrey Sanchez-Burks, a social psychologist at the University of Michigan Business School, underscored how strange this group is.

"People often describe cultural differences in terms of the exotic other, but rarely talk about why Americans are the way they are. But in my research comparing American relational styles to those of East Asian and Latin cultures, it's Americans who are the anomaly. So I actually shifted my research to focus on American culture."

The college student populations with which the bulk of psychological research is conducted are also an odd lot. Even among Americans, only 24 percent of those over age 25 have college degrees.

The good news for psychologists who want to do cultural psychology is this: You're already doing it.

Social psychologist Fathali Moghaddam, Georgetown University, has speculated that non-student populations would reveal a more striking cultural difference than purely academic groups, even though many studies have already documented cultural differences among college students.

"If you look at the details of life in modern universities across cultures, they are very similar to each other, and very different from those of life outside of universities. For example, university students in Istanbul read, listen to, and wear many of the same things as university students in Washington, DC. However, the lives of these students in Istanbul are quite different from those of people in the villages of western Turkey, just as the lives of university students in major American cities are quite different from those of people in other American contexts."

Oh, the Places You'll Go!

Perspective on your own culture's commitments, as well as insights into another's, requires the same first step: go away. Immerse yourself in the everyday business of living in another culture. It is only through the contrast of cultural systems that their operating principles become salient.

Cultural psychologists differ in their opinions of how deep the cultural immersion has to be before it imparts its wisdom. Psychological anthropologist Alan Fiske, University of California, Los Angeles, often recommends a lengthy stint of fieldwork, replete with language learning and participant observation.

"Not interviewing, not videotaping, but genuine participant observation [is the key]," Fiske said. "Culture consists mostly of practices, skills, and motives whose cognitive representation is primarily procedural, not explicit semantic knowledge. We learn about each other's cultures by participating in them, not by asking about them."

Psychologists often have to settle for less than ideal immersion, however, because psychological training often does not include time for such fieldwork. Many draw initial insights from their own cultural backgrounds and then supplement these insights by reading texts from anthropology, history, and sociology. Sanchez-Burks, for example, recommends reading Weber and de Tocqueville to understand European-American culture.

Psychologists can also take better advantage of the short bouts of travel that their discipline does allow. "Don't travel like a tourist," advised social psychologist Sheena Iyengar, Columbia University's Graduate School of Business. "Travel in a way that allows you to live more like the people there. Stay away from fancy hotels, which are basically the same wherever you go. If you can, try to stay in people's houses."

Another approach to studying cultural psychology is relying on the expertise of others. "Somebody on the team, at least at the outset, has got to be a native," said social psychologist and APS Fellow Richard Nisbett, University of Michigan. "Ideally, somebody on the team knows both cultures reasonably well, but sometimes it's enough to have one person who knows one culture and one who knows the other."

When considering possible cultural groups for research, budding cultural psychologists need not worry about encroaching upon other researcher's turf. "Most of the non-Western world is ripe for the picking," said Heine. There are also many under-explored populations within the United States. For example, Ying-yi Hong, a social psychologist at the University of Illinois, would like to see more research on bicultural, multicultural, and multiracial populations.

"These groups of people have often been neglected in previous research because they are viewed as not 'pure' enough to represent one culture," Hong said. "However, they are arguably the fastest growing population in many places because of increased mobility and migration. By investigating these individuals, we may be better able to understand how culture dynamically influences people's psychologies and how people negotiate their different cultural identities."

Oh, the Places You Might Not Go!

While cultural psychologists may find it easier to cross the globe in search of deep psychological insights than their mainstream counterparts, they may also find it harder to ascend the academic hierarchy.

"The greatest obstacle to doing cultural research," Moghaddam said, "is the publish-or-perish culture of academic psychology. Theoretically sound, culturally appropriate, and fine-tuned research with samples from at least two populations takes a long time. When you're doing that kind of research, it's very difficult

to churnout the number of articles necessary to survive in the system."

Even APS Fellow and Charter Member Harry Triandis, one of cross-cultural psychology's founding fathers, did not wholeheartedly pursue cultural research until he was comfortably tenured.

"When I first started my career, I focused my research on attitudes and attitude change," Triandis said. "That's how I got promoted. I became a professor first, and later I became a cross-cultural psychologist."

Heine enumerated some of the logistical barriers that cultural psychologists face in conducting their research. "After you have learned the cultural systems and languages in which you want to work, developed theory, and specified hypotheses, you then have to secure samples in both cultures," he said. "Unless you have a collaborator who is fully committed to the project, it can be difficult to find someone to help you collect data.... It can also be difficult to find a collaborator with the facilities that you require.

"As for [student] participants, you have to keep in mind that the school terms are at different times of the year in different countries, which can add significant delays to getting the data from the two samples, and further delays in running any follow-up studies. If participants are not students, or if the university does not have a subject pool (as is often the case outside of North America), unfavorable currency exchange rates can make studies very costly. There are also significant costs and challenges with creating materials that are appropriate in another culture, translating them and any open-ended data that you collect, and in training experimenters."

Having overcome these obstacles and produced exciting findings, many cultural psychologists still confront the fact that cultural psychology remains a somewhat marginalized discipline.

"Cultural psychology tends to be treated as non-essential in terms of hiring, curriculum development, and other central aspects of the discipline," Miller said. "It receives its own summary chapter in handbooks or texts, but is otherwise sometimes overlooked as a critical force in understanding basic psychological processes."

Despite these logistic and professional hurdles, a growing number of psychologists are pursuing cultural psychology. For them, its perils are outweighed by its powerful attractions, such as contributing to psychological functioning, engaging with ideas from other social sciences, hobnobbing with international colleagues, and having a good excuse for extensive travel.

Perhaps social psychologist Michael Bond, Chinese University of Hong Kong, best summarized the appeal and likely posterity of cultural psychology: "Cultural exploration has enough intellectual intrigue to occupy an academic lifetime," he said. "I am never bored, but constantly being stretched."

Author's Note: I would like to thank Susan T. Fiske for her contributions to the research for this article.

Ambition: Why Some People Are Most Likely to Succeed

A fire in the belly doesn't light itself. Does the spark of ambition lie in genes, family, culture—or even in your own hands? Science has answers

JEFFREY KLUGER

You don't get as successful as Gregg Anddrew shipp by accident. Shake hands with the 36-year-old fraternal twins who co-own the sprawling Hi Fi Personal Fitness club in Chicago, and it's clear you're in the presence of people who thrive on their drive. But that wasn't always the case. The twins' father founded the Jovan perfume company, a glamorous business that spun off the kinds of glamorous profits that made it possible for the Shipps to amble through high school, coast into college and never much worry about getting the rent paid or keeping the fridge filled. But before they graduated, their sense of drift began to trouble them. At about the same time, their father sold off the company, and with it went the cozy billets in adult life that had always served as an emotional backstop for the boys.

That did it. By the time they got out of school, both Shipps had entirely transformed themselves, changing from boys who might have grown up to live off the family's wealth to men consumed with going out and creating their own. "At this point," says Gregg, "I consider myself to be almost maniacally ambitious."

It shows. In 1998 the brothers went into the gym trade. They spotted a modest health club doing a modest business, bought out the owner and transformed the place into a luxury facility where private trainers could reserve space for top-dollar clients. In the years since, the company has outgrown one building, then another, and the brothers are about to move a third time. Gregg, a communications major at college, manages the club's clients, while Drew, a business major, oversees the more hardheaded chore of finance and expansion. "We're not sitting still," Drew says. "Even now that we're doing twice the business we did at our old place, there's a thirst that needs to be quenched."

Why is that? Why are some people born with a fire in the belly, while others—like the Shipps—need something to get their pilot light lit? And why do others never get the flame of ambition going? Is there a family anywhere that doesn't have its overachievers and underachievers—its Jimmy Carters and Billy Carters, its Jeb Bushes and Neil Bushes—and find itself wondering how they all could have come splashing out of exactly the same gene pool?

Of all the impulses in humanity's behavioral portfolio, ambition—that need to grab an ever bigger piece of the resource pie before someone else gets it—ought to be one of the most democratically distributed. Nature is a zero-sum game, after all. Every buffalo you kill for your family is one less for somebody else's; every acre of land you occupy elbows out somebody else. Given that, the need to get ahead ought to be hard-wired into all of us equally.

"For me, ambition has become a dirty word. I prefer hunger."

—Johnny Depp

And yet it's not. For every person consumed with the need to achieve, there's someone content to accept whatever life brings. For everyone who chooses the 80-hour workweek, there's someone punching out at 5. Men and women—so it's said—express ambition differently; so do Americans and Europeans, baby boomers and Gen Xers, the middle class and the well-to-do. Even among the manifestly motivated, there are degrees of ambition. Steve Wozniak co-founded Apple Computer and then left the company in 1985 as a 34-year-old multimillionaire. His partner, Steve Jobs, is still innovating at Apple and moonlighting at his second blockbuster company, Pixar Animation Studios.

Not only do we struggle to understand why some people seem to have more ambition than others, but we can't even agree on just what ambition is. "Ambition is an evolutionary product," says anthropologist Edward Lowe at Soka University of America, in Aliso Viejo, Calif. "No matter how social status is defined, there are certain people in every community who aggressively pursue it and others who aren't so aggressive."

Dean Simonton, a psychologist at the University of California, Davis, who studies genius, creativity and eccentricity, believes it's more complicated than that. "Ambition is energy and determination," he says. "But it calls for goals too. People with goals but no energy are the ones who wind up sitting on the couch saying 'One day I'm going to build a better mousetrap.' People with energy but no clear goals just dissipate themselves in one desultory project after the next."

> ## "Ambition is like love, impatient both of delays and rivals."
> **—Buddah**

Assuming you've got drive, dreams and skill, is all ambition equal? Is the overworked lawyer on the partner track any more ambitious than the overworked parent on the mommy track? Is the successful musician to whom melody comes naturally more driven than the unsuccessful one who sweats out every note? We may listen to Mozart, but should we applaud Salieri?

Most troubling of all, what about when enough ambition becomes way too much? Grand dreams unmoored from morals are the stuff of tyrants—or at least of Enron. The 16-hour workday filled with high stress and at-the-desk meals is the stuff of burnout and heart attacks. Even among kids, too much ambition quickly starts to do real harm. In a just completed study, anthropologist Peter Demerath of Ohio State University surveyed 600 students at a high-achieving high school where most of the kids are triple-booked with advanced-placement courses, sports and after-school jobs. About 70% of them reported that they were starting to feel stress some or all of the time. "I asked one boy how his parents react to his workload, and he answered, 'I don't really get home that often,'" says Demerath. "Then he handed me his business card from the video store where he works."

Anthropologists, psychologists and others have begun looking more closely at these issues, seeking the roots of ambition in family, culture, gender, genes and more. They have by no means thrown the curtain all the way back, but they have begun to part it. "It's fundamentally human to be prestige conscious,"

says Soka's Lowe. "It's not enough just to be fed and housed. People want more."

If humans are an ambitious species, it's clear we're not the only one. Many animals are known to signal their ambitious tendencies almost from birth. Even before wolf pups are weaned, they begin sorting themselves out into alphas and all the others. The alphas are quicker, more curious, greedier for space, milk, Mom—and they stay that way for life. Alpha wolves wander widely, breed annually and may live to a geriatric 10 or 11 years old. Lower-ranking wolves enjoy none of these benefits—staying close to home, breeding rarely and usually dying before they're 4.

Humans often report the same kind of temperamental determinism. Families are full of stories of the inexhaustible infant who grow up to be an entrepreneur, the phlegmatic child who never really showed much go. But if it's genes that run the show, what accounts for the Shipps, who didn't bestir themselves until the cusp of adulthood? And what, more tellingly, explains identical twins—precise genetic templates of each other who ought to be temperamentally identical but often exhibit profound differences in the octane of their ambition?

Ongoing studies of identical twins have measured achievement motivation—lab language for ambition—in identical siblings separated at birth, and found that each twin's profile overlaps 30% to 50% of the other's. In genetic terms, that's an awful lot—"a benchmark for heritability," says geneticist Dean Hamer of the National Cancer Institute. But that still leaves a great deal that can be determined by experiences in infancy, subsequent upbringing and countless other imponderables.

Some of those variables may be found by studying the function of the brain. At Washington University, researchers have been conducting brain imaging to investigate a trait they call persistence—the ability to stay focused on a task until it's completed just so—which they consider one of the critical engines driving ambition.

The researchers recruited a sample group of students and gave each a questionnaire designed to measure persistence level. Then they presented the students with a task—identifying sets of pictures as either pleasant or unpleasant and taken either indoors or outdoors—while conducting magnetic resonance imaging of their brains. The nature of the task was unimportant, but how strongly the subjects felt about performing it well—and where in the brain that feeling was processed—could say a lot. In general, the researchers found that students who scored highest in persistence had the greatest activity in the limbic region, the area of the brain related to emotions and habits. "The correlation was .8 [or 80%]," says professor of psychiatry Robert Cloninger, one of the investigators. "That's as good as you can get."

It's impossible to say whether innate differences in the brain were driving the ambitious behavior or whether learned behavior was causing the limbic to light up. But a number of researchers believe it's possible for the nonambitious to jump-start their drive, provided the right jolt comes along. "Energy level may be genetic," says psychologist Simonton, "but a lot of times it's just" Simonton and others often cite the case of Franklin D. Roosevelt, who might not have been the same

President he became—or even become President at all—had his disabling polio not taught him valuable lessons about patience and tenacity.

Is such an epiphany possible for all of us, or are some people immune to this kind of lightning? Are there individuals or whole groups for whom the amplitude of ambition is simply lower than it is for others? It's a question—sometimes a charge—that hangs at the edges of all discussions about gender and work, about whether women really have the meat-eating temperament to survive in the professional world. Both research findings and everyday experience suggest that women's ambitions express themselves differently from men's. The meaning of that difference is the hinge on which the arguments turn.

"Ambition makes you look pretty ugly."
—Radiohead

Economists Lise Vesterlund of the University of Pittsburgh and Muriel Niederle of Stanford University conducted a study in which they assembled 40 men and 40 women, gave them five minutes to add up as many two-digit numbers as they could, and paid them 50¢ for each correct answer. The subjects were not competing against one another but simply playing against the house. Later, the game was changed to a tournament in which the subjects were divided into teams of two men or two women each. Winning teams got $2 per computation; losers got nothing. Men and women performed equally in both tests, but on the third round, when asked to choose which of the two ways they wanted to play, only 35% of the women opted for the tournament format; 75% of the men did.

"Men and women just differ in their appetite for competition," says Vesterlund. "There seems to be a dislike for it among women and a preference among men."

"Ambition, old mankind, the immemorial weakness of the strong."
—Vita Sackville-West

To old-line employers of the old-boy school, this sounds like just one more reason to keep the glass ceiling polished. But other behavioral experts think Vesterlund's conclusions go too far. They say it's not that women aren't ambitious enough to compete for what they want; it's that they're more selective about when they engage in competition; they're willing to get ahead at high cost but not at any cost. "Primate-wide, males are more directly competitive than females, and that makes sense," says Sarah Blaffer Hrdy, emeritus professor of anthropology at the University of California, Davis. "But that's not the same as saying women aren't innately competitive too."

As with so much viewed through the lens of anthropology, the roots of these differences lie in animal and human mating strategies. Males are built to go for quick, competitive reproductive hits and move on. Women are built for the it-takes-a-village life, in which they provide long-term care to a very few young and must sail them safely into an often hostile world. Among some of our evolutionary kin—baboons, macaques and other old-world monkeys—this can be especially tricky since young females inherit their mother's social rank. The mothers must thus operate the levers of society deftly so as to raise both their own position and, eventually, their daughters'. If you think that kind of ambition-by-proxy doesn't translate to humans, Hrdy argues, think again. "Just read an Edith Wharton novel about women in old New York competing for marriage potential for their daughters," she says.

Import such tendencies into the 21st century workplace, and you get women who are plenty able to compete ferociously but are inclined to do it in teams and to split the difference if they don't get everything they want. And mothers who appear to be unwilling to strive and quit the workplace altogether to go raise their kids? Hrdy believes they're competing for the most enduring stakes of all, putting aside their near-term goals to ensure the long-term success of their line. Robin Parker, 46, a campaign organizer who in 1980 was already on the presidential stump with Senator Edward Kennedy, was precisely the kind of lifetime pol who one day finds herself in the West Wing. But in 1992, at the very moment a President of her party was returning to the White House and she might have snagged a plum Washington job, she decamped from the capital, moved to Boston with her family and became a full-time mom to her two sons.

"Being out in the world became a lot less important to me," she says. "I used to worry about getting Presidents elected, and I'm still an incredibly ambitious person. But what I want to succeed at now is managing my family, raising my boys, helping my husband and the community. In 10 years, when the boys are launched, who knows what I'll be doing? But for now, I have my world."

But even if something as primal as the reproductive impulse wires you one way, it's possible for other things to rewire you completely. Two of the biggest influences on your level of ambition are the family that produced you and the culture that produced your family.

There are no hard rules for the kinds of families that turn out the highest achievers. Most psychologists agree that parents who set tough but realistic challenges, applaud successes and go easy on failures produce kids with the greatest self-confidence.

What's harder for parents to control but has perhaps as great an effect is the level of privilege into which their kids are born. Just how wealth or poverty influences drive is difficult to predict. Grow up in a rich family, and you can inherit either the tools to achieve (think both Presidents Bush) or the indolence of the aristocrat. Grow up poor, and you can come away with either the motivation to strive (think Bill Clinton) or the inertia of the hopeless. On the whole, studies suggest it's the upper middle class that produces the greatest proportion of ambitious people—mostly because it also produces the greatest proportion of anxious people.

When measuring ambition, anthropologists divide families into four categories: poor, struggling but getting by, upper middle class, and rich. For members of the first two groups, who are fighting just to keep the electricity on and the phone bill paid, ambition is often a luxury. For the rich, it's often unnecessary. It's members of the upper middle class, reasonably safe economically but not so safe that a bad break couldn't spell catastrophe, who are most driven to improve their lot. "It's called status anxiety," says anthropologist Lowe, "and whether you're born to be concerned about it or not, you do develop it."

"Ambition is so powerful a passion in the human breast that however high we reach, we are never satisfied."

—Niccolo Machiavelli

But some societies make you more anxious than others. The U.S. has always been a me-first culture, as befits a nation that grew from a scattering of people on a fat saddle of continent where land was often given away. That have-it-all ethos persists today, even though the resource freebies are long since gone. Other countries—where the acreage is smaller and the pickings are slimmer—came of age differently, with the need to cooperate getting etched into the cultural DNA. The American model has produced wealth, but it has come at a price—with ambition sometimes turning back on the ambitious and consuming them whole.

The study of high-achieving high school students conducted by Ohio State's Demerath was noteworthy for more than the stress he found the students were suffering. It also revealed the lengths to which the kids and their parents were willing to go to gain an advantage over other suffering students. Cheating was common, and most students shrugged it off as only a minor problem. A number of parents—some of whose children carried a 4.0 average—sought to have their kids classified as special-education students, which would entitle them to extra time on standardized tests. "Kids develop their own moral code," says Demerath. "They have a keen sense of competing with others and are developing identities geared to that."

Demerath got very different results when he conducted research in a very different place—Papua, New Guinea. In the mid-1990s, he spent a year in a small village there, observing how the children learned. Usually, he found, they saw school as a noncompetitive place where it was important to succeed collectively and then move on. Succeeding at the expense of others was seen as a form of vanity that the New Guineans call "acting extra." Says Demerath: "This is an odd thing for them."

That makes tactical sense. In a country based on farming and fishing, you need to know that if you get sick and can't work your field or cast your net, someone else will do it for you. Putting on airs in the classroom is not the way to ensure that will happen.

Of course, once a collectivist not always a collectivist. Marcelo Suárez-Orozco, a professor of globalization and education at New York University, has been following 400 families that immigrated to the U.S. from Asia, Latin America and the Caribbean. Many hailed from villages where the American culture of competition is alien, but once they got here, they changed fast.

As a group, the immigrant children in his study are outperforming their U.S.-born peers. What's more, the adults are dramatically outperforming the immigrant families that came before them. "One hundred years ago, it took people two to three generations to achieve a middle-class standard of living," says Suárez-Orozco. "Today they're getting there within a generation."

So this is a good thing, right? Striving people come here to succeed—and do. While there are plenty of benefits that undeniably come with learning the ways of ambition, there are plenty of perils too—many a lot uglier than high school students cheating on the trig final.

Human history has always been writ in the blood of broken alliances, palace purges and strong people or nations beating up on weak ones—all in the service of someone's hunger for power There's a point at which you find an interesting kind of nerve circuitry between optimism and hubris," says Warren Bennis, a professor of business administration at the University of Southern California and the author of three books on leadership. "It becomes an arrogance or conceit, an inability to live without power."

While most ambitious people keep their secret Caesar tucked safely away, it can emerge surprisingly, even suddenly. Says Frans de Waal, a primatologist at the Yerkes Primate Center in Atlanta and the author of a new book, Our Inner Ape: "You can have a male chimp that is the most laid-back character, but one day he sees the chance to overthrow the leader and becomes a totally different male. I would say 90% of people would behave this way too. On an island with three people, they might become a little dictator."

But a yearning for supremacy can create its own set of problems. Heart attacks, ulcers and other stress-related ills are more common among high achievers—and that includes nonhuman achievers. The blood of alpha wolves routinely shows elevated levels of cortisol, the same stress hormone that is found in anxious humans. Alpha chimps even suffer ulcers and occasional heart attacks.

For these reasons, people and animals who have an appetite for becoming an alpha often settle contentedly into life as a beta. "The desire to be in a high position is universal," says de Waal. "But that trait has co-evolved with another skill—the skill to make the best of lower positions."

Humans not only make peace with their beta roles but they also make money from them. Among corporations, an increasingly well-rewarded portion of the workforce is made up of B players, managers and professionals somewhere below the top tier. They don't do the power lunching and ribbon cutting but instead perform the highly skilled, everyday work of making the company run. As skeptical shareholders look ever more askance at overpaid corporate A-listers, the B players are becoming

53

DONALD TRUMP

Achievements

Before he ever uttered the words "You're fired," Trump developed more than 18 million sq. ft. of Manhattan real estate, naming most of it after himself.

Early Signs Of Ambition

While in college, Donald read federal foreclosure listings for fun. It paid off: he bought his first housing project before he graduated.

BILL CLINTON

Achievements

Former U.S. President, current global celebrity.

Early Signs Of Ambition

At 16, he beat out some 1,000 other boys to win a mock state senate seat and a trip to Washington, where he knew "the action was." Once in the capital, he got himself into position to shake hands with his idol, President John F. Kennedy.

OPRAH WINFREY

Achievements

Her $1 billion media empire includes movies, a magazine and her talk show, now in its 20th year.

Early Signs Of Ambition

She could read at 2, and although she was just 5 when she started school, she insisted on being put in first grade. Her teacher relented. The next year young Oprah was skipped to third grade.

TIGER WOODS

Achievements

At 21, he was the youngest golfer ever ranked No. 1 in the world. Now 29, he holds the record for most prize money won in a career—$56 million and counting.

Early Signs Of Ambition

At 6, he listened to motivational tapes—"I will make my own destiny"—while practicing his swing in the mirror.

MARTHA STEWART

Achievements

The lifestyle guru rules an empire that includes one magazine, two TV shows, a satellite-radio deal, a shelf full of best sellers and a home-furnishings line at Kmart.

Early Signs Of Ambition

As a grade-schooler, she organized and catered neighborhood birthday parties because, she says, the going rate of 50¢ an hr. for babysitting "wasn't quite enough money."

VERA WANG

Achievements

She turned one-of-a-kind wedding gowns into a $300 million fashion business.

Early Signs Of Ambition

Although from a wealthy family, she spent her high school summers working as a sales clerk in a Manhattan boutique. After college, she landed a job at *Vogue* magazine, where she put in seven-day workweeks, rose quickly and became a senior editor at 23.

CONDOLEEZZA RICE

Achievements

The current Secretary of State and former National Security Adviser was 38 when she became Stanford University's youngest, and first female, provost.

Early Signs Of Ambition

A gifted child pianist who began studying at the Birmingham Conservatory at 10, the straight-A student became a competitive ice skater, rising at 4:30 a.m. to spend two hours at the rink before school and piano lessons.

SEAN COMBS

Achievements

Diddy, as he's now known, is a Grammy-winning performer and producer and a millionaire businessman with a restaurant, a clothing line and a marketing and ad agency.

Early Signs Of Ambition

During his days at Howard University, he learned about business by doing: he sold term papers and tickets to dance parties he hosted.

JENNIFER LOPEZ

Achievements

The former Fly Girl dancer has sold 40 million records, is the highest-paid Latina actress in Hollywood and has launched fashion and perfume lines.

Early Signs Of Ambition

When she signed with Sony Music, she insisted on dealing with its chief, Tommy Mottola. She told him she wanted "the A treatment. I want everything top of the line."

BRITNEY SPEARS

Achievements

Her first single and first four albums made their debut at No. 1. Since then she has sold 76 million records and amassed a $150 million fortune.

Early Signs Of Ambition

Spears used to lock herself in the bathroom and sing to her dolls. After each number, she practiced smiling and blowing kisses to her toy audience.

TOM CRUISE

Achievements

He's a movie superstar who gets $25 million a film, an accomplished actor with three Oscar nods and a gossip staple who has sold a zillion magazines.

Early Signs Of Ambition

After his first role in a high school musical, he asked his family to give him 10 years to make it in show business. Within four, he was starring in the surprise hit film *Risky Business*.

more highly valued. It's an adaptation that serves the needs of both the corporation and the culture around it. "Everyone has ambition," says Lowe. "Societies have to provide alternative ways for people to achieve."

Ultimately, it's that very flexibility—that multiplicity of possible rewards—that makes dreaming big dreams and pursu-

ing big goals worth all the bother. Ambition is an expensive impulse, one that requires an enormous investment of emotional capital. Like any investment, it can pay off in countless different kinds of coin. The trick, as any good speculator will tell you, is recognizing the riches when they come your way.

From *Time Magazine*, November 14, 2005, pp. 49-59. Copyright © 2005 by Time Inc. Reprinted by permission.

How to Keep Those New Year's Resolutions

Psychologists have identified successful ways of meeting self-determined goals, but they may not work if you're a perfectionist.

It's hard to take New Year's resolutions too seriously. We know they are more often breached than observed, so we make them, ironically, half-heartedly—or not at all. They epitomize "easier said than done."

Yet there is a meaty side to resolutions, which at other times of the year we simply call setting goals for ourselves. Many such goals are related to health. Getting more exercise, losing weight, quitting smoking—they perennially top the to-do lists. Much more than vanity is at stake. Study after study shows that almost anything that helps people make progress in those areas does wonders for their health.

Moreover, researchers who study the subject believe that doctors could tap into the psychology of goal attainment to help their patients be better about everything from taking their medications to eating more fiber to getting more sleep.

Even if health isn't involved directly, researchers have found that setting, pursuing, and achieving a goal pays off in improved mental health. This may be particularly true of Americans. Observers have long noted how fervently, if fitfully, Americans work at improving themselves. Now, of course, catering to the desire is a huge moneymaker: Publishers selling self-help books, educational institutions offering adult education classes, the diet industry hawking the greatest way to shed pounds—one way or another, they're all in the self-improvement business.

What Doesn't Work ...

Yet our best-laid plans often go awry. Researchers have found that people must structure goals correctly in order to meet them.

One common mistake is to have too many goals. Attention and willpower get split so many ways that little headway is made toward reaching any goal. And the longer your list, the greater the chance that the items on it will conflict. So if you've made 10 New Year's resolutions, start the year off right by trimming them back to three.

Another formula for failure is to set your sights on behaviors that are too vague ("I am going to be a better spouse"). In the health realm, telling yourself that you are going to eat more healthful foods this year, or that you're going to exercise more often, is probably not going to work.

A third pitfall is setting goals that are too lofty. That's one reason experts so often recommend brisk walking (a pace of three miles or more per hour) as a form of exercise. Not only are there good data showing that it has multiple health benefits, but brisk walking is also something that many people can do.

... And What Does

Matching values and goals. In one study, researchers recruited 59 students at McGill University in Montreal for a study of New Year's resolutions. The volunteers were asked to make three resolutions and then were e-mailed questions two weeks and a month later. (That's not very long for sticking with a resolution, but psychology experiments frequently have short time limits in order to get results.) Most of the goals were related to health, academic, or social ("I will call my family more often") achievements.

At the beginning of the study, the researchers asked the student volunteers to rate the following four statements about their motivations for their resolutions on a scale of 1 to 9, with 1 representing total disagreement and 9 complete agreement:

Because somebody else wants you to, or because you'll get something from somebody if you do

Because you would feel ashamed, guilty, or anxious if you didn't—you feel that you ought to strive for this

Because you really believe that it is an important goal to have—you endorse it freely and value it wholeheartedly

Because of the fun and enjoyment that the goal will provide you—the primary reason is simply your interest in the experience itself.

Psychologists have developed these questions to measure self-concordance—or how well people's goals match their interests and values, in contrast to goals that feel imposed either by external (as in #1) or internal (as in #2) pressures.

In this study and many others, goals that were self-concordant were more likely to be achieved. In other words, you're more likely to keep a resolution or achieve a goal if the motivation is coming from you and not someone else.

Put that way, there's a big "well, duh!" factor here. On the other hand, what's more murky than the origins of our motivations? But judging by the results of this and a number of other psychology experiments, if you want to make a successful resolution, you need to sort through the mess and pick wisely, focusing on goals that fit your values and desires.

Strategies, not just goals. Another recurring theme from goal-attainment research is that it's not enough to have a goal. You must come up with a strategy for reaching it that's rooted in practical steps. Psychologists have found that the best results seem to come when people tie the desired behaviors to common situations or events, or to habits they already have, so the new behavior becomes more or less automatic.

An early-morning exercise routine is a good example. For many people, the cue that it's time to get walking, jogging, or working out is waking up. They don't even have to think about it. Some people make pill taking automatic by putting their medications by their toothbrush.

So take a look at your New Year's resolutions. You need to pave the road of those good intentions for 2006 with concrete strategies about the where, the when, and the how—and then connect them to things you do already. The result could be a happier, healthier new year for you.

Perfectionists May Get Frustrated

Perfectionists are self-critical. So does that tendency get in the way of reaching goals? Or does the pursuit of perfection spur them on? Short answer: It depends.

Researchers have developed questionnaires to measure perfectionism in a personality. Fifty McGill students who participated in a study of New Year's resolutions (not the same study mentioned above) filled out one such questionnaire, the Multidimensional Perfectionism Scale.

When investigators analyzed how perfectionism affected the keeping of resolutions, they came up with a split verdict. In an article published in 2004 in the Personality and Social Psychology Bulletin, they reported that step-by-step plans for pursuing a goal (so-called implementation intentions) worked well for students with perfectionist tendencies if those tendencies were integral to their personalities.

But the practical steps backfired for students with perfectionism that was "socially prescribed," or driven by a need to reach expectations set by others. For those students, supposedly practical steps may stir up paralyzing self-criticism and excessive worry about what others think, according to one of the researchers, Theodore Powers, an associate professor at University of Massachusetts, Dartmouth.

Stand & Deliver

Do you check e-mail 100 times a day, only to answer two messages? Understanding why people really procrastinate is the key to purging that in-box and getting on with life.

MAIA SZALAVITZ

At the age of 37, Jared, a would-be professor in New York state, should be on tenure track at a university, perhaps publishing his second or third book. Instead, he's working on a dissertation in sociology that he'd planned to complete a decade ago. He's blown two "drop-dead" deadlines and is worried about missing a third. His girlfriend is losing patience. No one can understand why a guy they consider brilliant doesn't "just do it." Nor, for that matter, can Jared: "If I could change it, believe me, I would," he swears.

Jared is among the one in five people who chronically procrastinate, jeopardizing careers and jettisoning peace of mind, all the while repeating the mantra: "I should be doing something else right now."

Procrastination is not just an issue of time management or laziness. It's about feeling paralyzed and guilty as you channel surf, knowing you should be cracking the books or reconfiguring your investment strategy. Why the gap between incentive and action? Psychologists now believe it is a combination of anxiety and false beliefs about productivity.

Procrastinators may enjoy the adrenaline rush that comes with mailing taxes at 11:30 p.m. on April 15.

Tim Pychyl, Ph.D., associate professor of psychology at Carleton University in Ottawa, Canada, tracked students with procrastination problems in the final week before a project was due. Students first reported anxiety and guilt because they had not started their projects. "They were telling themselves 'I work better under pressure' or 'this isn't important,'" says Pychyl. But once they began to work, they reported more positive emotions; they no longer lamented wasted time, nor claimed that pressure helped. The results of this study will be presented at the Third International Conference on Counseling the Procrastinator in Academic Settings in August. Psychologists have focused on procrastination among students because the problem is rampant in academic settings; some 70 percent of college students report problems with overdue papers and delayed studying, according to Joseph Ferrari, associate professor of psychology at Chicago's DePaul University.

Pychyl also found that procrastination is detrimental to physical health. College students who procrastinate have higher levels of drinking, smoking, insomnia, stomach problems, colds and flu.

So why can't people just buckle down and get the job done?

False Beliefs

Many procrastinators are convinced that they work better under pressure, or they'll feel better about tackling the work later. But tomorrow never comes and last-minute work is often low quality. In spite of what they may believe, "Procrastinators generally don't do well under pressure," says Ferrari. The idea that time pressure improves performance is perhaps the most common myth among procrastinators.

Fear of Failure

"The main reason people procrastinate is fear," says Neil Fiore, Ph.D., author of *The Now Habit*. Procrastinators fear they'll fall short because they don't have the requisite talent or skills. "They get overwhelmed and they're afraid they'll look stupid." According to Ferrari, "Procrastinators would rather be seen as lacking in effort than lacking in ability." If you flunk a calculus exam, better to loudly blame it on the half-hour study blitz, than admit to yourself that you could have used a tutor the entire semester.

Perfectionism

Procrastinators tend to be perfectionists—and they're in overdrive because they're insecure. People who do their best because they want to win don't procrastinate; but those who feel they must be perfect to please others often put things off. These people fret that "No one will love me if everything I do isn't utter genius." Such perfectionism is at the heart of many an unfinished novel.

Master the Task

Never say "I must":

"People get stuck between their inner voices and use ineffective ways of motivation," says Neil Fiore. One voice says, "I should," another says, "I don't want to." Fiore recommends that instead you recognize you have a choice. Realizing that you have selected your goals helps shut down the conflict between "should" and "want." Sure, you don't have to study for the bar exam—but choosing not to could seriously crimp your plan to become an attorney.

Set realistic goals:

Resolutions like "I want to get in shape," often fail, but plans like "I will run three times a week at 7 a.m.," are more achievable. Break tasks down into small, manageable steps. When the house looks like a garbage dump, cleaning it may seem insurmountable. But tidying the bathroom for 15 minutes isn't so bad.

Schedule time off:

Fiore found that graduate students who completed dissertations in two years or less allowed themselves time for relaxation. Those who took three or more years tried to spend every minute researching and writing. They rebelled against the self-imposed drudgery, rendering themselves less effective in the long term.

Fight misguided impulses:

Don't succumb to myths such as "pressure improves performance." Set up a schedule that includes short-, medium- and long- term goals to avoid leaving everything until the last minute.

Be selective:

If you tend toward perfectionism, only do your absolute best when it matters. Every e-mail you send needn't be exquisitely composed; a book proposal, however, should be.

Please yourself first:

The more you cultivate a sense of self-worth in areas outside the procrastination prone domain (usually work or school), the less likely you will be to postpone tasks. Remember, no judgment of your work is ever the final verdict on you.

Seek professional help:

If procrastination is putting your study habits on hold, cognitive-behavioral therapy can be effective.

Self-Control

Impulsivity may seem diametrically opposed to procrastination, but both can be part of a larger problem: self-control. People who are impulsive may not be able to prioritize intentions, says Pychyl. So, while writing a term paper you break for a snack and see a spill in the refrigerator, which leads to cleaning the entire kitchen.

Punitive Parenting

Children of authoritarian parents are prone to procrastinate. Pychyl speculates that children with such parents postpone choices because their decisions are so frequently criticized—or made for them. Alternatively, the child may procrastinate as a form of rebellion. Refusing to study can be an angry—if self-defeating—message to Mom and Dad.

Thrill-Seeking

Some procrastinators enjoy the adrenaline "rush." These people find perverse satisfaction when they finish their taxes minutes before midnight on April 15 and dash to the post office just before it closes.

Task-Related Anxieties

Procrastination can be associated with specific situations. "Humans avoid the difficult and boring," says Fiore. Even the least procrastination-prone individuals put off taxes and visits to the dentist.

Unclear Expectations

Ambiguous directions and vague priorities increase procrastination. The boss who asserts that everything is high priority and due yesterday is more likely to be kept waiting. Supervisors who insist on "prioritizing the Jones project and using the Smith plan as a model" see greater productivity.

Depression

The blues can lead to or exacerbate procrastination—and vice versa. Several symptoms of depression feed procrastination. Decision-making is another problem. Because depressed people can't feel much pleasure, all options seem equally bleak, which makes getting started difficult and pointless.

MAIA SZALAVITZ is a freelance science writer and co-author of *Recovery Options: The Complete Guide: How You and Your Loved Ones Can Understand and Treat Alcohol and Other Drug Problems.*

UNIT 3

Problems Influencing Personal Growth

Unit Selections

Key Points to Consider

- Why do psychologists emphasize childhood? Should they, or are other developmental stages just as important?

- What factors most affect child development?

- Is the child really "father to the man"?

- What are some of the problems experienced by individuals as they progress through various developmental stages?

- Is there any such thing as a "good" death?

Student Web Site

www.mhcls.com/online

Internet References

Further information regarding these Web sites may be found in this book's preface or online.

Adolescence: Changes and Continuity
http://www.oberlin.edu/faculty/ndarling/adolesce.htm

Facts for Families
http://www.aacap.org/info_families/index.htm

Mental Health Infosource: Disorders
http://www.mhsource.com/disorders/

Mental Health Risk Factors for Adolescents
http://education.indiana.edu/cas/adol/mental.html

Suicide Awareness: Voices of Education
http://www.save.org

At each stage of development from infancy to old age, humans are faced with new challenges. The infant has the rudimentary sensory mechanisms for seeing, hearing, and touching but needs to begin coordinating incoming information into meaningful events. For example, early in life the baby begins to recognize familiar and unfamiliar people and usually becomes attached to the primary caregivers. As a toddler, the same child must master the difficult skills of walking, talking, and toilet training. This energetic, mobile, and sociable child also needs to learn the boundaries set on his or her behavior by others and society. As the child matures, not only do physical changes continue to take place, but the family composition may change when siblings are added, parents divorce, or mother and father work outside the home. Playmates become more influential, and others in the community, such as day-care workers and teachers, have an increasing influence on the child. The child eventually may spend more time at school than at home. The demands in this new environment require that the child sit still, pay attention, learn, and cooperate with others for long periods of time—behaviors perhaps never before extensively demanded of him or her.

In adolescence the body changes noticeably. Peers may pressure the individual to indulge in new behaviors such as using illegal drugs or engaging in premarital sex. Some older teenagers are said to be faced with an identity crisis when they must choose among career, education, and marriage. The pressures of work and family life exact a toll on less mature youths, while others are satisfied with the workplace and home.

Early adulthood, middle age, and old age may bring contentment or turmoil as individuals face career peaks, empty nests, advancing age, and perhaps the death of loved ones, such as parents or spouses. Again, some individuals cope more effectively with these events than do others.

At any step in the developmental sequence, unexpected challenges face individuals. These stressors include major illnesses, accidents, natural disasters, economic recessions, and family or personal crises. It is important to remember, however, that an event need not be negative to be stressful. Any major life change can cause stress. As welcome as weddings, new babies, and job promotions may be, they, too, can be stressful because of the changes in daily life that they demand. Each challenge and each alteration must be met and adjusted to if the individual is going to move successfully to the next stage of development. As you will read, some individuals continue along their paths unscathed; others do not fare so well.

This unit of the book examines problems in various stages of life from before birth to death. The unit commences with an article that provides a chronological look at issues of development. In "The Biology of Aging," Geoffrey Cowley offers an overview of age-related changes in various life eras. He also includes predictions about just how long humans can live.

Christine Gorman reviews the concept of childhood resilience. Resiliency is a child's ability to flourish despite a life filled with adversity. Not all children are resilient. Psychologists today are examining how some children become hardy as well as how to assist children who otherwise might not be.

"Kaleidoscope of Parenting Cultures" is a fascinating article about how parenting styles and parenting priorities differ among cultures. Hence, culture greatly influences a child's subsequent development. We would be remiss if an article on culture and its impact on early and middle childhood were not included here.

Many of today's school-aged children are fascinated by Harry Potter. In a very interesting article comparing Harry's school to modern schools, Margaret and Grace Zoller describe aspects of the Hogwarts School that they believe schools of today could and should adopt. These changes would motivate and inspire students to love learning.

Continuing our developmental theme, we next focus on adolescents and the abundant problems facing them—such as reading questionable material on the Internet. Many parents seem oblivious to modern technological environments and the deleterious effects to which their children are exposed. "The Divided Self" is an article that asserts teens are alienated and dispassionate because of the stream of media at their disposal.

Adulthood is the next developmental milestone of interest in this unit. As the baby boomers swell the ranks of the middle aged, some are bound to be disappointed in midlife while others will be content. In the first article on adulthood, obesity, which often becomes noticeable in middle age and which can wound an individual's self-image, is discussed. How to avoid middle-age spread and develop a healthier lifestyle is the focus of the first article in this series on adulthood.

More Americans are suffering from Alzheimer's disease than ever before. The exact cause of this debilitating brain disease is unknown, but the burden it places on families, caregivers, and American society is well known. Barbara Basler examines the science attempting to unravel the secrets of this enigmatic disorder.

The ultimate developmental stage is death. Death is a topic that both fascinates and frightens most of us. In "Good Life, Good Death," the veil of stigma that surrounds the issue of death is lifted. The article concerns "death awareness", something that might be uniquely human and which affects a multitude of our behaviors and attitudes.

The Biology of Aging

Why, after being so exquisitely assembled, do we fall apart so predictably? Why do we outlive dogs, only to be outlived by turtles? Could we catch up with them? Living to 200 is not a realistic goal for this generation, but a clearer picture of how we grow old is already within our reach.

GEOFFREY COWLEY

If only God had found a more reliable messenger. Back around the beginning of time, according to east African legend, he dispatched a scavenging bird known as the halawaka to give us the instructions for endless self-renewal. The secret was simple. Whenever age or infirmity started creeping up on us, we were to shed our skins like tattered shirts. We would emerge with our youth and our health intact. Unfortunately, the halawaka got hungry during his journey, and happened upon a snake who was eating a freshly killed wildebeest. In the bartering that ensued, the bird got a satisfying meal, the snake learned to molt and humankind lost its shot at immortality. People have been growing old and dying ever since.

The mystery of aging runs almost as deep as the mystery of life. During the past century, life expectancy has nearly doubled in developed countries, thanks to improvements in nutrition, sanitation and medical science. Yet the potential life span of a human being has not changed significantly since the halawaka met the snake. By the age of 50 every one of us, no matter how fit, will begin a slow decline in organ function and sensory acuity. And though some will enjoy another half century of robust health, our odds of living past 120 are virtually zero. Why, after being so exquisitely assembled, do we fall apart so predictably? Why do we outlive dogs, only to be outlived by turtles? And what are our prospects for catching up with them?

Until recently, all we could do was guess. But as the developed world's population grows grayer, scientists are bearing down on the dynamics of aging, and they're amassing crucial insights. Much of the new understanding has come from the study of worms, flies, mice and monkeys—species whose life cycles can be manipulated and observed in a laboratory. How exactly the findings apply to people is still a matter of conjecture. Could calorie restriction extend our lives by half? It would take generations to find out for sure. But the big questions of why we age—and which parts of the experience we can change—are already coming into focus.

The starkest way to see how time changes us (aside from hauling out an old photo album) is to compare death rates for people of different ages. In Europe and North America the annual rate among 15-year-olds is roughly .05 percent, or one death for every 2,000 kids. Fifty-year-olds are far less likely to ride their skateboards down banisters, yet they die at 30 times that rate (1.5 percent annually). The yearly death rate among 105-year-olds is 50 percent, 1,000 times that of the adolescents. The rise in mortality is due mainly to heart disease, cancer and stroke—diseases that anyone over 50 is right to worry about. But here's the rub. Eradicating these scourges would add only 15 years to U.S. life expectancy (half the gain we achieved during the 20th century), for unlike children spared of smallpox, octogenarians without cancer soon die of something else. As the biologist Leonard Hayflick observes, what ultimately does us in is not disease per se, but our declining ability to resist it.

Biologists once regarded senescence as nature's way of pushing one generation aside to make way for the next. But under natural conditions, virtually no creature lives long enough to experience decrepitude. Our own ancestors typically starved, froze or got eaten long before they reached old age. As a result, the genes that leave us vulnerable to chronic illness in later life rarely had adverse consequences. As long as they didn't hinder reproduction, natural selection had no occasion to weed them out. Natural selection may even *favor* a gene that causes cancer late in life if it makes young adults more fertile.

But why should "later life" mean 50 instead of 150? Try thinking of the body as a vehicle, designed by a group of genes to transport them through time. You might expect durable bodies to have an inherent advantage. But if a mouse is sure to become a cat's dinner within five years, a body that could last twice that long is a waste of resources. A 5-year-old mouse that can produce eight litters annually will leave twice the legacy of a 10-year-old mouse that delivers only four each year. Under those conditions, mice will evolve to live roughly five years. A sudden disappearance of cats may improve their odds of completing that life cycle, but it won't change their basic genetic makeup.

The First Years of Growth

In childhood the body is wonderfully resilient, and **sound sleep** supports the growth of tissues and bones. During the teenage years, **hormonal changes** trigger the development of sexual organs. Boys add **muscle mass**. Even the muscles in their voice box lengthen, causing voices to deepen. In girls, fat is redistributed to hips and breasts.

That is the predicament we face. Our bodies are nicely adapted to the harsh conditions our Stone Age ancestors faced, but often poorly adapted to the cushy ones we've created. There is no question that we can age better by exercising, eating healthfully, avoiding cigarettes and staying socially and mentally active. But can we realistically expect to extend our maximum life spans?

Researchers have already accomplished that feat in lab experiments. In the species studied so far, the surest way to increase life span has been to cut back on calories—way back. In studies dating back to the 1930s, researchers have found that species as varied as rats, monkeys and baker's yeast age more slowly if they're given 30 to 60 percent fewer calories than they would normally consume. No one has attempted such a trial among humans, but some researchers have already embraced the regimen themselves. Dr. Roy Walford, a 77-year-old pathologist at the University of California, Los Angeles, has survived for years on 1,200 calories a day and expects to be doing the same when he's 120. That may be optimistic, but he looks as spry as any 60-year-old in the photo he posts on the Web, and the animal studies suggest at least a partial explanation. Besides delaying death, caloric restriction seems to preserve bone mass, skin thickness, brain function and immune function, while providing superior resistance to heat, toxic chemicals and traumatic injury.

How could something so perverse be so good for you? Scientists once theorized that caloric restriction extended life by delaying development, or by reducing body fat, or by slowing metabolic rate. None of these explanations survived scrutiny, but studies have identified several likely mechanisms. The first involves oxidation. As mitochondria (the power plants in our cells) release the energy in food, they generate corrosive, unpaired electrons known as free radicals. By reacting with nearby fats, proteins and nucleic acids, these tiny terrorists foster everything from cataracts to vascular disease. It appears that caloric restriction not only slows the production of free radicals but helps the body counter them more efficiently.

Food restriction may also shield tissues from the damaging effects of glucose, the sugar that enters our bloodstreams when we eat carbohydrates. Ideally, our bodies respond to any rise in blood glucose by releasing insulin, which shuttles the sugar into fat and muscle cells for storage. But age or obesity can make our cells resistant to insulin. And when glucose molecules linger in the bloodstream, they link up with collagen and other proteins to wreak havoc on nerves, organs and blood vessels. When rats or monkeys are allowed to eat at will, their cells become less sensitive to insulin over time, just as ours do. But according to Dr. Mark Lane of the National Institute on Aging, older animals on calorie-restricted diets exhibit the high insulin sensitivity, low blood glucose and robust health of youngsters. No one knows whether people's bodies will respond the same way. But the finding suggests that life extension could prove as simple, or rather as complicated, as preserving the insulin response.

Another possible approach is to manipulate hormones. No one has shown conclusively that any of these substances can alter life span, but there are plenty of tantalizing hints. Consider human growth hormone, a pituitary protein that helps drive our physical development. Enthusiasts tout the prescription-only synthetic version as an antidote to all aspects of aging, but mounting evidence suggests that it could make the clock tick faster. The first indication came in the mid-1980s, when physiologist Andrzej Bartke outfitted lab mice with human or bovine genes for growth hormone. These mighty mice grew to twice the size of normal ones, but they aged early and died young. Bartke, now based at Southern Illinois University, witnessed something very different in 1996, when he began studying a strain of rodents called Ames dwarf mice. Due to a congenital lack of growth hormone, these creatures reach only a third the size of normal mice. But they live 50 to 60 percent longer.

As it happens, the mini-mice aren't the only ones carrying this auspicious gene. The island of Krk, a Croatian outpost in the eastern Adriatic, is home to a group of people who harbor essentially the same mutation. The "little people of Krk" reach an adult height of just 4 feet 5 inches. But like the mini-mice, they're exceptionally long-lived. Bartke's mouse studies suggest that besides stifling growth hormone, the gene that causes this stunting may also improve sensitivity to—you guessed it— insulin. If so, the mini-mice, the Croatian dwarfs and the half-starved rats and monkeys have more than their longevity in common. No one is suggesting that we stunt people's growth in the hope of extending their lives. But if you've been pestering your doctor for a vial of growth hormone, you may want to reconsider.

The Early Years of Adulthood

In many ways, the 20s are the prime of life. We're blessed with an efficient metabolism, **strong bones** and **good flexibility**. As early as the 30s, however, metabolism begins to slow and women's **hormone levels** start to dip. Bones may start to lose density in people who don't exercise or who don't get the vitamin D required for calcium absorption.

Growth hormone is just one of several that decline as we age. The sex hormones estrogen and testosterone follow the same pattern, and replacing them can rejuvenate skin, bone and muscle. But like growth hormone, these tonics can have costs as well as benefits. They evolved not to make us more durable but to make us more fertile. As the British biologist Roger Gosden observed in his 1996 book, "Cheating Time," "sex hormones are required for fertility and for making biological gender distinctions, but they do not prolong life. On the contrary, a price may have to be paid for living as a sexual being." Anyone suffering from breast or prostate cancer would surely agree.

The Joys of Middle Age

Around 40, people often start noticing gray hairs, mild **memory lapses** and difficulty focusing their eyes on small type. Around 51, most women will experience **menopause**. Estrogen levels plummet, making the skin thinner and bones less dense. Men suffer more **heart disease** than women at this age. Metabolism slows down in both sexes.

In most of the species biologists have studied, fertility and longevity have a seesaw relationship, each rising as the other declines. Bodies designed for maximum fertility have fewer resources for self-repair, some perishing as soon as they reproduce (think of spawning salmon). By contrast, those with extraordinary life spans are typically slow to bear offspring. Do these rules apply to people? The evidence is sketchy but provoc-

ative. In a 1998 study, researchers at the University of Manchester analyzed genealogical records of 32,000 British aristocrats born during the 1,135-year period between 740 and 1875 (long before modern contraceptives). Among men and women who made it to 60, the least fertile were the most likely to survive beyond that age. A whopping 50 percent of the women who reached 81 were childless.

Eunuchs seem to enjoy (if that's the word) a similar advantage in longevity. During the 1940s and '50s, anatomist James Hamilton studied a group of mentally handicapped men who had been castrated at a state institution in Kansas. Life expectancy was just 56 in this institution, but the neutered men lived to an average age of 69—a 23 percent advantage—and not one of them went bald. No one knows exactly how testosterone speeds aging, but athletes who abuse it are prone to ailments ranging from hypertension to kidney failure.

All of this research holds a fairly obvious lesson. Life itself is lethal, and the things that make it sweet make it *more* lethal. Chances are that by starving and castrating ourselves, we really could secure some extra years. But most of us would gladly trade a lonely decade of stubborn survival for a richer middle age. Our bodies are designed to last only so long. But with care and maintenance, they'll live out their warranties in style.

With RACHEL DAVIS

Childhood Is for Children

"More and more, it seems that we have lost sight of the 'child' in childhood and turned it into a joyless training camp for the adult world."

JOHANN CHRISTOPH ARNOLD

Despite all the talk about putting children first, our society is becoming increasingly hostile to its young. How different schools and homes would be if parents and educators would defend youngsters' right to a childhood, instead of fixating on their progress and success.

The pressure to excel is undermining childhood as never before. Naturally, parents have always wanted their offspring to "do well," both academically and socially. No one wants his or her kid to be the slowest in the class or the last to be chosen in a pick-up game. Yet, what is it about the culture we live in that has made that natural worry into such an obsessive fear, and what is it doing to our children? Why are we so keen to mold them into successful adults, instead of treasuring their carefree innocence?

Jonathan Kozol, a best-selling author and children's advocate, puts it bluntly: "Up to the age of 11 or maybe 12, the gentleness and honesty of children is so apparent. Our society has missed an opportunity to seize that moment. It's almost as though we view those qualities as useless, as though we don't value children for their gentleness, but only as future economic units, as future workers, as future assets and deficits."

Of all the ways in which we push kids to meet adult expectations, the trend toward high-pressure academics may be the most widespread, and the worst. I say "worst" because of the age at which we begin to subject them to it and the fact that, for some of them, school quickly becomes a place they dread and a source of misery they cannot escape for months at a time.

In my book, *Endangered: Your Child in a Hostile World*, I quote Melinda, a veteran preschool teacher in California: "We have parents asking whether their two-and-a-half-year-olds are learning to read yet, and grumbling if they can't. I see kids literally shaking and crying because they don't want to go in to testing. I've even seen parents dragging their child into the room."

Childhood itself has come to be viewed as a suspect phase. Children of all ages and means are being squelched on the playground and in class, not because they are unmanageable or unruly, but simply because they are behaving as youngsters should. Diagnosed with "problems" that used to be recognized as normal childhood traits—impulsiveness and exuberance, spontaneity and daring—thousands of kids are being diagnosed as hyperactive and drugged into submission.

I am referring, of course, to the widespread use of Ritalin and to the public's fascination with medicine as the answer to any and every problem. Given the fivefold increase in Ritalin prescriptions in the last decade, one has to wonder if it isn't being misused to rein in lively children who may not even have attention deficit-hyperactivity disorder. After all, much of what is designated as ADHD is nothing more than a defense against overstructuring—a natural reflex that used to be called letting off steam or, alternately, a symptom of various unmet emotional needs.

More and more, it seems that we have lost sight of the "child" in childhood and turned it into a joyless training camp for the adult world. We have abandoned the idea of education as growth and decided to see it only as a ticket to the job market. Guided by charts and graphs, and cheered on by experts, we have turned our backs on the value of uniqueness and creativity and fallen instead for the lie that the only way to measure progress is a standardized test.

Children ought to be stretched and intellectually stimulated. They should be taught to articulate their feelings, to write, read, develop and defend an idea, and think critically. However, what is the purpose of the best academic education if it fails to prepare young people for the "real" world beyond the confines of the classroom? What about those life skills that can never be taught by putting kids on a bus and sending them to school?

As for the things that schools are supposed to teach, even they are not always passed on. Writer John Taylor Gatto points out that, even though American pupils sit through an average of 12,000 hours of compulsory academic instruction, there are plenty who leave the system as 18-year-olds who still can't read a book or calculate a batting average—let alone repair a faucet or change a flat.

It is not just schools that are pressuring kids into growing up too fast. The practice of rushing them into adulthood is so widely accepted and so thoroughly ingrained that people often go blank when you voice concern about the matter. Take, for example, the number of parents who tie up their children's afterschool hours in extracurricular activities. On the surface, the explosion of opportunities for "growth" in areas like music and sports looks like the perfect answer to the boredom faced by millions of latchkey kids, but the reality is not always so pretty.

It is one thing when a child picks up a hobby, a sport, or an instrument on his or her own steam, but quite another when the driving force is a parent with an overly competitive edge. In one family I know, their daughter showed a genuine talent for the piano in the second grade, but by the time she was in the sixth, she wouldn't touch a keyboard for any amount of coaxing. She was tired of the attention, sick of lessons (her father was always reminding her what a privilege they were), and virtually traumatized by the strain of having been pushed through one competition after another. The pattern is all too familiar: ambitious expectations are followed by the pressure to meet them, and what was once a perfectly happy part of a youngster's life becomes a burden that is impossible to bear.

As an author, I became aware, after completing my first book, of something I had never noticed previously—the importance of white space. I am referring to the room between the lines of type, the margins, extra space at the beginning of a chapter, and/or a page left blank at the beginning of a book. It allows the type to "breathe" and gives the eye a place to rest. White space is not something you are conscious of when you read a book. It is what isn't there.

Just as books require white space, so do children. That is, they need room to grow. Nevertheless, too many children aren't getting that. The ancient Chinese philosopher Lao-Tzu reminds us that "it is not the clay the potter throws that gives the jar its usefulness, but the space within."

Certainly, there is nothing wrong with giving kids chores and requiring them to carry out the tasks on a daily basis. However, the way many parents overbook their children, emotionally and time-wise, robs them of the space and flexibility they need to develop at their own pace. They need stimulation and guidance, but also need time to themselves. Hours spent alone in daydreams or quiet, unstructured activities instill a sense of security and independence and provide a necessary lull in the rhythm of the day.

It is a beautiful thing to see kids absorbed in play. In fact, it is hard to think of a purer, more spiritual activity. Play brings joy, contentment, and detachment from the troubles of the day. Especially nowadays, in our hectic, time- and money-driven culture, the importance of play cannot be emphasized enough. Educator Friedrich Froebel, the father of the modern kindergarten, goes so far as to say that "a child who plays thoroughly and perseveringly, until physical fatigue forbids, will be a determined adult, capable of self-sacrifice both for his own welfare and that of others." In an age when fears of playground injuries and the misguided idea that play interferes with "real" learning has led approximately 40% of the school districts across the country to do away with recess, one can only hope that the wisdom of these words will not go unheeded.

Allowing youngsters the room to grow at their own pace does not mean ignoring them. Clearly, the bedrock of their security from day to day is the knowledge that we who care for them are always at hand, ready to help them, talk with them, give them what they need, and simply be there for them. How often, though, are we swayed instead by our own ideas of what they want or need?

Isn't the parental desire to have superstar or genius offspring in the first place just another sign of our distorted vision—a reflection of the way we tend to view children as little adults, no matter how loudly we may protest such a "Victorian" idea? The answer, of course, is to drop our adult expectations entirely, to get down on the same level as our children and look them in the eye. Only when we lay aside our ambitions for them will we begin to hear what they are saying, find out what they are thinking, and see the goals we have set for them from their point of view.

Obviously, every child is different. Some seem to get all the lucky breaks, while others have a rough time simply coping with life. One child consistently brings home perfect scores, while another is always at the bottom of the class. One is gifted and popular, while still another, no matter how hard he or she tries, is always in trouble and often gets forgotten. As parents, we must refrain from comparing our offspring with others. Above all, we must refrain from pushing them to become something that their unique personal makeup may never allow them to be.

Raising a "good" child is a dubious goal in the first place. Getting into trouble can be a vital part of building character. As the Polish pediatrician Janusz Korczak pointed out, "The good child cries very little, he sleeps through the night, he is confident and good-natured. He is well-behaved, convenient, obedient, and good. Yet no consideration is given to the fact that he may grow up to be indolent and stagnant."

It is often hard for parents to see the benefits of having raised a difficult child, even when the outcome is positive. Strange as it may sound, I believe that the more challenging the youngster, the more grateful the parents should be. If anything, the parents of difficult children really ought to be envied, because it is they, more than any others, who are forced to learn the most wonderful secret of parenthood: the true meaning of unconditional love. It is a secret that remains hidden from those whose love is never tested.

When we welcome the prospect of raising a problematic child with these things in mind, we will begin to see our frustrations as moments that can awaken our best qualities. Instead of envying the ease with which our neighbors seem to raise perfect offspring, we will remember that rule-breakers and children who show their horns often make more self-reliant and independent adults than those whose limits are never tried. By helping us to discover the limitations of "goodness" and the boredom of conformity, they can teach us the necessity of genuineness, the wisdom of humility, and the reality that nothing good is won without struggle.

"Unlearning" our adult mindsets is never easy, especially at the end of a long day, when children sometimes seem more of a bother than a gift. When there are kids around, things just don't always go as planned. Furniture gets scratched, flowerbeds trampled, new clothes torn or muddied, and toys lost or broken. Children want to have fun, to run in the aisles. They need space to be rambunctious, silly, and noisy. After all, they are not china dolls or little adults, but unpredictable rascals with sticky fingers and runny noses who sometimes cry at night. If we truly love them, we will welcome them as they are.

JOHANN CHRISTOPH ARNOLD is a children's advocate, family counselor, father of eight, and author of *Endangered: Your Child in a Hostile World*.

The Importance of Resilience

Why do some children bounce back from adversity better than others—and can that quality be taught?

CHRISTINE GORMAN

By all outward appearances, 11-year-old Quashone Perry was headed for jail or the morgue in 1989. An older brother ran with a tough crowd in the dangerous Miami neighborhood where they lived with their single mom, who worked long hours at two jobs and was barely getting by. On one particularly inauspicious day, a spat between rivals led to a drive-by shooting in which a bullet grazed Quashone. "The first thing that came to my mind was to go get my brother's gun and shoot back at the guy who did it," he recalls. Luckily for him, when he told his mother what he was planning to do, she not only talked him out of it but also quit her jobs and moved the family to a different part of Miami.

Fifteen years later, Perry's life is a blueprint for achievement. He graduated from college, is married and is starting his second semester of law school. And he owes some of that to, of all things, ballet. After the shooting, his mother insisted that he take ballet lessons after school. Perry, who loved football, was more than a little reluctant at first, but the encouragement and persistence of one teacher helped him master dance so well that he ended up playing leading roles in *The Nutcracker*. And that, in turn, gave him a new focus and perspective on his life. "It's scary to go back to where I used to live," he says. "It gives me the chills, how far I've come."

Why are some children like Perry able to overcome extreme circumstances—poverty, a parent's absence, a violent neighborhood—and find happiness while others are defeated by the mildest of setbacks? What allows people to start over after a horrific calamity—such as last month's tsunami in the Indian Ocean—and create a new life for themselves on the shattered foundations of the old one?

Psychologists use the word resilience to describe this ability to bounce back from adversity. "It's amazing what kids can go through," says Emmy Werner, a professor of human development at the University of California at Davis, who as a child suffered the saturation bombing of Germany during World War II. But whether the context is war, natural disaster or a more private hell, many of the same factors seem to play a role in whether children grow up to become successful adults. "Some of it is sheer luck, of course," says Werner, who began research-

ing resilience in youngsters in the 1950s, "and the scars will be there. But, terrible as it is to say, you adapt."

Some characteristics appear to be fundamental. The strength of the parental bond established in the first three years of life, for example, seems to set the tone for the rest of our days. Studies by Werner and others that follow children to adulthood show that parental bonds influence future success more than almost any other factor. So does being born with the right personality. A child with an easygoing temperament or a certain amount of intelligence appears to have an advantage.

But what of the external factors, the things you aren't born with? Can kids learn particular skills to help them overcome adversity? The answer is a qualified yes. You can't teach resilience, but researchers have identified some skills—such as developing a sense of autonomy or being a good reader—that increase the chances that a child will become a productive member of society. Belief systems—whether something as straightforward as believing you have a future or as nuanced as practicing a religious faith—also play a critical role.

Resilience, researchers agree, is a complex process that is in some ways as unpredictable as the weather. "This is not a one-dimensional thing," says Arthur Reynolds, a professor of social work at the University of Wisconsin. "There is a sort of chain reaction that leads to resilience later, and that chain reaction begins when children are very young."

A number of negative factors may weaken resilience. Among the most common in the U.S.: violence, physical or sexual abuse, direct exposure to alcoholism and removal from the home. As the major risk factors add up, so does the toll. "It's cruel to ask a man who has no bootstraps to pick himself up by his own bootstraps," says Mark Katz, a psychologist who heads a resilience program in San Diego. "If resilience is strength under adversity, then multiple-risk exposures—four or more—limit emotional endurance."

So much for the caveats. Even the most cautious researchers agree that luck and favorable genetics aren't everything. There are concrete things you can do to help a child grow up to be a relatively happy and successful adult. Indeed, as the more innovative children's programs in the U.S. demonstrate, many of the same elements show up again and again. Among them:

Hone a Talent Kids who are resilient have often found something to be better at than anyone else. Dance was the avenue for Perry—a skill that would set him apart. At the age of 12, he won a scholarship to study with Miami's Thomas Armour Youth Ballet. Perry rose through the ranks to become a professional dancer, a career he might resume after law school. "Ballet is not about instant gratification," says Ruth Wiesen, the group's director. "Sometimes it's very difficult for kids. They learn by showing up every day and working hard that success can be as simple as that."

Find a Champion It also helps to have a Ruth Wiesen in your life—someone who believes wholeheartedly in you, the way Wiesen has in Perry and hundreds of other budding ballet students. She recognized Perry's talent immediately, but she also saw that he needed extra attention, particularly when it came to attendance. "It was just my calling him to say, 'Come, come again and, O.K., come again' if he didn't show up for class," she says. Teachers make excellent champions, of course, but so do grandparents, coaches, police officers and janitors. The point is to take an interest and maybe have an expectation or two. Studies show that boys even more than girls need that external, emotional support and often fail to succeed without it.

Look Within Some things clearly are out of a child's control. But believing that everything—from passing a class to getting into a fight to becoming pregnant—is basically a question of luck tends to compound the problems. Fortunately, attitudes can change for the better. "Part of resilience is learning some skills, some tools to stay safe," says Jerry Moe, who works with children of alcoholics at the Betty Ford Centers in California and Texas. One technique Moe uses a lot is playing a game he calls wheel of misfortune, in which kids brainstorm on ways to handle situations like being yelled at by a drunken father or a mom's wanting to drive them somewhere when she's had three too many.

Be Your Own Recruiter "Get help" may be the most obvious piece of advice anyone can give a kid heading for trouble. But studies show that the most resilient kids have a way of drawing in other people to help them. Usually those boys and girls are open and engaging, not reserved and sullen. Perhaps they have a winning smile or have learned to develop a quick sense of humor. In other words, they make you want to help them and have become good enough judges of character that they know whom to tap to get the help they need. If one person lets them down, they find another. Some preschool programs pair a child who is adept at asking for help with one who isn't, so the second one can learn by imitation.

Help Others Another common thread among adults who rebound from adversity is that as children they were required to help others. Selfless acts that have no apparent reward—like giving up a seat on a bus to an older person or participating in a service project—seem to give children some perspective on their lives and troubles. It's another way of not being alone, not being the only person with a problem.

Make Better Parents This insight is central to the approach of the federally funded Child-Parent Centers, a Head Start–like program in Chicago. It goes way beyond persuading parents to volunteer at bake sales or help chaperone a field trip. Consider, for example, the Lorraine Hansberry Child-Parent Center in the city's North Lawndale section, where most of the families are poor and unemployment runs high. In addition to its preschool and elementary programs, the center offers parents and other caregivers classes designed to enhance parenting skills, including sessions on child development, how to talk with their kids, deal constructively with conflicts and the right way to help with homework. "Especially with the parents who spend a lot of time here, you can see them growing as they try to make themselves a better life," says Shelly Bailey, who is responsible for many of the parent classes. "We encourage them to go back to school, to strive for better things."

The results are striking, according to Wisconsin's Reynolds. For the past two decades, he has been following young people who graduated in 1985 from several of what were then 25 Child-Parent Centers in Chicago. (There are now 15.) As a group, they are much less likely than their peers to commit a crime or be the victim of one and are more likely to graduate from school on time. "If we provide education and family support for kids at high risk, it leads to great levels of success for kids," he says. "And if they get in that success stream, they often stay in it because of the positive early advantages."

Latonya Thomas, 32, and her two children Bryant, 14, and Shana, 7, are prime examples. All of them have attended classes at the Lorraine Hansberry center. "I love this program," says Thomas, who credits the center with instilling a love of school in her daughter and providing a strong foundation for her son, who is on the ninth-grade honor roll. As much as it has helped Bryant and Shana, however, Thomas acknowledges the changes it has made in her life as well. "I have more patience with the kids, I know how to talk to let them know I'm there for them," she says. Wouldn't she have done that anyway? "Yes," she says. "There's my way and their way. When I put them together, it works just fine." The center also inspired Thomas to upgrade her job skills, and she is studying to be a lab technician.

As these success stories illustrate, resilience is real, but it's not inevitable. Someone has to take a chance. Someone has to care. And a certain amount of time and treasure are required. We know human beings can survive many things. Otherwise we wouldn't be here. It's a lesson that is repeated in every generation. The ones who learn it best help one another muddle through. —*Reported by Sarah Sturmon Dale, Minneapolis, Wendy Grossman, Houston, Kathie Klarreich, Miami, Jeanne McDowell, Los Angeles and Leslie Whitaker, Chicago*

Kaleidoscope of Parenting Cultures

V<small>IDYA</small> T<small>HIRUMURTHY</small>

Educator: Immigrant parents from Asia in my class have a dogmatic parenting style and I don't know how to make them change their parenting style. They show little interest in the class when we discuss parenting issues. Should they not be expected to adapt to this culture? After all, it was their choice to move here.

Vidya: Should we expect them to change?

An uneasy silence pervaded the room full of experienced educators, who are grappling with similar situations. They are clueless as to how to approach it.

I will share here some observations I made of parents and children from over 27 countries who participated in a university preschool program. The emotionally enmeshed relationship between a Jewish parent and child, the teacher-taught behavior of an Indian father, the nonverbal relationship of a Brazilian couple with their child, the filial piety approach of a Chinese father, the friendly and playful demeanor of an African American mother, and the negotiation-oriented and self-explaining conduct of an Euro-American mother are descriptors of only a few characteristics observed among the preschool parents. I rely on a few examples to illustrate some cultural variations in parenting.

What is proper or improper behavior is based on cultural expectations and contexts (Brooks, 1999). Western cultures focus on the empowerment of individualism and autonomy in the child (Rudy, Grusec, & Wolfe, 1999). Freedom and individuality are the core values and parents do not view a child's defiance when asked to comply with a request as a threat. They may disagree with their child; nonetheless, they may still perceive the child's behavior as his/her way of asserting him/herself.

As a contrast, parents in most non-Western cultures believe in imposing absolute standards on their children. They value obedience and expect their children to respect authority. Their goal is to promote interdependency and cooperation. "Interdependence is promoted by fostering intense emotional bonds with children at an early age … children are motivated to cooperate and meet the needs of others, since [their activities] promote a sense of self-worth and emotional security"(Rudy et al., p. 302).

Defiance is the opposite of cooperation and a non-cooperative behavior is perceived as a threat to maintaining their family unity. Asian and Hispanic cultures typically value individualism less and collaboration and cooperation more. They exercise more control over the child to achieve these goals. But most Westerners perceive this approach as being demanding. They fear such parenting styles would result in "poor school achievement among Euro-Americans"(Chao, 1994, p. 1111). Yet, obedience is a virtue for the non-Western parents and they have implicit faith in punishment.

Similarly, Chinese and Asian parents equate parenting to teaching (Rudy et al., 1999). For example, an Indian father expected forceful cooperation rather than cooperation through negotiation when he instructed his son several times each morning to greet his teachers. "Beta (Son), say good morning to all your teachers and friends,"was a mantra he chanted. As a contrast to this, the Brazilian couple would enter very quietly and slip out of the classroom as though they would disturb the serenity of the class. They rarely exchanged greetings with the teacher or with other parents. Smith (1997) explains that Brazilians often use silence as a way to greet others. They seldom greeted or interacted with other parents when they entered the classroom in the morning.

When a child controls the behaviors of his parents, Baumrind (1991) calls it a permissive parenting style. The daily routine of a Jewish couple and their son lasted for about an hour. This little boy had a difficult time letting go of his parents. The observer noticed the emotional entanglement in their relationship—yet another characteristic of the permissive style. "Parents promote the child's assertion of his or her will: Israeli mothers, for example, are more likely than those in Japan to value disobedience when it is a reflection of the child's assertion of individuality"(Osterweil & Nagano, 1991, as cited by Rudy, Grusec, & Wolfe, 1999, p. 302). But what we must realize is that emotionally enmeshed behaviors are considered healthy in many cultures and it is believed to strengthen the bond between parents and children. It cannot be labeled as inappropriate parenting.

The communication patterns of most Euro-American parents were different from the rest. They got down to the eye-level of the children when talking with them. They spoke softly to their children and were non-intrusive. A few of them held their children on their laps or hugged them while they talked. Western culture promotes looking the speaker straight in the eye to show "interest and attention"(Smith, 1997, p. 349). Therefore, making eye contact is considered very important when communicating with others. This; is in stark contrast to many other cultures that teach their children not to establish such eye contact with elders and persons of authority because it is considered disrespectful.

The patterns of parental attitudes and behaviors exhibited in the preschool differed greatly across cultures. The cultural contexts in which parents grew up, the experiences they have had with their own parents, and the experiences they have with their own children affect parent cognition and behavior. Parents hold a mental representation of relationships, which they develop based on their own childhood experiences (Grusec, Hastings, & Mammone, 1994). It does not mean that parents passively accept and mirror the parenting styles of their parents. They filter through the behaviors and absorb only those that are in accordance with their individual beliefs. Thus, variations in approaches illustrate both cultural and individual differences in parenting styles.

Immigrants leave their lands, families, and cultural settings behind. Even though it was their choice to move here, they face an overwhelming challenge in adapting to new situations, land, and culture. Educators can state their expectations clearly and let the parents do it in their own way. As long as there is no abuse, we must strive to help parents maintain their cultural identities and be successful. As one of my students put it, our goal should be to support them in their parenting and help them gain a deeper understanding of our parenting styles.

References

Baumrind, D. (1991). Parenting styles and adolescent development. In R. M. Lerner, A. C. Petersen, & J. Brooks-Gunn (Ed.), Encyclopedia of adolescence (pp. 746–758). New York: Garland.

Brooks, J. (1999). The process of parenting (5th ed). Mountain View, CA: Mayfield.

Chao, R. K. (2004). Beyond parental control and authoritarian parenting style: Understanding Chinese parenting through the cultural notion of training. Child Development, 65, 1111–1119.

Grusec, J., Hastings, P., & Mammone, N. (1994). Parenting cognitions and relationships schemas. In J. Smetana (Ed.), Beliefs about parenting: Origins and developmental implications (pp. 5–19). San Francisco: Jossey-Bass.

Rudy, D., Grusec, J., & Wolfe, J. (1999). Implication of cross-cultural findings for family socialization. Journal of Moral Education, 28, 299–310.

Smith, T. J. (1997). Early childhood development. Upper Saddle River, NJ: Merrill.

—Vidya Thirumurthy,
International/Intercultural Committee

What American Schools Can Learn from Hogwarts School Of Witchcraft and Wizardry

Since they first appeared on these shores in 1997, the Harry Potter books have been lightning rods for criticism and praise for a variety of reasons. But since they are set in a school, what do they say about education? A mother and daughter share their insights.

MARGARET ZOLLER BOOTH AND GRACE MARIE BOOTH

The United States has been swept up in the Harry Potter phenomenon, with film adaptations, companion readers, and literary critique and analysis following in the wake of J. K. Rowling's series of books chronicling the adolescent wizard's adventures. In addition to sparking a resurgence in fiction pertaining to wizardry and the fantasy world, the series has introduced new words into the English language (e.g., "muggle" and "quidditch"). It has also touched off a reaction from conservative Christian institutions, which have called for banning the books in school libraries on the grounds that they glorify "wizardry" and are therefore anti-Christian. However, in spite of all the attention given to the literary worth of the novels, there has been very little analysis of the primary locus of the action, the Hogwarts School of Witchcraft and Wizardry, as an educational institution.

As my daughter Grace devoured each volume, finally prompting me to read the books out of parental self-defense, we began to discuss Hogwarts and the education that was being imparted to Harry Potter and his friends, Hermione and Ron. This discussion occurred naturally for us because Grace, as the daughter of two itinerant academic researchers, has become familiar with British educational institutions both in England and in various African nations. Notably, she has attended schools in Swaziland, a small kingdom in southern Africa that had been a British colony from the early to mid-20th century. Thus her school there was based on virtually the same structure and principles as those of Hogwarts.

Consequently, as we read the Harry Potter books we found ourselves analyzing the quality of the education that Harry was receiving at Hogwarts, at first somewhat episodically but then at a deeper level. Our discussions formed the basis of this analysis, which is presented from two educational perspectives—that of a 40-something and that of an 11-something. First, we compare and contrast the Hogwarts School of Witchcraft and Wizardry with the British model of education and then with the culture and structure of schools in the United States. Second, we look at Hogwarts from the perspective of an educational psychologist by analyzing the characteristics and quality of the teaching there in relation to contemporary theory and practice. Grace gives her views on the education at Hogwarts while I comment on her observations from an educator's perspective.

A Somewhat British Setting

Grace: I like the idea that there are different ages all together in one school. That way, the older ones can help take care of the younger ones, and the younger ones will learn things from the older kids.

In other words, Grace seems to like the idea that Harry does not attend a junior high school where all the students are grouped by age. Unlike the U.S. system, which often requires students to make two major transitions—from elementary to junior high and then to high school—the Hogwarts (British) model mandates only one institutional change. The fact that J. K. Rowling begins her series with Harry's 11th birthday is entirely appropriate for a series that takes place within a British-type school system. That is the year when English pupils make the transition from primary to secondary education. For Harry, this move is especially symbolic, as he not only moves from one educational level to the next but also passes from the world of muggles to the world of wizards. Once Harry enters the second level, he stays there until he is finished with secondary school. Hogwarts is based on the British model, which includes six forms, with the final one (a two-year course) preparing students for higher education. Consequently, the seven volumes planned for the series will neatly see Harry through his secondary years.

Grace's enthusiasm for "fun competition"— a system in which everyone works together toward a common goal—concurs with the research on cooperative learning and goal structures.

Grace's endorsement of the multi-age school structure with fewer transitions is supported by the education literature that reports that multiple transitions during the early adolescent school years are generally not beneficial for students, particularly for girls. The negative effects include declines in academic achievement, less participation in extracurricular activities, and a drop in self-esteem.[1] The negative effects of transitioning at this age result from both organizational discontinuities (changes in school structure) and social ones (changes in student population and relationships with teachers). Continuity seems especially important when students are experiencing other physical and cognitive changes.[2] Consequently, while Harry might fare better in a school system with multiple transitions than Hermione Granger, both of them would probably benefit from remaining in a single school setting for a longer time.

Grace: Each house (Gryffindor, Hufflepuff, Ravenclaw, and Slytherin) at Hogwarts is like a family. It is like a fun competition, but the competition is a good kind of contest, and there are members in your house to help you work together in that competition. And your house helps you along the way—like your family does.

Grace's idea of a "family" is an extension of the multi-age structure of Hogwarts. The structure of a family succeeds because the wiser, more experienced family members guide the less experienced ones. Furthermore, Grace's enthusiasm for "fun competition"—a system in which everyone works together toward a common goal—concurs with the research on cooperative learning and goal structures. First, the Hogwarts method of awarding "house points" for individual academic and behavioral achievements is a good example of a group contingency program that motivates all to do well, as all the students of each house benefit from each individual's successes.[3] Hogwarts students realize that individual achievement will also bring rewards and glory to their entire group or "house"; likewise, individual failings will hurt the common cause. The students' efforts culminate in the annual awards banquet, at which the house with the most points at the end of the year is honored. The award reinforces a cooperative goal structure that research has shown to contribute to success.[4]

Grace: Prefects are good because they lead their houses, especially the younger students. And if the young kids need help, they can help them. They also make sure that if something bad happens, like it does every year, the others don't worry about it. Even though every house works hard together to win competitions, it is important to have a leader.

Continuing on the theme of group cooperation, Grace is linking the learning process to peer interaction, including peer help and evaluation. These interactions are especially helpful when there are peers who are older or more knowledgeable to help guide the learning of the younger, less experienced students. This represents a line of thinking similar to that of Lev Vygotsky, who postulated that learning includes a strong social element and is best accomplished when peers are working together to solve a problem. A good example of Vygotsky's concept of "scaffolding" is the British school tradition of prefects, in which more experienced, older peers help younger students throughout the year.

When Harry, Ron, and Hermione entered Hogwarts, they needed regular guidance from the prefects and older students. They needed this guidance in every aspect of student life, including academic work, dining hall behavior, and understanding and mastering the school sport, quidditch. However, as time passed, the three needed less help from the prefects in negotiating the culture of Hogwarts. Nonetheless, the prefects occasionally did attempt to step in when they sensed that the three had gotten in over their heads and were unable to extricate themselves on their own.

A final point of comparison involves the importance of academic testing at Hogwarts. Not only do Hogwarts students spend a great deal of time studying for year-end exams at every grade level, they must also take the standardized Ordinary Wizardry Level exams (O.W.L.s) when they are 15 years of age. These exams, similar to the Ordinary level (O-level) exam in the British system, determine one's access to higher learning and direct students toward particular professions. The importance of these exams is made quite clear in book four when Harry's older friends, the Weasley twins, earn scores on their O.W.L.s below those expected by their mother and thus have to suffer the consequences both at home and at school. Grace's attitude toward these high-stakes tests is not surprising.

Grace: I don't like them because you might know everything about a subject, but you get so nervous about these O.W.L.s and then don't do well on them. When that happens, they do not really measure your real abilities. So I just don't think it is a very good idea. It is better to do tests and papers and presentations all the time because they test what you just learned in that chapter (like about Antarctica or something), but if you wait until later, you might forget about it all.

Pedagogical Practices: The Good, The Bad, and The Ugly

Grace: Professor Sprout is a good teacher because she lets the students experiment on plants. They do not just watch her do it. She always warns them first about the dangers involved with working with the deadly plants, which is good. But she still lets them do it even though some of the kids might make some mistakes. Professor McGonagall is also a good teacher because even though she is strict, she keeps the class interested by letting them experiment with transfigurations (like turning a match into a needle). Even though she first demonstrates the transfigurations, the students then get a chance to practice. Madame Hooch, the physical education teacher, is also good because she lets the students practice the sports for themselves. Even though the students sometimes might not get it right away (like flying broomsticks), she lets them make their own mistakes, sometimes get a little hurt, and figure it out.

While the recent emphasis on national exams has forced a more standardized curriculum on schools in England, teachers there have historically enjoyed a greater degree of pedagogical freedom in the classroom than have their European counterparts. This is also the case at Hogwarts, where teachers generally have free rein within their own classrooms regarding teaching methodology and textbook choice. This sovereignty, as in the United States, can result in high-quality teaching, but it also carries the danger of leaving the quality of some instruction wanting. Thus Grace has definite opinions about the quality of instruction at Hogwarts and about which teachers provide real learning experiences for their students.[5] Furthermore, she recognizes that the classroom setting is hardly the only place where effective learning happens at Hogwarts.

From her comments, it is clear that Grace appreciates an active, constructivist pedagogical approach to learning more than direct instruction. However, her analysis of the student-centered approach and its benefits for learning is actually quite complex. First, it is apparent from Grace's examples that hands-on experience and real-life activity are vital to learning. Each of the professors she mentions gives the students the opportunity to experiment and practice the topics that are to be learned. The students are not given plastic plants or make-believe broomsticks, but real-life materials to be used in real-world situated learning. These examples also show that Grace understands the dangers inherent in some constructivist, student-centered approaches. Nonetheless, she would prefer this approach to the safe, yet sometimes boring, teacher-centered strategies employed by some of the other professors.

Grace's examples also illustrate the strengths of both cognitive and social constructivist approaches to the learning process.[6] Her examples, which recognize the benefits of some demonstration and modeling, also incorporate notions from social cognitive theory. And they illustrate the need for teachers to provide guidance and cognitive apprenticeship to strengthen the individual skills of their students.

Grace recognizes that it is sometimes helpful for a teacher to first demonstrate an activity, such as how to turn a feather into a pen. Then, as the students experiment with their own wands, animals, potions, and other wizardry devices in the cognitive construction of witchcraft, they can model their actions on what they have observed. Piaget would agree with this approach.[7]

Likewise, many of the better teachers whom Grace identified provide the social climate necessary for constructivism according to the Vygotskian notion of peer cooperation and teacher/student scaffolding. The examples above illustrate the desire

students have to learn in cooperation with one another and to help their peers when they make mistakes (such as blowing things up in the lab).

The Vygotskian notion of teacher scaffolding is also present in Grace's analysis of Professor Flitwick.

> *Grace*: Professor Flitwick helps them out if they are having trouble. Professor Flitwick understands that Neville always seems to have a lot of problems. So Professor Flitwick takes the time to read over the instructions for him and explains it to him in a way that Neville can understand. But then Professor Flitwick encourages him and other students when they do something right. He compliments them, which is good.

Unfortunately, as is the case with any school, not every teacher at Hogwarts manages to successfully engage his or her students in constructivist, meaningful learning experiences.

> *Grace*: Professor Gilderoy Lockhart is not very good because he always just talks about himself on and on and on. He even gave his class a quiz about himself. He doesn't really teach them. He says he's so good, but then he doesn't really know how to do things. Professor Bins is boring, and that is why the students do not like to go into his history class. All he does is talk on and on. The only time it was exciting was when Hermione asked an interesting question, which shocked the professor because all the students finally listened.

Rowling has re-created the stereotypically boring history teacher in Professor Bins, who continues to live so deeply in the past that he "was their only ghost teacher [who] hadn't noticed he was dead." Bins epitomizes ineffective teaching, as his "routine has not varied in the slightest" since the day he died, and he reads from his notes "in a flat drone like an old vacuum cleaner."[8] Bins exemplifies direct but counterproductive instruction. While there is a time and place for the lecture method, good teachers know when to use it, how to alternate it with other teaching methods, and how to craft an exciting lecture that both engages the students and leaves them wanting more.

> *Grace*: Professor Snape is bad because he is only nice to the students in his house (Slytherin). And if anyone does something wrong, like blows something up, he punishes them, like gives them a detention. He does not even let them explain themselves. When Professor Snape teaches, he just talks at the students, on and on, and does not let them say much.

Here, Grace hits upon several characteristics of poor teaching, some of which have to do as much with attitude and style as with specific pedagogical practices. Ned Flanders has discovered in his analysis of classroom interaction that a teacher with an indirect style is one who "accepts children's feelings, uses praise and encouragement, and uses pupils' ideas." By contrast, a teacher with a direct style is one who "tends to lecture, to give directions, and to criticize pupils."[9] Research has found that an indirect style leads to a higher level of school achievement and a more positive student attitude toward school and academic work. Unfortunately, Snape seems to exhibit all the negative traits of the direct approach to teaching, most notably with his seeming enthusiasm for criticizing his students in a manner intended to wound.

Real-Life Learning

Grace: What Harry, Ron, and Hermione learn in real life (about Voldemort and stuff) is also very important, and they have to do it by themselves. Even though they might learn more important things by solving the big problems in their real lives, they also do use the spells that they have learned in class in order to help solve the mystery. Like in the second book, they learn about the polyjuice potion. After that they are able to figure out how to transfigure themselves into other people and then secretively find out information. So even though Professor Snape is a bad teacher, they did learn something from him which was useful later. They also learned levitations, luminations, and the disarming spell, which are just examples of some things they learned in a classroom but then used in real life.

Grace recognizes the need for school learning, but especially that which is relevant and useful to real life. The three heroes of the series constantly find themselves in the process of discovery learning, in which they experience real problems for themselves and must discover how to solve each one without the aid of teachers or other authorities at school. However, all schools should provide their students with the proper support that will guide them through the "process of knowledge-getting."[10] And in truth, Harry, Ron, and Hermione certainly become experts in the process of knowledge-getting as the stories progress.

The real-life problems that Harry, Hermione, and Ron must solve in each book are perfect examples of learning involving problems in real-life settings (real to the wizard world). When the three are faced with a mystery, they naturally take on the investigation as a cooperative activity. While they may have been slow to join forces during the first book, their increasing ease at slipping into their cooperative roles is facilitated by their success at problem solving.

The three exhibit many of the traits that research on cooperative learning has found to be effective. First, each member naturally takes on a specific role within the group. While Harry often assumes the role of the leader, he does not monopolize it, as all three are equally highly motivated to work and learn. Harry often reflects on their progress more than do Ron and Hermione, but this is largely because he often has more information than the others and thus is able to think things through productively. Hermione takes on the role of academic investigator, or what some researchers refer to as the "coach," as she continuously slips into the library to conduct background research. She also plays the vital role of the tough inquisitor of the other two, in which capacity she steers them (especially Harry) away from serious pitfalls. While Ron frequently employs specific skills, such as his mastery of wizard's chess in the first book, he also very often takes on the role of an "encourager"

and is the one who guides the problem-solving process by asking the right questions.[11] This seemingly instinctive group work of Harry, Hermione, and Ron illustrates the concept of "cooperative scripting."

Rowling has ingeniously included within this small group many of the elements that education literature espouses to be beneficial in cooperative work. Groups that are heterogenous in nature tend to be more successful in developing varied ideas and investigating problems from different perspectives. Harry, Ron, and Hermione's group is mixed in regard to gender, socioeconomic status (one of Ron's most important characteristics is that he is from a low-income family), ethnicity (as demonstrated by the classifications of "pure bloods" and "mudbloods"), and academic achievement (the overachiever Hermione and the average Harry and Ron). The students' varied backgrounds, abilities, and skills contribute significantly to their ability to perform independent work fueled by individual motivation toward the achievement of their group goal.

Additional critiques of the type of schooling Harry is receiving at Hogwarts are possible, as is further comparative analysis of this somewhat British institution (e.g., a comparison of the "Ministry of Magic" with the British Local Education Authorities). However, Grace's personal awareness of the nuances of British schooling is limited to her own short-term experiences in various institutions. While Harry continues to learn and grow both in and out of the classroom and in the muggle and wizard worlds, he must compare and contrast his various learning environments and, in the end, take the best from each as he matures. Like Harry, Grace will also learn within and outside the confines of a classroom and in various cultural contexts. She too will partake in meaningful constructivist learning but will also experience her share of Professor Bins. In the end, both Vygotsky and Piaget would agree that, as Grace and Harry both acquire more educational experiences, there will be more opportunities for cross-cultural comparisons.

References

1. Dale A. Blyth, Roberta G. Simmons, and Steven Carlton-Ford, "The Adjustment of Early Adolescents to School Transitions," in Rolf E. Muus and Harriet D. Porton, eds., *Adolescent Behavior and Society*, 5th ed. (Boston: McGraw-Hill, 1998).
2. Lorin W. Anderson et al., "School Transitions: Beginning of the End or a New Beginning," *International Journal of Educational Research*, vol. 33, no. 4, 2000, pp. 325–39.
3. Robert E. Slavin's work on group structure is summarized in his own textbook, *Educational Psychology: Theory and Practice*, 7th ed. (Boston: Allyn and Bacon, 2003).
4. Ibid.
5. This article was written prior to the publication of the fifth Harry Potter book. Avid readers of the series will have noted that the theme of teacher evaluation can be taken even further with the fifth book, as it explores the notion of what makes a good teacher more directly than the others.
6. Summaries of constructivist perspectives can be found in various introductory educational psychology textbooks.
7. James P. Byrnes, *Cognitive Development and Learning in Instructional Contexts* (Boston: Allyn and Bacon, 2001).
8. J. K. Rowling, *Harry Potter and the Chamber of Secrets* (New York: Scholastic Press, 1999), p. 148.

9. David Fontana, *Psychology for Teachers* (London: Macmillan, 1995), p. 388.
10. Jerome Bruner, *Toward a Theory of Instruction* (New York: Norton, 1966).
11. Descriptions of the dynamics of cooperative work can be found in almost any basic educational psychology text. See, for example, John W. Santrock, *Educational Psychology* (Boston: McGraw-Hill, 2001), for a concise summary of the advantages of role-playing.

MARGARET ZOLLER BOOTH is an associate professor in the Educational Foundations and Inquiry Program at Bowling Green State University, and her daughter **GRACE MARIE BOOTH** is a student at St. Aloysius School, Bowling Green, Ohio. They jointly presented this article as a paper at the annual meeting of the Midwest/Northwest Comparative and International Education Society, Pittsburgh, November 2002.

The Divided Self

Inside the World of 21st-century Teens

RON TAFFEL

For decades before and after World War II, children all over the United States hung out, had slumber parties, made crank phone calls, and played sports unsupervised. They didn't need the help of adults to set up play dates or hand out certificates of participation. As we know all too well by now, we no longer live in that world. What's less apparent is that, despite the appearance of greater parental involvement and psychological sophistication, most adults are just as clueless about the "second family" of their children's peer group and adolescent pop culture as they ever were.

A fundamental psychological shift further separates the experience of today's children from that of previous generations. Decades ago, most kids carried parents around inside, whether they wanted to or not. Through endless channels, parents constituted a deeply felt, internal presence, however neurotic and oppressive it might sometimes have been. But what I encounter again and again in my practice is the startling reality that many parents have become psychically extruded from the inner lives of their children. While helicopter dads and soccer moms have become more and more adept at *managing* the logistical challenges of 20th-century family life, they're often too frenetically busy to exert an emotionally magnetic presence in the internal landscape of a child's world.

Increasingly, kids feel the fabric of connection tearing. From an early age, they've learned that most of the time they spend with their families could best be described by the old movie line "Hello, I must be going!" They "get" that life with mom or dad is a series of transitions, interrupted conversations, and moments hurried along so that the next activity can go on as planned.

But obvious overscheduling and invisible disconnection from parents is only part of what's changed. While at first glance, 21st-century adolescents appear impossibly cool—cooler than we could have ever been ourselves—teens today are running hot. They're not just hormonally hot, but hot with cultural forces that have redefined the nature of their consciousness and experience of selfhood. Millennium kids live in a context that spawns fragmentation, what I call a "divided-self" experience: cool and often cruel on the surface, they hide surprisingly healthy passions beneath.

The Fast and the Furious

Most of the kids I see are buried under a crazy quilt of digital connections every single moment of every single night. A typical evening can be spent on the computer engaging in five online discussions at once, talking on a cell phone while waiting those interminable nanoseconds for a response, listening to a burned CD, with a TV on in the background, and, naturally, focusing on homework at the same time.

"Hey mom, don't get all unhinged, can't you see I'm doing my work!!!" yells 12-year-old John, looking very cool as he effortlessly moves from one screen to another. But talk to John the next day and he's depleted by his conversations of the night before. Trying to return every instant message, he's gotten into several arguments with friends that'll need to be tackled throughout the schoolday. It happened so fast, John doesn't really know what hit him.

Thirteen-year-old Dawn says to me: "We were hanging out in the schoolyard. All of a sudden, Perry started screaming at me. She said I was obviously ¥bi,' my best friend is a ¥man-whore,' and, anyway, how could anyone want to be friends with a slut like me?"

"Did anything go on just before, between you?" I ask.

"No. It came out of nowhere. But this is what happens all the time. Don't you know that, Dr. Taffel?"

I do know. Every day in my practice, I hear about such sudden bursts of unmediated anger or acting out. While parents do logistical somersaults on the margins of connection, their children surf down the slopes of media-stimulated consciousness, habitually split off from their own feelings. When emotions do cross the divide into awareness, the experience is often jarring and white hot. With a hundred friends bumping into each other on MySpace or e-mailing each other on AIM, all of a sudden, some spaghetti of interpersonal energy sticks to the wall and splatters everyone around.

Listen to the dialogue between 21st-century kids and you can't help but be affected by split-second shifts from cool-sounding inanities— "wazzup, g2g, lol"—to hair-raising accusations and eruptions of raw bile, seemingly coming out of nowhere. Self-regulation or even an awareness of their easily triggered emotions isn't the strong suit of a "just do it" generation outfitted with cool fiber-circuitry that transmits instantaneous heat.

Sex and the Great Divide

Sex play is another way that 21st-century kids experience the divide with their deeper emotions. Casual sex is no longer reserved for "bad" girls and boys. Elementary and middle-school kids show me astonishingly graphic text messages every day. In city and suburban neighborhoods, middle-school "cum parties" are a weekend occurrence, the meaning of which needs no explanation. "Rainbow contests," however, might require clarification: girls wear different color lip gloss, and the boy who ends up with the most colors on his penis is declared the winner. "HJ" is a commonly used elementary and middle-school term for hand-job, which is replacing quaint bumping and grinding on the dance floor. Same-sex permutations—with girls experimenting with the "L word" (for teen boys, homophobia is more rampant than I've ever seen)—are becoming a common rite of passage, again with no relationship necessary. Sexual encounters are frequently recorded and blogged, making a once-intimate experience into mass-marketed public property.

As disconcerting as all this may be, the combination of impulsiveness and emotional flatness with which many 21st-century kids express their sexuality makes a great deal of sense. Girls feel freer to be casually active if they can avoid removing their clothes and publicly revealing a far-from-thin-enough body. Commitment-shy kids loaded down with anxieties about "safe sex" flock to instant action that requires no clumsy, time-consuming protection. And the increased use of SSRIs among teens may inadvertently disconnect sexual drive from passion, just as it does with many adults. Regardless of exact cause, the result is the same: more teens doing more kinds of sex at earlier ages, but without the deep-down, desperate yearning we often equate with adolescence.

Good Night and Good Luck

Hundreds of parents have told me how their teenagers go to sleep: they need mom or dad lying by their sides or they stay on-line under the sheets, with cell phones nestled on their chests or watching TV with a buddy miles away. "It seems like my kids have no ability to amuse themselves, even for a few moments," says one discouraged parent after another.

Kids are divided not only from their emotions (until they're engulfed by them), they're often split off from their internal fantasy lives. Imagination mediates and regulates emotional experience. But why should 21st-century children even need an internal world of self-soothing or self-stimulating fantasies? After all, from the second they get up until late in the evening, kids have an endless stream of readymade, fantasy-rich, interactive images to play with.

This is one of the simple but unarticulated reasons that many parents have such trouble getting 21st-century kids to go to bed at night. From the moment kids put down their heads, they don't know what to do with themselves. They're bored. This is the first time all day that they've had to endure a moment without external stimulation to fill their minds and fuel their fantasies

The End of History

Some years ago, after gazing at far too many blank faces, I stopped asking children in initial interviews: "So where do your parents and grandparents come from?" I don't know why I hung on for so long, except that decades ago, my supervisors had instilled in me the belief that drawing a genogram was a sacred rite of the consulting room.

Parents aren't just far off in the sense of harried daily connection. They're far away in terms of their own children's knowing any deep background about them. Knowledge of family history caused a lot of heat between previous generations. Many of us vehemently disagreed with our parents politically. We heard endless oral histories of their adventures ("Please, not that story again!!!"). And we may have expended enormous energy trying to get away from their oppressive authority or dysfunction. But there was at least a nascent understanding of who they were and where they came from; for better or worse, their life struggles had historical depth.

Except for that random first- or second-grade assignment to "interview" parents, most kids haven't got a clue as to their roots, and parents are so used to their own historical irrelevance they hardly even notice. Generally, kids have no more interest in the history of their family than they seem to have in the history of the world, if declining scores in this academic area are an accurate indicator. The distant past is yesterday or last week, especially for teens. This gives kids little understanding of who they are from a longitudinal perspective, making it more difficult for them to maintain a coherent sense of self within the moment-to-moment shape-shifting that's so natural to them today.

Ask kids what their parents do for a living and they'll most likely mention job titles they don't understand. The majority of kids today haven't got the foggiest idea of what their parents do that enables them to afford the iPod, mp3 player, and cell phone their children so crave. This isn't because 21st-century kids are craven and selfish. It's a superficiality fostered by the abstractions of modern living, as well as by the misguided attempts of many enlightened parents, at all ends of the socioeconomic spectrum, not to burden their children with knowledge about what's required to earn a living. Instilling deep gratitude for the efforts made by the adults who provide for them has been sacrificed to a widespread fear of inflicting pathological guilt on children—the great bugaboo of modern-day parenting. This leaves children disconnected not only from their parents' common work struggles, but also from the perseverance and determination that daily survival requires.

The Loss of Passion

It's sometimes been almost unbearable for me to realize how scary it is for many kids to reach down and connect to an idiosyncratic passion that might separate them from the crowd. With a constant eye on pop culture, kids of all ages are "scared straight" into cultivating a veneer—to dress right, get the right stuff, and become voracious consumers. They're seduced into worshipping physical perfection; to create at all costs, a flawless body "to die for." They're slowly intimidated out of talking about internal experience, which would be soothing, and instead dispense the hollow wisdom or cruel wit of mass-market psychobabble. They're increasingly bullied by national legislation to measure up on standardized tests, from preschool through high school, often without understanding the material and without acquiring a love of learning.

The real teen secrets I learn about in therapy aren't about sex, drugs, or rock 'n' roll, which are often already "blogged" in cyberspace. They're about nonpop-culture passions: secret journals, drawings, and art that no one has seen, or a stash of fantasy stories.

The kid culture itself has defined passion—to be enthusiastic about some activity or topic—as uncool. Kids with idiosyncratic passions are widely portrayed as geeks, and are rarely found in the popular crowd. The Johnson Institute followed thousands of children and found that they tend to give up personal interests during the transition between elementary and middle school. Kid-cool is often a facade hiding interests left behind—passion that can't be expressed.

When looked at in this way, some of teens' most troubling behaviors become more understandable. What do kids do in the often persecutory, competitive world of the 21st century as a result of being divided from themselves? Well, they demand from insecure parents endless supplies, with a sense of entitlement so unmodulated, it can be breathtaking. They diss and humiliate without much warning or empathic care for their impact on the other. They try to break through to internal numbness with the heat of binge-drinking—10 drinks ("pregaming" as it's called) aren't unusual *before* the evening begins. They push their estranged body-as-commodity to raging excess: starving, purging, and criticizing themselves mercilessly. They cut—carving up an arm or leg while expressing an anger so submerged it isn't even felt. They gleefully submit to tattoos: imagination and internal imagery writ large for the world to see. They pierce—a searing penetration toward the inside core that simultaneously makes a hard-edged statement of cool to the ever-watchful eye of the peer group and the pop culture.

Strategies for Breaking Through

Our job as helping professionals, then, is daunting but within our reach. It's to feel the passion beneath the cool, to recognize how split off 21st-century kids are from themselves, and to understand that therapy with adolescents needs to change fundamentally. We may not have the power to alter the techno-pop culture that defines so much of teen experience today, but by focusing treatment squarely on how to engage adolescents in a vital relationship, we can make an enormous difference in their lives.

If we can truly connect with the children we work with, the impact can be infectious, spreading outside the office and helping to heal the inner divide that keeps them cut off from themselves and others. To engage these 21st-century kids, though, we must go far beyond what we were officially trained to do and

move closer to what we secretly say and do, often beyond the gaze of supervisors and even our colleagues.

Working with teens is difficult enough, but we're too often our own worst enemies in the treatment room. For starters, the blandly modulated tone of therapist-speak is destined to make even the most well-meaning practitioner shrink into a tiny speck on the multiplex screen of an adolescent's mind. To put it bluntly, most models make us way too boring to be noticed by a generation in love with special effects, let alone remembered once they leave our offices. With adolescents, the "edge of relatedness," as psychoanalyst Darlene Ehrenberg calls it—the place where two people feel and touch each other emotionally—must be particularly edgy for them to even register your presence.

Our training too often works against this, smoothing out our edges, inhibiting our genuine reactions to the outrageous stories we hear from teens every day in our practice. For instance, Peter is planning a date in an abandoned garage with a complete stranger he met in cyberspace. Theo, who's 10, is teased relentlessly for being "gay." Louis and friends regularly smoke pot in the bathroom at his middle school, next to kids who purge themselves as a group activity.

It would seem impossible *not* to react to descriptions of such activities with a full range of feelings: outrage, sadness, shock, fear, relief, and so on. Yet, most of us are constrained by our training from expressing edgy feelings to clients. To stay three-dimensional and get kids' attention, however, you must go against those invisible constraints and in a responsible way—using your own beliefs, style, and words—respond in a fashion your teen client absolutely can't miss. Anything less is just static in a gigahertz, high-tech world. For most of us, learning to respond in a real manner to today's teens means engaging first in a quick, internal dialogue between what we feel like saying and the voice of our therapy training.

When Peter first told me about his online dating scheme to meet someone in an abandoned garage, I yelled (silently berating myself for worrying too much), "Are you out of your mind?!" To Louis, who smoked up in his middle school, I instinctively commented (though not without hesitating several moments), "Are you trying to drive me insane?" To Ernie, who told me that he really liked a girl and that every adult he knew had warned him that high school relationships are doomed, I said in a hushed voice (all the while concerned about the intensity of this message), "With all my heart, I believe there's a chance for you and Chloe to make it. It really is possible."

The words aren't unusual; it's the strength of the emotions they carry that's important. But regardless of differing approaches, we consistently flatten our feelings because we consider them unprofessional or nontherapeutic. Yet, in every one of these situations, I finally got kids to hear me.

Sometimes words, no matter how dramatic, aren't enough, though. In this hyperkinetic world, physical movement loosens lips and is often necessary to get kids' attention. Again, treatment constraints make this easier to say than do—most of us are "participant-observers," stuck on our own clinical thrones.

It took me almost two decades to get up from my chair and out of the constricting habits of my practice. I was working with a withdrawn, young adolescent girl, Lisa, who mumbled the few words she said. Failing in school, she was diagnosed as ADD, oppositional, and selectively mute. Partly to prevent myself from going mad, I suggested that we walk around the room a bit, just to shake things up a little. I thought maybe our stuck psychical positions might be loosened by a physical change.

Lisa liked the idea, and I found myself trailing behind her with my notebook. She'd mumble and I'd yell, "What? What did you say?" The more I yelled as I walked behind her, the more she began to laugh and yell back at me. This ambling approach to therapy made a far greater impression on me than on Lisa, who took to it naturally, as have dozens of other kids with whom I now move about the office, as if we are on a psychological road trip.

Many times I've gotten across my feelings by leaving the consulting room—another therapy taboo. When Brian repeatedly told me, with a grin on his face, about prank-calling older people, I said: "Brian, you seem unable to think about the effect you're having on these people. You know what? This sickens me a little; I have to take a break from you for a minute." When I returned a few minutes later, Brian was finally willing to talk about the mean way he often treated his parents and friends.

Humor, a therapeutic tool mostly unexplored in clinical training, can provide a lightning bolt of connection to sophisticated 21st-century teens. Given the endless menu of cartoon comedy—*The Simpsons, Family Guy, South Park*—and the everyday banter of adolescent life, it's a wonder that we do not get how necessary this is to create engagement that leads somewhere. Fourteen-year-old Adam came to his therapy session with a glum look. Rudderless much of the time and an aficionado of nonstop television, he looked even flatter than usual, and with good reason—he'd just returned from the doctor, who'd said that one testicle was enlarged. Fearing the worst, we proceeded aimlessly through the session until I wondered out loud (*Should a therapist be joking about this, I thought?*) whether an enlarged testicle might require a change in his TV-viewing habits. Maybe he'd need to switch to a new kind of couch, with a cutout section so he'd feel more comfortable. Instead of getting angry, Adam seized on this and began to speculate that he might soon require a wheelbarrow to move through the wide hallways of his suburban school, or even might need to call ahead to announce his arrival. I joined in and we were off to the races, with Adam jumping up and down, doing improv about how everyday living might be affected by this new challenge—routines that had us both rolling on the floor.

The crisis passed, thankfully with no health consequences, but the stand-up part of our sessions became a connecting ritual—a means for Adam to start expressing his feelings about his lack of popularity at school and discomfort at home. While discussing serious issues, we continued to make each other laugh, and the pleasure he got from his hysterical impersonations of celebrities and everyone in his life, including me, ultimately led him to seek out roles in his town's theater group—no small step for a coarse, pop-obsessed adolescent. Adam still needed to learn the boundary between humor and empathy, especially with friends and parents, but the jokes that punctuated our sessions helped break through his emotional divide.

The sanctity of session length is another artificial encumbrance that works against kids' ability to hear. Teen consciousness is so fragmented that it's simply grandiose to believe they remember a thing we say even two minutes after our most "important" pronouncements. So, if you're trying to make a point you don't want to get lost, why stick to the sacrosanct 45- to 50-minute session? As long as we fill out insurance and agency forms accurately, charge less, or make up the lost time, there's nothing inviolate about the "treatment hour." Especially with teens, cutting the session short to let a comment sink in or lengthening it to let a situation play out, helps grab their attention.

Aiden, a 16-year-old, was stuck on the notion that his girlfriend had to give him oral sex. If she didn't, it meant she really didn't care about him. More important, he was not getting what he thought every other guy was getting, casually or from girlfriends. "If she's not going to give me head, I'll break up with her!" he kept saying. He simply couldn't get past this thought, and his already damaged self-esteem was plummeting.

I let Aiden know that, although I understood, his wish was the exact opposite of what was involved in becoming a man. The debate became very heated, but I wasn't worried about the fireworks. I wanted one message to get through: that Aiden needed to go for an entire weekend without turning oral sex into a huge fight with his girlfriend.

Every aspect of creating engagement described here became part of this session—I was emotionally expressive about my beliefs, we moved around the room a lot as we talked, I left twice to get my bearings, we yelled at each other, and we joked around. Finally, I moved closer, sat on the floor, and spoke to Aiden very, very quietly. At last, he seemed to "get" how this artificial pressure was impacting him and his girlfriend. I immediately stopped the session. I didn't want this hard-won insight to be buried by the next inevitable distraction.

Instead of finishing the session, we scheduled a 15-minute meeting before the weekend, so we could discuss the importance of this decision again. To my surprise, I found out at the brief follow-up that Aiden had just talked to his father about sex for the first time ever, initiating an essential adult connection that helped him navigate the high-risk teen choices that came up every day for years.

The Fascination of Boring Detail

Creating genuine engagement with teens often requires paying attention to exactly the kind of mindless detail we've been taught to think of as "avoidance." But in work with adolescents, the nitty-gritty nonsense of everyday life is the most direct pathway to a meaningful connection. "I can't believe you're interested in this stuff," one teen after another remarks to me. Even though I've learned the clinical value of the most seemingly trivial conversation, it took every bit of faith in this viewpoint to stick with the following interaction.

Amanda, a 14-year-old told me, "I just hung out this weekend. Maggie snuck out in this really cool black tank top. Her parents haven't seen it. And Alice wore these new pants, like around her hips, with a big belt."

Restraining myself from moving toward significant issues, I said, "What about you? What did you wear?"

"I had on these new shoes. I have them on today. You wanna see them?"

I fought my impatience with this clinical dead-end as Amanda displayed her new shoes, pointing out their various features—color, the height of the heel, the special laces.

Far from being the neutral observer, I reacted to each aspect she remarked on, ending with the shallowest observation I could muster, "It sounds like you guys wanted to look pretty good."

"Yeah, there's this new girl," Amanda responded. "Kelly. She's a real bitch. All the guys like her."

Instead of asking, "How do you feel about this new girl?" I remained just as deeply grounded in the superficial, replying, "Oh. Who else was there?"

Amanda mentioned a few of the boys.

Reigning myself in from the inevitable therapeutic query about feelings, I stooped to: "So what was everybody else wearing?"

To my surprise, Amanda perked up even more and said, "Well just about everybody had on stuff that showed off their tattoos and piercings, because that's what Kelly's into. She's got a few that her parents don't even have a clue about. Her mom knows about her belly-button ring, but Kelly's also got her nipple pierced."

Now I was in a real clinical dilemma: I could barely resist the temptation to explore the therapeutic gold of mother-daughter relationships, secrets, etc. But I held firm and stuck to the trivial, asking, "So where did you guys go?"

We continued on this road to nowhere, discussing the mall, its new stores, and which tattoos Amanda thought were the best. Spurred on by my unflagging interest in the details most adults shut off, Amanda unexpectedly opened up about a serious decision. "Well, there's one tattoo I was thinking of. I'd get it on my hip. It's really small and my mom would never see it, because, even if I was wearing a thong, it couldn't really be seen."

I veered once again from inquiring about thoughts or feelings and instead asked Amanda to describe the tattoo.

All of a sudden the discussion, which I'd certainly have kept a secret from that imaginary supervisor on my shoulder, took a turn. Amanda said, "But just when I was about to do it, I got in a fight with Maggie. She said I was being a poser, and I was getting a tattoo just because Kelly is now the queen and I'm trying to be like her." Amanda then added, "The big thing is she had her tongue pierced."

Finally, my first traditional therapeutic response: "Do you think that's a good idea, this tongue piercing?"

Amanda was then eager to talk. "Well, she can do it, but I'm scared. For her, it's all about hooking up. The boys really like it. But I'm just not ready for that, I don't think, so I'm just going to go for the tattoo instead."

We were now engaged at a very different level. In a not-so-subtle nod to her motivation I asked, "Are you going for the tattoo to look better, so you can find someone to hook up with, or to pose? Maybe Maggie was right. What's the tattoo for?"

"I don't know," Amanda sadly replied. "I have to think about what Maggie said. I don't know if I'm just doing it so Kelly will

let me in. She's got everybody else . . . it feels like I don't have the friends I used to."

"You're right," I responded, genuinely moved. "Who don't you have anymore? Who's gone?"

The talk had moved from the truly trivial—malls, clothes, and shoes—to tattoos, hooking up, connections with other kids, and all the way to issues of abandonment and betrayal. It turned out that what was really disturbing Amanda was the friends she'd lost. Over the next two weeks, the core of our work became everyone who'd moved into a tight circle around Kelly, leaving Amanda behind. Our discussions then began to center on her losses in general, and the decisions she needed to make about how to stay true to herself.

Discovering Passion

We need to challenge another barrier to engagement, opening the walls of therapy to the superficialities of teen life—e-mails, video games, music, magazines, photographs, and television. If dreams were the royal road to the unconscious according to Freud, pop culture pursuits are the road to the split-off inner world of today's teens. By inviting their interests into therapy, you create a theme for sessions and set the stage for the development of real engagement that can lead to passion and depth.

Juliet was 14 when I first met her. She was dealing with an affective/anxiety disorder. Being physically magnetic and haughtily cool, she was a lightning rod for her small-town teen drama and gossip. At the same time, she was angrily fixated on the popularity pecking order; enough so that she "delicately" cut herself to alleviate her emptiness and despondency.

After I encouraged her to do so several times, Juliet arrived with printouts of recent e-mail arguments. It was clear to me at once how well she was able to express herself in writing. As we pored over these e-mails, I reacted to the style as well as the content of her communications, and writing became a theme of our relationship. Against my better clinical judgment, we read articles from pop magazines. Soon I learned that these stories reminded Juliet of her friends' secret issues, as well as her own. Then, she began bringing in her friends to meet me; secondhand written descriptions had turned into three-dimensional people about whom I could now truly engage.

As writing moved from a hidden to a central pursuit, Juliet joined the school newspaper, focusing on real-life adolescent issues "that adults had better face." She didn't immediately become a model teenager; she went through years of frightening ups and downs as she learned how to regulate her sharply shifting moods. But throughout the bumpy process, writing became the vehicle for containing her emotions and expressing her previously buried, true self.

Demanding Empathy

Another incorrect notion that ties up clinicians and parents is that unconditional love means accepting everything teens say, or their self-esteem will suffer a profound injury. Quite the contrary, healing engagement requires that teens emerge from their self-centered world and learn what it means to empathize with adults. Although this is a reversal from the mantra of post–World War II childrearing and treatment, decades ago, psychoanalyst D. W. Winnicott stated that empathy toward adults (moving beyond blame of one parents) was a sign of maturity.

The psychological establishment has recognized Winnicott's wisdom, but mostly in a horizontal direction. Schools focus on peer-to-peer empathy—a major component of anti-bully programs and social-emotional modules. However, they still largely ignore the idea of empathy toward therapists or parents. Seeing the adults around them as alien, two-dimensional beings without feelings leaves kids feeling mean and out of control, oblivious to the hurtful impact of their words and actions. The therapeutic relationship is an opportunity to create empathic engagement, which is also a means for teens to recognize their own buried humanity and passion.

Sixteen-year-old Mike's "me-first" behavior got him into trouble every day, reaching a climax as graduation from middle school increased his usual self-preoccupation. He wanted the celebration to be held in his home. His mother initially agreed, but as the day got closer, she started freaking out about having so many people in her small house. She began talking about renting a cheap space in a nearby community center—which infuriated Mike because he was afraid his friends wouldn't think it was cool enough.

In our meeting, I told Mike that I agreed with his mother. Not unexpectedly, he howled about the unfairness of it all.

But then I shifted the focus, surprising myself by saying, "I want you to understand what graduation felt like from my side."

Mike considered this a violation of 21st-century teen rights. "What about my side. You're not getting it!"

I responded with unexpected intensity, "I do understand. I was so self-conscious about how I looked to my friends that I didn't even want pictures taken at my graduation. But I lost that one, just like you're going to lose this one, too."

Mike responded: "That's totally different. You can rip up pictures afterwards. I'll have these memories my whole life."

"Look," I insisted, "I want you to try to see it from my perspective; what it felt like for me." And here's where I really moved away from the training I still hold sacred: "Hey, it's never just about your feelings. In here, mine count, too!"

Around and around we went for the entire session. But the focus was now entirely different; we'd made a drastic U-turn, so Mike might empathize with me and how self-conscious I'd felt as an adolescent. After we parted, I was filled with doubt about this change of therapeutic direction. A couple of days later, I received a surprising call from Mike's mother. "I don't know what you did," she said, "but for the first time, Mike let me explain how frightened I was; that I just couldn't handle this party at home. He didn't agree to the other location, but at least he tried to hear me."

No wave of emotional intelligence swept over Mike; we continued to struggle as I worked to get him to treat me and others more empathically. But this episode created a beginning awareness that he wasn't the absolute the center of the world and was the start of his slow crawl out of the loser-outcast group.

My father died when I was 22—still an adolescent in today's terms. His passing was so sudden that I went cold, so numb I didn't shed a tear. One night several months after his death, I dreamt about him. "Ronnie," he said to me, "do you remember when I sculpted circus animals for you?" He reached out with his hand, tenderly giving me the soft clay it held. I could see his heart in his eyes, and I touched his face. I woke up in tears, and continued to cry every morning for months after.

The next day, I bought some clay and began sculpting. Two months later, I fell in love for the first time, with a girl who mysteriously came over to me offering a sip from a container of milk. The sudden connection I experienced in that dream and the burst of creativity that followed were no accident. It's also no accident that the vast majority of kids I engage in the ways I've described here fall in love for the first time or discover an enduring passion.

Engagement is the essence of what we must create in therapy. These fragmented times call for nothing less than consulting rooms filled with life. Although overcoming the constraints in our treatment approaches isn't a simple matter, it's clear to me that no treatment model—whether psychodynamic, systemic, cognitive, dialectic-behavioral, or goal directed—can long ignore the human engagement our kids so desperately need.

We can help adolescents to heal. Without even knowing it, super-cool 21st-century teens are waiting to discover the genuine heat of their own inner lives—yearning to feel the heart and passion just beyond the divide.

RON TAFFEL, Ph.D., is chairman of the board of the Institute for Contemporary Psychotherapy in New York. He's author of *Breaking Through to Teens: Psychotherapy for the New Adolescence* and *The Second Family: How Adolescent Power Is Challenging the American Family*. Contact: rivervue83@aol.com. Letters to the Editor about this article may be e-mailed to: letters@psychnetworker.org

Staving Off Middle-Age Spread Requires Portion Control and Plenty of Exercise

Jill Wendholt Silva

Before last summer, playwright/actor Philip blue owl Hooser had the necessary girth to play Alfred Hitchcock in Late Night Theatre's "The Birds."

In theatrical reviews he's been described as "larger than life," "slow moving" and "physically imposing…moving about the stage like a great ocean liner."

Hooser, a 41-year-old Choctaw Indian, weighed 335 pounds, and the slow, steady spread of middle age was only adding to his midsection.

"I just kept buying bigger clothes," he says.

It's a refrain many baby boomers know. Sixty-five percent of American adults are considered overweight or obese, and the nation's expanding midsection cuts across gender, age, race and ethnicity.

Maintaining a healthy weight in the adult years can be an uphill battle. As the metabolism slows, the risk of becoming overweight continues to increase until age 60. A weight gain of more than 20 pounds increases the risk for heart disease, certain types of cancer, Type 2 diabetes, stroke, arthritis, breathing disorders and depression.

Health officials from the surgeon general on down are eager to get a handle on what many are calling a health crisis of epidemic proportions: 300,000 deaths each year are associated with obesity, and the economic cost in the United States was about $117 billion a year.

Some experts are calling obesity "the next tobacco." In terms of health, health-care costs and quality of life, only nutrition and physical activity come close to the importance that tobacco does," says Margo Wootan, director of nutrition policy for the Center for Science in the Public Interest, a nutrition advocacy group based in Washington, D.C.

"If you want to prevent disease, you have to deal with diet, inactivity and tobacco because they're responsible for two-thirds of all premature deaths."

Yet physicians and dietitians say a climate of political correctness has made it difficult to tell adults what they don't want to hear: It's time to take responsibility for what and how we eat.

"If you eat too much, you will get fat. It's an absolute equation," says K. Dunn Gifford, executive director of Oldways & Preservation Exchange Trust, a Boston-based nonprofit nutrition think tank.

Achieving a healthy body mass index or BMI—a ratio of height to weight used to determine fitness—requires relearning restraint, rethinking portion sizes and removing the social barriers that keep us from nutritional balance.

But how?

Real people eat food. They don't eat nutrition. That's where researchers find lifestyle practices are frequently out of sync with our knowledge and beliefs about good nutrition.

As the Pendulum Swings

Eager to be cast in more varied roles, Hooser started a low-carbohydrate/high-protein diet last summer.

"I gotta tell you, the way I eat makes people mad. Some people say, 'It's just wrong,'" Hooser says during lunch as he laps up a decadent cream sauce with his spoon, carefully skirting a molded mound of rice at the center of his plate.

Wrong because he's indulging in meat and cream, which are high in saturated fat. Wrong because instead of eating six to 11 grains servings a day, as recommended by the USDA's Food Guide Pyramid, Hooser ate just two grain servings a week and limited his fruit intake.

A shift in focus from low-fat to low-carbohydrate diets has put the public and some experts in the nutrition community at odds.

"It's very controversial topic," says Holly Wyatt, an assistant professor of medicine at the University of Colorado Center for Human Nutrition. "Most people feel strongly one way or another."

CU recently received a grant from the National Institutes of Health to study the Atkins diet, a low-carbohydrate/high-protein diet that has been around since the '70s but has never undergone rigorous scientific scrutiny.

Meanwhile, low-fat diet proponents insist that removing plant sources from the diet because they contain carbohydrates is encouraging people to eat more animal proteins. Animal products contain higher amounts of saturated fat, the "bad" fat, which has been linked to heart disease.

Which Diet Is the *Right* Diet?

The optimum diet probably lies somewhere between the '90s fat-free Snackwells and the '00s protein-rich T-bone steak. It also depends on a person's genetic predisposition for certain diseases and overall lifestyle habits.

Despite swings of the dietary pendulum, the truth is still this: There is no magic pill. At every age, good nutrition is about eating a wide variety of foods in moderation (especially more fruits and vegetables), avoiding high-fat and high-sodium foods and exercising daily.

"If nutrition guidelines have not seized public attention, it may be because they seem so obvious. Eat more fruit and vegetables. Nothing could be more self-evident," says Marion Nestle, a professor of human nutrition at the New York University and the author of *Food Politics: How the Food Industry Influences Nutrition and Health* (University of California Press, 2002).

Flaws In the Design

A simple, easily recognizable icon, the decade-old USDA Food Guide Pyramid is designed to give at-a-glance nutrition information. Food groups are arranged in a highly graphic, hierarchical structure with recommended servings listed under each.

But critics are quick to point out the pyramid's flaws. For instance, there is no explanation about what constitutes a serving size, nor does it differentiate between monounsaturated and polyunsaturated (the good fats) and saturated or trans fats (the bad fats). By encouraging people to eat from all the food groups every day, the message appears to be "eat more" when we should really be eating less.

"To put it bluntly, current conventional dietary guidelines and messages are a failure," Gifford says. "Eating and drinking behaviors at birth are instinctive in all living things. *Healthy* eating and drinking, however, is a choice. It is a learned behavior and must be taught."

In the past dietitians have been seen as finger-wagging naysayers. Perhaps understandably, the public often tunes out messages that do not fit their lifestyles or their tastes. A 2002 American Dietetics Association survey found that 63 percent of consumers agreed with the statement: "It seems like I am always hearing information about what not to eat rather than what I should eat." Only 37 respondents agreed with the statement when posed two years earlier.

The Basics of Good Nutrition

The average adult already knows quite a bit about health and nutrition. A study for Rodale Press found that nutrition news tops the list of subjects adults are interested in, rating higher than national, local and even sports news. Yet there are wide gaps and plenty of confusion to go around.

"You can eat the (USDA Food Guide) pyramid requirements and still have a bad diet if you choose five servings of white bread, a couple of eggs, some apples and corn," says Barbara Lohse Knous, associate professor at K-State Research and Extension. "Eating from the pyramid does not guarantee a healthy intake, but not following it pretty much guarantees you won't have a healthy intake."

So here are the basics:

- *Eat more fruits and vegetables*—At 4.4 servings a day, most Americans are getting close to the recommended "5 A Day," a national program to increase fruit and vegetable consumption sponsored by the National Cancer Institute. But last fall the recommended servings went up—from five to nine.

  A good rule of thumb is to "colorize" diet by choosing vividly colored fruits and vegetables that are rich in antioxidants. Filling up on large amounts of fruits and vegetables can help keep hunger pangs at bay.

- *Eat good fats*—Since 1990 the Dietary Guidelines outlined by the USDA continue to recommend no more than 30 percent of calories from fat with no more than 10 percent from saturated fat, but it's important not to shun all fats. Some fat in the diet is essential to proper bodily functioning, and monounsaturated fats such as those found in foods such as avocados and nuts contain healthful phytochemicals.

- *Eat fewer carbohydrates*—Americans have tended to overdose on "bad" carbohydrates in recent years. Refined and processed grain products make up the bulk of the American diet. Instead, eat more whole grains. Look for the words "whole grain" as the first ingredient on nutrition labels.

- *Moderate protein*—The verdict is out on whether the Atkins diet is a useful tool for weight reduction. That said, few people can follow a true "diet" for the rest of their lives. Instead, most dietitians recommend consuming moderate amounts of protein. The protein source need not be meat. Try beans and legumes.

- *Portion control*—Americans have super-sized their meals to the point they no longer know what an appropriate portion size is. A 2002 survey by the American Dietetic Association has found 68 percent of respondents overestimated the serving size of cooked vegetables, 55 percent overestimated pasta and 54 percent overestimated a serving of meat.

- *Learn to cook*—The only way to really know what's in your food is to take control and prepare your own food.

- *Become a mindful eater*—Eat slower. Eat at a table. Eat with seasons so food is at its peak of freshness.

- *Exercise*—The link between diet and exercise is a crucial piece of the weight-management puzzle. Most experts are recommending at least an hour of brisk exercise a minimum of five times a week for optimum health, but health benefits accrue with as little as 30 minutes a day.

Detours on the Road

Forty-year-old females who are educated are the most likely to consume the recommended five servings of fruit and vegetables each day. But when asked to define the appropriate serving size of raw, leafy vegetables, most adults surveyed by the American Dietetic Association overestimated the proper amount. (One cup is considered a serving of raw, leafy vegetables.)

NYU's Nestle uses an order of fast-food french fries to illustrate how portion sizes have become grossly inflated. From 1950 to 1970, the usual serving size was 2 ounces of french fries or 200 calories. By the 1980s the serving size had doubled. And by 2002, the serving size had ballooned to 6.1 ounces, tipping the scales at a whopping 610 calories.

But whether you're a soccer mom carpooling kids, a businessman between appointments or an actor juggling a frenzied schedule of rehearsals and performances, quick, inexpensive grab-and-go fare is often hard to resist.

In the last three decades, American families have increasingly relied on restaurants. In 1970, 26 percent of food dollars were spent on restaurant meal and foods prepared away from home, according to CSPI. By 1993, 46 percent of our food dollars were spent outside the home for a total of one-third of our daily calories.

A restaurant entree can easily provide half a day's calories, saturated fat and trans fat, or sodium. Include an appetizer, drink and dessert, and you may consume a whole day's calories, saturated and trans fat, and sodium in a single meal.

Breaking down the barriers to better eating will require Americans to bypass the drive-through and make a detour to the kitchen. Even better if that detour includes a stop at the gym or a walk around the block.

Making Lifestyle Changes

As a playwright, Hooser spends the bulk of each day sitting in front of a computer screen writing.

Last summer he began walking for exercise, shedding 90 pounds and dropping his waist size from 54 to 38 inches. Now he walks from his Westport apartment to his job at Crown Center four times a week and has begun looking for other exercises that will help him build lean body mass.

With a boost in energy, Hooser says his mood has improved. "I can feel the health difference of not having to lug a friend around with me," he says.

Hooser chats online with others in the "low carb community" who urge him to "take it one bite at a time." He has begun cooking more. He even swaps recipes on the Internet with other dieters and boasts of making a "mean" gratin-style cauliflower dish that mimics the silky smooth taste of twice-baked potatoes.

Potatoes have long been a favorite of Hooser's. He still eats them, just not as often. As the potato vs. cauliflower swap illustrates, not all foods are created equal.

About one-third of Hooser's diet comes from carbohydrates, and he now consumes moderate amounts of protein, in line with the USDA recommendation. But unless you're overweight or obese, many health experts say forget about counting carbohydrates and proteins. Focus on a diet heavy on fruits and vegetables instead.

Not only is color-rich produce high in fiber and low in fat, it's also loaded with health-giving phytochemicals high in antioxidants. Antioxidants are thought to protect against heart disease, cancer, age-related cognitive decline, cataracts and macular degeneration. To get the maximum benefit, variety is the key. Eating apples and oranges is good, but over the long haul it won't provide the same protection as a diet that also includes blueberries, kale and sweet potatoes.

Meanwhile, Hooser's latest party trick—sucking in his gut until his pants fall down—is getting rave reviews. When he reaches "the century mark" he plans on throwing himself a party.

"I don't really advocate the way I eat to anybody, but it's working for me. I'm happy eating this way," he says.

As Hooser likes to say—"YMMV."

Your mileage may vary.

Lost & Found

Promising therapy for Alzheimer's draws out the person inside the patient

BARBARA BASLER

The woman wore a plain housedress and a big apron, its pockets stuffed with plastic checkers. Head down, eyes blank, she shuffled aimlessly around the activity room. Cameron Camp, a research psychologist who was visiting this assisted living home in Kentucky, watched the 70-year-old woman for a moment. Then, he recalls, "I went up to her and gave her one of our books—the one on Gene Kelly, the dancer—and asked her to please read a page."

He pauses, remembering the woman and the skeptical staff—and the very next moment.

"She took the book and read aloud—clear as a bell," Camp says with a smile. "A shocked staffer turned to me and said, 'I didn't even know she could speak. That's a miracle.'"

Camp heads the Myers Research Institute in Beachwood, Ohio, and his cutting-edge work with patients in all stages of Alzheimer's has left him improbably upbeat—because he sees miracles like this day after day.

His research is part of a sea change in the care of Alzheimer's patients who are in the later stages of the disease: "Ten to 15 years ago these people were institutionalized, and their care involved physical or chemical restraints," says Kathleen O'Brien, vice president of program and community services for the Chicago-based Alzheimer's Association, which, with the National Institutes of Health, has helped fund Camp's work.

Psychologist Cameron Camp says patients live in the moment. "Our job is to give them as many good moments as we can."

"Today," she says, "more than 70 percent of those with Alzheimer's are cared for in the family home, and we talk about controlling the disease and enhancing daily life for those who have it."

Alzheimer's, the most common form of dementia in people over the age of 65, affects 4.5 million Americans. An irreversible brain disorder, the disease robs people of their memory and eventually impairs most of their mental and physical functions.

While research typically focuses on preventing Alzheimer's or delaying its progress in the early stages, some medical specialists and long-term care professionals are investigating activities that will help patients in the later stages.

"We can't stop cell death from Alzheimer's," Camp explains. "But at any stage of dementia there is a range of capability. If you give people a reason to get out of bed, activities that engage and allow them to feel successful, they will be at the top of their game, whatever it is."

Camp, 53, began his research 10 years ago when he looked at the activities developed for young children by the educator Maria Montessori, whose "method" is followed today in Montessori schools around the world. There, children learn by manipulating everyday objects like balls, seashells and measuring spoons in highly structured activities that engage children but rarely allow them to fail.

Camp adapted these kinds of exercises for older people with dementia, tailoring them to the individual's background and interests, and found he could draw out the person inside the patient.

"Suddenly, they just wake up, come alive for the moment," he says.

That happened to Mary Anne Duffy's husband when they took part in Camp's research. James Duffy, 77, has Parkinson's disease and dementia and is confined to a wheelchair in a nursing home in Mentor, Ohio.

"James loved woodworking," Duffy says, "and he liked fixing things, so the researcher brought him a small box to paint, nuts and bolts to put together, puzzles." Before her husband began the activities, she says, he "just sat there, nodding off."

But when he was working a puzzle or painting a box, "James actually smiled—something I hadn't seen for a long time," Duffy says. "And he would talk. That was amazing."

People with Alzheimer's "live in the moment, and our job is to give them as many good moments as we can," Camp says. "We need to be thinking about these people in a new way. Instead of focusing on their problems and deficits, we need to ask what strengths and abilities remain."

People had assumed, for instance, that the woman with the checkers in her apron pockets was too impaired to read. But studies have found that reading is one of the very last skills to fade away. "It's automatic, almost a reflex," Camp says.

"If the print is right," he says as he flips through one of his specially designed books with big, bold letters, many Alzheimer's patients can read.

One goal of Camp's work has been to turn his research into practical how-to guides for professional and family caregivers. Published by the Myers Research Institute, the guides have been translated into Chinese, Japanese and Spanish.

While long-term care residences may have some activities for dementia patients—like coloring in a picture or listening to a story—often they don't have activities "that are meaningful, that call on an adult's past," Camp says. "And even people with Alzheimer's are bored if an activity isn't challenging or interesting."

Much of Camp's research is with residents at Menorah Park Center for Senior Living in Beachwood, which is affiliated with Myers Research. After Alzheimer's patients were given the large-print books that he and his colleagues developed, many could read aloud and discuss the books.

A brief biography of Leonardo da Vinci, for instance, talks about some of his wildly imaginative inventions, like a machine that would let soldiers breathe underwater so they could march underneath enemy ships, drill holes in their hulls and sink them.

"It's a wonderful, wacky idea," Camp says. "Dementia patients react to it just as we do. They love it. They laugh, they shake their heads. They talk about it."

E ducation Director Lisa P. Gwyther of the Bryan Alzheimer's Disease Research Center at Duke University Medical Center recalls visiting a facility where she saw Alzheimer's patients themselves teaching some of the simple activities they had learned to preschool children. "I was so impressed with the dignity and the purpose and the fun that was observable between the older person and younger child," she says. Camp's work has been rigorously studied in a number of small pilot projects, she adds, "which means this is a reliable, valid method."

At Menorah Park, Camp and his team look at what basic skills remain in those with dementia: Can the person read, sort, categorize, manipulate objects? Then they customize activities for those skills.

"We had one man who loved baseball," Camp says. "We had him sort pictures of baseball players into American and National leagues. Another man who loved opera sorted titles into operas by Puccini and operas by Verdi."

The activities help patients maintain the motor skills needed to feed themselves or button buttons. They also trigger memories, then conversations that connect the patient and the caregiver.

People with dementia won't consciously remember the activity from one session to the next. But, Camp says, "some part of them does remember, and eventually they will get bored. So you can't have them match the same pictures each time."

It doesn't matter if patients make mistakes, Camp adds. "What's important is that they enjoy the process."

Mike Skrajner, a project manager for Myers Research who monitored an Alzheimer's reading group at Menorah Park, recalls one morning when the group was reading a biography of Gene Kelly and came to the part where Kelly tells his father he is quitting law school—to take ballet lessons. "They stopped right there and had a great conversation about how they would react to that news," he says. "It was a wonderful session, and at the end they all wound up singing 'Singin' in the Rain.'"

Manipulating everyday objects helps patients maintain skills for feeding themselves or brushing their teeth.

Camp's research shows that people who engage in such activities tend to exhibit fewer signs of agitation, depression and anxiety.

George Niederehe, acting chief of the geriatrics research branch of the National Institute of Mental Health, which is funding some of Camp's work, says a large study of patients in long-term care facilities is needed for definitive proof of the effectiveness of Camp's approach. But his method could be as helpful to caregivers as it is to people with Alzheimer's, he says, because it would improve "staff morale, knowing they can do something useful for these patients." And that, he adds, would enhance the overall environment for staff and residents alike.

One vital part of Camp's theory—like Montessori's—is that residents need activities that give them a social role, whether it's contributing at a book club or stirring lemonade for a party.

The Menorah Park staff worked with one patient, a former mailman, who loved folding pieces of paper stamped with "Have a Nice Day!" He stuffed the notes into envelopes and delivered them to other residents.

"What we try to do," Camp says, "is let the person you remember shine through the disease, even if it's only a few moments a day."

To Learn More

- To download samples of Cameron Camp's activities for dementia patients, go to www.aarp/bulletin/longterm.
- The caregiver's manual "A Different Visit" costs $39.95 plus shipping, and the special large-print books for Alzheimer's patients cost $5.95 each (or six copies for the price of five) plus shipping. To order, go to www.myersresearch.org, or write Myers Research Institute, 27100 Cedar Road, Beachwood, OH 44122.
- For general information, go to the Alzheimer's Association website at www.alz.org.

For nine simple habits you can adopt that may delay dementia, see the September-October issue of *AARP The Magazine*.

Reprinted from *AARP Bulletin*, September 2005, pp. 10-11, 17. Copyright (c) 2005 by American Association for Retired Persons (AARP). Reprinted by permission.

Good Life, Good Death

The only way to learn from the reaper is to accept he's there.

No one knows exactly when, but as the old song says, everybody's gotta go sometime. Indeed, 155,000 people die on the planet every day—from famine, illness, violence, war, neglect, accidents, bad judgment, and old age. While death is a voyage that awaits us all, not everyone gets the same noisy sendoff when they depart. Compare the frenzy earlier this year around the demise of the pope and Terri Schiavo with Americans' relative ignorance of the rising body count in Iraq. The fact is that we live in an era simultaneously obsessed with death and in denial about it—a paradox that affects us all. We hope this section will give readers a chance to think about how to balance the fear of dying with its power to make us better at the art of living.

—The Editors

LAINE BERGESON

"Hello, Laine?" my doctor's voice sang out cheerily from the answering machine, "Your test results came back today and it looks like you have a growth on your pancreas. Give a call if you have any questions, Hope you have a great afternoon!"

Did I have questions? Since pancreatic cancer is medical jargon for "goner," I had several: What kind of growth? What would happen next? And how could I have a possibly fatal diagnosis? Dying, after all, is for the bit players in our tightly scripted lives. You and I, dear reader, the stars of the romantic comedies airing nightly in our imaginations, will never die.

On one level we know that isn't true, of course. Humans are gifted with the ability to contemplate their own demise, and this weird blessing infuses every moment of life with the inevitability of death. That said, we're remarkably good at making our date with death seem so far away we doubt we'll have to keep it. If an event pierces our defenses and makes our mortality vivid, we quickly return to living as we usually live, as if the odds against death are stacked in our favor.

To deny death, for all its initial comfort (unless you're a Russian novelist), is to deny an essential part of life. Throughout the ages, students of the human condition have suggested that reconciling ourselves to death can open a window into our deepest nature, and only by accepting death will we lead a truly fulfilling life. And what happens if we don't? The answer to that question could have special importance in an age of terror attacks and preemptive war—the cultural equivalents of bad news from the doctor.

At 29, I've had my shot at wrestling with these issues. My parents gifted me with a genetic disorder that, according to the medical elite (except my optimistic acupuncturist), will take me down short of the normal span. I co-parented a beloved boxer dog who, within a week of being asked to write this piece (as if on some cosmic cue), died of a massive heart attack in his apparent prime. My father also died too young. By the end, holding his purple hand, I could see tumors rising up beneath his skin, an image that brings to mind what Zen teacher Suzuki Roshi reportedly said about his terminal cancer: ""Well, it wants to live, too."

Most people aren't so calm in the face of "mortality salience"—modern science-speak for the moments when we realize death awaits us. According to studies, pointed reminders of death are more likely to trigger unsavory behaviors, including a puritanical conformism that drives us to defend our worldview and to punish others who threaten it—if only in our minds.

Curiously, an awareness of death also drives us to seek out ways to bolster our self-esteem. Researchers say that even little ways of feeling better about ourselves (like flattery or shopping) are strangely effective in lulling us back into forgetting our ultimate fate.

To deny death, some busy themselves with tasks only the living can do, like trimming cuticles or alphabetizing the condiments in the pantry.

Some say our efforts to manage the terror of death can be used to explain a range of human activity, from the rise of culture and religion to American patriotic fervor after the attacks on 9/11. As noted by Kate Douglas in *New Scientist* magazine

(Aug 28, 2004), not all researchers buy what is known as "terror management theory," or TMT, "but nobody doubts that we do react in interesting ways when confronted with death."

Long before Western science got interested, mystics and sages have sought to live well with our mortality, tapping its potential to liberate our better traits while sidestepping its equally potent ability to turn us into rigid creeps. From death anxiety and its contradictions, "the most sublime, creative, and spiritually uplifting aspects of our nature emerge," says Daniel Liechty, a theology and peace studies scholar and a professor of social work at Illinois State University, quoted in *Science & Spirit* (March/April 2005). But that's also from where "the most primitively reactive, paranoid, and violent aspects of our nature emerge." The Zen master's equanimity with his fatal disease springs from a centuries-old discipline of clear-eyed gazing at the frightened self's response to its annihilation. And Zen is only one of many traditions, religious and secular, that have sought to teach us how to deal with death.

As the tragic cycle of violence that began with 9/11 enters its fifth year, that event has come to be seen as an entire era's near-death experience. Many would say the result is a world hardened into absolutism, where myopic foreign policy is de rigueur. Instead of encouraging creativity and enlightenment, the fear of death, amplified by the modern media, creates panic as well as political leaders who garner power by promising the kind of psychic safety that only rigid ideology can provide. In other words, we're watching the paradox of death awareness play out on a global scale.

My doctor, it turns out, is prone to hyperbole: the polyp was on my gall bladder, not my pancreas, and it appears benign. With the happy news of my new lease on life, I quickly forgot my medical scare and returned to the comforting distractions of life.

To deny death, some fall back on righteousness, some busy themselves with crucial tasks only the living can do, like trimming cuticles or alphabetizing the condiments in the pantry. A rare few reach peace with death and remain unconcerned by the ego's final erasure.

I'm not one of those people. Life has served me up a lot of loss—from beloved creatures already gone, to dear friends about to go, to the terrifying thought we all share that today will be the day we get paved over by an errant city bus, and all our chances to eat Oreos, and play with our chocolate Labs, and watch inane TV, and be madly in love, and be intellectually challenged, and be free, and alive, and beautiful, will be gone. I have no idea what to do with this odd knowledge. Any prescription I might offer would be someone else's.

Death is like an unmapped land—a place our minds can't fully comprehend, but on the perimeters of which we are summoned to both new spiritual depths and sheer terror. Maybe our only call, both for ourselves and for our culture in denial, is to acknowledge this strange tension and learn to live with it. As others have noted, intelligence is the ability to hold two opposing ideas in mind at one time. Perhaps living an honest life means having the ability to do the same with death.

LAINE BERGESON is assistant editor at *Utne*.

Reprinted by permission from *Utne Reader* (September/October 2005, pp. 48-50).

UNIT 4
Relating to Others

Unit Selections

Key Points to Consider

- How do others influence our self-perceptions?

- How do our own self-perceptions influence others or the way we interact with them?

- What factors enhance our interpersonal relationships?

- What factors detract from our interpersonal relationships?

- How does the culture from which we come influence our interactions with others?

- Can we really "catch" a behavior from someone else? How so?

Student Web Site

www.mhcls.com/online

Internet References

Further information regarding these Web sites may be found in this book's preface or online.

Emotional Intelligence Discovery
http://www.cwrl.utexas.edu/~bump/Hu305/3/3/3/

The Personality Project
http://www.personality-project.org/personality.html

People can be seen everywhere in groups: couples in love, parents and their children, teachers and students, gatherings of friends, religious groups, theatergoers. People hold much influence on one another when they congregate in groups.

Groups spend a great deal of time communicating with members and nonmembers. The communication can be intentional and forceful, such as when protesters demonstrate against a totalitarian regime in a far-off land. Or communication can be more subtle, for example, when a young woman sweetly touches the hand of her boyfriend as he passes by.

In some groups, the reason a leader emerges is clear—perhaps the most skilled individual in the group is elected leader by the group members. In other groups, for example during a spontaneous nightclub fire, the qualities of the rapidly emerging, perhaps self-appointed leader are less apparent. Nonetheless, the followers flee unquestioningly in the leader's direction. Even in dating couples, one person may seem to lead or be dominant over the other.

Some groups, such as large businesses, issue formal, written rules and discipline members for rule breaking. Other groups, families or trios of friends, for example, possess fewer, less for-malized rules, but their rules are still quickly learned by and are important to all members.

Certain groups are large but seek more members, such as nationalized labor unions. Other groups seek to keep their groups small and somewhat exclusive, such as teenage cliques. A few groups exist that are almost completely adversarial with other groups; youth gangs may come to mind. Other groups pride themselves on their ability to remain cooperative, such as neighbors who band together in adjoining community crime watches.

Psychologists are so convinced that interpersonal relationships are important to the human experience that they have intensively studied groups. There is ample evidence that contact with other people is a necessary part of human existence. Research has shown that most individuals do not like being isolated from others. In fact, in laboratory experiments causing total isolation for extended periods, participants begin to hallucinate the presence of others. In prisons, solitary confinement is often used as a form of punishment because of its adversive effect. Additional research has shown that people who must wait under stressful circumstances prefer to wait with others, even if the others are total strangers, rather than wait alone.

This unit examines small and therefore fairly intimate interpersonal relationships such those among friends and married couples. The next unit examines the effects of a much larger group, specifically, American society.

In the first article, "Mirror, Mirror: Seeing Yourself as Others See You," the author discusses how others perceive you. Accurately gauging how others judge you is important to traversing the social world *and* helping you establish your self-identity. Inaccurate perceptions can create a myriad of psychological and social problems for an individual.

In the next series of articles, various factors that enhance or inhibit our relationships with others are discussed. The next two articles review a fairly important concept—emotional intelligence or EQ. Emotional intelligence relates to our ability to get along with and be sensitive to other people's needs and emotions. It also enables to interpret accurately our own feelings and needs. Emotional intelligence therefore is important to our success in interpersonal interactions.

A related ability is the capacity to discern the self from others. Some individuals, however, carry this tendency too far. In an extreme way, they grossly differentiate their *own group* from *other groups*, known respectively as the in-group and the out-group.

This tendency is particularly strong relative to racial or ethnic groups. In "Us vs. Them," Raphael Cushnir criticizes this propensity and suggests ways we can stop being so judgmental of others and the groups to which they belong.

Our self-concept and our ability to distinguish ourselves from others are important to interpersonal relationships. However, developing *healthy* relationships goes beyond simply knowing others and deciding whether they are similar or different from us. Two articles address this point. In "Relationships, Human Behavior, and Psychological Science," the authors review research that demonstrates all the positive ways interpersonal connectedness is good for us. A companion article on friendships, "Budding Friendships Fill Out the Family Tree," contends that close friendships are filling the void left by social mobility and the geographic move away from nuclear families. Good friends in faraway places offer the same social support and therefore positive health outcomes offered by good families.

In "Contagious Behavior," the author contends that certain behaviors, beyond yawns, are passed ("caught") from one person to another—often without anyone's awareness. Even psychogenic (loosely, imaginary) illnesses can be thusly contagious.

Mirror Mirror: Seeing Yourself as Others See You

To navigate the social universe, you need to know what others think of you—although the clearest view depends on how you see yourself.

CARLIN FLORA

I gave a toast at my best friend's wedding last summer, a speech I carefully crafted and practiced delivering. And it went well: The bride and groom beamed; the guests paid attention and reacted in the right spots; a waiter gave me a thumbs-up. I was relieved and pleased with myself. Until months later—when I saw the cold, hard video documentation of the event. * As I watched myself getting ready to make the toast, a funny thing happened. I got butterflies in my stomach all over again. I was nervous for myself, even though I knew the outcome would be just fine. Except maybe the jitters were warranted. The triumph of that speech in my mind's eye morphed into the duller reality unfolding on the TV screen. My body language was awkward. My voice was grating. My facial expressions, odd. My timing, not quite right. Is this how people saw me? * It's a terrifying thought: What if I possess a glaring flaw that everyone notices but me? Or, fears aside, what if there are a few curious chasms between how I view myself and how others view me? What if I think I'm efficient but I'm seen as disorganized? Critical, but perceived as accepting?

While many profess not to care what others think, we are, in the end, creatures who want and need to fit into a social universe. Humans are psychologically suited to interdependence. Social anxiety is really just an innate response to the threat of exclusion; feeling that we're not accepted by a group leaves us agitated and depressed.

Others always rate you one point higher than you rate yourself on a scale of physical attractiveness.

The ability to intuit how people see us is what enables us to authentically connect to others and to reap the deep satisfaction that comes with those ties. We can never be a fly on the wall to our own personality dissections, watching as people pick us apart after meeting us. Hence we are left to rely on the accuracy of what psychologists call our "metaperceptions"—the ideas we have about *others'* ideas about us.

The Bottom Line: It Comes Down to What You Think About Yourself

Your ideas about what others think of you hinge on your self-concept—your own beliefs about who you are. "You filter the cues that you get from others through your self-concept," explains Mark Leary, professor of psychology at Wake Forest University in Winston-Salem, North Carolina.

Our self-concept is fundamentally shaped by one person in particular: Mama. How our mother (or primary caregiver) responded to our first cries and gestures heavily influences how we expect to be seen by others. "Children behave in ways that perpetuate what they have experienced," says Martha Farrell Erickson, senior fellow with the Children, Youth and Family Consortium at the University of Minnesota. "A child who had an unresponsive mother will act obnoxious or withdrawn so that people will want to keep their distance. Those with consistently responsive mothers are confident and connect well with their peers."

As an infant scans his mother's face he absorbs clues to who he is; as adults we continue to search for our reflections in others' eyes. While the parent-child bond is not necessarily destiny, it does take quite a bit to alter self-concepts forged in childhood, whether good or bad. People rely on others' impressions to nurture their views about themselves, says William Swann, professor of psychology at the University of Texas, Austin. His research shows that people with negative self-concepts goad others to evaluate them harshly, especially if they suspect the person likes them—they would rather be right than be admired.

The Top Line: You Probably Do Know What People Think of You

But it's likely you don't know any one person's assessment. "We have a fairly stable view of ourselves," says Bella DePaulo, visiting professor of psychology at the University of California at Santa Barbara. "We expect other people to see that same view immediately." And they do. On average there is consensus about how you come off. But you can't apply that knowledge to any one individual, for a variety of reasons.

For starters, each person has an idiosyncratic way of sizing up others that (like metaperceptions themselves) is governed by her own self-concept. A person you meet will assess you through her unique lens, which lends consistency to her views on others. Some people, for example, are "likers" who perceive nearly everyone as good-natured and smart.

Furthermore, if a particular person doesn't care for you, it won't always be apparent. "People are generally not direct in everyday interactions," says DePaulo. Classic work by psychologist Paul Ekman has shown that most people can't tell when others are faking expressions. Who knows how many interactions you've walked away from thinking you were a hit while your new friend was actually faking agreeability?

And there's just a whole lot going on when you meet someone. You're talking, listening and planning what you're going to say next, as well as adjusting your nonverbal behavior and unconsciously responding to the other person's. DePaulo calls it "cognitive busyness."

Because of all we have to contend with, she says, we are unable to effectively interpret someone else's reactions. "We take things at face value and don't really have the means to infer others' judgments." Until afterward, of course, when you mull over the interaction, mining your memory for clues.

Context is Key

While our personalities (and self-concepts) are fairly consistent across time and place, some situations, by their very structure, can change or even altogether wipe out your personality. You might feel like the same old you wherever you are, but the setting and role you happen to be playing affect what people think of you. Suppose you describe yourself as lighthearted and talkative. Well, no one could possibly agree if they meet you at your brother's funeral.

What Type of Person Can Handle Feedback ...

Are you open to experience? Are you, say, perennially taking up new musical instruments or scouting out-of-the-way neighborhoods? If so, your curiosity will drive you to learn new things about the world and yourself. You'll be inclined to ask people how you're doing as you embark on new challenges, and you will gather a clearer idea of how you come off to others, says David Funder, professor of psychology at the University of California at Riverside.

How to Solicit a Character Critique (Yours!)

Muster your courage and set up an "exit interview" if you're left wondering why a relationship went south, in a spirit of fact-finding—that is, without hostility—contact your ex and ask for an honest and kind discussion of how things went awry. You're not looking to get your ex back (or get back at your ex) but to gather information to prevent lightning from striking twice. Ask questions ("What could I have done better?") and listen. Be sure you don't use the conversation to justify your old behavior.

People endowed with the trait of physical awareness have a keen sense of how they present themselves. If you are concerned with the observable parts of personality—voice, posture, clothes and walk—as an actor would be, says Funder, "you will control the impression you give, and your self-perception will be more accurate." If, for example, you slouch but don't know it, your droopy posture registers in the minds of those you meet and enters into how they see you—unbeknownst to you.

If you are someone who craves approval, you will tend to think you make a positive impression on other people. And generally, you will, says DePaulo.

People who have learned to regulate their emotions are in a much better position to know what others think of them, says Carroll Izard, professor of psychology at the University of Delaware: "They are able to detect emotions on others' faces and to feel empathy." If you are either overwhelmed with feelings or unable to express them at all, it becomes difficult to interpret someone else's response to you. Learning to give concrete expression to your feelings and to calm yourself in highly charged moments will give you a much better grip on your own and others' internal states.

Those with personalities that feed the accuracy of their metaperceptions are handsomely rewarded. "The more accurate you are about how others perceive you, the better you fare socially," says Leary. "Think of a person who thinks he's really funny but isn't. He interprets polite laughter as genuine laughter, but everyone is on to him and annoyed by him."

... And What Kind of Person Rejects Feedback

There are people who behave in ways that prevent them from getting direct feedback from others, which renders them less able to know how they come off. Maybe you're a boss who is prickly and hostile in the face of criticism. Or a student who bursts into tears over a bad evaluation. Either way, coworkers and teachers will start leaving you in the dark to fumble over your own missteps.

Such demeanor may even encourage others to lie to you, says DePaulo. You may project a fragility that makes others afraid they will break you by offering honest criticism.

> **Too much concern about what others think of you can only constrict behavior and stifle the spirit.**

Narcissism also blocks metaperception. Instead of wincing, as "normal" subjects do, when forced to see themselves on-screen, narcissists become even more self-biased, finds Oliver John, professor of psychology at the University of California at Berkeley. When he and his team videotaped people diagnosed as pathological narcissists, a group absorbed with themselves, their subjects loved watching the footage and uniformly thought they came off beautifully! The finding underscores how fiercely we defend our self-concepts, even if they reflect psychological instability.

Shyness: A Double Whammy

If you are socially anxious (otherwise known as shy), you likely fret that you don't come off well. Unfortunately, you're probably right. Shy people convey unflattering impressions of themselves, says DePaulo. But not for the reasons they think. People don't see them as lacking in smarts, wit or attractiveness but as haughty and detached. When you're anxious, you fail to ask others about themselves or put them at ease in any way, which can be seen as rude and self-centered.

In a way, many shy people are self-centered, points out Bernie Carducci, psychologist at Indiana University Southeast and author of *Shyness: A Bold New Approach*. They imagine that everyone is watching and evaluating their every move. They think they are the center of any social interaction, and because they can't stand that, they shut down (unlike an exhibitionist, who would relish it). Socially anxious people are so busy tracking what others think that they can't act spontaneously. Still, many people find them endearing, precisely because they don't hog attention.

The Powerful and the Beautiful

Neither group gets accurate feedback. "People are too dazzled or intimidated to react honestly to them," says Funder. Michael Levine, the head of a Hollywood public relations agency, has run up against many such people, who end up with a deluded sense of self thanks to a coterie of sycophants. If you are among the bold and the beautiful, he says, you must invite feedback by playing on the fact that people want desperately to be liked by you. "You must let them know that your approval is conditional upon their honesty with you."

Don't Worry—You're Not See-Through

The traits others judge us on fall roughly into two categories—visible and invisible. Funder has found that others notice our visible traits more than we ourselves do (the eye, after all, can't see its own lashes, as the Chinese proverb goes). You would rate yourself higher on the characteristic of "daydreams" than others would—simply because they cannot easily discern whether or not you're a daydreamer. They'll tend to assume you're not.

> **There's always a trade-off between how good you want to feel—and what you want to know.**

The good news, however, is that on a scale of physical attractiveness, others always rate you about one point higher than you rate yourself. This applies to "charm," too—another characteristic you can't easily convey to yourself, one that others naturally have a better window onto. "Imagine trying to be charming while alone on a desert island," Funder observes.

One common concern is that internal states are evident for all to see. In a study where subjects did some public speaking and then rated their own performances, the anxious ones in the group gave themselves a low rating, thinking that their inner churning was apparent to all. But audiences reported that they did just fine.

"Invisible" traits aren't entirely invisible—at least not to close friends. But an anxious friend would still rate herself higher on worry than we would.

The invisible/visible trait divide helps explain why people agree more on your positive attributes than your negative ones, says Eric Turkheimer, professor of psychology at the University of Virginia.

"First of all, people are less honest about their own negative traits," he says, "and many of these are 'stealth' traits. You'd have to know someone really well to have any thoughts on whether or not he 'feels empty inside,' for example."

Self-Awareness: A Blessing and a Curse

There is one sure way to see yourself from others' perspective—on videotape (as I did post-toast). But remember, the image is still filtered through your self-concept—it's still you watching you. Paul Silvia, assistant professor of psychology at the University of North Carolina at Greensboro, points to an experiment in which psychologically healthy adults watched tapes of themselves giving group presentations. They described it as quite sobering. They cued into their faults and judged themselves much more harshly than they would have had they relied on their own impressions of the experience. You evaluate yourself much more critically when you are self-aware, because you are focused on your failure to meet internal standards.

If I watch myself on tape, I'm not only viewing with my self-concept in mind, I'm comparing "me" to my "possible selves," the "me's" I wish to become. Here is where an unbridgeable gap opens up between people: I will never have a sense of anyone else's possible selves, nor they mine.

So, should we just rely on our memories of events, protective of self-esteem as they are, and eschew concrete documentation of ourselves? Not necessarily, says Silvia. But the dilemma reveals how self-awareness is a double-edged sword. Self-awareness furnishes a deep, rich self-concept—but it also can be paralyzing, warns Leary, author of *The Curse of the Self." Self-Awareness, Egotism and the Quality of Human Life*. "It leads you to overanalyze others' reactions to you and misinterpret them."

Many of the most unpleasant shades on our emotional palettes—embarrassment, shame, envy—exist solely in the interpersonal realm. We cannot feel them until we are self-aware enough to worry what others think about us. These emotions are supposed to motivate us to cut out potentially self-destructive behaviors. But, Leary points out, given the brain's natural bias toward false alarms, people feel overly embarrassed. Too much concern about what others think can only constrict behavior and stifle the spirit.

Do You Really Want to Know How You Come Off?

Report cards and annual reviews give you information on your performance in school and at work. But you'll rarely be treated to a straightforward critique of your character—unless someone blurts one out in a heated argument or you solicit it directly. "You could always ask a family member or someone else who knows you are stuck with them to tell you honestly what they think of you," says Funder. Publicist Levine took this approach a bit further when he asked several ex-girlfriends to each list three positive and three negative aspects of being in a relationship with him. "There was some consistency in their answers," he says. "It was challenging to take it in, but really helpful."

"There's always a trade-off between how you want to feel and what you want to know," says DePaulo. If ignorance is bliss, maybe it's best to trust someone's instinct to protect you. "But there are times when you really need accurate feedback," she says, "such as when you are trying to decide if you would be good in a certain career."

Perhaps the delicate balance between feeling good about yourself and knowing exactly how you come off is best maintained not by all those elusive "others." Maybe it's maintained by your most significant ones, the people who will keep you in line but appreciate you for who you are, not just for the impressions you leave behind.

Feeling Smart: The Science of Emotional Intelligence

A new idea in psychology has matured and shows promise of explaining how attending to emotions can help us in everyday life

DAISY GREWAL AND PETER SALOVEY

Over the past decade almost everyone tuned in to American popular culture has heard the term *emotional intelligence.* As a new concept, emotional intelligence has been a hit: It has been the subject of several books, including a best seller, and myriad talk-show discussions and seminars for schools and organizations. Today you can hire a coach to help you raise your "EQ," your emotional quotient—or your child's.

Despite (or perhaps because of) its high public profile, emotional intelligence has attracted considerable scientific criticism. Some of the controversy arises from the fact that popular and scientific definitions of emotional intelligence differ sharply. In addition, measuring emotional intelligence has not been easy. Despite these difficulties, research on emotional intelligence has managed to sustain itself and in fact shows considerable promise as a serious line of scientific inquiry. It turns out that emotional intelligence can indeed be measured, as a set of mental abilities, and that doing so is an informative exercise that can help individuals understand the role of emotions in their everyday lives.

Ten years after the appearance of that bestselling book and a *TIME* magazine cover that asked "What's your EQ?" it seems sensible to ask what is known, scientifically, about emotional intelligence. In the history of modern psychology, the concept represents a stage in the evolution of our thinking about the relation between passion and reason and represents an important outgrowth of new theories of intelligence. Work in this subfield has produced a four-factor model of emotional intelligence that serves as a guide for empirical research. In this article we will explain ways of assessing emotional intelligence using ability-based tests and some of the findings that have resulted from this method.

Before "Emotional Intelligence"

Philosophers have debated the relation between thought and emotions for at least two millennia. The Stoics of ancient Greece and Rome believed emotion far too heated and unpredictable to be of much use to rational thought. Emotion was also strongly associated with women, in their view, and therefore representative of the weak, inferior aspects of humanity. The stereotype of women as the more "emotional" sex is one that persists today. Even though various romantic movements embraced emotion over the centuries, the Stoic view of emotions as more or less irrational persisted in one form or another well into the 20th century.

But many notions were upended during the rapid development of modern psychology in the 20th century. Setting the stage for a new way of thinking about emotions and thought, psychologists articulated broader definitions of intelligence and also new perspectives on the relation between feeling and thinking. As early as the 1930s, psychometrician Robert Thorndike mentioned the possibility that people might have a "social intelligence"—an ability to perceive their own and others' internal states, motivations and behaviors, and act accordingly. In 1934 David Wechsler, the psychologist whose name today attaches to two well-known intelligence tests, wrote about the "nonintellective" aspects of a person that contribute to overall intelligence. Thorndike's and Wechsler's statements were, however, speculations. Even though social intelligence seemed a definite possibility, Thorndike admitted that there existed little scientific evidence of its presence. A similar conclusion was reached by psychometric expert Lee Cronbach, who in 1960 declared that, after half a century of speculation, social intelligence remained "undefined and unmeasured."

But the 1980s brought a surge of new interest in expanding the definition of intelligence. In 1983 Howard Gardner of Harvard University became famous overnight when, in the book *Frames of Mind,* he outlined seven distinct forms of intelligence. Gardner proposed an "intrapersonal intelligence" very similar to the current conceptualization of emotional intelligence. "The core capacity at work here," he wrote, "is access to one's own feeling life—one's range of affects or emotions: the capacity instantly to effect discriminations among these feelings and, eventually, to label them, to enmesh them in symbolic codes, to draw upon them as a means of understanding and guiding one's behavior."

Is "emotional intelligence," then, simply a new name for social intelligence and other already-defined "intelligences"? We hope to clear up this thorny question by explaining just what we attempt to measure when assessing emotional intelligence. Certainly it can be seen as a type of social intelligence. But we prefer to explicitly focus on the processing of emotions and knowledge about emotion-related information and suggest that this constitutes its own form of intelligence. Social intelligence is very broadly defined, and partly for this reason the pertinent skills involved have remained elusive to scientists.

Emotional intelligence is a more focused concept. Dealing with emotions certainly has important implications for social relationships, but emotions also contribute to other aspects of life. Each of us has a need to set priorities, orient positively toward future endeavors and repair negative moods before they spiral into anxiety and depression. The concept of emotional intelligence isolates a specific set of skills embedded within the abilities that are broadly encompassed by the notion of social intelligence.

Emotion and Thinking

New understandings of the relation between thought and emotion have strengthened the scientific foundation of the study of emotional intelligence. Using a simple decision-making task, neurologist Antonio R. Damasio and his colleagues at the University of Iowa have provided convincing evidence that emotion and reason are essentially inseparable. When making decisions, people often focus on the logical pros and cons of the choices they face. However, Damasio has shown that without feelings, the decisions we make may not be in our best interest.

In the early 1990s Damasio had people participate in a gambling task in which the goal is to maximize profit on a loan of play money. Participants were instructed to select 100 cards, one at a time, from four different decks. The experimenter arranged the cards such that two of the decks provided larger payoffs ($100 compared to only $50) but also doled out larger penalties at unpredictable intervals. Players who chose from the higher-reward, higher risk decks lost a net of $250 every 10 cards; those choosing the $50 decks gained a net of $250 every 10 cards.

One group of participants in this study had been identified as having lesions to the ventromedial prefrontal cortex of the brain. Patients with this type of brain damage have normal intellectual function but are unable to use emotion in making decisions. The other group was normal, meaning that their brains were fully intact. Because there was no way for any of the players to calculate precisely which decks were riskier, they had to rely on their "gut" feelings to avoid losing money.

Damasio's group demonstrated that the brain-lesion patients failed to pay attention to these feelings (which he deems "somatic markers") and subsequently lost significantly more money than the normal participants. Therefore, defects in the brain that impair emotion and feeling detection can subse-

quently impair decision-making. Damasio concluded that "individuals make judgments not only by assessing the severity of outcomes, but also and primarily in terms of their emotional quality." This experiment demonstrates that emotions and thought processes are closely connected. Whatever notions we draw from our Stoic and Cartesian heritages, separating thinking and feeling is not necessarily more adaptive and may, in some cases, lead to disastrous consequences.

The Four-Branch Model

The term "emotional intelligence" was perhaps first used in an unpublished dissertation in 1986. One of us (Salovey), along with John D. Mayer of the University of New Hampshire, introduced it to scientific psychology in 1990, defining emotional intelligence as "the ability to monitor one's own and others' feelings, to discriminate among them, and to use this information to guide one's thinking and action."

Some critics have seen the concept of emotional intelligence as a mere outgrowth of the late-20th-century Zeitgeist—and indeed, as we reflect in the conclusion to this article, today the term has a vibrant pop-culture life of its own. But within psychology, the concept developed out of a growing emphasis on research on the interaction of emotion and thought. In the late 1970s psychologists conducted experiments that looked at a number of seemingly unrelated topics at the interface of feeling and thinking: the effect of depression on memory, the perception of emotion in facial expressions, the functional importance of regulating or expressing emotion.

Emotional intelligence is one of the concepts that emerged from this work. It integrates a number of the results into a related set of skills that can be measured and differentiated from personality and social skills; within psychology it can be defined as an intelligence because it is a quantifiable and indeed a measurable aspect of the individual's capacity to carry out abstract thought and to learn and adapt to the environment. Emotional intelligence can be shown to operate on emotional information in the same way that other types of intelligence might operate on a broken computer or what a photographer sees in her viewfinder.

Interested in helping the field of emotions develop a theory that would organize the numerous efforts to find individual difference in emotion-related processes, Salovey and Mayer proposed a four-branch model of emotional intelligence that emphasized four domains of related skills: (a) the ability to perceive emotions accurately; (b) the ability to use emotions to facilitate thinking and reasoning; (c) the ability to understand emotions, especially the language of emotions; and (d) the ability to manage emotions both in oneself and in others. This four-branch emotional intelligence model proposes that individuals differ in these skills and that these differences have consequences at home, school and work, and in social relations.

Perceiving and Using Emotions

The first domain of emotional intelligence, *perceiving emotions,* includes the abilities involved in identifying emotions in faces, voices, pictures, music and other stimuli. For example, the individual who excels at perceiving emotions can quickly tell when his friend is upset by accurately decoding his friend's facial expressions.

One might consider this the most basic skill involved in emotional intelligence because it makes all other processing of emotional information possible. In addition, our skill at reading faces is one of the attributes humans share across cultures. Paul Ekman of the University of California, San Francisco showed pictures of Americans expressing different emotions to a group of isolated New Guineans. He found that the New Guineans could recognize what emotions were being expressed in the photographs quite accurately, even though they had never encountered an American and had grown up in a completely different culture.

But emotion perception does vary across individuals. A study by Seth D. Pollak at the University of Wisconsin-Madison in 2000, for example, demonstrated that physical abuse might interfere with children's ability to adaptively perceive facial expressions.

Pollak asked abused and nonabused children, aged 8 to 10, to come into the laboratory to play "computer games." The children were shown digitally morphed faces that displayed emotional expressions that ranged from happy to fearful, happy to sad, angry to fearful, or angry to sad. In one of the games, the children were shown a single picture and asked to identify which emotion it expressed. Because all the faces expressed varying degrees of a certain emotion, the investigators were able to discover how the children perceived different facial expressions. They found that the abused children were more likely to categorize a face as angry, even when it showed only a slight amount of anger.

In addition, Pollak measured the brain activity of the children while completing this task using electrodes attached to their scalps. The abused children also exhibited more brain activity when viewing an angry face. This research shows that life experiences can strongly shape the recognition of facial expression. We can speculate that this difference in likelihood to perceive anger may have important consequences for the children's interactions with other people.

The second branch of emotional intelligence, *using emotions,* is the ability to harness emotional information to facilitate other cognitive activities. Certain moods may create mind-sets that are better suited for certain kinds of tasks.

In a clever experiment done during the 1980s, Alice Isen of Cornell University found that being in a happy mood helps people generate more creative solutions to problems. Isen brought undergraduates into the laboratory and induced either a positive mood (by showing them comedy clips) or a neutral mood (by showing them a short segment from a math film).

After watching one of the films, each student was seated at an individual table and given a book of matches, a box of tacks and a candle. Above the table was a corkboard. The students were given 10 minutes to provide a solution to the following challenge: how to affix the candle to the corkboard in such a way that it would burn without dripping wax onto the table. Those students who had watched the comedy films, and were therefore in a happier mood, were more likely to come up with an adequate solu-

tion to the problem: They realized that the task can be easily accomplished by emptying the box, tacking it to the wall and using it as a platform for the candle. It appears that emotional intelligence can facilitate certain tasks; the emotionally intelligent person can utilize pleasant feelings most effectively.

Understanding and Managing Emotion

Mayer and Salovey classified the third and fourth branches of the emotional intelligence model as "strategic" (rather than "experiential") intelligence. The third branch, *understanding emotions,* is the ability to comprehend information about relations between emotions, transitions from one emotion to another, and to label emotions using emotion words. A person who is good at understanding emotions would have the ability to see differences between related emotions, such as between pride and joy. The same individual would also be able to recognize, for instance, that irritation can lead to rage if left unattended.

Boston College psychologist Lisa Feldman Barrett has demonstrated that the ability to differentiate one's emotional states has important implications for well-being. Feldman Barrett and her colleagues asked a group of 53 undergraduates to keep a daily diary of their emotions for two weeks. Specifically, they assessed the most intense emotional experience they had each day by rating the intensity of their experience of nine emotions, represented by words, on a scale from 0, *not at all,* to 4, *very much.* Four of the emotion words related to positive emotion (happiness, joy, enthusiasm, amusement); five related to negative emotion (nervous, angry, sad, ashamed, guilty).

Feldman Barrett and her colleagues then calculated the correlations between reported experiences of positive emotions and also looked at how correlated were reported experiences of negative emotions. A subject whose reports of positive emotions are highly correlated is perceiving less differentiation between positive states. Similarly, larger correlations between the reports of each negative emotion indicate less differentiation between negative states.

At the end of the study, all participants completed a questionnaire assessing the extent to which they engaged in various emotion-regulation strategies during the previous two weeks (for example, "talking to others"). Greater differentiation between positive emotional states had no effect on regulation strategies. But differentiation of negative states clearly did. That is, participants who were able to more specifically pinpoint *what* negative emotion they were feeling each day also engaged in more strategies for managing their emotions. This shows that the ability to distinguish and label emotions may represent an important skill in learning how to handle emotions successfully.

The fourth branch of emotional intelligence is the ability to manage one's emotions as well as the emotions of others. This skill of *managing emotions* is perhaps the most commonly identified aspect of emotional intelligence. Emotional intelligence is far more than simply being able to regulate bad moods effectively. It can also be important to maintain negative emotions when needed. For example, a speaker trying to persuade her audience of some injustice should have the ability to use her own outrage to stir others to action.

An example of how using different strategies for managing emotions can have different consequences is found in the work of James S. Gross of Stanford University, in experiments during the mid-1990s. Gross showed undergraduates video clips from medical procedures, such as amputation, that elicit disgust. The students were divided into three different groups. In the suppression condition, the students were instructed to hide their emotions during the film as much as possible by limiting their facial expressions. In the reappraisal condition, students were instructed to view the film as objectively as possible and to remain emotionally detached from what they were seeing. The third group was given no special instructions before viewing the film. All of the students' reactions to the films were recorded by video camera, and their physiological reactions, such as heart rate and skin conductance, were also measured. In addition, participants were asked to make self-reports of their feelings before, during and after watching the film.

The students in the suppression and reappraisal conditions had strikingly different experiences from watching the film. In the suppression condition, participants were able to successfully reduce the outward experience of their emotions by reducing their facial expressions and other behavioral reactions to the film. However, they showed heightened physiological arousal and reported feeling as much disgust as controls. The participants in the reappraisal condition reported lower levels of disgust upon watching the film while not displaying any heightened physical arousal (compared to controls). Gross's work demonstrates that there might be important, and sometimes hidden, physical costs for those individuals who chronically suppress expression of their negative emotions; nevertheless, monitoring and evaluating one's emotions may be strategically useful.

Measuring Emotional Intelligence

Any attribute being suggested as a form of intelligence must meet the standards of psychometrics, the field of psychological measurement. Scientists must be able to show that tests do not merely capture personality traits or information about other abilities. Three approaches to measuring emotional intelligence have been used: self-report tests, reports made by others and ability-based tests. Self-report tests were developed first and continue to be widely used, owing to the ease with which they can be administered and scored. Test-takers agree or disagree with items that attempt to capture various aspects of perceived emotional intelligence. For example, the popular Self-Report Emotional Intelligence Test (SREIT), authored by Nicola Schutte, asks respondents to rate how much they agree with such items as "I have control over my emotions," and "(other people find it easy to confide in me.)"

Reports made by others are commonly collected using "360" instruments. People who frequently interact with one another (such as friends and colleagues) are asked to rate one another's apparent degree of emotional intelligence. These instruments commonly contain items similar to those used in self-report tests, such as the statement "This person has control over his or her emotions."

Unfortunately, self-report tests assess self-estimates of attributes that often extend beyond definitions of emotional intelligence. They tend to incorporate facets of personality and character traditionally measured by existing personality tests.

Assessing emotional intelligence through self-report measures also presents the same dilemma one would face in trying to assess standard analytic intelligence by asking people, "Do you think you're smart?" Of course most people want to appear smart. Also, individuals may not have a good idea of their own strengths and weaknesses, especially in the domain of emotions. Similarly, although reports made by others seem more promising in providing accurate information, they are also highly vulnerable to biased viewpoints and subjective interpretations of behavior.

In an attempt to overcome these problems, the first ability-based measure of emotional intelligence was introduced in 1998 in the form of the Multi-factor Emotional Intelligence Scale (MEIS). An improved and professionally published version of the MEIS, from which problematic items were eliminated, was released in 2002 in the form of the Mayer-Salovey-Caruso Emotional Intelligence Test (MSCEIT, named for Mayer, Salovey and collaborator David R. Caruso of the EI Skills Group).

The MSCEIT consists of eight different tasks—two tasks devoted to each of the four branches of emotional intelligence. For example, the first branch, perceiving emotions, is tested by presenting participants with a photograph of a person and then asking them to rate the amount of sadness, happiness, fear etc. that they detect in the person's facial expression. Skill in using emotions is tested by having people indicate how helpful certain moods, such as boredom or happiness, would be for performing certain activities, such as planning a birthday party. The understanding-emotions portion of the test includes questions that ask participants to complete sentences testing their knowledge of emotion vocabulary and how emotions can progress from one to another. The test section addressing the fourth branch, managing emotions, presents participants with real-life scenarios. Participants are asked to choose, from several options, the best strategy for handling the emotions brought up in each scenario. After completing the MSCEIT, scores are generated for each of the four branches as well as an overall total score.

How Good Is the Test?

Marc A. Brackett of Yale University and Mayer calculated the extensive overlap between self-report tests of emotional intelligence and commonly used tests of personality. Many studies of personality are organized around The Big Five model of personality; they ask participants to self-rate how much they exhibit the following traits; neuroticism, extraversion, openness, agreeableness and conscientiousness.

Brackett and Mayer administered scales assessing The Big Five to a group of college students along with the MSCEIT and the SREIT. They found that scores on Big Five personality traits were more highly correlated with participants' scores on the

SREIT than on the MSCEIT. The trait of "extraversion," for example, had a correlation of 0.37 with scores on the SREIT but only correlated 0.11 with scores on the MSCEIT. Therefore, it appears that self-report tests of emotional intelligence may offer limited information about a person above and beyond standard personality questionnaires.

The biggest problem one faces in trying to use an ability-based measure of emotional intelligence is how to determine correct answers. Unlike traditional intelligence tests, emotional intelligence tests can lack clear right or wrong solutions. There are dozens of ways one could handle many emotion-laden situations, so who should decide which is the emotionally intelligent way of doing things? Intrinsic to the four-branch model of emotional intelligence is the hypothesis that emotional skills cannot be separated from their social context. To use emotions in a useful way, one must be attuned to the social and cultural norms of the environment in which one interacts. Therefore, the model proposes that correct answers will depend highly upon agreement with others of one's own social group. Furthermore, experts on emotion research should also have the ability to identify correct answers, since scientific methods have provided us with good knowledge on correct alternatives to emotion-related problems.

Consequently, the MSCEIT is scored using two different methods: general consensus and expert scoring. In consensus scoring, an individual's answers are statistically compared with the answers that were provided by a diverse worldwide sample of 5,000 respondents aged 18 or older who completed the MSCEIT prior to May 2001. The sample is both educationally and ethnically diverse, with respondents from seven different countries including the United States.

In the consensus approach, greater statistical overlap with the sample's answers reflects higher emotional intelligence. In expert scoring, a person's answers are compared with those provided by a group of emotion experts, in this case 21 emotion investigators elected to the International Society for Research on Emotions (ISRE).

The amount of overlap between consensus and expert scoring has been carefully examined. Participants' responses have been scored first using the consensus method and then the expert method, and these results are then correlated with each other. The average correlation between the two sets of scores is greater than 0.90, indicating sizable overlap between the opinions of experts and the general consensus of test-takers. Laypeople and emotion experts, in other words, converge on the most "emotionally intelligent" answers. The scores of the experts tend to agree with one another more than do those of the consensus group, indicating that emotion experts are more likely to possess a shared social representation of what constitutes emotional intelligence.

The MSCEIT has demonstrated good reliability, meaning that scores tend to be consistent over time and that the test is internally consistent. In sum, given its modest overlap with commonly used tests of personality traits and analytic intelligence, the MSCEIT seems to test reliably for something that is distinct from both personality and IQ.

Putting Research to Work

Research on emotional intelligence has been put to practical use with unusual Speed. The reason may be simple: Experiments suggest that scores on ability-based measures of emotional intelligence are associated with a number of important real-world outcomes.

Emotional intelligence may help one get along with peers and supervisors at work. Paulo N. Lopes of the University of Surrey in the United Kingdom spearheaded a study conducted at a Fortune 500 insurance company where employees worked in teams. Each team was asked to fill out surveys that asked individuals to rate other team members on personal descriptors related to emotions such as, "This person handles stress without getting too tense," or "This person is aware of the feelings of others."

Supervisors in the company were also asked to rate their subordinates on similar items. Everyone who participated in the study also took the MSCEIT. Although the sample of participants was small, employees who scored higher on the MSCEIT received more positive ratings from both their peers and their supervisors. Their peers reported having fewer conflicts with them, and they were perceived as creating a positive atmosphere at work. Supervisors rated their emotionally intelligent employees as more interpersonally sensitive, sociable, tolerant of stress and possessing more leadership potential. Higher scores were also positively associated with rank and salary in the company.

Emotional intelligence may also be important for creating and sustaining good relationships with peers. A different study conducted by Lopes and his collaborators asked German college students to keep diaries that described their everyday interactions with others over a two-week period. For every social interaction that lasted at least 10 minutes, students were asked to record the gender of the person they interacted with, how they felt about the interaction, how much they had wanted to make a certain impression, and to what extent they thought they succeeded in making that impression.

Scores on the using-emotions branch of the MSCEIT were positively related to how enjoyable and interesting students found their interactions to be, as well as how important and safe they felt during them. Scores on the managing-emotions branch seemed most important in interactions with the opposite sex. For these interactions, students scoring high on managing emotions reported more enjoyment, intimacy, interest, importance and respect. In addition, managing emotions was positively related to the students' beliefs that they had made the desired impression on their opposite-sex partners (coming across as friendly, say, or competent).

Brackett also investigated how scores on the MSCEIT relate to the quality of social relationships among college students. American college students completed the MSCEIT along with questionnaires assessing the quality of their friendships and their interpersonal skills, In addition, these students were asked to recruit two of their friends to evaluate the quality of their friendship. Individuals scoring high in managing emotions were rated as more caring and emotionally supportive by their friends. Scores on managing emotions were also negatively related to friends' reports of conflict with them. In another recent study by Nicole Lemer and Brackett, Yale students who scored higher in emotional intelligence were evaluated more positively by their roommates; that is, their roommates reported experiencing less conflict with them.

Emotional intelligence may also help people more successfully navigate their relationships with spouses and romantic partners. Another study headed by Brackett recruited 180 young couples (mean age 25 years) from the London area. The couples completed the MSCEIT and then filled out a variety of questionnaires asking about aspects of the couples' relationships, such as the quality of the interactions with their partners and how happy they were with the relationship. Happiness was correlated with high scores for both partners, and where one partner had a high score and the other a low score, satisfaction ratings tended to fall in the intermediate range.

The Future of Emotional Intelligence

Context plays an important role in shaping how these skills are put into action. We can all name people—certain notable politicians come to mind—who seem extremely talented in using their emotions in their professional lives while their personal lives seem in shambles. People may be more adept at using the skills of emotional intelligence in some situations than in others. A promising direction for future research is a focus on fluid skills rather than crystallized knowledge about emotions.

Although it has proved valuable so far as a test of general emotional intelligence, the MSCEIT requires refinement and improvement. We view the MEIS and the MSCEIT as the first in a potentially long line of improved ways of assessing emotional abilities.

We believe research on emotional intelligence will be especially valuable if focused on individual differences in emotional processes—a topic we hope will continue to generate more empirical interest. The science of emotion thus far has stressed principles of universality. Ekman's work on faces, mentioned above, and similar cross-cultural findings offer important insights into the nature of human emotional experience. However, in any given culture, people differ from one another in their abilities to interpret and use emotional information. Because individual deficits in emotional skills may lead to negative outcomes, anyone interested in improving emotional skills in various settings should focus on how and why some people, from childhood, are better at dealing with emotions than others. Such knowledge provides the hope of being able to successfully teach such skills to others.

The Popularization of "EQ"

Media interest in emotional intelligence was sparked by *New York Times* science writer Daniel Goleman's bestselling book *Emotional Intelligence* in 1995. In October of the same year came the *TIME* magazine cover and additional media coverage proclaiming emotional intelligence the new way to be smart and the best predictor of success in life.

The late 1990s provided the perfect cultural landscape for the appearance of emotional intelligence. The latest in a string of IQ controversies had broken out with the 1994 publication of *The Bell Curve,* which claimed that modern society has become increasingly stratified not by money, power or class, but by traditionally defined intelligence.

The Bell Curve was read as advocating a view that intelligence is the most important predictor of almost everything that seems to matter to most people: staying healthy, earning enough money, even having a successful marriage. Yet half the population, by definition, has below-average IQs; moreover, IQ is seen as difficult to change over one's lifespan. For many readers, *The Bell Curve* contained an extremely pessimistic message. As if to answer the growing fear that a relatively immutable IQ is the primary predictor of success in life, Goleman's book on emotional intelligence included the phrase, "Why it can matter more than IQ," right on the cover. The public responded favorably to this new promise, and the book soon became a staple on airport newsstands worldwide.

Skepticism over narrow definitions of the word "intelligence" resonated powerfully with a public that seemed to agree that something else—something more intangible—may more strongly determine the quality' of one's life. Evidence that the Scholastic Aptitude Test (SAT), which is highly correlated with IQ, fails to predict academic success especially well beyond the first year of college continued to fuel interest in how emotional skills, or something else beside traditional intelligence, may more significantly determine one's future accomplishments. Americans have always prided themselves on a strong work ethic; the motto that "slow and steady wins the race" represents an attitude that fits well with public conceptions of emotional intelligence as a mark of good character. Americans also have a strong collective self-image of equality, which popular views of emotional intelligence support by characterizing success as dependent on a set of skills that anyone can learn.

Goleman's book continues to be one of the most successful and influential of its genre, and other trade books concerned with emotional intelligence (or EQ, as it is referred to in the popular literature) have appeared in recent years. More than just a passing fad, or temporary backlash against standardized testing, emotional intelligence has captured the long-term interest of employers and educators. In just a few years, what started as a somewhat obscure area of science-driven research in psychology burgeoned into a multi-million-dollar industry marketing books, tapes, seminars and training programs aimed at increasing emotional intelligence.

Popularization has in some cases distorted the original scientific definition of emotional intelligence. Many people now equate emotional intelligence with almost everything desirable in a person's makeup that cannot be measured by an IQ test, such as character, motivation, confidence, mental stability, optimism and "people skills." Research has shown that emotional skills may contribute to some of these qualities, but most of them move far beyond skill-based emotional intelligence. We prefer to define emotional intelligence as a specific set of skills that can be used for either prosocial or antisocial purposes. The ability to accurately perceive how others are feeling may be used by a therapist to gauge how best to help her clients, whereas a con artist might use it to manipulate potential victims. Being emotionally intelligent does not necessarily make one an ethical person.

Although popular claims regarding emotional intelligence run far ahead of what research can reasonably support, the overall effects of the publicity have been more beneficial than harmful. The most positive aspect of this popularization is a new and much needed emphasis on emotion by employers, educators and others interested in promoting social welfare. The popularization of emotional intelligence has helped both the public and research psychology reevaluate the functionality of emotions and how they serve humans adaptively in everyday life. Although the continuing popular appeal of emotional intelligence is both warranted and desirable, we hope that such attention will stimulate a greater interest in the scientific and scholarly study of emotion. It is our hope that in coming decades, advances in cognitive and affective science will offer intertwining perspectives from which to study how people navigate their lives. Emotional intelligence, with its focus on both head and heart, may adequately serve to point us in the right direction.

Bibliography

Bechara, A., H. Damasio and A. R. Damasio. 2000. Emotion, decision making and the orbitofrontal cortex. *Cerebral Cortex* 10:295–307.

Brackett, M. A., and J. D. Mayer. 2003. Convergent, discriminant, and incremental validity of competing measures of emotional intelligence. *Personality and Social Psychology Bulletin* 29:1147–1158

Daniasio, A. R. 1994. *Descartes' Error, Emotion, Reason, and the Human Brain.* New York: Putnam.

Ekman, P. 1980. *The Face of Man: Expressions of Universal Emotions in a New Guinea Village.* New York: Garland STPM Press.

Feldman Barrett, L., J. Gross, T. Christensen and M. Benvenuto. 2001. Knowing what you're feeling and knowing what to do about it: Mapping the relation between emotion differentiation and emotion regulation. *Cognition and Emotion* 15:713–724.

Gardner, H. 1983. *Frames of Mind.* New York: Basic Books.

Goleman, D. 1995. *Emotional Intelligence.* New York: Bantam Books.

Gross, J. J. 1998. Antecedent and response focused emotion regulation: Divergent consequences for experience, expression, and physiology, *Journal of Personality and Social Psychology* 74:224–237,

Isen, A. M., K. A. Daubman and C. P. Nowicki. 1987. Positive affect facilitates creative problem solving, *Journal of Personality and Social Psychology* 52:1122–1131

Lopes, P. N., M. A. Brackett, J. Nezlck, A. Schutz, I. Sellin and P. Salovey. 2004. Emotional intelligence and social interaction. *Personality and Social Psychology Bulletin* 30:1018–1034.

Lopes, P. N., S. Côté, D. Grewal, J. Kadis, M. Gall and P. Salovey. Submitted. Evidence that emotional intelligence is related to job performance, interpersonal facilitation, affect and attitudes at work, and leadership potential.

Mayer, J. D., and P. Salovey. 1997. What is emotional intelligence? In *Emotional Development and Emotional Intelligence: Educational Implications,* ed. P. Salovey and D. Sluyter, pp. 3–31. New York: Basic Books.

Mayer, J. D., P. Salovey and D. Caruso. 2002. *The Mayer-Salovey-Caruso Emotional Intelligence Test (MSCEIT).* Toronto: Multi-Health Systems, Inc.

Mayer, J. D., P. Salovey, D. R. Caruso and G. Sitarenios. 2003. Measuring emotional intelligence with the MSCEIT V2.0. *Emotion* 3:97–105.

Pollak, S. D., and S. Tolley-Schell. 2003. Selective attention to facial emotion in physically abused children. *Journal of Abnormal Psychology* 22:323–338.

Salovey, P, and J. D. Mayer. 1990. Emotional intelligence. *Imagination, Cognition, and Personality* 9:185–211.

Salovey, P, J. D. Mayer and D. Caruso. 2002. The positive psychology of emotional intelligence. In *Handbook of Positive Psychology,* ed. C. R. Snyder and S. J. Lopez, pp. 159–171. New York: Oxford University Press.

DAISY GREWAL is a doctoral student in the social psychology program at Yale University. She received her B.A. in psychology from the University of California, Los Angeles in 2002 and her M.S. in psychology from Yale in 2004. Her research focuses on gender stereotypes and prejudice, particularly in organizational contexts. **PETER SALOVEY,** who earned his Ph.D. from Yale in 1986, is Dean of Yale College and Chris Argyris Professor of Psychology at Yale, where he directs the Health, Emotion, and Behavior Laboratory and holds additional professorships in management, epidemiology and public health, and social and political studies. His research emphases are the psychological significance and function of mood and emotion, and the application of principles from social and personality psychology to promoting healthy behavior. Address for Salovey: Yale University, Department of Psychology, 2 Hillhouse Avenue, New Haven, CT 06520-8205. Internet for both: daisy.grewal@yale.edu.peter.salovey@yale.edu

From *American Scientist*, July/August 2005, pp. 330–339. Copyright © 2005 by American Scientist, magazine of Sigma Xi, The Scientific Research Society. Reprinted by permission.

What's Your Emotional IQ?

Emotional intelligence can affect your mental and physical health, as well as those around you.

MELISSA ABRAMOVITZ

On March 5, 2001, 15-year-old Andy Williams brought a 22-caliber pistol to school at Santana High School in Santee, California. With a smile on his face, he used the gun to kill two students and injure 13 other people. When later asked why he did it, Williams revealed that he'd had enough of his schoolmates' teasing, taunting, and ostracism because he was small and scrawny.

Some of Williams' friends reported that, prior to the shooting, the boy frequently drank alcohol and used illegal drugs. He also made repeated threats to shoot students at the school, but no one took these threats seriously. "I didn't think he was like that," said one boy who had laughed off Williams' promises to kill others.

Both Andy Williams' horrific act and his friends' lack of insight into his true intentions and feelings are frightening examples of how the lack of emotional intelligence can have disastrous consequences. Williams' inability to cope productively with his feelings of anger and rejection led him to endanger himself and others with drugs and violence. In a similar manner, his friends' unwillingness or inability to detect the desperation in his threats prevented them from stopping him from carrying out his deadly plans.

What Is EI?

Emotional intelligence, or EI, is similar to cerebral intelligence, except that it involves awareness and insight into emotions rather than into other mental functions. Emotional IQ, also known as EQ (emotional quotient), refers to measurements of an individual's ability to understand and manage his or her emotions and interpersonal relationships.

Although many of the ideas related to EI and EQ were originally applied to business and leadership skills, these concepts are also relevant to everyday living and health. EI and EQ affect many aspects of an individual's mental and physical well-being, as well as the ability to get along with others, to make wise life style choices, and to succeed in school, athletics, careers, and other areas.

Recent studies indicate that programs which seek to prevent violence, teen smoking, drug abuse, pregnancy, and dropping out of school are most effective when they address the elements of emotional intelligence. Indeed, according to the Center for the Advancement of Health in Washington, D.C., "Nearly half of the nation's premature deaths are attributable to controllable behavioral factors, such as using tobacco, alcohol, and illegal substances and engaging in risky sex." The center concludes that to be effective, a program must integrate behavioral and psychological perspectives with biomedical interventions.

Experts say that developing emotional intelligence can help you avoid both short-term injury risks and long-term illnesses such as heart disease, liver disease, and some cancers. These hazards are often a result of substance abuse and other dangerous lifestyle choices that go along with out-of-control emotional stress. Says Jan Wallender, Ph.D., "The way we feel and think and relate to others definitely has an impact on our biology, our health, and our disease experience."

The Elements of EI

Daniel Goleman, Ph.D., a well-known psychologist, has written extensively on the subject of EI and has identified five basic elements: self-awareness, managing emotions, motivating oneself, empathy, and social skills. Goleman and other EI experts point out that these elements are not automatically set in stone at birth, but instead can be learned and improved upon throughout a person's lifetime. Accordingly, many schools and businesses now offer EI training programs to help students and employees learn about and master these five aspects of dealing effectively with everyday challenges to emotional stability.

1. Self-awareness refers to the ability to recognize and identify your feelings. The EI experts emphasize that it's important to be able to recognize emotions such as anger or love in order to act appropriately. Bullies, for example, generally do not recognize their own feelings of insecurity or unhappiness and behave aggressively toward others as a result. One way that everyone can improve self-awareness is to verbalize emotions rather than ignore them. If you're angry, say "I'm angry" and explain why. If you're frightened, admit it, at least to yourself. Trying to appear tough and invincible at all times is OK only for legendary superheroes who don't have to live with their emotions the way real people do.

2. Managing your emotions involves using techniques for handling all sorts of feelings in a productive and appropriate manner. If your best friend suddenly informs you she has a new best friend, for example, most likely you will feel hurt, angry, and jealous. If you don't manage these emotions wisely, you might do something that you would probably regret. By effectively managing your emotions, though, hopefully you could take a deep breath, count to 10, control your desire to tell her off, and muster the strength to say something like, "I'm sorry you made that choice. I value our friendship and hope we can discuss this sometime."

3. Motivating oneself builds on managing your emotions to the extent that you can delay the immediate gratification of an impulse and can maintain a positive outlook. Studies show that individuals who are able to restrain themselves from immediately fulfilling a desire are more optimistic and successful in school, athletics, careers, and interpersonal relationships. This is due in part to using self-restraint, which is an important indicator of how someone responds to challenges. If you flunk a math test and say, "I'll never pass math, so I'm going to quit going to class," you will definitely not improve your math skills. If, however, you realize that going for tutoring can help you do better in the future, you have a good chance of passing the course and of applying these perseverance skills to other areas of your life.

4. Empathy is being sensitive to and understanding other people's feelings. Some individuals seem to have a natural ability to empathize, but this, like the other elements of EI, can be learned. To hone your empathy skills, try "putting yourself in someone else's shoes" and asking yourself how you would feel in his or her situation. Another useful technique is to focus on "reading" people's facial expressions and other body cues to gauge their true feelings. For example, observing the face and body language of a guy who says "I'm not scared"—yet exhibits wide-eyed terror and hunches his shoulders forward—will help you realize that this guy is definitely scared.

5. Social skills refers to an individuals's ability to interact with others in a positive and productive manner. Actually, if you do your homework on the other four elements of EI and master those concepts, you should be in pretty good shape in the social skills department. People who are self-aware, successfully manage their emotions, are motivated, and are able to empathize are generally quite adept in social situations.

How EI Affects the World

While emotional intelligence is certainly not a cure-all for the ills that exist in the world, it is an important factor in many global and personal issues. Road rage, child and spousal abuse, and school shootings are just a few of the serious problems in our society that raising people's EI can address. Experts point out that children and teens are especially vulnerable to the dangers of what psychologists call "emotional malaise." To combat this problem, many schools are including emotional-awareness training in their programs.

You alone have the power to improve your emotional intelligence with practice and effort. And becoming aware of your

Test Your Emotional IQ

How would you deal with these emotional intelligence issues?

1. After a classmate dies in a car accident, you
   a. tell yourself it couldn't happen to you.
   b. realize you are feeling intense fear and sadness.
2. You've just been offered a beer at a party. Your friend Jamie says you're a wuss if you don't chug it. You don't want to be a wuss, so you
   a. drink the beer.
   b. politely refuse since you promised your parents there would be no alcohol at the party.
3. When you feel depressed, you
   a. cry and feel sorry for yourself.
   b. try to find a positive distraction like volunteering at a homeless shelter.
4. Your best friend just got dumped by his girlfriend. You
   a. tell him it doesn't matter.
   b. understand he's feeling depressed and encourage him to talk about it.
5. You hardly know anyone on your new hockey team. You
   a. request a transfer to a team where you know more people.
   b. look forward to getting to know the new people.

How did you do?

If you answered with a's, your emotional IQ needs some work. You are having trouble recognizing and managing your own emotions and recognizing other people's emotions. If you chose mostly b's, it means your emotional IQ is way up there! You are most likely successfully recognizing and managing your emotions and have good interpersonal relationships skills.

emotional intelligence can be beneficial not only to your own health and happiness, but it can also help make the world a more civilized and peaceful place.

For Review

1. Define emotional intelligence. (It is similar to cerebral intelligence, except it involves awareness and insight into emotions rather than other mental functions. EQ is a measure of an individual's ability to understand and manage his or her emotions and interpersonal relationships.)

2. Summarize the five elements of emotional intelligence. (They include self-awareness—the ability to recognize and identify your feelings; managing emotions—using techniques for handling all sorts of feelings in a productive and appropriate manner; motivating oneself—ability to manage your emotions well enough to be able to delay immediate gratification of an impulse and to maintain a positive outlook; empathy—being sensitive to and understanding other people's feelings; and hav-

ing social skills—the ability to interact with others in a positive, productive manner.)

Activity

Based on the five elements of emotional intelligence in the article, have students work in groups of three or four to write a skit in which a fellow student demonstrates a fairly low emotional intelligence. Have them act out the skits for the class and allow them to critique and make observations on the EI of the characters as they saw it. Then allow the authors of each skit to rewrite it to demonstrate improved EI skills.

Us vs. Them

Some people push our buttons by what they do or even who they are. These seven steps lead away from criticizing and rejecting, and toward the healing power of forgiving and forgetting.

RAPHAEL CUSHNIR

People bug me. All kinds of people. Like the guy who takes up two parking spaces for his SUV. Or the kids who toss beer cans along my favorite hiking trail.

Okay, let me be more honest. I actually feel hateful toward these people. When I think about them, my stomach clenches and my eyes narrow and I feel an ugly surge of, well, hate. It doesn't last that long, and I don't identify with it, yet still, for that one quick moment when I'm awash in hate's fury, I just want to wring their necks.

Why does this matter? Because I'm supposed to be a "spiritual teacher." After a successful career as a Hollywood screenwriter and filmmaker, my life fell apart, my heart broke wide open, and now I write books on happiness and love and travel around the country trying to teach people how to achieve them. Does that make me a hypocrite? I'll let you decide. But one thing is certain: it makes me a human being.

Human beings love to hate. Even more, they love to judge. While hate is a feeling, judgment is its rationale. We allow ourselves the perverse pleasure of our hatred when we decide that those who elicit it are evil, or some kind of threat, or that they've wronged us. Even when we're not actually in the direct experience of hate, we still thrive on enumerating all the reasons that these people are different from us, less than us.

> **Sometimes, those of us who pride ourselves on personal growth, who think we're beyond judgment, turn out to be the most judgmental of all.**

Of course, I've exaggerated to make a point. Often, what accompanies our judgments is just irritation or annoyance, rather than full-blown hatred. That's certainly the case with the personal examples above. But such low-grade judgments can actually be even more toxic than the hate-fueled variety. This is because they're able to proliferate beneath our radar. Not only

can we be unaware that they exist, but we may even deny them outright. Sometimes, those of us who pride ourselves on personal growth, who think we're beyond judgment, turn out to be the most judgmental of all.

The Bible admonishes, "Judge not lest ye be judged." But in my experience it's impossible not to judge. We all do it, all the time. And it hurts us far more than those we judge. It isolates us, makes us small, and bars us from our spiritual essence. None of this, however, is a problem. In fact it's an opportunity. Recognizing our judgments, and working with them skillfully, is how we cultivate compassion. And cultivating compassion, I believe, is the key to well-being.

An Open and Shut Case

Think of someone you love. Choose a person whose very name brings about an automatic inner smile. Next, invite all the emotions and sensations associated with this person to fill you up completely. Then turn your attention to your body and notice what you feel. Chances are you feel open, flowing, a little more connected to yourself and the world around you. This state of being, which we'll refer to Expansion, is what allows us to be fully present in any moment or situation. It's also the pathway to our greatest wisdom and creativity.

Now think of someone truly reprehensible. Whether part of your own life or a public figure, make sure this is a person whom you judge harshly. Next, invite all that judgment to fill you up completely. Then turn your attention to your body and notice what you feel.

Chances are you feel scrunched up, shut down, a little less connected to yourself and the world around you. This state of being, which we'll refer to as Contraction, is what limits our presence in any moment or situation. In a contracted state, we're unable to gain access to the breadth and depth of our perspective, or to cultivate peace of mind.

Most of the time, we exist somewhere between the opposing poles of expansion and contraction. But taken together, these two simple exercises point toward an important principle: judgment makes us feel bad. And when we feel bad, it's much harder to be our best.

Caveman Logic

Even if this principle were well understood, however, it wouldn't be enough to make us surrender our most closely held judgments. That's because there's an instinctive part of our brains that functions in a strictly binary fashion. All it knows is yes/no, good/bad, us/them. Psychologists refer to this aspect of thought as "primitive splitting." When we're expanded, such primitive splitting easily gives way to a more nuanced outlook. But when we're contracted, primitive splitting takes hold of us like a hypnotic trance.

The first key in breaking this trance is awareness. Once we realize the impact of primitive splitting, it becomes natural to regard virtually every judgment with suspicion.

I experienced this awareness for the first time in my early thirties. It was Thanksgiving dinner. Something was said and I suddenly felt furious with both my parents. In my mind they weren't just bad; they were all bad. This wasn't a new feeling, but with a recent understanding of primitive splitting, I was no longer willing to indulge myself. It just didn't feel right anymore to stay up late, nibbling leftovers, dissecting my parents' shortcomings with equally disdainful siblings.

Still, I couldn't let go of my judgments just by force of will. I needed the help of my fiancée. Both of us had spent time in the film industry, so I put it to her this way: "When I watch characters in a movie, no matter how despicable their actions I can always see them as whole. I can appreciate the personal histories that led them to their transgressions. But I just can't seem to do that with Mom and Dad. So help me, describe them for me as if they were totally fictional."

But in my experience it's impossible not to judge. We all do it, all the time. And it hurts us far more than those we judge. It isolates us, makes us small, bars us from our spiritual essence.

It worked like magic. The trance broke. By imagining them cinematically, I was able to view my parents with sudden expansion. They still had flaws, of course, just like me and everyone else, but they weren't my own mind-made monsters anymore.

There Is No Them

Once we're aware of primitive splitting, it's easier to look more closely at two related fallacies of the judgmental mind. The first is our tendency to group people we disagree with into an opposing camp. This creates the "them" in us vs. them. It may include those of a different religion, political view, gender, sexual

preference, aesthetic, subculture, personality type, class, ethnicity, culture, location, lifestyle, or even just a single opinion or trait that veers from ours.

The main result, when we group people in this way, is that we feel better than them. It may be a temporary salve, but underneath this illusion of superiority is a sense of separation. Separation always leads to contraction, which is at the heart of why judgment feels so bad. (Plus, even if we actually were "better" than those we judge on some ultimate moral scale, the very act of our judging, ironically, would serve to erase that distinction once and for all.)

One example of how this works is when someone cuts us off in traffic. Usually, even if we don't like to admit it, our initial fit of pique leads to an automatic mental tirade such as Those damn [fill in ethnic group]! Or fat people. Or rich people. Or tourists. After such an outburst, whether shouted silently or at full volume, there may be a momentary satisfaction. The results of such condemnation, however, far outweigh any benefit.

Another example is in an exercise that I routinely include at workshops after days of bonding and mutual support have brought everyone close together. At this point I ask participants to look around the room and imagine that every person they see holds a viewpoint on abortion that's vehemently opposed to their own. Then I ask them to notice if just this imaginary division of opinion creates a sense of superiority, separation, and contraction. The answer is always yes.

But this exercise, helpful as it is, carries within it the second and related fallacy of the judgmental mind. Whenever we lump people into a "them" of any variety, there's an assumption that all those in the group are basically the same. We may call them Palestinians, or lawyers, or tree huggers, or fundamentalists. Though it's necessary to use such labels to communicate, at the same time they're always false. Only from a distance do any two individuals seem alike. While they may share certain key characteristics, there are also millions of distinctions—inherited, learned, chosen—that make them absolutely unique.

Therefore, at best, labeling any type of "them" is a dangerous convenience. In addition to perpetuating contraction, it dulls our wisdom and distorts our interactions. This is true at every level of society, from governments to organizations to families to the secret corners of our own minds.

There Is No Us

At this point, you may be thinking that the readers of *Spirituality & Health* probably need to hear this message far less than most people. You may conclude, as the saying goes, that I'm preaching to the choir. But as someone who travels extensively to churches all across the country, I can tell you with certainty that there is no choir.

By that I mean the following: just as it's a fallacy to think of any opposing group as a uniform "them," it's also a fallacy to think of any of our own communities as a unified "us." There is no such thing as preaching to the choir because there is no choir. This idea can be hard to swallow, because we want there to be an "us." In the core of our being we need to belong. We gain strength in numbers, even when those numbers add up to a small minority. It feels so reaffirming to hear a sermon or stump speech from someone who powerfully puts forth our view, the right view.

And yet, every alliance is temporary. Every coalition is provisional. Every group, no matter how seemingly stable, is in constant flux. It's no surprise that the most successful and dynamic churches I visit are also the ones most in turmoil. Powerful groups are comprised of powerful personalities, and sooner or later cohesion gives way to discord. Sub-groups and splinter groups are always just around the bend. That's why there are Blue Dog Democrats and Log Cabin Republicans, Reform Jews and Liberation Theologists. That's why your diehard group of college friends may not be so tight anymore, and why a reading group that bonds over the shared love of one book may break apart in dissension over another.

Once we're able to embrace that there is no fixed "us," it's no longer as necessary to identify with our judgments, to base our sense of self on who and what we include, exclude, champion or deride. And that's when the real work can begin, when we're finally ready to use our judgments as tools for growth and healing.

The More Aware You Are of Your Judgments, the Easier it Gets to Relax Them

Sit down and take yourself through these steps. You can use them any time judgment surfaces in your life.

Step 1—Judge Away

You've already done this earlier, in the contraction exercise. As you reprise it now, by focusing on someone or something that you find reprehensible, stay with the process until you can easily locate the resulting contraction in your body. Make sure it's palpable, discernibly unpleasant.

Step 2—Melt the Armor

Take your attention off the subject of your judgment and place it fully upon the contraction. Don't try to understand it, change it, or make it go away. Instead, simply keep your attention focused on the sensation of the contraction as it appears in your body. If your mind wanders, gently bring it back. See if you can approach the contraction with a sense of openness, genuine interest and caring.

When you do this, the contraction always releases. It may take a just a moment or a few minutes, but sooner than you imagine the dissolving contraction brings you face to face with the emotion it's been trying to protect you from.

Step 3—Feel Your Way Open

Notice what you're feeling right now—in your body. Is it anger? Frustration? Powerlessness? Hurt? Where do you feel it? In the same place as the contraction, or elsewhere? Is it warm or

cool? Sharp or diffuse? Is it possible to keep your attention on the emotion with the same openness, interest and caring that you brought to the contraction?

If you're able to do this, even for a short while, the emotion will take your cue and begin to flow freely. At this point a number of things may happen. For a time it may become more intense. Or it may disappear. Or it may yield to a more primary emotion. If you began feeling angry, for example, that anger may become hurt, or grief, or humiliation.

No matter what happens in this particular instance, it will arise within a state of expansion. Even if the emotions are difficult to experience, the expanded state in which they occur, as we've seen, is preferable to remaining shut down.

Step 4—Revisit the Villain

After the most intense emotions have passed, and you feel a resulting calm, bring your attention back to the subject of your previous judgment. Are you able to do so without re-experiencing the same intense contraction? If so, you've given yourself a great gift. You've come to know, firsthand, that what often fuels our biggest judgments is a wellspring of unfelt emotion. Once those emotions are felt, the judgment no longer has the same power to cut us off from life.

That's why our judgments of others can be so valuable for growth: they're like flashing neon signs pointing directly to our own stuck places.

If revisiting the "villain" makes you just as contracted as before, don't despair. You may just have a substantial backlog of unfelt emotion and need to repeat steps one through three. Since letting go of judgments can't be rushed, it's important to be patient, and to avoid judging yourself for the amount of time it naturally takes. In addition, the remaining three steps may also help you get unstuck.

Before describing them, however, I'd like to spend a moment discussing a prevalent idea regarding judgment. You may often hear that your judgments of others are projections, and that they reflect some kind of similar transgression in yourself. If you're particularly contracted by people who are cruel, for example, there may be ways that you are unconsciously cruel. Or, perhaps, you may have a hidden cruel streak just dying to get out.

Sometimes, just recognizing such a connection can be liberating, and can take the rebounding sting out of our judgments. In my experience, however, we're not usually able to experience the full benefit of such reflection as long as a reservoir of unfelt emotion still exists. Emotion is the key. That's why feeling it, which for many of us is a lost art, is the most direct route to a more expansive life.

Step 5—Face Off

If one or more of your judgments continue to linger, imagine that the offending party is right in front of you. Without any distance for either of you to hide behind, speak in complete truthfulness about the situation. Scream your words if necessary, paying no mind to civility or political correctness. Keep coming back to your own feelings—I'm so furious! I feel betrayed! My heart is breaking!—so that rather than staying mired in the accusations, you're able to release your own pain.

Step 6—See the Child

To further encourage your expansion, picture the offending party as a newborn, as a toddler, as a student on the first day of school. Did he or she deserve your judgment then? What traumas would have been necessary to lead from childhood innocence to such depravity? Even if you believe in pure evil, that monsters are born rather than made, what must it be like to bear such a curse?

Most of the people we judge clearly are not monsters, and in fact, are much like us. But whatever we hold against them usually stems from some experience or circumstance out of their original control. They're not so much acting in response to the present situation as re-acting to what happened long ago. Recognizing this doesn't make them less responsible, but it may make us a little more likely to soften.

Step 7—Trade Places

Finally, if you still need a little more help, step into the shoes of the person you judge. For just a minute or two, pretend that you are that person, and try to experience the situation from his or her perspective. It's not the person's beliefs or justifications that matter, but how it really feels to live that particular life.

If suddenly you're awash in a painful emotion such as hatred, negativity or bitterness, see if you can touch the awful wounds that gave rise to it. If you encounter a complete lack of feeling, attempt to grasp whole stretches of time so frozen and vacant.

Discernment

As we've explored, the greatest barrier to compassion is judgment. Yet some people in the world seem to have earned our judgment. Rapist, abusers, murderers, terrorists—matter how wounded they may be, their misdeeds can be so heinous that it seems wrong to regard them with compassion.

But one of the best ways to understand compassion is as loving care. It doesn't mean that the recipients of our compassion haven't done wrong to themselves and others. Nor does it deny that they may have committed hideous crimes, deserve serious punishment, and even death according to some. In other words, it's possible to condemn people's actions and still feel compassion toward them.

When that happens, your judgment becomes discernment. What's the difference? With discernment, you're able to remain in a fully expanded state while still possessing a specific opinion, belief or value. Your point of view is no longer hurtful to you. In the expansiveness that follows, you're able to see the offending party, and indeed the whole world, with much greater clarity.

Whoever you've judged, whether as distant as a president or as close as your immediate family, imagine being able to wish them all healing, peace, and a heart as open as your own—and see how you feel.

RAPHAEL CUSHNIR is the author of *Unconditional Bliss: Finding Happiness in the Face of Hardship* and *Setting Your Heart on Fire: Seven Invitations to Liberate Your Life*. For more information, visit heartonfire.org.

From *Spirituality and Health*, May/June 2005, pp. 42-47. Copyright © 2005 by Raphael Cushnir. Reprinted by permission of the author.

Relationships, Human Behavior, and Psychological Science

Extensive evidence attests to the importance of relationships for human well-being, and evolutionary theorizing has increasingly recognized the adaptive significance of relationships. Psychological science, however, has barely begun to consider how relationships influence a broad array of basic social, cognitive, emotional, and behavioral processes. This article discusses contemporary theory and research about the impact of relationship contexts, citing examples from research on social cognition, emotion, and human development. We propose that the validity and usefulness of psychological science will be enhanced by better integration of relationship contexts into theories and research.

A recent cartoon in the *New Yorker* depicts a middle-aged, probably long-married couple reading quietly in their living room. The man turns to his wife and says, "I can't remember which one of us is me." This cartoon embodies an idea whose time has come in the psychological sciences: that human behavior varies significantly depending on relationship +contexts and the cognitive, emotional, and social mechanisms that have evolved for recognizing, evaluating, and responding to those contexts—who else is present and who else is affected by, or has had an effect on, present circumstances. This idea follows from the uncontroversial but often overlooked fact that most human activity involves coordinating one's actions with the actions of others, and that the relative success or failure of such coordination is a principal determinant of productivity and well-being, whether in families, friendships, organizations, neighborhoods, or societies.

Psychological science rarely integrates relationship contexts into its theories and research. One reason for this gap has been the historical focus of psychology on the behavior of individuals. Another has been a shortage of valid concepts, empirical knowledge, and rigorous methods for introducing relationship processes into mainstream psychological research. Recent advances in relationship science—empirical research on relationship processes and their effects—suggest that this void may soon be filled. A virtual explosion of research has provided analytical and methodological tools that allow most psychological or behavioral processes to be investigated from a relationship perspective. The premise of this article is that such investigations will advance the completeness and accuracy of psychological science.

HARRY T. REIS AND W. ANDREW COLLINS

Why Relationships Matter

Abundant evidence attests that associations, often powerful ones, exist between the quality and quantity of relationships and diverse outcomes, including mortality rates, recovery from coronary artery bypass surgery, functioning of the immune system, reactions to stress, psychiatric disturbance, and life satisfaction. These effects do not appear to be artifacts of personality, temperament, behavior, or lifestyles, but instead reflect the direct influence of relationship events on biological processes (e.g., Kiecolt-Glaser & Newton, 2001).

How did the processes by which relationship events affect human biology evolve? Many accounts posit that living and working in small, cooperative groups has been the primary survival strategy for the human species, because social organization buffered early humans from the dangers of the natural environment. Thus, it was adaptive for the human mind to develop a series of mechanisms—Bugental (2000) called them the "algorithms of social life"—for regulating social relations. Social organization is composed of interlocking relationships among individuals within a social network.

Although no definitive list of innate systems for regulating social relations and responding to social circumstances exists, many processes of long-standing interest among behavioral researchers are likely candidates: cooperation and competition, adherence to social norms, coalition formation, attachment, face perception, social inclusion and exclusion, communication of emotion, romantic jealousy, empathy, and commitment, for example. These processes are not applied equally to all of an individual's contacts, but rather are applied selectively, depending on the existing relationship and the particular problem to be solved. People become psychologically attached primarily to caregivers and intimates, and cooperation predominates within in-groups. Social interaction involves determining what sort of relationship exists and therefore which processes are most relevant. Growing evidence that these processes are manifested in nonhuman species and that they are governed to some extent by nonconsciously regulated neurobiological systems suggests that responsiveness to relationship contexts is deeply wired into human architecture.

Relationships may be characterized in terms of the properties that describe the involved parties' interdependence with each other—the manner in which individuals alter their behavior in order to coordinate with others' actions and preferences. Thus, persons in relationships respond (or not) to each other's wishes, concerns, abilities, and emotional expressions; they modify their behavior to be together (or not); they allocate tasks between themselves; they react to each other's behaviors and circumstances, misfortune, and happiness; and they take the fact of their interdependence into account in organizing everyday life and longer-term plans. Central to most conceptualizations of relationship is the idea that these patterns of mutual influence are more informative about relationships than are nominal categories (e.g., spouses, co-workers, friends) or simple static descriptors (e.g., length of acquaintance, nature or degree of affect).

Evidence for differential effects of relationship contexts is available in many areas of research. We next describe three such areas to illustrate the importance of such evidence for psychological science.

Social Cognition

Much research has investigated the cognitive processes by which individuals perceive, interpret, and respond to their social environments. In most such studies, no relationship exists between the subjects and the objects of thought, who are often, for example, strangers, hypothetical people described by the experimenter, famous persons, or social groups. Even when a relationship does exist, its possible influence on the results obtained is rarely considered. This approach tacitly implies that the principles governing cognition about people who are familiar or close do not differ materially from the principles governing cognition about acquaintances and strangers (or, for that matter, inanimate objects). Increasingly, theory and research challenge this assumption.

Take, for example, one of the most robust social-cognitive phenomena: the *self-serving attributional bias*, which refers to the fact that people give themselves more credit for success and less responsibility for failure than they give strangers. This bias, reported in virtually every textbook in the field, is not observed when the self is compared with close relationship partners, who are accorded the same attributional generosity as is the self (Sedikides, Campbell, Reeder, & Elliot, 1998). Other phenomena that reflect self-serving biases also vary depending on the closeness of the relationship.

Another example concerns the well-documented self-referential effect: the enhancement of memory when information is encoded with reference to the self, rather than, for example, another person. This effect is significantly smaller when the other person is an intimate rather than a stranger or acquaintance (Symons & Johnson, 1997). Partners in close or committed relationships typically adopt an interdependent frame of reference ("we," rather than "you

and I"), perhaps because, following the logic of a connectionist model, close relationships entail a greater number of direct connections and overlapping links than distant relationships do (Smith, Coats, & Walling, 1999). Even more suggestive is a recent neural imaging study (Lichty et al., 2004) showing substantial overlap—most strongly, in the right superior frontal gyrus and prefrontal cortex—in the brain regions activated by hearing one's own name and hearing the name of a close friend, but no overlap in the areas of activation associated with hearing one's own name and hearing the name of a familiar (but not close) other person. The degree of overlap in the own-name and close-friend conditions was more pronounced to the extent that the relationship with the other was experienced as a close relationship.

Relationship context may also influence social cognition when the close partner is not present. A long-standing and sophisticated program of experimentation has shown that representations of significant others from one's past may affect one's inferences, recollections, evaluations, and feelings about a new acquaintance when the new acquaintance resembles the significant other (and thereby activates mental schemas associated with the preexisting relationship; Andersen & Chen, 2002).

It has long been recognized that social cognition is designed to facilitate the individual's transit through social life. These and similar studies represent an advance in psychological science, demonstrating that which particular social-cognitive process is activated, and the output of its operation, depends critically on the nature of the ongoing relationship between the cognizer and relevant others. Moreover, Bugental (2000) has argued that evolved brain mechanisms tend to be specialized, perhaps as distinct modules, to fit the varying role requirements of different relationship contexts. If so, humans' extraordinary capacity to quickly recognize (within milliseconds) close friends or even distant acquaintances expedites activation of different cognitive processes with different partners.

Emotion

Ever since Darwin emphasized the social communicative function of emotion in the survival of species, researchers have recognized that emotions have both evolutionary significance and relevance to social life. It is thus somewhat ironic that "interpersonal functions [of emotion] have generally been given short shrift in comparison to intrapersonal functions ... [although most researchers] believe that emotions are brought into play most often by the actions of others, and, once aroused, emotions influence the course of interpersonal transactions" (Ekman & Davidson, 1994, p. 139). Although not all interpersonal transactions involve partners in ongoing relationships, many do. Consequently, many researchers now acknowledge that affect should be examined in its relationship context.

Several emotions are intrinsically relationship-specific; they are unlikely to arise outside of relationships (e.g., jealousy, maternal and romantic love, grief over loss). For most other emotions, the likelihood, intensity, and nature of expression typically are influenced by the individual's relationship with the target of the emotion. For example, a rude bus driver likely elicits a weaker and different response than a rude spouse, junior colleague, or teenaged daughter. This observation accords with the definition of emotion as a response to environmental events that have significance for personal well-being. Different relationships necessarily imply different consequences for personal well-being.

Diverse studies demonstrate links between the emotion-eliciting power of situations and their relationship context. For example, the intensity of elicited emotions, particularly the so-called hot emotions, varies with the closeness of a relationship. This pattern can be explained by Berscheid and Ammazza-lorso's (2001) emotion-in-relationships model, according to which expectancy violations are the cause of emotion. The more interdependent two persons are, the stronger, more numerous, and more consequential their expectations of each other, and thus, the more intense the emotions they elicit. Moreover, people's willingness to communicate about emotional experience depends on their relationship with the person with whom they are communicating. Studies conducted by the first author and his colleagues indicate that people are more willing to express both positive and negative emotions to the extent that a relationship is intimate, trusting, and communal (i.e., a relationship in which partners are responsive to each other's needs), regardless of whether the emotion was triggered by the partner or someone else. Similarly, emotional displays may be suppressed when the emotion is perceived to have relationship-impairing potential. For example, East Asians are more likely than European Americans to suppress certain emotion displays, perhaps reflecting their greater potential to harm relationships in collectivist than in individualist cultures. Although the tendency to experience emotion is widely believed to be hard-wired, behavioral responses to emotion-eliciting events may be shaped to a significant extent by interactions within close relationships.

A further example of the links between emotion and relationship context is that in communal relationships, relative to less caring ones, individuals are more likely to show empathic compassion for a partner's misfortune, better understand each other's emotions (the occasional instance of motivated misunderstanding notwithstanding), and are more likely to share in each other's emotional experience through such processes as emotional contagion, physiological synchrony, vicarious arousal, and rapport (Clark, Fitness, & Brissette, 2001).

Thus, attention to relationship contexts advances understanding of emotional experience and expression.

Relationships and Development

Rudimentary social interaction skills are evident at birth, or soon thereafter. Newborns attend to the faces of members of their species. Other innate mechanisms for relating to others (e.g., attachment, or a proximity-seeking bond between child and caregiver) begin to emerge shortly after birth. Infants contribute to these early relationships by orienting clearly and consistently to their caregivers, and caregivers contribute by attending closely to their infants' behavior and emotions. Patterns of exchange and interdependence are apparent from the early weeks of life. A key sign of the importance of early relationships is that infants reliably turn to caregivers for reassur-

ance and confidence in the face of threatening or stressful circumstances, a phenomenon known as the secure base. A critical mass of research now shows that these and other such abilities provide an essential infrastructure for many vital activities (relating to other people, exploring the environment, striving for achievement, solving problems creatively, caring for children and other people in need, engaging in health-promoting behavior) throughout life. Moreover, it is increasingly evident that the development of these abilities (and their underlying psychological traits) depends on the child's early relationships.

Caregiver-child pairs vary in the degree to which their relationships readily and unambiguously provide the secure base and the resulting emergent sense of security. Existing evidence indicates a substantial degree of continuity between early experiences and diverse relationships during childhood, adolescence, and adulthood. Discontinuities between earlier and later relationships typically are related to pronounced disruptions or stressors in the intervening years. Several explanations have been suggested for these temporal links. One possibility is that unsatisfying or restricted early relationships disrupt normal development, in turn affecting later behavior and relationships. Research with nonhuman species and with human children reared in orphanages with inadequate care arrangements has shown that even minor deprivation of contact with responsive individuals results in abnormal development of the brain and hormonal systems that regulate coping with stress (Gunnar, 2000). One researcher (Siegel, 1999) has even proposed that the "mind" develops at the intersection of neurophysiological processes and interpersonal relations. A more limited possibility is that early relationships are key sources of expectations about social relations. These "residues" of early relationships have been found repeatedly to be related to the characteristics of later relationships in childhood, adolescence, and adulthood (Roisman, Madsen, Hennighausen, Sroufe, & Collins, 2001). Little evidence supports one popular alternative hypothesis—that the long-term implications of attachment security are better attributed to individual differences in temperament (Thompson, 1998).

The evidence is compelling that relationships are significant in nearly every domain of activity. From infancy to old age, having friends and relating successfully to other people is associated with desirable outcomes in virtually all human domains: school, work, coping with negative events, adaptation during life transitions, parenthood, self-worth, and emotional well-being (Hartup & Stevens, 1997). This fact underscores the adaptive significance of relationships in human evolution and highlights the need to study development as a process that unfolds in relational contexts.

Concluding Comment

Diverse emerging evidence indicates that relationship contexts have the potential to influence a diverse array of cognitive, emotional, and behavioral processes. Important challenges remain if these trends are to be cultivated into a systematic body of knowledge. Chief among these challenges is the necessity for identifying and evaluating the boundaries for relationship-context effects, and articulating their operation in a theoretically integrated way: To what extent do which different interpersonal circumstances affect the operation of which processes? Similarly, which individual differences moderate the degree to which interpersonal circumstances influence relationship outcomes and their behavioral effects? Other key questions for further advances in this area of research concern mechanisms. Although the evidence we have cited is suggestive, it remains to be determined how the external reality of relating is translated into the internal reality of basic cognitive, emotional, and biological processes. Finally, the rudimentary theoretical and methodological tools currently available must be supplemented by additional, even more sophisticated models and techniques. Such work promises to allow psychological science to more fully capitalize on a cherished axiom: that behavior is a product of the interaction between the properties of the person and the properties of the environment. To individuals, few features of the environment have greater salience or impact than whom they are with (or thinking about), and the nature of their relationship with that person. Fuller integration of the role of relationship contexts at all levels of psychological theorizing, research, and application is likely to augment the validity and utility of psychological science.

Recommended Reading

Berscheid, E. (1999). The greening of relationship science. *American Psychologist, 54,* 260–266.
Collins, W.A., & Laursen, B. (Eds.). (1999). *Minnesota Symposium on Child Psychology: Vol. 30. Relationships as developmental contexts.* Mahwah, NJ: Erlbaum.
Hinde, R.A. (1997). *Relationships: A dialectical perspective.* East Sussex, England: Psychology Press.
Kelley, H.H., Berscheid, E., Christensen, A., Harvey, J., Huston, T., Levinger, G., McClintock, E., Peplau, L.A., & Peterson, D. (1983). *Close relationships.* New York: Freeman.
Reis, H.T., Collins, W.A., & Berscheid, E. (2000). The relationship context of human behavior and development. *Psychological Bulletin, 126,* 844–872.

References

Andersen, S.M., & Chen, S. (2002). The relational self: An interpersonal social-cognitive theory. *Psychological Review, 109,* 619–645.10.1037//0033-295X.109.4.619
Berscheid, E., & Ammazzalorso, H. (2001). Emotional experience in close relationships. In M. Hewstone & M. Brewer (Eds.), *Blackwell handbook of social psychology* (**Vol. 2,** pp. 308–330). Oxford, England: Blackwell.
Bugental, D. (2000). Acquisition of the algorithms of social life: A domain-based approach. *Psychological Bulletin, 126,* 187–219.10.1037//0033-2909.126.2.187
Clark, M., Fitness, J., & Brissette, I. (2001). Understanding people's perceptions of relationships is crucial to understanding their emotional lives. In M. Hewstone & M. Brewer (Eds.), *Blackwell handbook of social psychology* (**Vol. 2,** pp. 253–278). Oxford, England: Blackwell.
Ekman, P., & Davidson, R. (Eds.). (1994). *The nature of emotion: Fundamental questions.* New York: Oxford.
Gunnar, M.R. (2000). Early adversity and the development of stress reactivity and regulation. In C. Nelson (Ed.), *Minnesota Symposium on Child Psychology: Vol. 31. The effects of adversity on neurobehavioral development* (pp. 163–200). Mahwah, NJ: Erlbaum.
Hartup, W.W., & Stevens, N. (1997). Friendships and adaptation in the life course. *Psychological Bulletin, 121,* 355–370.10.1037//0033-2909.121.3.355
Kiecolt-Glaser, J., & Newton, T. (2001). Marriage and health: His and hers. *Psychological Bulletin, 127,* 472–503.10.1037//0033-2909.127.4.472
Lichty, W., Chyou, J., Aron, A., Anderson, A., Ghahremani, D., & Gabrieli, J. (2004, October). *Neural correlates of subjective closeness: An fMRI study.* Poster presented at the annual meeting of the Society for Neuroscience, San Diego, CA.
Roisman, G.I., Madsen, S., Hennighausen, K., Sroufe, L.A., & Collins, W.A. (2001). The coherence of dyadic behavior across parent-child and romantic relationships as mediated by the internalized representation of experience. *Attachment & Human Development, 3,* 156–172.10.1080/14616730110056946
Sedikides, C., Campbell, W., Reeder, G., & Elliot, A. (1998). The self-serving bias in relational context. *Journal of Personality and Social Psychology, 74,* 378–386.
Siegel, D.J. (1999). *The developing mind: Toward a neurobiology of interpersonal experience.* New York: Guilford.
Smith, E.R., Coats, S., & Walling, D. (1999). Overlapping mental representations of self, in-group, and partner: Further response time evidence and a connectionist model. *Personality and Social Psychology Bulletin, 25,* 873–882.
Symons, C., & Johnson, B. (1997). The self-reference effect in memory: A meta-analysis. *Psychological Bulletin, 121,* 371–394.10.1037//0033-2909.121.3.371
Thompson, R.A. (1998). Early sociopersonality development. In W. Damon (Series Ed.) & N. Eisenberg (Vol. Ed.), *The handbook of child psychology* (**Vol. 3,** pp. 25–104). New York: Wiley.

Acknowledgments—We gratefully acknowledge the enormous contributions of Ellen Berscheid to the conceptual framework from which this article emerged.

Budding Friendships Fill Out the Family Tree

In a mobile society, sometimes it's the people we choose who help us feel rooted

SHARON JAYSON

Cheryl and Richard Hazeltine love their family, but this year they plan to spend Christmas with friends instead.

The Hazeltines, both 63, discovered how important friends could be 35 years ago when they moved from New Jersey to Austin, where Richard joined the physics faculty at the University of Texas.

"I lived far away from my parents and aunts and uncles and sisters and was being dropped into a foreign land," recalls Cheryl, who teaches informal classes on gardening. "My friends have become very strong for my support locally."

For a growing number of Americans, the idea of family extends beyond the old definition of blood ties.

In many ways, friends are the new family. They're there to commiserate with you, celebrate with you and provide the kind of everyday emotional support that humans crave. When family is distant—whether physically or emotionally—friends fill the vacuum, especially at the holidays.

"Friends certainly don't supplant my family," Cheryl Hazeltine says. "We see our family a lot."

But going home for the holidays was always a challenge.

"It was, 'Are we spending enough time with the family? Can we visit our friends now? Is everybody getting in their equal time?'"

This year, they spent Thanksgiving at the beach with two other couples—an annual tradition started 10 years ago—and will spend Christmas with one of those couples at a lodge at Big Bend National Park in western Texas. They'll visit their son and his family in Iowa in February.

"Most years we do Christmas with the family, but every now and then we take a different course," Cheryl says.

A range of demographic factors has increased the importance of friends in our lives. According to the Census Bureau, moving has become common, with almost 20% of moves being to another state. Americans marry later and have children later than they did a generation ago; those Waltons-esque images of large, close, multigenerational families are increasingly rare. About one in two marriages end in divorce. More than 25% of households today are composed of singles—the most common household type.

Friends are stepping in where only family once trod, serving in roles as important as godparents to new babies or as basic as standby transportation for schoolchildren in need of a ride. And research conducted in Australia suggests that good friends, rather than close family ties, may help you live longer in old age.

When there are no living relatives or there's an estrangement from family, friends can play an even more central role. Among some gay people, for example, close friends provide an alternative familial community, especially when relatives don't accept a family member's homosexuality.

"My friends are definitely a surrogate family," says Jasmyne Cannick, 28, a legislative adviser from Los Angeles who is a lesbian.

"Even if your family is accepting of your sexual orientation, there is a limit," she says. "Your families want you to come home, but they might not necessarily want you to bring your partner."

Rather than Christmas, Cannick says she celebrates Kwanzaa, an African-American cultural festival, with her friends.

"My friends are very traditional, even though they are gay," she says. "Holidays are a big deal. It's a very lavish spread."

John Perry of San Francisco says he relied more on friends than family until he and his partner of nine years adopted a son and created what he terms a "conventional unconventional family."

Unlike some gay men who have strained family relations, Perry, 41, who is in marketing communications, says they would be with his extended family for the holidays if they lived in the same city.

An 'Undermined' Institution

But some traditionalists look askance at today's broader view of what constitutes family.

"The institution of the family has been weakened and undermined steadily over the past 40 years," says Christian psychologist James Dobson, author of 36 books and founder of the non-profit Focus on the Family, whose mission is to "preserve traditional values and the institution of the family."

"The homosexual-activist movement has achieved striking success in changing the way families are perceived in the culture," he says in an e-mail interview. "Friends are priceless to us, but they can never replace families."

Relationship researchers say there's no evidence that friendship endangers families.

"The family has been pretty resilient when you think of how many people are divorced, and we still have family ties," says Rebecca Adams, a sociology professor at the University of North Carolina-Greensboro and editor of the journal Personal Relationships. "Maybe it was never quite the way people thought it was."

But Pepper Schwartz, a professor of sociology at the University of Washington, does see evidence that family ties are not what they used to be.

"I do think family—as being the center of one's universe—has weakened," she says. "It's hard to find three generations of the same family in the same town anymore. You have more in common with people who are approximal to you—friends, neighbors, colleagues. They know you in ways your family ceases to know you."

Michael Niederhausen, 29, is close with his three younger brothers and every year visits family in Atlanta for both Thanksgiving and Christmas, but it was his friends in McLean, Va., who helped him over a recent romantic breakup.

"These are people I hang out with," he says. "And it makes it easier to talk with them. I tell my brothers things, but it's a different kind of connection."

Whether friends play a larger role in our lives than in the past is unclear because sociologists have little empirical data, Adams says.

"We don't know if they have become more important because we don't know if they've been important before," she says. "The concern about families becoming less important was expressed more in the '50s when residential mobility increased a great deal."

Since that time, "we went through the scholarly literature and decided that the death of the family had been exaggerated."

New research conducted in the United Kingdom supports what many U.S. experts on friendship say: It's not an either/or situation. Families aren't endangered by friendship. Friends and family complement rather than compete.

"Friends can be family, and family can be friends," says British sociologist Ray Pahl of the Institute of Social and Economic Research at the University of Essex.

Pahl's decade-long analysis of the annual British Household Panel Study, based on 10,000 respondents, was published in September in the British Journal of Sociology. He examined questions about respondents' relationships with their three best friends.

"What we've shown is this process of suffusion—family becomes more friend-like and friends become more family-like," says Pahl, co-author of a book titled *Rethinking Friendship*, due summer [2006].

Pahl says the evidence is clear that these findings, though collected in Britain, apply to other cultures, including the USA.

"It's extremely important in the modern world that people who are moving about and changing their jobs and changing their homes have the capacity to make new friends," Pahl says. "People who don't make friends easily or are too much tied in a traditional way to the family are disadvantaged."

After a divorce, for example, friends are often more important than family. "They are less likely to be judgmental about whose fault it was," he says. And, in times of illness, friends provide "less emotionally charged support."

"Very often people don't want to worry family if they're ill," he says. "They say, 'My mother worries so much, it makes me more ill.'"

Jan Yager, a Stamford, Conn., sociologist and author, says friendships may be viewed as a more important relationship when family ties are less pronounced.

"There is this rather Pollyanna-ish view of friendship," she says. "Since we choose friends, they are wonderful people in our lives. And since you don't choose your relatives, they may not be someone you want to hang out with."

Friendly Health Benefits

As new family-like groups are being created from cadres of friends, the benefits are clear both physically and emotionally.

Research has long shown that people with well-developed friendship networks live longer than people who don't. Several studies have shown that people who have at least one close friend have greater resistance to illness and speedier recoveries and lower incidences of mental illness.

For older adults, friendship is actually more important to psychological well-being than family relationships.

Research published this year in the Journal of Epidemiology and Community Health suggests that a network of friends is more beneficial to your health than family support, at least among the very old. Data from the Australian Longitudinal Study of Aging, which from 1992 through 2002 monitored the health and well-being of almost 1,500 people 70 and older, suggest that close contact with children and relatives had little impact on survival rates, but those with the strongest network of friends lived longer.

Stephanie Tucker, 23, of Seattle, will spend this Christmas with friends rather than going home to her family in New Philadelphia, Ohio, about 30 minutes from Akron. She works for a proprietary school and is a graduate student. She says her friends, all young professionals, are in the same position. They had to choose a holiday vacation either at Thanksgiving or Christmas and went home for a long Thanksgiving break.

But with Christmas looming, Tucker says the reality of her first holiday away from home is beginning to hit.

"I'm a little bit disappointed," she says. "I'd love to see my parents over Christmas. I knew moving out here that the distance was going to be an issue. We'll spend a lot of time with phone calls and e-mails over the holiday. I'll maybe be a little regretful as it gets closer."

Nurturing Empathy

How seeing the world through another's eyes not only makes a child compassionate but helps him learn right from wrong

JULIA GLASS

On mellow summer evenings, my neighbor Holly Lance and I used to get our 2-year-old sons together outside for "run them bone tired" playdates. One evening, as they were sprinting and cavorting with typical pinball momentum, Holly's son, Stefan, burst into tears. Holding his elbow in obvious pain, he collapsed in his mother's arms. My son approached his inconsolable playmate with a look of alarm. He watched Stefan cry for a few seconds, then walked to a nearby wall, bumped his head against it, and erupted into sobs to rival Stefan's.

I had never seen Alec do anything so peculiar. Was he trying to upstage his friend? It was Holly who said, "What a sweet thing to do!" And then I saw that Alec had clearly been attempting—if somewhat clownishly—to comfort someone he loved. I'd long since begun to encourage Alec's verbal, physical, and musical abilities, but what about his emotional abilities? Should I be nurturing this flair for compassion? I wondered.

"At its simplest, empathy means feeling the same thing another person's feeling; at its most sophisticated, it's understanding his entire life situation," says Martin Hoffman, Ph.D., professor of psychology at New York University and author of *Empathy and Moral Development: Implications for Caring and Justice.*

It's empathy that leads us, as adults, not just to help out friends and family but also to stop for a driver stranded by the side of the road, point a bewildered tourist in the right direction, even water a thirsty tree. Without it, our species would probably be extinct, says Hoffman. It is also a key to moral internalization—our children's increasing ability, as they grow, to make decisions by themselves that weigh others' needs and desires against their own.

Given the importance of this attribute, here's how to recognize empathy's earliest signs and encourage it to blossom.

The root of empathy is linking what an emotion feels like for you with what it feels like for others.

Born to Connect

There you are squeezing melons in the produce aisle, your 1-year-old babbling blissfully away, when a baby over in the snack-foods section starts to wail. All too predictably, so does yours. Experts believe that such copycat grief may be an emotional reflex that helps "train" our nature toward a more genuine form of compassion.

"The root of empathy is being able to recognize a link between what it feels like for you to be in a particular emotional state and what that feels like for another person, and it looks as if we're born with a primitive form of that kind of identification," says Alison Gopnik, Ph.D., a psychology professor at the University of California at Berkeley and coauthor of *The Scientist in the Crib.* "Even within an hour of birth, babies will try to make the same facial expression they see someone else making." Over the next few months, infants strive to coordinate their gestures and vocalizations as well as their expressions with those of adults around them.

At about 9 months, a baby begins to pay attention to how others feel about things. Confronted with an unfamiliar object—a toy robot or pureed squash—he'll instantly look at Mom to read her take. If she looks apprehensive, he'll hold back; if she looks pleased, he'll probably dive right in. While this reveals a new depth of perception, it also shows that babies have yet to grasp the most fundamental principle of civilized society: Each of us is a separate being with individual proclivities and feelings. You can't comprehend the feelings of another person until you grasp the concept that there is such a thing as another person.

You Are You, I Am I: Discovering Others

"For most of the first year, babies are pretty confused about what's going on around them," says Hoffman. "If they see another baby fall down and need comfort from his mother, they'll cry and need comfort too."

About midway through the second year, most toddlers begin to recognize themselves in a mirror—seeing themselves as unique, distinct objects. They now see other people as separate—but only physically. They have yet to learn that different people have different inner states as well. So when one toddler sees another in distress, her instinct is to fetch her own mother rather than her playmate's, to placate the child with her own favorite toy. She'll recognize the suffering as belonging to someone else but can't imagine any appropriate remedy other than the one that would suit her. This impulse is one of the most common early signs of what we recognize as genuine empathy, and it may continue even after kids gain a greater sense of what makes other people tick.

3 Empathy Busters

"Empathy is innate, but you can stunt its development," says psychologist Martin Hoffman, Ph.D. Try not to:

Overindulge. Just as an authoritative, "because I said so" style of parenting may prevent children from understanding the whys and wherefores of considerate behavior, so may overly permissive parenting. Kids raised without enough limits may come to feel very entitled—and entitlement, which focuses on the self, is anything but empathic.

Smother. Empathizing with another's strong feelings sometimes requires keeping a respectful distance, especially when a child needs to retreat for a time with a difficult emotion, such as shame or guilt. Resist the urge to try to protect kids from such strong emotions.

Stress competition. "In middle-class America, consideration of others is valued very highly," says Hoffman, "but so is individual achievement." For the first few years of life, those two values rarely collide; mothers may compare kids' developmental milestones, for instance, but such competition takes place mainly between parents. Come the school years, that changes.

"If a kid does excel, it's normal to feel some empathic distress for friends who don't do as well," says Hoffman, but many parents just want their kids to feel good about succeeding and don't acknowledge their empathy. Likewise, students who perform poorly need a more compassionate response than a dose of tutoring and a well-meant "You'll do better next time." The competition won't go away; what's important is to recognize its dark side and discuss how it affects your child's feelings toward peers.

Encouraging Compassion

"Showing affection to kids helps them feel secure and loved," says psychologist Hoffman, "and that contributes to their ability to feel consideration for others. Being a model of empathy—actively helping others—is also important." Beyond these fairly obvious gestures, you can encourage compassion if you:

•**Discipline in ways that invoke natural empathy.** By the end of the second year, scoldings constitute some two-thirds of all parent-child interactions, says Hoffman. And much of the offending behavior involves situations in which the child hurts or upsets someone else.

When your child is the transgressor, it's important not just to let him know he was wrong but also to be specific about the consequences of his actions. Saying, "You made me angry when you poured your milk on the table because now I have to mop it up and we don't have any more" or "You hurt his feelings when you grabbed that airplane—how would you feel if he grabbed it from you?" is an essential step toward making a child feel both guilt for the behavior and responsibility for how other people feel. In time, the ability to anticipate that guilt can motivate kids to "do the right thing."

•**Encourage conciliatory gestures.** Ask your child to apologize or give the person he hurt a hug, pat, or kiss.

•**Don't stifle his emotions.** Adults may try too quickly to "fix" a child's bad feelings—to distract him from sadness with treats, negotiate to thwart his anger, or otherwise derail an emotion that may help teach him the less pleasant aspect of human nature. This doesn't mean you have to accept misbehavior in the name of letting your child "feel"; part of learning to be empathic is learning that we can't act on every emotion we have.

•**Make feelings a topic of discussion.** When you see other people in different situations, ask your child to imagine what those people might be feeling. And don't limit yourself to real life. Talk about your child's emotional response to books, TV shows, and videos.

•**Revel in role-playing games.** "They let kids feel what it's like to be somebody else—a daddy, a baby," says psychologist Alison Gopnik, Ph.D. "That's important to empathy. When my son was three, I'd say, 'I'm going to be Alexei, and you be Mommy.' I'd be difficult and carry on, and he'd say things like 'You can't do that! It's going to be a big mess and I'm going to have to clean it up!' It was a great way to work out some of our conflicts."—J.G.

When 4-year-old Shai Karp's mother was rushed to the hospital for an appendectomy, he went along and sat with her as she was being checked in for surgery. "He'd brought his favorite stuffed animal, Tumby—short for the 'tumble dry low' on its label," says his mother, Judy Wilner. "As I sat there, feeling miserable, Shai insisted I keep Tumby with me that night."

Somewhat ironically, the age at which this type of generosity arises is exactly when, behaviorally speaking, the Tubby custard hits the fan. Because just as toddlers are trying to learn how to make other people feel better, they're also learning how to make other people—most notably, their parents—feel decidedly worse. And it's not just, as I used to think, that Mother Nature throws in these random adorable moments to pacify our rage; the two tendencies are closely intertwined.

The Altruistic Twos?

Toward the end of the second year, children begin to understand that other people have thoughts, feelings, and wants different from their own—often through a process of trial and error. When a toddler trying to comfort his friend sees that his own favorite toy doesn't do the trick, he'll try the friend's favorite toy instead or he'll fetch the friend's mom.

This stage marks a primitive but true form of empathy, says Hoffman, one when children not only start to recognize the different experiences of other people but also, when necessary, reach out to them. "Empathy isn't just a feeling; it's a motive," he stresses. Whether we're throwing a bridal shower or helping a friend cope with a death in the family, empathy spurs us to partake in someone else's experience. We don't always act on the urge, but when we do, it often makes us feel good.

Preschoolers begin to perceive subtler feelings, such as that a classmate may be sad because he misses his parents.

This eventful early age is also a period of intensive experimenting to find out what makes people different from one another. "It's around age two that we begin to see children perform these lovely altruistic acts—and do things precisely because we don't want them to," says Gopnik. "The same impulse that leads a child to think, 'Mom's crying, I'm not; I can comfort her,' also leads to 'Mom doesn't want me to touch that lamp; I can touch that lamp, I'm going to touch it.' If you think about what we want to encourage—understanding how other people feel—the 'terrible twos' is a part of that." (For more on promoting this understanding, see "Encouraging Compassion.")

Toward a More Mature Compassion

From this point on, children refine and enlarge their perspective on other people's inner lives. In the preschool years, says Hoffman, they begin to perceive more subtle, removed feelings—such as that a classmate may be sad because he misses his parents. They also learn that a single event can lead to different reactions from different people. Sometime between ages 5 and 8—having grasped their own gender and ethnic identity—they begin to look at each person around them as having a distinct personal history and to consider its influences on that person's experiences and feelings. "They also start to see how having different personalities makes people react differently, and they begin to take that into account when dealing with people," adds Gopnik.

Children are now on the threshold of what Hoffman says is a highly sophisticated form of empathy—empathy for another's experience beyond the immediate situation, a skill that we work on for the rest of our lives. They can see that some people have generally happy or sad lives, and they can begin to empathize with entire groups of people (the homeless, earthquake victims, firefighters battling an inferno).

Last Thanksgiving a friend's 4-year-old daughter had a poignant moment. "AnnaBess walked into the kitchen when her father was dressing the turkey," recalls her mother, Wendy Greenspun. "She started crying and said, 'Daddy, that turkey doesn't want to be dead! He wants to be alive! He wants to be with his friends.' She was extremely upset for almost an hour." Whether or not AnnaBess was expressing an unusually precocious empathy, this much is clear: She was saddened by another creature's hardship, and her outrage occurred spontaneously—without prompting by anyone else.

For when it comes to raising empathic children, says Hoffman, parents need not fret about following some rule book or missing a narrow window of opportunity. "The beauty of empathy," he says, "is that it comes naturally. It doesn't have to be forced. You need only nourish it."

JULIA GLASS recently won her third Nelson Algren Fiction Award and a fellowship in writing from the New York Foundation for the Arts.

From *Parenting*, June/July 2001, pp. 72. Copyright © 2001 by Julia Glass. Reprinted by permission of the author.

Contagious Behavior

Shirley Wang

On a fall morning in 1998, a teacher at a Tennessee high school noticed the smell of gas in her classroom and soon felt dizzy and nauseous. Some of her students then reported feeling ill as well, and they were transported by ambulance to a nearby hospital. As concerned staff and students watched them go, some of them started feeling sick, too.

That day, 100 people showed up in the emergency room with symptoms they believed to be associated with the exposure to gas at the school. But the illnesses could not be explained by medical tests. Extensive environmental tests conducted at the school concluded that no toxic source could be the cause, according to results published in the *New England Journal of Medicine*.

What occurred was real illness, although not caused by germs or fumes, according to Timothy F. Jones, lead author of the paper and deputy state epidemiologist at the Tennessee Department of Health.

"It was not an infection, but it was certainly transmitted," Jones said.

It was a phenomenon known as *mass psychogenic illness*, in which symptoms are passed from person to person among people who are visible to one another.

"You get sick because you see someone else getting sick," said Jones.

Mass psychogenic illness is an extreme example of the more general phenomenon of contagious behavior: the unconscious transmission of actions or emotions from one individual to another.

Our everyday lives are filled with examples of how we "catch" even subtle emotions and complex behaviors, such as happiness and anger, bulimic symptoms, and depression, from other people. Psychologists, anthropologists, and neuroscientists have studied how and why such contagion occurs.

Contagion appears to involve both biological and social processes. It is pervasive, and yet we are often unaware of the influence of other's emotions and behaviors on our own—which is particularly striking because the consequences of contagious behavior can be significant.

Do You Feel Like I Feel?

The contagious quality of mood and emotion has been perhaps the most widely studied of all the different forms of contagion.

People are extremely good at picking up on other people's emotions—both negative and positive—without consciously trying.

APS Fellow and Charter Member Elaine Hatfield, professor at the University of Hawaii and a pioneer in the study of emotional contagion, became interested in the topic when wondering how clinicians were being affected by their patients' moods, particularly when patients were not articulating their feelings.

In the lab, she and her colleagues studied whether people catch the emotions of others, and to what extent they pay attention to explicit, verbal descriptions of feelings compared to nonverbal facial and postural cues as their source of emotional information.

In one study, participants watched a videotape of a target person describing a positive or negative memory. The tape continued to show the target as he viewed his own taped description. The target expressed surprise at the emotion showing on his face, and he felt very different than how he appeared on tape.

The participants then assessed the target's emotion, as well as their own. Hatfield and her team found that the participants rated the target's emotion largely based on his words. That is, if the target said he felt much sadder than he looked, participants rated him as quite sad.

However, when participants rated their own emotion, they were much more similar to the emotion expressed by the target's nonverbal cues. It appeared that the participants' mood was affected by the target—but they responded to his displayed emotion, not his stated one.

This suggests that if we think we begin to feel an emotion when interacting with another individual, it's quite possible that person is also feeling the same emotion.

"We're reflecting what they feel," Hatfield said. "If we feel irritated at a client, the client is irritated at us or something else."

Thomas Joiner, professor at Florida State University, has found that not only are negative moods contagious, but depressive symptoms—such as sleep problems and thoughts about death—also appear to spread over time.

Unfortunately, Joiner said, it's not a two-way street. While it would be wonderful if an individual's nondepressed mood could ease the mood of a depressed person, the direction of contagion doesn't usually go that way.

Mood Rings

Still, the good news is that emotional contagion can be used constructively to promote behavior change.

Sigal Barsade, associate professor at the University of Pennsylvania, brought groups of participants into a lab to complete a simulated managerial exercise. The group included a research confederate who was either positive or negative, and who exerted high or low energy.

Examining both participants' self-reported mood and independent video coders' ratings, Barsade found that individuals grouped with the positive mood confederates became more positive over time, while those in the other condition became, as expected, more negative.

"We aren't emotional islands," said Barsade. "People are sort of walking mood conductors and we need to be aware of that."

The positive-emotional-contagion groups experienced increased cooperation, less conflict, and improved perceived performance compared to those in the negative condition.

In fact, the group emotional experience was so powerful that in some groups the participants ended up exchanging phone numbers after the study, according to Barsade.

"It's critical that people understand emotional contagion is not just a self-contained phenomenon that ends with the 'catching' of the emotion," she said. "This contagion then influences our cognition and behavior—and we often don't even realize the process is happening."

Mechanisms of Contagion

There are multiple paths through which contagion can occur, and several processes interact to produce the phenomenon.

On a biological level, we are built to mimic others. Recent research shows that humans, like monkeys, have certain types of neurons that fire when simply watching someone else carry out an action, even when we ourselves are not doing the same thing. Such neurons help prime us to understand and identify with other people.

Say, for instance, you are sitting at home intently watching a football game on television, and you really like the team's quarterback. When he makes a long pass, you would likely show some electrical signal in our own arm as well, according to APS Fellow and Charter Member John Cacioppo, director of the Center for Cognitive and Social Neuroscience at the University of Chicago. You've identified with that player and, as part of that, you have an actual physiological reaction to his action.

"Synchrony is necessary in social animals," said Cacioppo, a past member of the APS Board of Directors. "This synchrony is fundamental to not only having that emotional back and forth, but also to basic correspondence. One really does resonate physiologically."

Physiologic mimicking occurs with facial expressions, and is often so subtle that we ourselves don't even realize we're doing it, but it is important to our social interactions.

Laugh and the World Laughs With You

"Essentially the bottom line is that people, in almost a monkey-see monkey-do kind of way, are wired up to imitate others' faces and voices," said Hatfield.

Such seems to be the case with laughter, considered a particularly contagious behavior. Laughter is highly stereotyped—it is generally similar across people—and hard to interrupt mid-stream. Once it starts, it has a tendency to run its course to completion, according to Robert Provine, a professor at the University of Maryland-Baltimore County.

We appear to have an almost automatic laugh reaction in response to others' laughter—think laugh tracks on television shows—and it's hard to laugh while alone. His research shows that we are 30 times more likely to laugh in the presence of other people than by ourselves.

In fact, laughing alone can serve as an alert to others that a person may not be in touch with reality, according to Provine. Imagine the villain on television who laughs maniacally to himself. Generally we are much better at inhibiting laughter than producing it on command.

"Laughter is a social relationship between people," said Provine. "The essential ingredient is another person."

Imitating others' behavior is only part of what makes emotion contagious. According to one theory, we infer our emotion from our expressions and behaviors. We smile, therefore we must be happy.

Alternatively, we may use the emotions and behaviors of others as a means of social comparison, to gauge how we should be feeling and acting in a particular situation.

Matching others may also be one way to show empathy, or just "I like you," according to Hatfield.

Researchers have brought couples into the lab and observed their behavior. Those who like each other behave more similarly. Conversely, "if a couple is out of sync, they don't like each other as much," said Cacioppo.

Infection or Selection

One question that arises in conducting work on contagion among individuals who already know each other, such as roommates or couples in a romantic relationship, is whether individuals who are already more similar to each other in affect tend to seek each other out—a selection effect—rather than truly being "infected" by the other person's moods.

Both processes appear to occur: People do tend to seek out those who are more similar to them, but they are also influenced by others' emotions and actions.

"People who are similar will think and interpret the information similarly," said Thomas Sy, assistant professor at California State University Long Beach, who studies how leadership status affects group emotions and productivity. The same action, like crossing one's arms, might be interpreted very differently by people who work in a corporate setting versus a clinical one.

In Sy's studies on group behavior, he finds that not only do individuals' moods shift toward their leader, but that the variation in emotion between group members decreases over time. Individuals end up feeling not just better or worse, but more similar to each other.

"It makes a lot of sense that if I want to be part of this group, I will think and act and behave—and in this case feel—like the rest of my group members," said Sy.

Our experiences over the years also help build scripts, or routines, that we tend to then perform in a particular situation. When a script is enacted, it triggers a set of behaviors with a high degree of automaticity, according to Raymond Novaco, professor of psychology and social behavior at the University of California, Irvine, whose research focuses on anger and aggression.

In the case of road rage, repeated exposure to other people's behavior on the roads may form a script that aggression is appropriate when driving.

"The contagion notion is diffusion," said Novaco. "Part of the spreading is that it makes salient various scripts for aggressive behavior on the roadways."

But road "rage" may be a misnomer. Anger—an emotion—can be a trigger for aggression, defined as an act intended to harm, but need not be present for the behavior to occur.

This is likely to be the case in general: Changes in emotion may impact behavior but behavioral contagion can occur without emotional contagion.

Yet the very basic underlying process between emotional and behavioral contagion may be the same. Our facial muscles twitch, and we infer that we are happy. We see someone looking ill, we feel our internal bodily sensations—perhaps our heart is beating rapidly or we're breathing shallowly because we're anxious about the situation—and we interpret these signs that we are about to pass out because we also took in the gas fumes.

Communicable Dis-ease

There are a number of personality and situational factors that both strengthen and weaken the likelihood that contagion will occur.

Although we are wired to respond to other people, there is also a tremendous amount of variability in individuals' ability to transmit their emotions to others. More outgoing and expressive individuals tend to be better transmitters, or more successful at having you feel what they feel, according to Hatfield.

Think about the person in the office who is hard to feel happy around when he or she is upset. That person may not criticize or denigrate you, but you might start feeling miserable nonetheless. Chances are this individual communicates feelings very strongly, perhaps by scowling or sighing deeply. By noticing that person's mood, consciously or not, one may be more likely adopt it.

This expressiveness can be taught, said Cacioppo. And, we can still be affected even if we know that people are intentionally trying to influence us, as in the case of cheerleaders at a pep rally.

On the other side, more easily infected people tend to be more observant of others, and may be of lower status in the situation.

"You have to actually pay attention to the person to be able to clue in to what's going on," said Barsade.

There are also conditions under which contagion is more likely to spread.

Disinhibitory situational factors, such as anonymity and ease of escape, can increase the likelihood of a behavior's occurrence—especially those that are typically considered inappropriate, like aggression, which people typically try to minimize—according to Novaco.

Despite the pervasive nature of contagion, we often don't attribute changes in mood or behavior to the people around us. Barsade explicitly asks her participants after experiments what factors they think might have influenced their performance. Hardly anyone mentions the moods of other people.

Awareness may be important, however.

"The person who's aware can start to control it, modulate it," said Sy. "Some people are able."

If parents have a bad day at work, they may be able to consciously tell themselves they shouldn't let the interaction with the boss affect how they treat their children.

"If they're not aware of that and they go home and they don't know it's the boss that caused it, they might shift that blame to their kids," said Sy. "When it's conscious, you have a better chance of controlling how it's going to impact you."

However, we are surprisingly bad at controlling emotions, according to Hatfield; and even when we can modulate our moods we tend to be able to do so only in spurts.

Hatfield cites the example of being with family during the holidays. You can remain pleasant with your family and resist feeling irritable for a couple of hours, but after that you'll probably be yearning for the hotel where you can take a nap.

However, if one continues to remain in that stressful situation, "people start getting tired, and then start mimicking other people's behavior. It's a surprisingly short time."

Rooted in biology but supported by social and situational factors, contagion—whether of nausea or of happiness—is a powerful process and an almost unavoidable fact of being human.

On the other hand, if people want to avoid being infected, what's an easy way to try and foil the attempt?

"Be oblivious," said Hatfield. "Fifteen-year-old boys are great at it."

SHIRLEY WANG is a freelance writer in New Haven, Connecticut.

UNIT 5

The Individual and Society

Unit Selections

Key Points to Consider

- What are some of the social changes affecting our society?

- How are gender roles changing? Or are they?

- What role do poverty and race play in how the individual adjusts to society and interact with others?

- How have the Internet and other technologies changed American culture?

- What types of traumas and disasters have Americans faced recently? How have the traumas affected the average American?

- Can personal growth really occur as a result of trauma or disaster?

Student Web Site

www.mhcls.com/online

Internet References

Further information regarding these Web sites may be found in this book's preface or online.

AFF Cult Group Information
   http://www.csj.org/index.html

National Clearinghouse for Alcohol and Drug Information
   http://www.health.org

The passing of each decade brings changes to society. Some historians have suggested that changes are occurring more rapidly than in the past. In other words, history appears to take less time to occur. How has American society changed historically? The inventory is long. Technological advances can be found everywhere. Not long ago, few people knew what "user-friendly" and text message signified. Today these terms are readily identified with the rapidly changing computer and cell phone industries.

Forty-five years ago, Americans felt fortunate to own a 13-inch black and white television that received three local stations. Now people feel deprived if they cannot select from 250 different worldwide channels on their big, wide-screen, digital sets. Thankfully, today we can transmit an e-mail to the other side of the world faster than we can propel a missile to the same place.

In the Middle Ages, Londoners worried about the bubonic plague. Before vaccines were available, people feared polio and other diseases. Today much concern is focused on the transmission and cure of avian flu, the discovery of more carcinogenic substances, and the greenhouse effect. In terms of mental health, psychologists see few hysterics, the type of patient seen by Sigmund Freud in the 1800s. Psychosomatic ulcers and drug addictions are more common today.

Nearly every popular magazine carries a story or two bemoaning the passing of the traditional, nuclear family and the decline in "family values." And as if these spontaneous or unplanned changes were not enough to cope with, some individuals are intentionally trying to change the world. Witness the continuing dramatic changes in the Middle East or the individuals who write computer viruses or worms that wreak havoc with personal and commercial computing systems. This list of societal transformations, while not exhaustive, reflects society's continual demand for adaptation and change by each of its individual members.

This unit addresses the interplay between the individual and society (or culture) in producing the problems each creates for the other. The first article tackles an endlessly evolving issue—men's and women's gender roles. As role expectations change, the demands on and the need to adjust by the individual grow. Women today are essentially expected to be more masculine (e.g. help bring income home) and men are encouraged to be more sensitive and nurturing (e.g. spend quality time with the children). These new demands compete with the way children traditionally were reared and thus can create much anguish for them as adults. Sean Elder explores these issues in "The Emperor's New Woes."

Prejudice is another obstacle in our society. Psychologists believe that prejudice, for example racism, still exists in the U.S. today; it is just more subtle and more covert than in the past. The article, "Fiftieth Anniversary: Brown v. Board of Education," reviews the history of racism and discrimination in America and chronicles whether indeed racism has diminished since this landmark case.

You probably believe that America is an affluent country; it is indeed, especially when compared to other countries, for example those in Africa. We still, however, have families that live below the poverty level in the United States. Poverty keeps people poor and not just with respect to their prosperity; poverty also contributes to psychosocial stress and to unhealthy lifestyles. Finding ways to improve the well-being of the poor is the focus of "Sick of Poverty by Robert Sapolsky."

Working life is also changing for the American adult. Most of today's jobs demand more from workers; thus, home lives often suffer. Cynthia Thompson claims that many American organizations are in denial about their negative effects on family life. There are, however, solutions to work-home conflicts that she shares with the reader.

In this unit, we should also examine large scale social strife. Three such events which have dominated our lives of late have been the threat of natural disasters, pandemics, and wars. The first article in this series is about pandemics and how psychologists can help officials better communicate with the public. Effective and well-framed messages are important to keeping society safe and healthy.

The final article of the unit relates to war. Recent wars in Iraq and Afghanistan have heightened our sensitivity to this issue. Christopher Munsey, writing for the *Monitor on Psychology*, describes the terrible psychological effects of war on all of us—soldiers, their families, and civilians alike.

The Emperor's New Woes

Man is no longer king of his domain. He's now supposed to be an equal partner—and a good listener, too. Blindsided by the escalating emotional demands of marriage, guys wonder how love became a no-win proposition.

SEAN ELDER

Last year I was asked by the editor of a men's magazine to write a story about intimacy in relationships. His was one of those publications that advise the American man how to flatten his stomach and increase his chest size—that look, in other words, like a lot of women's magazines. I spoke to the requisite marriage experts: psychologists and sociologists who had stared into the murk of modern male-female relations. Though I tried to steer my sources toward simple declarative sentences and do-it-yourself answers, the editor was not happy.

"Couldn't you just give it to us in bullet points?" he asked. "We want a step-by-step guide on how to be emotionally intimate with your woman."

Therein lies a précis of the principal dilemma in marriage today. Men have come to accept—even celebrate—their wives' careers and paychecks while learning, step-by-step, how to bathe the baby and baste the turkey. But there is no Julia Child-style primer on closeness, no chart with diagrams: Insert A into slot B, and there you go. Intimacy achieved. Let's go have a cold one.

It would be funny if it weren't so painful. "It's probably the real cause of half of all divorces," according to Sam Margulies, a divorce mediator in Greensboro, North Carolina, and author of several books on the subject of marital breakups. The changes in women's lives—their roles, ambitions, opportunities—have been considered from every angle. But men's lives have changed too, in ways that are more confusing, more contradictory and often less welcome. Men did not ask to have their roles redefined. Now, they're looking for an instruction manual complete with fine print—and a translator's guide as well.

"Very few women could compare their lives to their mothers' and say, 'We look pretty similar,'" says Steven Nock, a professor of sociology at the University of Virginia who has studied what marriage means to men. "Women have so many dramatically different options in their lives. But where are men taking their cues about what it means to be a husband or a father? There is much less discussion in our society about that."

The guidelines for being a good husband used to be simple: provide, protect, maybe trim the hedges now and then. Now wives still want all that in a mate—and more. Today's wife wants a confidante and soul mate as well.

The requirements changed with no warning, and many husbands feel blindsided. Most men were raised with the idea that making it in the outside world is how you score points at home. For many women that also still holds true. It's not as though they want men to be less goal-oriented or less interested in money. They're asking for a breadwinner *and* a best friend.

But the skills needed to be a successful soldier or CEO are literally antithetical to the caring-sharing sort. Success and even heroism are still measured by a man's ability to compartmentalize, desensitize, act decisively and sacrifice himself. "The essence of masculinity is that what it takes to get love makes us distant from love," says Warren Farrell, San Diego-based author of *Why Men Earn More* and *Why Men Are the Way They Are*. "That is the male dilemma in a nutshell."

"Men are beside themselves," Farrell continues. "There is a fundamental contradiction: If [a man] is successful at work he has really prepared himself to be unsuccessful at home. He's damned if he does and damned if he doesn't."

Marriage Changes Everything

Most men accept that and even welcome the transition. Men recognize that marriage requires compromise and sacrifice—but their beliefs about what's most important are surprisingly traditional, and not necessarily in line with women's beliefs. In his sociological research, Nock followed more than 6,000 young men for decades, gathering data on their social lives, careers and habits. His conclusion is that most men undergo a profound personal transformation when they marry. It is a passage into manhood in an era when the very definition of manhood is in flux. "Marriage changes men because it is the venue in which adult masculinity is developed and sustained," he writes in *Marriage in Men's Lives*.

A married man works longer hours, moves up the career ladder faster and earns more money than his single peers. He spends more time with his relatives. He donates less to charity; he spends less time hanging out with his buddies and more time in formal social organizations like business and civic associations.

A husband even *thinks* differently. "The way men view the world and their place in it changes in the act of marrying," says Nock. "Marriage makes people more conventional. If they are religious, they become more devout. They acquire the trappings of property owners, which makes them more conservative. They're less likely to engage in risky or deviant behaviors. Entering into this traditional arrangement has the effect of making men more traditional." A wedding is more than an expression of love; it's a public declaration that a man plans to abide by a set of social expectations about male adulthood. The seriousness with which men approach marriage and the lengths they are willing to go in order to be better husbands are some of the best evidence we have that men take commitment seriously and are willing to do what is expected of them to make marriage work.

For a lot of husbands trying to rise to the demands of their 21st-century wives, the lessons of intimacy are worse than rocket science. They're poetry.

But there's a catch. Nock believes that since he conducted his research in the 1990s, women's expectations have expanded to include greater intimacy. While conducting his research, he says, "I was focused more on ordinary expectations." He believes that emotional expectations may now be the most central part of marriage.

"Even a generation ago, if a man was a good breadwinner and he had no profoundly negative attributes, if every night he came home, had a martini and watched TV all night, then went to bed, he was fine," says marriage and family therapist Terry Real, author of *How Do I Get Through to You? Closing the Intimacy Gap Between Men and Women*. Now the job description has been expanded to include listening and that least measurable of skills, empathizing. Today, simply not cheating on your wife or beating your kids doesn't make you a good husband and father.

Real says he counsels a lot of men who would prefer the bullet-point version of how-to-achieve-intimacy-now. "I say to them, 'She wants you to be more relationship-skilled than you were raised to be. You're a smart guy—this isn't rocket science.'" But for a lot of husbands trying to rise to the demands of their 21st-century wives, the lessons of intimacy are worse than rocket science. They're *poetry*.

When husbands realize what their wives are asking for, the reaction isn't "'I didn't know that you wanted that, too,'" says Margulies. "It's more like 'I don't understand what the hell you're talking about.'" It's not a question of miscommunication, of Mars and Venus. It's a matter of new specifications, of women wanting something more than a traditional husband who, by definition, was removed and even remote. "In a nutshell, women want their husbands to act like girlfriends," Margulies says.

"I wish it were that simple," says Nock. "I don't think we can say, 'Okay, men, here's what you need to do to become better

husbands.'" A lot of men would prefer such clear coordinates—even if it meant acting like a girlfriend.

While the conflicted desires of women have created some of this tension, society sends its own mixed signals. Time and feminism have chipped away at the granite facade of traditional masculinity, but old monuments don't fall easily. The last presidential election, after all, was in part a referendum on what kind of father or husband we want for our country. And did not the simple, stubborn, somewhat unintelligible fellow with the apparently traditional marriage best the more nuanced, flexible, loquacious gent with the strong, independent wife? John Kerry was chastised for windsurfing on Nantucket while George Bush was off whacking weeds in the hot Texas sun.

"What's so ludicrous about windsurfing?" asks Real. "It's effete—which is another way of saying it's feminine." Yet guys are forced to contend with such inane stereotypes. (Have you ever tried windsurfing? It's about as easy as riding a shark.)

Worst of all, women are often complicit in the stereotyping. If a single woman goes to a party, says Farrell, her friends don't push her toward the sensitive schoolteacher—they urge her to chat up the banker. "People don't say, 'Look at that man, he's really listening to a woman, asking her questions and drawing her out,'" says Farrell. "You don't get introductions like that, even though you would be introducing the woman to the type of man who would be a wonderful husband and father. Instead the host will say, 'That fellow is an intern at Mt. Sinai Hospital.'"

For men, actual physical proximity is often as good as intimacy ("I'm here, aren't I?"), while women want something more demonstrative.

So we end up with men wary of the shifting rules of marriage, wondering what's in it for them. The weary white-collar salaryman, having worked his 60-hour week while making time for his daughter's piano recital, may well wonder about the poetry lessons his wife is threatening him with. Suddenly an evening of video games or ESPN doesn't sound so bad, even if it means eating a TV dinner. Hungry-Man meals have gotten a lot better over the years—and they're still nicely compartmentalized, with clear bullet-point instructions on the back of the box.

For the Most Part, Our Parents and grandparents did not worry much about the emotional content of marriage. My parents lived through the Great Depression and the second World War. When their marriage ended in divorce in the 1960s, I doubt either of them thought, "If only we had achieved greater intimacy!" It's not that they were stronger or better than we are today, or that our demands and complaints aren't legitimate. The lack of emotional connection certainly killed many marriages, and the right to personal fulfillment was part of what drove the women's movement—which in turn changed marriage for the better.

But on the communication score, most men are still playing catch-up with women. To care about someone else's feelings you have to be in touch with your own, and getting in touch with your feelings is not something we've been raised to think of as essential, or even admirable. Collectively, we don't have a lot of positive examples of an open, questioning, emotional hero. Hamlet, who was certainly introspective, was neither husband nor father; he died, quite conveniently, before facing either of those hurdles.

"It's not so much that men can't provide the emotional support that women want as that men and women define emotional support differently," according to Nock. "As marriages become more focused on emotion and happiness, men and women are defining closeness in somewhat different terms." For men, actual physical proximity is often as good as intimacy ("I'm here, aren't I?"), while women want something more demonstrative.

Just look at how men and women communicate with members of their own gender. I have seen my wife sit down knee-to-knee with one of her close friends and unload, with no preamble or pretext of doing anything else besides perhaps drinking a glass of wine or cup of tea. Guys, for the most part, need some distraction in order to talk about feelings.

Two summers ago, while visiting some old friends in France (and how is that for effete?), my wife marveled at how my longtime pal Randy and I reconnected after not seeing each other for years. We sat knee-to-knee as well—with our iBooks linked, swapping music files. But what she did not hear was us comparing notes on aging—his mother had passed away, mine was ailing—or our marriages, topics we would not have easily broached otherwise. It's as though men need something to do with their hands.

Having established that some men are willing to try to meet women halfway, it's safe to ask what women can do for men. Sex is seriously underrated as a passport to that communicative country a lot of wives want to explore. While some women seem to resent the fact that their husbands want them, and want to be wanted back, the very act (as opposed to talk) allows a lot of men to be more emotionally available. And it, too, gives us something to do with our hands.

"The complaints I hear from men are about their spouses not taking their sexual needs seriously enough," says Mark Epstein, a psychiatrist in private practice in New York and author of *Open to Desire: Embracing a Lust for Life*. "Men become vulnerable when they are sexually engaged. Maybe if women didn't feel demeaned or objectified by male sexuality they wouldn't have to push it away so much. They could start to feel it as more of a form of communication." He acknowledges that many women may see it as more work—but isn't that what they're asking of their men? Sex is one area where men and women can explore differences without yielding their individual identities. "One thing that has to happen in a couple is that each one has to make room for the other's desire," says Epstein, "which is different from the way you experience it. You can approach it but never totally understand it."

Women can cut men a bit of slack, and try to empathize with these rough creatures (remember *Beauty and the Beast?*) rather than change them. They can also adjust their expectations. As Farrell says, "If you expect a man to be a killer and be home on time for dinner, you will end up feeling depressed about your partnership."

After all, men have quickly become masters at another kind of intimacy: fatherhood. Many contemporary fathers feel that they are an upgrade from the previous version. Warm, loving, generous fathers are lionized in the culture rather than scorned, points out Terry Real. "The current generation of men is much better as fathers than their fathers were," he says, "but it's not clear to me that we're much better husbands than our fathers were." The difference is that much less risk is involved in being vulnerable or intimate with your child than there is with your mate. The relationship of parent and child is not that of equals, and while we may have a lot of expectations of our children, we generally don't look to them for complete emotional fulfillment.

Truth be known, most men want the same thing from their mates that their wives are looking for in their husbands. They want to be understood by them, even if it means understanding themselves first. There is plenty of evidence that men want and need marriage as much as women do and are willing to learn new dance steps. Just put them in bullet points, and let us lead sometimes.

50th Anniversary

Brown v. Board of Education

Oliver Brown was fed up. His daughter, Linda, a Topeka, Kan., third-grader, had to walk two miles each day through a railroad switchyard to get to and from her black elementary school when a better school stood just seven blocks away. Brown had tried to enroll her in the much-closer white school, but the principal refused. The situation was nothing new for America's black citizens in the early 1950s, but Brown obtained the right help at the right time. With the aid of McKinley Burnett, the head of Topeka's branch of the National Association for the Advancement of Colored People, Brown's case would eventually become the landmark court decision for *Brown v. Board of Education,* leading to the eventual desegregation of public schools and serving as the impetus for the civil rights movement.

According to the Supreme Court decision delivered by Chief Justice Earl Warren on May 17, 1954, "In these days, it is doubtful that any child may reasonably be expected to succeed in life if he is denied the opportunity of an education. Such an opportunity, where the state has undertaken to provide it, is a right which must be made available to all on equal terms."

DEBBIE O'LEARY

Integration has been a slow and often painful process as schools and communities across the country have worked to eliminate various forms of inequity and incorporate strategies to academically prepare students of all races, ethnicities, and cultures.

Now, 50 years after the decision of *Brown v. Board of Education* was handed down, historians and citizens question whether it has had its intended effect. While the education of African-American children was inadequate due to black schools being under-funded, understaffed, and undersupplied, many wonder if much has actually changed.

"There's a new theme in the historical assessment of pre-*Brown* segregated schools," says Donald Warren, professor in educational leadership and policy studies. "Historians are pointing to the fact that a lot of positives from segregated schools were lost during desegregation."

The fallout included lost jobs for black teachers and the closing of African-American schools that were created from the ground up by caring and committed community members.

Integration has presently hit another stumbling block as some public schools today remain segregated or are becoming re-segregated.

Although the Supreme Court could lawfully mandate integration, it could not integrate Americans' hearts. As African-American students moved into white schools, the residing white students initiated a mass departure from schools and communities. In 1954, 83 percent of students in the Indianapolis Public School system were white. Today, that number has dropped to approximately 31 percent. Indianapolis is not alone in this statistic. The numbers are comparable or worse nationwide.

According to Chalmer Thompson, associate professor in counseling and educational psychology, as white students moved out to other areas, a tension was created in African-American communities. "It became clear that having 'too many' blacks in one school was uncomfortable for whites, and many accepted the idea that the greater the proportion of blacks, the more problems academically," she says. "Desegregation was important to society. But the problem that came with desegregation was that white lawmakers and communities didn't listen to what black advocates were saying. Black advocates didn't merely want blacks to integrate into white schools, they also wanted teaching that dealt with racial injustice and other forms of oppression."

Integration has presently hit another stumbling block as some public schools today remain segregated or are becoming re-segregated. According to Suzanne Eckes, assistant professor in educational leadership and policy studies, during the 1990s there were three Supreme Court decisions that made it easier for school districts to lift their desegregation decrees by proclaiming they had eliminated the vestiges of past discrimination.

"As it currently stands, lower courts have been given carte blanche in determining whether a school district has achieved

Race Riot Conjures Different Memories for Whites, Blacks

Throughout the summer of 1943, bloody race riots were triggered across the nation's cities, including Indianapolis, Detroit, New York, Los Angeles, Mobile, Philadelphia, Baltimore, St. Louis, Washington, D.C., and Beaumont, Texas.

During world War II, Beaumont experienced rapid population growth, housing and food shortages, and forced workplace integration. These circumstances were already causing racial tensions when a white woman lied about being raped by a black man. Approximately 4,000 people rioted, resulting in the mobilization of the State and National Guard, as well as the Texas Rangers. Many blacks were assaulted, three people were killed—two blacks and one white—and hundreds of thousands of dollars worth of damage was reported.

Educational Leadership and Policy Studies Professor Donald Warren, who grew up in Beaumont, the riot's genesis, asking what, in general, they remembered about life on the homefront during World War II. "The subjects talked about the many patriotic acts they participated in, but not one of the subjects remembered the race riots," he says. When Warren reminded them of the riot, they were shocked that they had forgotten.

The results were much different when he asked black citizens the same questions. According to Warren, blacks were haunted by memories of terror, but also of how they protected themselves during the riot. Historians had often reported that blacks were passive during the Beaumont riot, but according to the subjects Warren interviewed, they were anything but passive. "They fought back in very clever ways, arming themselves and working to help each other escape dangerous parts of the city," he says.

Witnesses recalled that one of the black men killed was an army inductee who was waiting at the bus terminal. He was beaten and killed by the rampaging mob as police stood by and watched.

"It was a jarring contrast between what happened and what was supposed to happen during the patriotism of World War II and our democratic crusade across the world."

Web Site Helps Teachers Develop Social Justice Curriculum

In order to promote problem-based historical inquiry in high school social studies classes, a Web site is being created that will enable teachers to share curriculum and activities on a broader range of social justice and historical issues.

Located at www.pihnet.org, Persistent Issues in History Network allows teachers to use a set of tools to develop their own units. The project, which is a partnership between Tom Brush, associate professor in instructional systems technology, and Auburn University's John Saye, will provide students with an opportunity to grapple with social issues and look for new strategies to promote a more just society. "Problem-based historical inquiry will help prepare students to be more effective citizens by not just knowing the past, but also by being able to make competent, knowledgeable decisions as adults," Brush says.

Through funding from the National Endowment for the Humanities and support from IU, Auburn, and the School of Education's Center for Research on Learning and Technology, Brush and Saye have been working with 20 teachers from across the United States to formulate a set of curricula and activities for the site. Teachers identified the civil rights movement as a subject that would enable them to promote and implement certain strategies in social justice. It was also a subject for which teachers said they severely lacked materials.

"Because we tend to minimize the overall historical perspective anyway, PIHN will give teachers the tools to expand the curriculum to allow students to struggle with all aspects of the civil rights movement," he says. The site currently contains a civil rights database with 1,500 primary and secondary sources. According to Brush, the site will soon branch out with more materials on the Spanish Conquest, post–Civil War reconstruction, and world history.

unitary status," says Eckes. "They have lifted desegregation decrees across the country when the vestiges of discrimination may not have been eliminated. In order to take a more fair approach to lifting desegregation decrees, more guidance is needed from the court in determining what is meant by vestiges of discrimination."

While the political arena struggles to eliminate remnants of racism and inequity, the School of Education holds fast to its mission of preparing teachers to successfully instruct all students. By incorporating multiculturalism into the curriculum, faculty members have amplified their focus on preparing students of all races and ethnicities to teach in diverse classroom settings throughout the country.

Teacher-education students at IUPUI attend classes within the urban school setting in order to interact with students of differing abilities and cultural backgrounds. According to Monica Medina, lecturer at IUPUI, this provides students a greater comfort level and increased sense of civic engagement and responsibility.

"When our students walk into schools, they assume students will come dressed like they are, with hats and coats and socks, etc. They are surprised when they see kids who aren't dressed appropriately," she says.

During the first semester of courses at IUPUI, cohorts must address issues of social justice and inequality they may not even know existed. According to Bob Osgood, associate professor in educational foundations, many students entering the teacher-education program are comfortable with their self-perceptions and are surprised when their own prejudices and stereotypes are revealed.

Goodwill Ambassadors Serve as International Contacts

Goodwill Ambassadors are a group of student who volunteer to answer questions, address concerns, and form new friendships with international students who are interested in coming to the School of Education. They represent all five academic department: curriculum and instruction, instructional systems technology, language education, educational leadership and policy studies, and counseling and educational psychology. The Web site, located at www.education.indiana. edu/~edfolks/goodwill, receives approximately 3,000 hits per year.

Studies Find Disproportionate Minority Representation in School Discipline

A recent study indicates students of color are disciplined more severely for less serious infractions and for less objective, more judgmental reasons.

In a paper presented at the School to Prison Pipeline Conference for the Harvard Civil Rights Project, the Center for Evaluation and Education Policy (formerly the Indiana Education Policy Center) reported significant minority over-representation in office referral, suspension, expulsion, and corporal punishment in almost all 50 states.

According to Russ Skiba, associate professor in counseling and educational psychology and a faculty researcher at CEEP, researchers have consistently found a significant difference in disciplinary measures attributable to race, even when controlling for possible explanations such as socioeconomic status and differences in rates of misbehavior.

In one study published recently in *Urban Review,* Skiba and his colleagues found that African Americans were more often disciplined for subjective infractions, such as loitering, disrespect, and threats. In contrast, white students were more likely to be disciplined for more clear-cut violations, including smoking, obscene language, leaving school without permission, and vandalism.

Research has shown that school discipline is a complex phenomenon. Student behavior is only the starting point in a process that includes the discretion of the individual teacher and the institution as a whole. If the outcomes of that process include racial disparity, Skiba notes, then it makes sense to explore to what extent classroom and schoolwide disciplinary strategies are contributing to continuing inequity in our schools and society.

"There is an amazing consistency in the research finding disproportionate minority representation in school discipline," says Skiba. "After 25-plus years, it's important to ask ourselves why the issue of disproportionate punishment has not yet been seriously addressed in policy or practice."

Cume Promotes Best Practices in Urban Education

The Center for Urban and Multicultural Education has a history of seeking to maximize equity and quality in urban schools by supporting the development of learning conditions that are inclusive and respectful of diversity. CUME, which functions as the research and development center of the Indiana University School of Education at IUPUI, is dedicated to understanding and improving education in metropolitan areas, where schools serve most of the nation's poor and cultural and linguistic minorities.

"CUME was created in 1979 to provide the School of Education with a voice in the nation's longstanding debate about the role and function of public education in our cities," explains CUME director Jeffrey Anderson. "For most of its early years, CUME functioned as a desegregation assistance center serving the Midwest region. Through conferences, seminars, training workshops, and symposia, the center disseminated information on such topics as discrimination in schools and the condition of urban and multicultural education in the nation."

While the general mission remains unchanged, today CUME's focus is to promote research to practice in ways that support successful school and community outcomes within the urban context. To put this mission into practice, CUME focuses on community engagement, leadership, learning and culture, and assessment and instruction.

"Most students come from racially homogenous backgrounds with little cross-cultural experience," says Osgood. "The first Block of classes can be very uncomfortable. The goal is to encourage people to listen and communicate honestly but respectfully. The first step is confronting the issues and getting them out on the table."

Students gain awareness through their coursework and assignments addressing issues of inequity. "They see that racism is much more subtle and pervasive than they previously thought," Osgood continues. "Most are astounded when they see the differences in resources, and they subsequently develop a passion and commitment to social justice and diversity." The result has been an increased number of education students wanting to teach in the Indianapolis Public Schools system.

It has also been rewarding for the children in the professional development schools with which students work. "The kids love having our students come into their classes," Medina says. "It provides them valuable one-on-one time with an educator, plus our students are closer to their age, so they feel more of a peer-related bond."

Another primary objective for the School of Education is to attract more minority teachers who can serve as role models to minority students as well as provide other teachers assistance in navigating cultural barriers. Kipchoge Kirkland, assistant professor in curriculum and instruction, works with Project TEAM

Minorities Often Receive Unfair Mental Health Treatment

Uninformed and unfair racial treatment is pervasive in the mental health system. According to Charles Ridley, a professor in the Department of counseling and Educational Psychology and a licensed psychologist, ethnic minority clients, compared to their white counterparts, are more likely to receive an inaccurate diagnosis, terminate prematurely, receive an inappropriate or less preferred treatment, be assigned to a junior rather than senior professional, and report greater dissatisfaction with their treatment.

But, says Ridley, much of this unfair treatment is unintentional. "Many people equate racism with racial prejudice and bigotry," he says. "They understandably believe that the unfair treatment accorded to individuals from minority groups is attributable to devious motives, bigotry, and hatred. Actually, a great deal of unintentional racism is motivated by a desire to be helpful."

Ridley cites examples of unintentional racism as that which often occurs when the therapist tries to address a perceived problem without establishing a working alliance with the client, and the client views the line of questioning as stereotypical. "The therapist, however, is in a position of power and is socially sanctioned to make a judgment about the client that carries weight and has serious consequences," he explains. "In observing the agitation of the client, the therapist mistakenly judges the reaction as a psychological disorder when in reality it is a healthy response to an unhealthy stimulus. All along, the therapist thinks he or she is doing the right thing."

Known as pseudo-transference, this is one of several therapist actions that results in African-American males' being assigned the diagnoses of paranoid schizophrenia ore than any other group. "Statistically, the prevalence of this diagnosis to this population is highly improbable," says Ridley.

It was also found in a recent study that Caucasian therapists, but not miority therapists, avoid any discussion of race with their minority clients. The therapists probably did not want to offend their minority clients or appear multiculturally incompetent. "Here the intentions are not malicious, but their professional behaviors are counterproductive," he says.

Latino Students Face Unique Barriers in Transition to Higher Education

Latino college students face many barriers in their academic careers. Universities can help these students stay in school by following several guidelines. According to Vasti Torres, associate professor in educational leadership and policy studies, administrators should let go of the myth that Latinos do not value education. "This is a myth brought on by the fact the many Latino parents do not know how to support their sons and daughters in college," Torres explains.

Like many first-generation college students, Latino students must explain to their parents why they have less time to have job or help with siblings. Therefore, universities should provide culturally sensitive orientations for parents. Administrators should also recognize that policies based on retention research may not be culturally sensitive, such as the evidence that first-year students do better living on campus. This may actually serve as a deterrent to immigrant Latino students. Officials also should make sure that Latino students are aware of the educational and social support services provided by the institution. In addition, says Torres, university officials should seek to understand issues that are culturally sensitive and language that could be misinterpreted, as well as create supportive environments.

"Students who are trying to find others like them or working to better their Spanish language skills need environments where these activities are valued and visible," Torres says.

---

students to help them become culturally competent educators. Project TEAM (Transformative Education Achievement Model), serves to prepare teachers for culturally diverse student populations.

"We can all draw upon our lived experiences, but it doesn't always translate to teaching," Kirkland explains. "Students must examine their own ethnic identities. Once they are able to put their feelings into perspective, they are then able to see how connections can be made within the curricula and among community, students, families, and other teachers. Students learn the importance of becoming part of the academic and cultural community."

Another aspect of inequality that is often left out of the discussion is economic injustice and class stratification. "As a society, we are uncomfortable admitting we're stratified by class," says Judith Chafel, professor in curriculum and instruction. "Many Americans believe that anyone in our country can succeed through hard work and determination. We fail to acknowledge the social-structural reasons for poverty. Issues of power, class, and economic injustice should be an integral part of the multicultural conversation."

The principal indicator for determining whether *Brown* has succeeded in ensuring equal educational opportunity for every student may be found in the achievement gap. According to the most recent assessment by the Indiana State Teachers Association, the achievement gap for blacks, whites, and Latinos indicates equity has not been realized. In IPS, Indiana Statewide Testing for Educational Progress pass rates for white children in grades 3, 6, 8, and 10 are 51 percent, compared to 36 percent for black students and 42 percent for Latinos.

Much work needs to be done, but faculty in the School of Education on both the Bloomington and Indianapolis campuses are committed to ensuring equitable education is possible through high-quality teacher preparation and innovative research that addresses issues of diversity and fairness.

Study Examines How Indiana Communities Deal With Migrant Populations

Although there is Indiana legislation stating that all K–12 schools should provide bilingual and bicultural education, most school districts are unaware of the law. While some communities have taken it upon themselves to provide these services, or at least some form of English as a second language, there is a monumental need for informed research to shape best practices for transnational migrants.

According to Bradley Unger Levinson, associate professor in education leadership and policy studies, a current study will help determine how Indiana communities where Latinos have recently settled have dealt with the arrival of these newcomers and how the newcomers have been faring. The study reframes the question of migrant education through a focus on the quality of civic life, social incorporation, and academic engagement for newcomer Latinos in three Indiana regions.

Along with an analysis of what Indiana has done, this focus on regions will help determine best practices for welcoming transnational migrants into the community and providing their children equal educational opportunities. "Policies and practices that build trust and academic skills greatly enhance student engagement and achievement," Levinson says.

In previous pilot study of an Indianapolis middle school, Levinson discovered that many newly arrived Latino youth were cynical or disaffected with school, while some highly acculturated Latino youth did better. This contradicts most research findings, which have found stronger pro-school attitudes among recently arrived immigrant students. "Contributing in part to such disaffection," he says, "was a high rate of geographic mobility and uncertainty about long-term citizenship and identity. These factors converged with local practices that didn't adequately address their needs."

The consequences of this increasing transnational circuit in terms of identity, aspirations, and educational engagement have not been adequately studied, Levinson sys. "Nor have studies addressed the ways in which states, towns, and school districts enact policies and practices that link schools with other community agencies of socialization to integrate newcomers," he adds. "All these factors are needed to ensure a student's educational achievement is not compromised."

Sick of Poverty

New studies suggest that the stress of being poor has a staggeringly harmful influence on health

ROBERT SAPOLSKY

Rudolph Virchow, the 19th-century German neuroscientist, physician and political activist, came of age with two dramatic events—a typhoid outbreak in 1847 and the failed revolutions of 1848. Out of those experiences came two insights for him: first, that the spread of disease has much to do with appalling living conditions, and second, that those in power have enormous means to subjugate the powerless. As Virchow summarized in his famous epigram, "Physicians are the natural attorneys of the poor."

Physicians (and biomedical scientists) are advocates of the underprivileged because poverty and poor health tend to go hand in hand. Poverty means bad or insufficient food, unhealthy living conditions and endless other factors that lead to illness. Yet it is not merely that poor people tend to be unhealthy while everyone else is well. When you examine socioeconomic status (SES), a composite measure that includes income, occupation, education and housing conditions, it becomes clear that, starting with the wealthiest stratum of society, every step downward in SES correlates with poorer health.

This "SES gradient" has been documented throughout Westernized societies for problems that include respiratory and cardiovascular diseases, ulcers, rheumatoid disorders, psychiatric diseases and a number of cancers. It is not a subtle statistical phenomenon. When you compare the highest versus the lowest rungs of the SES ladder, the risk of some diseases varies 10-fold. Some countries exhibit a five- to 10-year difference in life expectancy across the SES spectrum. Of the Western nations, the U.S. has the steepest gradient; for example, one study showed that the poorest white males in America die about a decade earlier than the richest.

So what causes this correlation between SES and health? Lower SES may give rise to poorer health, but conversely, poorer health could also give rise to lower SES. After all, chronic illness can compromise one's education and work productivity, in addition to generating enormous expenses.

Nevertheless, the bulk of the facts suggests that the arrow goes from economic status to health—that SES at some point in life predicts health measures later on. Among the many demonstrations of this point is a remarkable study of elderly American nuns. All had taken their vows as young adults and had spent many years thereafter sharing diet, health care and housing, thereby controlling for those lifestyle factors. Yet in their old age, patterns of disease, incidence of dementia and longevity were still significantly predicted by their SES status from when they became nuns, at least half a century before.

Inadequate Explanations

So, to use a marvelous phrase common to this field, how does SES get "under the skin" and influence health? The answers that seem most obvious, it turns out, do not hold much water. One such explanation, for instance, posits that for the poor, health care may be less easily accessible and of lower quality. This possibility is plausible when one considers that for many of the poor in America, the family physician does not exist, and medical care consists solely of trips to the emergency room.

But that explanation soon falls by the wayside, for reasons made clearest in the famed Whitehall studies by Michael G. Marmot of University College London over the past three decades. Marmot and his colleagues have documented an array of dramatic SES gradients in a conveniently stratified population, namely, the members of the British civil service (ranging from blue-collar workers to high-powered executives). Office messengers and porters, for example, have far higher mortality rates from chronic heart disease than administrators and professionals do. Lack of access to medical attention cannot explain the phenomenon, because the U.K., unlike the U.S., has universal health care. Similar SES gradients also occur in other countries with socialized medicine, including the health care Edens of Scandinavia, and the differences remain significant even after researchers factor in how much the subjects actually use the medical services.

Another telling finding is that SES gradients exist for diseases for which health care access is irrelevant. No amount of medical checkups, blood tests and scans will change the likelihood of someone getting type 1 (juvenile-onset) diabetes or rheumatoid arthritis, yet both conditions are more common among the poor.

The next "obvious" explanation centers on unhealthy lifestyles. As you descend the SES ladder in Westernized societies, people are more likely to smoke, to drink excessively, to be obese, and to live in a violent or polluted or densely populated neighborhood. Poor people are also less likely to have access to clean water, healthy food and health clubs, not to mention adequate heat in the winter and air-conditioning in the summer. Thus, it seems self-evident that lower SES gets under the skin by increasing risks and decreasing protective factors. As mordantly stated by Robert G. Evans of the University of British Columbia, "Drinking sewage is probably unwise, even for Bill Gates."

What is surprising, though, is how little of the SES gradient these risk and protective factors explain. In the Whitehall studies, controlling for factors such as smoking and level of exercise accounted for only about a third of the gradient. This same point is made by studies comparing health and wealth among, rather than within, nations. It is reasonable to assume that the wealthier a country, the more financial resources its citizens have to buy protection and avoid risk. If so, health should improve incrementally as one moves up the wealth gradient among nations, as well as among the citizens within individual nations. But it does not. Instead, among the wealthiest quarter of countries on earth, there is no relation between a country's wealth and the health of its people.

Thus, health care access, health care utilization, and exposure to risk and protective factors explain the SES/health gradient far less well than one might have guessed. One must therefore consider whether most of the gradient arises from a different set of considerations: the psychosocial consequences of SES.

Psychosocial Stress

Ideally, the body is in homeostatic balance, a state in which the vital measures of human function—heart rate, blood pressure, blood sugar levels and so on—are in their optimal ranges. A stressor is anything that threatens to disrupt homeostasis. For most organisms, a stressor is an acute physical challenge—for example, the need for an injured gazelle to sprint for its life or for a hungry predator to chase down a meal. The body is superbly adapted to dealing with short-term physical challenges to homeostasis. Stores of energy, including the sugar glucose, are released, and cardiovascular tone increases to facilitate the delivery of fuel to exercising muscle throughout the body. Digestion, growth, tissue repair, reproduction and other physiological processes not needed to survive the crisis are suppressed. The immune system steps up to thwart opportunistic pathogens. Memory and the senses transiently sharpen.

But cognitively and socially sophisticated species, such as we primates, routinely inhabit a different realm of stress. For us, most stressors concern interactions with our own species, and few physically disrupt homeostasis. Instead these psychosocial stressors involve the anticipation (accurate or otherwise) of an impending challenge. And the striking characteristic of such psychological and social stress is its chronicity. For most mammals, a stressor lasts only a few minutes. In contrast, we humans can worry chronically over a 30-year mortgage.

Unfortunately, our body's response, though adaptive for an acute physical stressor, is pathogenic for prolonged psychosocial stress. Chronic increase in cardiovascular tone brings stress-induced hypertension. The constant mobilization of energy increases the risk or severity of diseases such as type 2 (adult-onset) diabetes. The prolonged inhibition of digestion, growth, tissue repair and reproduction increases the risks of various gastrointestinal disorders, impaired growth in children, failure to ovulate in females and erectile dysfunction in males. A too-extended immune stress response ultimately suppresses immunity and impairs disease defenses. And chronic activation of the stress response impairs cognition, as well as the health, functioning and even survival of some types of neurons.

An extensive biomedical literature has established that individuals are more likely to activate a stress response and are more at risk for a stress-sensitive disease if they (a) feel as if they have minimal control over stressors, (b) feel as if they have no predictive information about the duration and intensity of the stressor, (c) have few outlets for the frustration caused by the stressor, (d) interpret the stressor as evidence of circumstances worsening, and (e) lack social support—for the duress caused by the stressors.

Psychosocial stressors are not evenly distributed across society. Just as the poor have a disproportionate share of physical stressors (hunger, manual labor, chronic sleep deprivation with a second job, the bad mattress that can't be replaced), they have a disproportionate share of psychosocial ones. Numbing assembly-line work and an occupational lifetime spent taking orders erode workers' sense of control. Unreliable cars that may not start in the morning and paychecks that may not last the month inflict unpredictability. Poverty rarely allows stress-relieving options such as health club memberships, costly but relaxing hobbies, or sabbaticals for rethinking one's priorities. And despite the heartwarming stereotype of the "poor but loving community," the working poor typically have less social support than the middle and upper classes, thanks to the extra jobs, the long commutes on public transit, and other burdens. Marmot has shown that regardless of SES, the less autonomy one has at work, the worse one's cardiovascular health. Furthermore, low control in the workplace accounts for about half the SES gradient in cardiovascular disease in his Whitehall population.

Feeling Poor

Three lines of research provide more support for the influence of psychological stress on SES-related health gradients. Over the past decade Nancy E. Adler of the University of California, San Francisco, has explored the difference between objective and subjective SES and the relation of each to health. Test subjects were shown a simple diagram of a ladder with 10 rungs and then asked, "In society, where on this ladder would you rank yourself in terms of how well you're doing?" The very openness of the question allowed the person to define the comparison group that felt most emotionally salient.

As Adler has shown, a person's subjective assessment of his or her SES takes into account the usual objective measures (education, income, occupation and residence) as well as measures of life satisfaction and of anxiety about the future. Adler's provocative finding is that subjective SES is at least as good as objective SES at predicting patterns of cardiovascular function, measures of metabolism, incidences of obesity and levels of stress hormones—suggesting that the subjective feelings may help explain the objective results.

This same point emerges from comparisons of the SES/health gradient among nations. A relatively poor person in the U.S. may objectively have more financial resources to purchase health care and protective factors than a relatively wealthy person in a less developed country yet, on average, will still have a shorter life expectancy. For example, as Stephen Bezruchka of the University of Washington emphasizes, people in Greece on average earn half the income of Americans yet have a longer life expectancy. Once the minimal resources are available to sustain a basic level of health through adequate food and housing, absolute levels of income are of remarkably little importance to health. Although Adler's work suggests that the objective state of being poor adversely affects health, at the core of that result is the subjective state of feeling poor.

Being Made to Feel Poor

Another body of research arguing that psychosocial factors mediate most of the SES/health gradient comes from Richard Wilkinson of the University of Nottingham in England. Over the past 15 years he and his colleagues have reported that the extent of income inequality in a community is even more predictive than SES for an array of health measures. In other words, absolute levels of income aside, greater disparities in income between the poorest and the Wealthiest• in a community predict worse average health. (David H. Abbott of the Wisconsin National Primate Research Center and I, along with our colleagues, found a roughly equivalent phenomenon in animals: among many non-human primate species, less egalitarian social structures correlate with higher resting levels of a key stress hormone—an index for worse health—among socially subordinate animals.)

Wilkinson's subtle and critical finding has generated considerable controversy. One dispute concerns its generality. His original work suggested that income inequality was relevant to health in many European and North American countries and communities. It has become clear, however, that this relation holds only in the developed country with the greatest of income inequalities, namely, the U.S.

Whether considered at the level of cities or states, income inequality predicts mortality rates across nearly all ages in the U.S. Why, though, is this relation not observed in, say, Canada or Denmark? One possibility is that these countries have too little income variability to tease out the correlation.

Some critics have questioned whether the linkage between income inequality and worse health is merely a mathematical quirk. The relation between SES and health follows an asymptotic curve: dropping from the uppermost rung of society's ladder to the next-to-top step reduces life expectancy and other measures much less drastically than plunging from the next-to-bottom rung to the lowest level. Because a community with high levels of income inequality will have a relatively high number of individuals at the very bottom, where health prospects are so dismal, the community's average life expectancy will inevitably be lower than that of an egalitarian community, for reasons that have nothing to do with psychosocial factors. Wilkinson has shown, however, that decreased income inequality predicts better health for both the poor and the wealthy. This

result strongly indicates that the association between illness and inequality is more than just a mathematical artifact.

Wilkinson and others in the field have long argued that the more unequal income in a community is, the more psychosocial stress there will be for the poor. Higher income inequality intensifies a community's hierarchy and makes social support less available: truly symmetrical, reciprocal, affiliative support exists only among equals. Moreover, having your nose rubbed in your poverty is likely to lessen your sense of control in life, to aggravate the frustrations of poverty and to intensify the sense of life worsening.

If Adler's work demonstrates the adverse health effects of feeling poor, Wilkinson's income inequality work suggests that the surest way to feel poor is to be made to feel poor—to be endlessly made aware of the haves when you are a have-not. And in our global village, we are constantly made aware of the moguls and celebrities whose resources dwarf ours.

John W. Lynch and George A. Kaplan of the University of Michigan at Ann Arbor have recently proposed another way that people are made to feel poor. Their "neomaterialist" interpretation of the income inequality phenomenon—which is subtle reasonable and, ultimately, deeply depressing—runs as follows: Spending money on public goods (better public transit, universal health care and so on) is a way to improve the quality of life for the average person. But by definition, the bigger the income inequality in a society, the greater the financial distance between the average and the wealthy. The bigger this distance, the less the wealthy have to gain from expenditures on the public good. Instead they would benefit more from keeping their tax money to spend on their private good—a better chauffeur, a gated community, bottled water, private schools, private health insurance. So the more unequal the income is in a community, the more incentive the wealthy will have to oppose public expenditures benefiting the health of the community. And within the U.S., the more income inequality there is, the more power will be disproportionately in the hands of the wealthy to oppose such public expenditures. According to health economist Evans, this scenario ultimately leads to "private affluence and public squalor."

This "secession of the wealthy" can worsen the SES/health gradient in two ways: by aggravating the conditions in low-income communities (which account for at least part of the increased health risks for the poor) and by adding to the psychosocial stressors. If social and psychological stressors are entwined with feeling poor, and even more so with feeling poor while being confronted with the wealthy, they will be even more stressful when the wealthy are striving to decrease the goods and services available to the poor.

Social Capital

A third branch of support for psychosocial explanations for the relation between income inequality and health comes from the work of Ichiro Kawachi of Harvard University, based on the concept of "social capital." Although it is still being refined as a measure, social capital refers to the broad levels of trust and efficacy in a community. Do people generally trust one another and help one another out? Do people feel an incentive to take care of commonly held resources (for example, to clean up graffiti in public parks)? And do people feel that their organizations—such as unions or tenant associations—actually have an impact? Most studies of social capital employ two simple measures, namely, how many organizations people belong to and how people answer a question such as, "Do you think most people would try to take advantage of you if they got a chance?"

What Kawachi and others have shown is that at the levels of states, provinces, cities and neighborhoods, low social capital predicts bad health, bad self-reported health and high mortality rates. Using a complex statistical technique called path analysis, Kawachi has demonstrated that (once one controls for the effects of absolute income) the Strongest route from income inequality to poor health is through the social capital measures—to wit, high degrees of income inequality come with low levels of trust and support, which increases stress and harms health.

None of this is surprising. As a culture, America has neglected its social safety nets while making it easier for the most successful to sit atop the pyramids of inequality. Moreover, we have chosen to forgo the social capital that comes from small, stable communities in exchange for unprecedented opportunities for mobility and anonymity. As a result, all measures of social epidemiology are worsening in the U.S. Of Westernized nations, America has the greatest income inequality (40 percent of the wealth is controlled by 1 percent of the population) and the greatest discrepancy between expenditures on health care (number one in the world) and life expectancy (as of 2003, number 29).

The importance of psychosocial factors in explaining the SES/health gradient generates a critical conclusion: when it comes to health, there is far more to poverty than simply not having enough money. (As Evans once stated, "Most graduate students have had the experience of having very little money, but not of poverty. They are very different things.") The psychosocial school has occasionally been accused of promulgating an anti-progressive message: don't bother with universal health care, affordable medicines and other salutary measures because there will still be a robust SES/health gradient after all the reforms. But the lesson of this research is not to abandon such societal change. It is that so much more is needed.

Overview/Status and Health

- Researchers have long known that people with low socioeconomic status [SES] have dramatically higher disease risks and shorter life spans than do people in the wealthier strata of society. The conventional explanations—that the poor have less access to health care and a greater incidence of harmful lifestyles such as smoking and obesity—cannot account for the huge discrepancy in health outcomes.
- New studies indicate that the psychosocial stresses associated with poverty may increase the risks: of many illnesses. The chronic stress induced by living in a poor, violent neighborhood, for example, could increase one's susceptibility to cardiovascular disease, depression and diabetes.

- Other studies have shown a correlation between income inequality and poor health in the U.S. Some researchers believe that the poor feel poorer, and hence suffer greater stress, in communities with wide gaps between the highest and lowest incomes.

The Good and Bad Effects of Stress

The human body is superb at responding to the acute stress of a physical challenge, such as chasing down prey or escaping a predator. The circulatory, nervous and immune systems are mobilized while the digestive and reproductive processes are suppressed. If the stress becomes chronic, though, the continual repetition of these responses can cause major damage.

Effects of Acute Stress

Brain Increased alertness and less perception of pain
Thymus Gland and Other Immune Tissues Immune system readied for possible injury
Circulatory System Heart beats faster, and blood vessels constrict to bring more oxygen to muscles
Adrenal Glands Secrete hormones that mobilize energy supplies
Reproductive Organs Reproductive functions are temporarily suppressed

Effects of Chronic Stress

Brain Impaired memory and increased risk of depression
Thymus Gland and Other Immune Tissues Deteriorated immune response
Circulatory System Elevated blood pressure and higher risk of cardiovascular disease
Adrenal Glands High hormone levels slow recovery from acute stress
Reproductive Organs Higher risks of infertility and miscarriage

More to Explore

Mind the Gap: Hierarchies, Health and Human Evolution. Richard Wilkinson. Weidenfeld and Nicolson, 2000.

The Health of Nations: Why Inequality Is Harmful to Your Health. Ichiro Kawachi and Bruce P. Kennedy. New Press, 2002.

The Status Syndrome. Michael Marmot. Henry Holt and Company, 2004.

Why Zebras Don't Get Ulcers: A Guide to Stress, Stress-Related Diseases and Coping. Robert Sapolsky. Third edition. Henry Holt and Company, 2004.

ROBERT SAPOLSKY is professor of biological sciences, neurology and neurological sciences at Stanford University and a research associate at the National Museums of Kenya. In his laboratory work, he focuses on how stress can damage the brain and on gene therapy for the nervous system. In addition, he studies populations of wild baboons in East Africa, trying to determine the relation between the social rank of a baboon and its health. His latest book is *Monkeyluv and Other Essays on Our Lives as Animals* [Scribner, 2005].

Work-life: Organizations in Denial

While work-family programs may provide some employees with useful resources, they do not address the root causes of work-life imbalance and often are not integrated into employers' strategic goals.

Cynthia A. Thompson

Changes in the demographic nature of the American workforce over the past few years, coupled with increasingly demanding employers trying to compete in a global economy, have increased the number of employees struggling to meet both work and family obligations. Dual-earner couples and single parents, for example, report significantly higher levels of conflict between their jobs and family lives than did employees in 1977 (Bond et al. 2003). Some of that increased conflict results from employees working longer hours: Since the late 1970s, the combined number of weekly work hours of dual-earner couples with children under 18 at home increased from 81 to 91 (Bond et al. 2003).

Although not everyone who attempts to juggle multiple work and non-work roles experiences conflict, a large number of employees do. Unfortunately for these employees, work-family conflict is often associated with job and life dissatisfaction, depression, anxiety, anger/hostility, hypertension, greater alcohol consumption and substance abuse, and perceptions of a lower quality of life. There are also unhealthy consequences for work organizations, including increased absenteeism, tardiness, and turnover as well as more widespread interest among employees in finding new employment (Eby et al. 2004).

For these reasons, as well as the desire to be perceived as "family friendly," work organizations increasingly are implementing policies and programs to provide employees with resources to help them manage their lives. These resources are of four types:

- Time-based resources help employees manage time pressures and conflicts and include flexible scheduling (e.g., flextime, job sharing, and telecommuting) and leave policies (e.g., parental leave, reduced work hours, and a phased return to work).
- Information-based resources are designed to provide information to employees to help them make better decisions about child care, elder care, health issues, managing time, etc. They include resource and referral programs, intranets and/or work/life Web sites,

dependent care provider fairs, support groups, and stress and time management seminars.
- Money-based resources provide financial assistance (e.g., flexible spending accounts and adoption assistance) to help employees manage dependent-care responsibilities.
- Finally, direct service resources (e.g., childcare services, after-school programs, and so-called concierge services that deliver and pick up employees' clothes from dry cleaning establishments, ship packages, and order dinners for delivery) are designed to help employees manage the day-to-day balancing act between work and family responsibilities.

These programs and policies are certainly a big improvement over the way businesses operated not so long ago, when organizations were designed around the prototypical "male breadwinner" model—a man with a wife at home to manage the domestic front so that he could focus his attention and energy on his job. But despite the growing popularity of "family-friendly" initiatives, organizations today are still designed around the notion that the best employees can and should put their jobs first. And therein lies the problem. Family-friendly initiatives, while helpful to many, do not go far enough toward helping all employees have a balanced life. Clearly, organizations are in denial about what really needs to be done to help workers fulfill their work and family obligations.

Barriers to Supportive Workplaces

One of the biggest barriers stems from how organizations define and reward success. For managerial and professional employees, success is defined not just as mastery of one's job but as movement up the hierarchy toward higher and higher levels of management. In addition, successful employees are those who show primary commitment to work or career, often by putting up with excessive time demands that presumably reflect the requirements of the job but often do not (Bailyn 1993). For example, some employees put in "face time" to demonstrate their commitment, staying late even though their work is completed.

These perceived demands and ways of thinking about success are reinforced by work organizations' reward systems, which sometimes include awards for "dedication." Many employees thus work long hours, place their job before their family, and put in face time to demonstrate their commitment, when these behaviors are not a requirement of the job itself but a requirement of a demanding culture. Career-oriented employees who might like to telecommute or work reduced hours fear they will commit career suicide by doing so. Thus, in many organizations, work-life programs go unused and unappreciated.

Another barrier is that some organizations implement impressive work-life programs but fail to measure whether they are having the intended effect(s) or are even being used. Because recent research shows that family-friendly initiatives may not be as important to employees as the extent to which the organizational culture supports work-life balance (Allen 2001; Thompson et al. 1999), organizations must determine whether the culture supports benefit use. My research suggests that supportive work-family cultures are more likely to make employees feel comfortable about using family-friendly benefits like flex-time, since they are less likely to worry about negative career consequences. In addition, employees who work in a supportive culture have higher levels of commitment to their employer, fewer thoughts about quitting, higher job satisfaction, and less work-family conflict (Allen 2001; Thompson et al. 1999).

The basic problem with work-life initiatives is that they do not solve the root cause of employee work-life imbalance. To be sure, employees who have access to flexible work arrangements experience less interference between their jobs and family lives (Bond et al. 2003). But offering flexible work hours does not change the underlying structure of how work is organized or executed. Flexible work hours may help employees manage the demands of work and family, but they do not address the total number of hours required, unpredictability in work routines, unsupportive managers, last-minute overtime demands, unreasonable work loads, etc. Work-life programs make organizations look family-friendly without requiring them to consider deeper, more fundamental issues—how jobs are designed, how work is coordinated, and how organizational rewards are determined.

Finally, when work-life programs are not considered in concert with the organization's strategic goals and are instead offered simply to compete with other employers, managers and supervisors are less likely to support their implementation and use. Without top management support, employees may encounter resistance from managers to using work-life benefits as well as face inadequate technical support, poorly defined policies and procedures for participating, and motivational systems that may be inconsistent with the new way of working (Nord et al. 2002).

Moving Beyond Work-family Programs

While it is important for organizations to continue offering work-life programs—they provide many employees with necessary resources and support for integrating work and life, and they may contribute to employee perceptions that their organization is supportive—deeper solutions to work-life imbalance must be considered. First, organizations must determine the source, or root cause, of work-life imbalance. Is it the rigidity of work schedules or the unpredictability of work demands? Is it unreasonable work loads? Do supervisors and managers support the work-life policies offered?

We must go beyond assessments that simply ask about family and personal needs that might conflict with work. We need to monitor the psychosocial environment to determine which business units have employees who are chronically stressed due to heavy work demands and little control (Shain 2004). We need to analyze job processes, coordination mechanisms, reward systems, and actual requirements of jobs. We need to ask whether there is another way to accomplish a job or task, whether we really need all the travel that we require of our professional employees, and whether we really need 7:00 a.m. breakfast meetings. We need to consider how we can measure and reward job performance without relying on face time.

Second, in creating a truly supportive culture, work-life efforts must be linked to an organization's overall strategy so that work-life balance is considered essential to business success. More specifically, an organization should consider linking work-life efforts to strategic goals of increasing employee commitment and job and career satisfaction and decreasing employee turnover, absenteeism, job strain, and poor health.

Third, top managers must embrace a vision for the organization that supports work-life balance, then communicate this vision through the company's mission statement, intranet, newsletters, and e-mail announcements. Furthermore, top and mid-level managers must model new behaviors or at least be supportive of alternative ways of working. Management support is crucial for any culture change to take place.

In addition, because supervisors play a key role in helping employees integrate work and family (Allen 2001; Thompson et al. 1999), organizations should require training programs that educate managers and supervisors about the benefits of supporting employees' work-life needs. These programs should help managers develop flexibility, new kinds of coordination, the ability to delegate responsibilities and evaluate performance based on deliverables versus face time, and self awareness about how they might be contributing to a culture of overwork. Some organizations go a step further and hold managers accountable by rewarding them for being supportive of their subordinates' efforts to combine work and family.

As organizations become larger and more diversified with respect to their markets and products, there is no doubt that competitive pressures and customer demands make it dysfunctional for some business units to offer flexible or reduced work hours. Such claims should be evaluated skeptically, however, as they may simply be justifications for managers' inertia or resistance to needed change. Indeed, given human nature it is likely that such claims will be made more frequently than not. Hiring an outside consultant to critically evaluate job requirements and work processes may be necessary to ensure objectivity.

It is possible, of course, that a business unit's culture of long hours and heavy work loads reflects real demands and constraints that cannot be changed without threatening the survival of the business. If so, organizations should ensure that realistic job previews are offered to job candidates. In this way, job candidates can decide whether their personal values and priorities match the demands of the job.

In addition, because employees' values and priorities change as life circumstances change, work organizations should also offer flexible career paths to allow workers to migrate internally toward more supportive business units. It is also important that workers who opt for a more flexible schedule not be stigmatized and be able to return to more demanding jobs in the future. In this way, organizations can retain employees rather than lose them to more supportive competitors.

At the most fundamental level, organizations must focus on work culture and work processes, not on projecting an image of being family friendly. They also must consider the ways in which outdated assumptions influence the total number of hours employees are expected to work as well as where they work, when they work, and how they work (Rapoport et al. 2002). What can't be denied is that work-family conflict is a very real problem for many employees in today's fast-paced, global environment, and work-life programs are only the beginning of the solution.

References

Allen, T. D. 2001. "Family-supportive work environments: The role of organizational perceptions." Journal of Vocational Behavior (58) 414–435.

Bailyn, L. 1993. Breaking the mold: Women, men and time in the new corporate world. New York: The Free Press.

Bond, T. J., C. A. Thompson, E. Galinsky, and D. Prottas. 2003. Highlights of the 2002 National Study of the Changing Workforce. New York: Families and Work Institute.

Eby, L. T., W. J. Casper, A. Lockwood, C. Bordeaux, and A. Brinley 2005. "Work and family research in IO/OB: Content analysis and review of the literature (1980–2002)." Journal of Vocational Behavior (66): 124–197.

Nord, W R., S. Fox, A. Phoenix, and K. Viano. 2002. "Real-world reactions to work-life balance programs: Lessons for effective implementation." Organizational Dynamics (30): 223–238.

Rapoport, R., L. Bailyn, J. K. Fletcher, and B. H. Pruitt. 2002. Beyond work-family balance: Advancing gender equity and workplace performance. San Francisco: Jossey-Bass.

Shain, M. 2004. "Benchmarking the psychosocial environment." Journal of Employee Assistance 34 (4): 32–33.

Thompson, C. A., J. Andreassi, and D. Prottas. 2005. "Work-family Culture: Key to reducing workforce-workplace mismatch?" In Bianchi, S. M., L. M. Casper, and R. Berkowitz Kind (eds.), Workforce/Workplace Mismatch? Work, Family, Health and Well-Being, 117–132. Mahwah, N.J.: Lawrence Erlbaum Publishers.

Thompson, C. A., L Beauvais, and K. S. Lyness. 1999. "When work-family benefits are not enough: The influence of work-family culture on benefit utilization, organizational attachment, and work-family conflict." Journal of Vocational Behavior (54): 392–415.

CYNTHIA THOMPSON is a professor in the Zicklin School of Business at Baruch College in New York. She can be reached by e-mail at ThompCUNY@aol.com.

From *Journal of Employee Assistance*, Vol. 35, Issue 2, May 2005, pp. 7-9. Copyright © 2005 by Employee Assistance Professionals Association, Inc. (EAP). Reprinted by permission.

Life-Saving Communication

If a flu pandemic strikes, psychologists' expertise could help keep society running and ensure that the people who need treatment get it.

CHRISTOPHER MUNSEY

A U.S. House of Representatives briefing called for more attention to the role social science research can play in communicating with the public, as part of the national strategy for dealing with a potential flu pandemic.

Rep. Brian Baird (D-Wash.), a committee member and clinical psychologist, hosted the briefing in December, pointing out that if a flu pandemic occurs, it is unlikely there will be sufficient vaccines or antiviral drugs to slow its spread.

"Social distancing, effective communication and other public health measures will be our only realistic line of defense, and this is the realm of social science," he said.

The briefing, sponsored by Rep. Bart Gordon (D-Tenn.), ranking member of the Committee on Science, featured presentations from three experts, including psychologist and APA Fellow Baruch Fischhoff, PhD, Clete DiGiovanni, MD, a physician and scientist with the Defense Threat Reduction Agency, and Monica Schoch-Spana, PhD, a medical anthropologist at the University of Pittsburgh's Center for Biosecurity.

Worldwide, health officials worry that the H5N1 avian flu virus, which has caused outbreaks among poultry flocks in Asia and Europe, will evolve into a form easily transmissible from person to person. Since 1997 when the virus was first detected in Hong Kong, there have been cases of bird-to-human transmission, usually among people living and working near poultry flocks. So far, about half of the people who have been infected by the H5N1 virus have died.

With no vaccine yet developed to protect people against such an outbreak, containing it may depend on enlisting the public's cooperation in public health measures to control its spread. The potential toll in human life from such a flu pandemic could be high. Historically, the 1918–1919 flu pandemic was the deadliest, killing as many as 50 million people worldwide, including more than 500,000 Americans.

If and when the next influenza pandemic strikes, knowledge about effectively communicating with people about health risks could help government authorities stem the death toll and keep society functioning, the panelists agreed.

Based on research about how people best evaluate risk and respond to threats, psychologists can help public decision-makers craft effective messages, said Fischhoff at the briefing.

The public needs clear, concise and truthful messages about the scope of a pandemic and information about what they can do to stem its spread, experts said.

Sending the Right Message

Among the most important social science research findings on effective communication in such situations is the need to speak with candor, said Fischhoff, a social and decision sciences professor at Carnegie Mellon University and past-president of the Society for Risk Analysis.

"People want to know the truth, even if it's worrisome," said Fischhoff during his remarks at the briefing. "They want to know what they're up against in order to have the best chance of figuring out what to do for themselves, their loved ones and those they're responsible for."

Besides candor, Fischhoff included the following points as key to effective communication:

- People absorb only a limited amount of new information at a time, so messages should include only the most critical facts.
- People have difficulty understanding how small risks mount up over repeated exposure, so messages have to reflect that weakness.
- Audiences must be treated respectfully to avoid provoking emotional reactions that can interfere with well-reasoned decisions.

To design effective messages, Fischhoff recommends officials pull together experts from four groups, specifically: specialists in social services, law and education; experts in risk and decision-making; psychologists and cognitive scientists who can identify audience beliefs; and communications specialists who can ensure that the messages get through to the right audiences.

At the briefing, DiGiovanni supported Baird's contention that communicating with the public, and public health measures, represent the best available choice for dealing with a flu pandemic.

"In the absence of pharmacological agents to deal with pandemic influenza, we're going to have to rely on public health measures to control its spread in the human population," DiGiovanni said.

In her statement, Schoch-Spana called for more attention to the role that civic groups and social networks could play in responding to such a pandemic, given the way people mobilize on their own to confront crises in their communities.

False Positives

Fischhoff's emphasis on giving people information is echoed by other psychologists studying risk communication, such as Len Lecci, PhD, a psychology professor at the University of North Carolina, Wilmington, who studied people's reactions to the anthrax attacks in the fall of 2001.

With fellow psychology professor Dale Cohen, PhD, Lecci and a team of students evaluated people after asking them to read news articles about the event, in which someone deliberately spread anthrax spores through the mail to media figures and congressional offices. Of the 22 people infected by anthrax, five died.

Locally, Lecci and his students found high levels of fear about anthrax, despite the fact that there were no recorded cases of infection anywhere near the university. His findings and other psychological research illustrate the damage that fear can cause: Too many people may think they are sick and seek medical attention, bogging down the medical system and preventing those who are really infected from getting treatment.

To prevent those problems, messages about a flu pandemic from authorities should be specific about what's understood about the outbreak, where outbreaks have occurred and steps people can take in their daily lives to reduce their risk of exposure, he says.

The goal of such communication, says Lecci, is warning the public about the threat, motivating everyone to take steps to avoid infection and emphasizing information about who is most at risk, so that treatment remains concentrated on people who might actually be infected.

"If it really is a high-threat situation," says Lecci, "we make sure the public perceives it as a high-threat situation, and ideally, we give them something to do"—such as recommending hygiene measures to avoid infection or listing symptoms of the feared condition that they can evaluate themselves for. That helps reduce anxiety and keeps people functioning, he said.

Communication Failures

Psychological research can inform decision-makers about better ways to communicate with the public. One example that has not benefited from such research is the U.S. Department of Homeland Security's (DHS) color-coded terrorist attack alert system, says Roxane Cohen Silver, PhD, a trauma researcher and professor of psychology and social behavior at the University of California Irvine, currently serving on a senior advisory committee for DHS.

The system is color-coded to communicate terror risk, with green for "low" risk rising to red for "severe" risk. The system wasn't designed for alerting the public, she says, but as a way to advise law enforcement agencies about conditions for possible terrorist strikes in the aftermath of Sept. 11, 2001. Silver says that system is flawed because it tells people that there's a terrorist threat, but doesn't give them specific actions they can take in response.

If no attacks occur after repeated warnings, she says, and if those warnings don't advise specific actions for responding to a threat, people may stop listening to them.

"If the messages are not appropriately framed, if they're not seen as trustworthy, if they're not tied to something people can do, I think they will be dismissed or not attended to appropriately," she says.

If a flu pandemic occurs, telling people some actions they can take to control its spread is an important aspect of helping them maintain their psychological health, she says. Giving people a way to focus on taking action helps them adjust and prepare for unsettling events, Silver says.

People will want to know about measures they can take to lessen their chances of contracting flu and their family's risk, she says.

And keeping people healthy psychologically will help keep society functioning in the event of a flu pandemic by encouraging people to "press forward" with their daily lives.

"Feeling some sense of control facilitates coping," she says.

Soldier Support

Psychologists help troops handle the stresses of combat in Iraq and the anxieties of coming home.

CHRISTOPHER MUNSEY
Monitor Staff

L ast fall near the city of Ar Ramadi in Iraq, the strain of combat was beginning to overwhelm a platoon from an Army unit supporting infantry pursuing insurgents, says Lt. Col. Kathy Platoni, PsyD, an Army psychologist. The soldiers were worn down by a constant toll of attacks from insurgents, pushed close to the edge of panic by fear.

"They were afraid to die, because so many of them had," Platoni says.

The insurgents' most frequent method of attack came via improvised explosive devices (IEDs), bombs planted by insurgents on roads and highways used by U.S. forces, but other soldiers had been killed or wounded by small arms fire, rocket-propelled grenades and sniper bullets. "They watched their beloved fellow soldiers being blown up all the time, burning to death right in front of them," she says.

Concerned about the soldiers' ability to continue functioning given their level of fear and sheer physical exhaustion, Platoni worked with the unit's leadership to give many of them a 48-hour reprieve from operations.

During the break, the soldiers got a chance to sleep, take a shower, eat a hot meal and talk to mental health professionals about their experiences, if they wanted to talk. Following the brief respite, the soldiers returned to their duties, still facing constant danger, but better able to manage their fears and concentrate on the job at hand.

Platoni, a mobilized Army reservist and private practitioner in Beavercreek, Ohio, organized the reprieve project with fellow soldier and mental health specialist Sgt. George McQuade during a 10-month stint working at forward operating bases in Iraq last year. Nicknamed FOBs in military lingo and scattered across Iraq, the bases are where U.S. servicemen and -women live and operate from while serving in the country.

The need for psychological services, she says, is evident in the sobering statistics: As of mid-March, 2,302 service members had been killed in action in Iraq and more than 17,124 had been wounded. Every day in Iraq, psychologists like Platoni are helping soldiers, Marines, sailors and airmen cope with the traumatic effects of combat and the stresses of living and working far from home and family in austere, dangerous conditions. They're also helping service members adjust to life after Iraq when they return home.

How Therapy Is Delivered

In fact, the Army has redoubled its mental health efforts, making psychologists and combat stress-control teams more accessible to deployed soldiers, instituting more stress-control training for deploying soldiers and surveying individual units for problems.

For example, working with the Marines, Navy medicine has adopted a new approach called OSCAR, for Operational Stress Control and Readiness. Instead of assigning a Navy psychologist from outside the unit's existing medical support staff, the program matches psychologists with Marine regiments in the months before a deployment, continuing during a rotation in Iraq, then back home, so that closer relationships can be built between psychologists and a unit's leadership.

Psychologists across military branches say their goal is keeping service members mentally focused during deployment and fostering resilience that encourages service members to rely on both their individual and unit strengths. Keeping soldiers or Marines focused can help them stay sharp in a hazardous environment requiring constant vigilance, psychologists say.

Often, doing that requires psychologists to get out from behind a desk in the larger, relatively more secure FOBs and experience firsthand what some service members see patrolling the roads and neighborhoods of Iraqi cities and towns every day.

"Just living in this environment can be overwhelming."

Bret Moore
U.S. Army

Different Types of Stress

Psychologists say service members encounter two broad kinds of stress in Iraq. The first is combat stress, created by directly experiencing roadside bomb explosions, suicide vehicle bomber attacks and combat operations. Besides the threat of IEDs, service members also have to deal with the unnerving threat of lethal mortar and rocket attacks targeting service members where they work and sleep.

The second is operational or deployment stress, created by being deployed overseas and working in harsh conditions. Service members live with very little privacy and typically sleep jammed together in tents, trailers and bunkers, all while enduring an outside environment with temperatures topping 130 degrees in the summer and cold rain and mud in the winter.

And while the immediacy of e-mail makes it much easier for family members to stay in touch, it sometimes exacerbates stress when spouses relay bad news and expect help with financial problems and kids in trouble back home.

Psychologists say they help service members cope with the different types of stress in a number of ways. Working from a FOB in northern Iraq, Army Capt. Bret Moore, PsyD, is the officer-in-charge of a three-person preventive team from the 85th Medical Detachment, making care available to about 5,000 soldiers. "Just living in this environment can be overwhelming," Moore says.

The Army deals with soldiers experiencing combat stress using a set of precepts, BICEPS. The acronym stands for:

- *Brevity.* Treatment will be short, addressing the problem at hand.
- *Immediacy.* An intervention will take place quickly, before symptoms worsen.
- *Centrality.* Treatment will be set apart from medical facilities, as a way to reduce the stigma soldiers might feel about seeking mental health services.
- *Expectancy.* A soldier experiencing problems with combat stress is expected to return to duty.
- *Proximity.* Soldiers are treated as close to their units as possible and are not evacuated from the area of operations.
- *Simplicity.* Besides therapy, the basics of a good meal, hot shower and a comfortable place to sleep ensure a soldier's basic physical needs are met.

All told, Moore says about 98 percent of soldiers sent to restoration areas come back to their units.

If a soldier isn't sent to a restoration area for 48- to 72-hour respite, Moore says he's only got enough time for between five and six therapy sessions with each soldier. The therapy's goal is keeping the soldier with his or her unit and functioning, he says. Moore uses a variety of techniques, ranging from cognitive-behavioral therapy to handing out CDs explaining deep breathing and other relaxation practices. To strengthen resiliency, he advises soldiers to exercise every day—preferably through a team sport—to eat balanced meals and to sleep when they can, he says.

It's not just Army psychologists helping care for soldiers. Another psychologist, Air Force Capt. Michael Detweiler, PhD, runs a life skills support center at an overseas base in Southwest Asia.

Detweiler describes himself as the only mental health provider for about 10,000 service members, mostly Army and Air Force personnel. Besides assisting soldiers in dealing with trauma, he often helps service members get along better.

"We live with the same people we work with...so the same people who drive you crazy at work are the same people you live with," Detweiler says.

Other important roles for psychologists in Iraq are helping leaders understand morale problems or handle interpersonal difficulties within units. Navy psychologist Lt. Cmdr. Gary Hoyt, PsyD, served with two Marine regimental combat teams in 2004 in Iraq, during which he regularly went out on patrols. Being present and exposed to the same dangers helped him earn the trust of junior enlisted Marines.

If the tempo of operations was too high, if they weren't getting enough sleep or if they were struggling with the big-picture "whys" of their mission in Iraq, Hoyt says he heard about it. With his access to leaders, Hoyt served as a conduit for those concerns, letting battalion-level officers know what was bothering junior Marines.

"There's no way they're going to hear this input directly from the junior ranks," he says. Besides talking to senior leadership, Hoyt says he stressed education and training of small-unit leaders about combat stress so Marines could spot problems themselves and help each other tackle them before the problems worsened.

Follow-up Care Strengthened

Besides offering mental health treatment for deployed soldiers, the Army also seeks to detect symptoms of post-traumatic stress disorder or other combat-related psychological problems when they return home, says Col. Bruce Crow, PsyD, the Army's chief psychologist. Currently, the best estimates are that about 15 percent of soldiers returning from Iraq will show symptoms of post-traumatic stress, Crow says.

As part of a militarywide initiative, all service members receive a health screening about 90 days after they return home. In addition, all soldiers and their families can tap into counseling through the Deployment Cycle Support Program.

Aiding in this effort is Lt. Col. Platoni, who works with returning combat soldiers on adjusting to life in the civilian world.

UNIT 6

Enhancing Human Adjustment: Learning to Cope Effectively

Unit Selections

Key Points to Consider

- What are some of the common problems we face as we adjust to the demands of the modern world?

- What are the various forms of intervention for individuals experiencing problems of adjustment?

- What are the advantages and disadvantages of these interventions?

- What form of treatment would you least like: psychotherapy or medication? Why?

- How do emotional states affect physical health?

- Do you think humans can find a perpetual state of happiness or does happiness occur at the moment?

Student Web Site

www.mhcls.com/online

Internet References

Further information regarding these Web sites may be found in this book's preface or online.

John Suler's Teaching Clinical Psychology Site
http://www.rider.edu/users/suler/tcp.html

Health Information Resources
http://www.health.gov/nhic/Pubs/tollfree.htm

Knowledge Exchange Network (KEN)
http://www.mentalhealth.org

Mental Health Net
http://www.mentalhealth.net

Mind Tools
http://www.mindtools.com/

NetPsychology
http://www.psychology.info/

On each college and university campus a handful of students experience overwhelming stress and life-shattering crises. One student learns that her mother, living in a distant city, has terminal cancer. Another receives the sad news that his parents are divorcing. A sorority blackballs a young woman who was determined to become a "sister"; she commits suicide. The sorority members now experience overwhelming guilt.

Fortunately, almost every campus houses a counseling center for students; some universities also offer assistance to employees. At the counseling service, trained professionals are able to offer aid and therapy to troubled members of the campus community.

Many individuals are able to adapt to life's vagaries, even to life's disasters. Other individuals flounder. They simply do not know how to adjust to change much less to disaster and chaos. These individuals sometimes seek temporary professional assistance from a therapist or counselor. These professionals then must decide how and when to intervene. Very few individuals, fortunately, require long-term care.

There are as many definitions of maladjustment as there are mental health professionals. Some practitioners define mental illness as "whatever society cannot tolerate." Others define it in terms of statistics: "If a majority does not behave that way, then the behavior signals maladjustment." Some professionals suggest that an inadequate self-concept is a symptom of maladjustment while others cite a lack of contact with reality. A few psychologists claim that to call one individual ill suggests that the rest are healthy by contrast, when, in fact, there may be few real distinctions among people.

Maladjustment is not only difficult to define, it is difficult to treat. For each definition, a theorist develops a treatment strategy. Psychoanalysts press clients to recall their dreams, their childhood, and their intrapsychic conflicts in order to analyze the contents of the unconscious. Humanists encourage clients to explore all of the facets of their lives in order to become less defensive.

Behaviorists are usually concerned with observable and therefore treatable symptoms or behaviors. For behaviorists, no underlying causes are postulated to be the roots of adjustment problems. Other therapists, namely psychiatrists (who are physicians by training), may utilize these therapies and add drugs or psychosurgery to the regimen.

This brief list of interventions raises further questions. For instance, is one form of therapy more effective, less expensive, or longer lasting than another? Is one disorder better treated by one particular form of therapy? Who should make the diagnosis, and who should provide the treatment? If two experts disagree on the diagnosis and treatment, how do we decide which professional is correct? These questions continue to be debated.

Some psychologists question whether professional intervention is necessary at all. In one well-publicized but highly criticized study, researcher Hans Eysenck was able to show that spontaneous remission rates were as high as therapeutic "cure" rates. You, yourself, may be wondering whether professional help is always necessary. Can people be their own healers? Is support from friends as productive as professional treatment? Do people naturally adjust over time?

The first article offers a brief introduction to the subject of mental disorder. Writing for *The Scientist*, Douglas Steinberg discusses mental disorders and how neuroimaging is bringing greater understanding to professionals and lay persons. Brain imaging offers one means by which professionals can predict who is at risk for a particular disorder or even for suicide.

After this introductory article, we proceed to an article on interventions. Two means for helping individuals cope better are the use of psychotropic medications and psychotherapy. Psychotropic drugs are not without side effects, some very debilitating. An important study reported in *Consumer Reports* and reprinted in the second article of this unit reveals that psychotherapy (the talking cure) can be just as effective as medications.

The next article is about general health and its complex relationship to general well-being. Scientists have shown that various chronic, negative emotions can indeed have a deleterious effect on our well-being—both physical and psychological. Alice Lesch Kelly reviews this scientific evidence and by so doing demonstrates that the immune system and the psyche are inextricably linked. She concludes that balanced emotional states write the bottom line for good mental and physical health.

The final article in the unit ends the anthology on an upbeat note. Positive psychology is sweeping across modern psychological research and thought. In this last article, Richard Handler describes this new movement and relevant research as well as his personal study of it. He ends by noting how positive psychology has affected his own growth and adjustment.

Brain Imaging Struggles for Psychiatric Respect

Researchers Seek a High-tech Way to Customize Drug, Talk, and Surgical Treatments for Various Disorders.

DOUGLAS STEINBERG

Psychiatrists can draw upon long clinical experience with adult patients to surmise why antidepressant medications foster suicidal thoughts and behavior in some children, as the US Food and Drug Administration warned this fall. Treatment often restores a person's ability to act purposefully, including self-destructively, before it improves his or her mood. In the weeks separating these two stages, a few desperately sad but resolute patients are attracted to suicide. Unfortunately, doctors have no systematic way to judge who is in danger.

Brain imaging might eventually provide such a test. For 20 years, psychiatrists and neurologists have applied positron emission tomography (PET), the imaging technology based on injections of slightly radioactive tracers, to chart metabolism and blood flow in the troubled human brain. The premise is that concentrations and movements of these tracers reflect idiosyncratic patterns of neuronal activity characteristic of a psychiatric disorder. Depression and obsessive-compulsive disorder (OCD) have been particularly well investigated.

One longtime cheerleader for this field is Eric R. Kandel, the Nobel Prize-winning Columbia University neuroscientist who did a psychiatric residency in the early 1960s. "I think there's a renaissance of interest in the biology of psychotherapy ... because of the ability to image the brain," he enthused on Charlie Rose's TV talk show this past September. Work has focused not only on psychotherapy (talk-based treatments) but also on serotonin-reuptake-inhibitor (SRI) drugs and psychosurgery. Meanwhile, psychiatric-treatment research is beginning to apply functional magnetic resonance imaging (fMRI), a radioactivity-free technology. Like some PET scans, fMRI tracks increased blood flow and presumably neuronal activity.

Though this field's first order of business has been to determine which brain changes are inextricably linked to therapeutic effects, the ultimate hope is to use imaging to predict which treatment will best suit a specific patient. Lewis R. Baxter Jr., a psychiatry professor at the University of Florida in Gainesville, envisions a scenario in which a brain scan will indicate, "Yes, Mrs. Jones, you have Type 27B depression, and this is the drug or therapy you should take." Baxter continues, "I believe, with a little bit of luck, we'll be there in OCD before—I'll go out on a limb here—before this decade is over."

Psychiatric brain imaging, however, must first overcome various practical and scientific obstacles. The stakes in this struggle are high for some mental-health professionals and patients. Selecting one treatment over others with equivalent statistical efficacy is now mostly a process of "just trial and error," contends Scott L. Rauch, director of psychiatric neuroimaging research at Massachusetts General Hospital in Boston. "There's little to guide us about what the likelihood of response is for a given patient." He asks, "Wouldn't it be wonderful if we could send that patient for a [predictive] imaging test?"

Talk versus drugs

OCD is a disorder in which a person is relentlessly hounded by intense feelings that something is amiss—germ-laden hands, for example—and must be rectified immediately. During the 1990s, PET work by Baxter and colleagues at the University of California, Los Angeles, established that OCD is marked by elevated metabolism in the orbital frontal cortex and right caudate nucleus. Studies also demonstrated that behavioral therapy and SRI drugs can lessen these abnormalities, and correlations were found between treatment responses and different patterns of brain metabolism.

OCD is a relatively well-defined, homogeneous condition. Major depressive disorder, in contrast, is considered a group of illnesses. Not surprisingly, PET images reveal a bewildering array of brain abnormalities. Metabolic signals from imaging, nevertheless, are "pretty well behaved," says Helen S. Mayberg, a psychiatry and neurology professor at Emory University School of Medicine in Atlanta. "They change with treatment, and they change differently when people get better than when they don't."

Mayberg and colleagues at the University of Toronto recently published a PET paper detailing how cognitive-behavior therapy (CBT) affected depressed patients. Lasting several months, CBT uses homework assignments and guided practice to identify relationships between a patient's thoughts, feelings, and behaviors. The researchers found that when 14 subjects responded to CBT, glucose metabolism decreased in certain cortical regions and increased in the hippocampus.[1] In an earlier study of 13 other depressed subjects, the SRI drug paroxetine (Paxil) had the opposite effects on those same areas. Several cortical areas affected by CBT, but not by the drug, involve "self-actualization, self-reference, and reappraisal of information," notes Mayberg.

In 2001, a team of scientists, including Baxter, compared paroxetine treatment of depression with interpersonal therapy (IPT), a conversational approach that is less structured than CBT and deals with themes including social deficits, role disputes and transitions, and grief. PET scans showed metabolic dissimilarities between the 10 subjects who chose to take medication and the 14 who opted for IPT[2] but these variations were not identical to those detected by Mayberg. "My suspicion would be that, if not different patient populations, it's the different treatments," Baxter muses about the divergent findings. "[IPT and CBT] really do focus on different aspects of depression."

Cost-Effective Applications

Though these studies suggest potential brain markers for effective treatment, imaging's clinical applicability still elicits much skepticism from psychiatrists. One qualm stems from a PET scarfs price tag of several thousand dollars. "Suppose you found a pattern of cerebral metabolism that indicated that you really did have a better chance with medication than psychotherapy, or vice-versa," says Michael E. Thase, a psychiatry professor at the University of Pittsburgh School of Medicine. "The cost of that test might actually be more than the cost of treatment." (Psychoanalysis, which can last many years, is not a standard therapy for depression.)

Thase acknowledges, however, that brain imaging might be cost-effective when the treatment options include electro-convulsive therapy (ECT) or psychosurgery. Harold Sackeim, a psychiatry and radiology professor at Columbia University College of Physicians and Surgeons in New York, is now using PET to track cerebral blood flow at patients' second ECT session. His goal is to be able to predict who will eventually benefit from shock treatment.

Massachusetts General Hospital is among a handful of US medical centers performing anterior cingulotomies, operations in which neurosurgeons lesion a cortical area in patients with intractable depression and OCD. But only about half of patients who undergo this operation respond positively. Using PET, Rauch and his colleagues discovered that responders with depression have higher presurgical metabolism in the left subgenual prefrontal cortex and left thalamus.[3] Another study found that presurgical metabolism in OCD responders is elevated in a part of the right posterior cingulate cortex.[4] This area connects to all nodes of the abnormal circuit that is OCD's hallmark.

Rauch hopes to replicate these small studies, but patient accrual is slow because surgeons at Mass General perform only about a dozen cingulotomies each year. "Obviously, as the data set gets

larger and the findings persist, then confidence grows" about using PET to decide for or against surgery, Rauch says. Meanwhile, he has begun to collect imaging data on deep-brain stimulation, a newer surgical approach to treating depression and OCD.

What especially concerns Rauch is data reproducibility, which can be elusive when the focus is a heterogeneous syndrome like depression. Wayne C. Drevets, a psychiatrist and senior investigator at the National Institute of Mental Health (NIMH), finds that he can boost reproducibility of PET results by scanning only patients with recurrent or early-onset depression or a family history of the disease. He and his NIMH boss, Robert B. Innis, are starting to image an even more exclusive sample: people with genetic polymorphisms linked to depression. The downside is that Drevets cannot examine the effects of talk-based treatments. "People who have recurrent major depressive episodes that meet our inclusion criteria typically don't respond to psychotherapy," he explains.

Non-Pet Projects

No research strategy, of course, applies universally; consider PET, for example. David R. Rosenberg, a professor of child psychiatry at Wayne State University School of Medicine in Detroit, specializes in OCD and depression in children, whose developing nervous systems cannot be exposed to even the scant radioactivity of a PET scan. Instead, his team uses an MRI-based technology called proton magnetic resonance spectroscopy. It allows scientists to monitor changes in both anatomy and neurochemistry.

Rosenberg is launching two imaging studies that will compare medication and CBT treatment of 100 children with OCD and 100 with depression. Similarly sized control groups, which will not receive sham treatments, should signal whether any brain-pattern changes observed in patients "are different from the changes that a healthy adolescent would just have over time," he says.

Rosenberg's team has also initiated pilot fMRI projects. "Our hope, on these higher-power MRI machines, which can do things faster, is that we can do all three studies—the functional, the chemical, and the structural—in the same child in the same scanning session," he states. "But we're not quite there yet."

Other investigators also mention current or prospective fMRI projects, but few papers have been published describing the fMRI effects of psychiatric treatments. Unlike PET, fMRI requires subjects to perform some task during the scan, so protocols typically require patients to look at emotion-provoking stimuli. Brain imaging then reveals blood-flow responses in depressed subjects before and after treatment, or compared to nondepressed controls.[5]

Magnetic-resonance research, however, could soon become far more sophisticated. Last September the University of Illinois at Chicago (UIC) inaugurated what it describes as the world's most powerful MRI machine for examining humans. Containing a 50-ton, 9.4 Tesla magnet, the device will facilitate psychiatric studies, predicts Keith R. Thulborn, a professor of radiology, physiology, and biophysics at UIC. (State-of-the-art clinical scanners currently use 3 Tesla magnets.)

"Where brain dysfunction happens is at the level of the biochemistry that supports the function," Thulborn explains. The new machine should allow biochemists to "move beyond looking at just a water or fat signal, which is what conventional MRI is based on." More specifically, scientists should be able to track the fate of injections of two rare nonradioactive isotopes: carbon-13, ultimately incorporated into carbon dioxide during glucose metabolism, and oxygen-17, incorporated into water during oxidative phosphorylation. The machine should also be able to measure sodium and phosphorus concentrations, which can indicate metabolism and tissue death.

Simplistic Interpretation?

PET technology is also advancing, as more radioligands are developed and spatial resolution shrinks to about four millimeters. But as imager and reagents improve, doubts persist as to what exactly they reveal. Do changes in brain scans during psychiatric treatment show the abatement of symptoms or the elimination of a disorder's causes?

"A lot of the interpretation of that [imaging] work, in my own view, has been somewhat simplistic," asserts Sackeim. The field's biggest problem, he continues, "is that it's largely correlational." To experimentally establish cause-and-effect relationships, Sackeim envisions curing psychiatric disorders by engineering particular brain patterns, not by drugs or talk therapy, but by focal techniques such as transcranial magnetic stimulation.

Mayberg contends that psychiatric brain imaging has moved slightly beyond the correlational stage. Noting that "we have markers that tell us that people who get better on therapy have brain-network states that are different from people who do well on drug," she describes the next generation of studies as randomizing patients to drug, psychotherapy, or placebo, and then seeing "whether or not you properly predicted outcome."

Nevertheless, no imaging study is apparently imminent that will tackle the link between antidepressant drugs and suicide. One difficulty is disentangling preexisting suicidal tendencies from those triggered by drugs. Suicidal patients usually receive medications whose effects on brain scans would swamp the effects of any endogenous abnormality, remarks Drevets. To skirt this confounding factor, he and David A. Brent, at the University of Pittsburgh, are conducting a PET study of unmedicated depressed people. Some of the subjects formerly considered killing themselves; others were never seriously suicidal. Drevets expects that this pilot project, which measures cerebral blood flow and serotonin-receptor concentrations, will be finished in about a year.

References

1. K. Goldapple et al., "Modulation of cortical-limbic pathways in major depression," *Arch Gen Psychiat*, 61:34–41, 2004.
2. A. L. Brody et al., "Regional brain metabolic changes in patients with major depression treated with either paroxetine or interpersonal therapy," *Arch Gen Psychiat*, 58:631–40, 2001.
3. D. D. Dougherty et al., "Cerebral metabolic correlates as potential predictors of response to anterior cingulotomy for treatment of major depression," *J Neurosurg*, 99:1010–7, 2003.
4. S. L. Rauch et al., "Cerebral metabolic correlates as potential predictors of response to anterior cingulotomy for obsessive compulsive disorder," *Biol Psychiat*, 50:659–67, 2001.
5. C. H. Fu et al., "Attenuation of the neural response to sad faces in major depression by antidepressant treatment: a prospective, event-related functional magnetic resonance imaging study," *Arch Gen Psychiat*, 61:877–89, September 2004.

DOUGLAS STEINBERG (dsteinberg@the-scientist.com)

From *The Scientist*, December 6, 2004, pp. 17-19. Copyright © 2004 by The Scientist. Reprinted by permission.

Are We Becoming a Nation of Depressives?

By many estimates depression has become the scourge of Western Man. Already the fourth leading cause of disability in the workforce, it is projected to reach Number Two by the year 2020 (after respiratory infections).

KEVIN TURNQUIST

Psychiatrists have taken the position that this apparent increase in depression is just a mirage. We'll argue that this much depression has always been present in the population. The party line is that it is simply better diagnosis and the decreased stigma associated with our treatments that is responsible for the climbing numbers of depressed people. Some of us remain unconvinced.

Research indicates that in any given year over seventeen million Americans experience major depression. Fifteen percent of our population (twenty percent if you are an American woman) are diagnosed with depression at some point in their lifetimes. The treatment of depression has become an enormous industry in this country. Sales of antidepressant medications are at over 13 billion dollars per year and have tripled in the U.S. in just a decade. In many parts of the country people wait for several months or longer for a fifteen-minute appointment with their psychiatrist so that they can continue to receive their antidepressant pills. Family practitioners are dispensing even more of these medications than the psychiatrists. Yet the consistent message to the treaters of depression is that only a small portion of the people who are suffering from depression are receiving treatment for it. Countless others are suffering and it is our responsibility to bring treatment—almost always in the form of expensive new medications—to the untreated.

This view of depression raises questions in the minds of many observers. Why should this disorder be on the rise despite the treatment efforts of several generations of psychiatrists and the combined resources of multi-billion dollar pharmaceutical companies? Is there something new about depression itself or does this represent a problem inherent in modern western society? How did humans manage to get through life before Prozac was introduced? Fortunately, some preliminary answers to these questions are beginning to emerge. Startling discoveries from basic research in neuroscience have forced us to begin thinking about the problem of depression in new and different ways. Before looking at these new findings, however, a review of how we got to our present state of affairs may be worthwhile.

Part of the helping profession's difficulty in dealing with depression is that we have never really understood what would cause one person to be depressed while a neighbor in similar circumstances remains symptom free. A number of explanatory theories have had their day: anger turned inward results in depression; depression is a reaction to real or imagined loss; depression represents the gap between our real view of ourselves and our unconscious, idealized version of how our lives should be; depression is a genetically inherited disorder; depression is a result of "chemical imbalances" in neurotransmitter systems that can only be understood by trained psychiatrists. Since each of these models undoubtedly have some truth in them, any new model of depression will have to explain why each of these diverse viewpoints has led to the relief of suffering in at least some individuals.

Clouding our view of depression even further is the fact that bona fide depression can arise from variety of "physical" causes. Pancreatic cancer, heart attacks, strokes, thyroid problems, side effects of a host of nonpsychiatric medications, even changes in exercise routines have all been clearly linked to the onset of depression in some individuals.

Modern psychiatry has dealt with this uncertainty about the root cause of depression largely by ignoring it. The sequence of *Diagnostic and Statistical Manuals* released by the American Psychiatric Association have been, by design, heavy on description and devoid of explanatory theories. The most recent manual requires that at least five of nine key symptoms be present for at least two weeks for major depression to be diagnosed: depressed mood, decreased interest in activities, significant weight loss or gain, disturbed sleep patterns, being physically agitated or slowed down, fatigue, feelings of worthlessness or excessive guilt, decreased ability to concentrate or make decisions, and recurrent thoughts of death or suicide. The manual does make the provision that if these symptoms are "clearly due to a medical condition" the diagnosis of major depression is not given. Otherwise, if you've experienced five of these nine symptoms for at least two weeks you qualify as a depressed person.

The APA's treatment recommendations do acknowledge that some depressions of lesser severity may be treated successfully with *either* medication or psychotherapy but, in practice, if you receive a diagnosis of major depression in an American psychiatrist's office a prescription for an antidepressant medication is almost certain to follow. Today this translates into a prescription for Prozac or one of it's chemical cousins (the serotonin specific reuptake inhibitors or "SSRI" medications like Paxil, Zoloft, Celexa, Luvox, and the like). This new generation of antidepressants has been so much safer and easier to use that it is now rare for psychiatrists to prescribe any of the older, "tricyclic" antidepressants that were the mainstay of treatment until the late 1980's. Millions of Americans take these new medications each day, usually showing some benefit from the treatment. Yet a number of problems make this very common equation of *five-of-nine depressive symptoms = treatment with a newer antidepressant*t rather problematic.

First of all, there is no research to suggest that these newer—and dramatically more expensive—medications are more effective in reducing depressive symptoms than the older ones. In fact, just the opposite seems to be the case. In severe depressions the "tricyclics" prove to be a bit more effective than the new drugs. It is the decreased frequency of side effects that have fueled the upsurge in use of the new medications. But that very tolerability has led to their being prescribed for a host of new maladies: mild depression, phobias, obsessions, post-traumatic stress symptoms, anxiety disorders of any kind, eating disorders, excessive shopping, hair pulling, skin picking, religious scrupulosity, sexual disorders, gambling, aggression, environmental sensitivities, and slow eating. It is difficult to imagine a single human problem that American psychiatrists have not reported as being successfully treated with SSRI's .

This wide-ranging effectiveness raises important questions about whether these drugs could possibly have a specific beneficial action in each of these disorders or whether some other overriding but unrecognized action is at work. The most plausible idea encountered so far is that these medications induce some sort of fundamental shift in the relationships between areas of the brain involved with thought and those involved with emotion. Perhaps SSRI 's decrease the emotional response to mental events so that chronic worries, obsessions, sad thoughts, and the like do not result in emotional responses of the usual magnitude. This effect has been likened to turning the brightness knob on your television all the way up. Everything is brighter but there isn't much contrast. Days can feel pretty much the same regardless of their events. Some experience this as a welcome relief from mental anguish; others have described it as "soul robbing".

Compounding matters further is the fact that all sorts of therapies have proven beneficial in reducing depressive symptoms.

Psychotherapy looks as good or better at relieving depression, especially at one year follow up, as antidepressant drugs. Exercise is a powerful and well recognized antidepressant. St. John's Wort and other herbal preparations are widely used as antidepressants in some parts of the world. Artificially lengthening the short days of winter with phototherapy lights has dramatic antidepressant effects for some individuals. Some have found that even exposing the back of the knees to such lights can treat depression. Depriving a person of an entire night's sleep is an old but effective antidepressant therapy. While this is just a partial list of effective alternatives to antidepressant medication, it is unlikely that you would hear mention of any of them in a psychiatrist's office these days.

In reality, the newer antidepressant drugs are such a main stay of treatment for depression that alternatives are rarely considered. The fact that these drugs offer only a 20–30% improvement over treatment with placebos (sugar pills) isn't a common topic of discussion in the office. Nor are patients routinely told that even if they do respond well to antidepressants they might have a great deal of difficulty discontinuing them, even several years down the road.

In some patients stopping SSRI's may result in a variety of symptoms including depression, insomnia, nightmares, anxiety, headache, nausea and even neurological effects such as restlessness and tingling sensations. The Internet abounds with personal tales of people who have been on antidepressants for years and can't get off them no matter what they do. Some also find that they have to increase their dosage over time or add a second antidepressant to maintain the same degree of benefit—"Prozac poop out" as it is known in the trade. By diagnostic criteria used in the third *Diagnostic and Statistical Manual* this need for increasing doses (tolerance) and the emergence of significant adverse effects when the medication is stopped (withdrawal) were sufficient to qualify a compound as an addictive drug. Definitions change. We now speak of "antidepressant discontinuation effects" rather than "withdrawal" and the suggestion that these drugs may be addictive is not particularly welcome in psychiatric circles.

So a brief and simplistic assessment of the modern psychiatrist's position on depression would be that we really don't know what causes depression. We don't know why it should be increasing in our population. We don't know why it responds to so many types of treatment. We don't know how our medications work but we're happy that they do.

It is very difficult to understand depression and it's treatment without consideration of economic factors. Psychiatrists can make an excellent living doing nothing else but prescribing SSRI's to people who endorse having five or more depressive symptoms. If, like a great many prominent American psychiatrists of today, you also receive money directly from the pharmaceutical companies for speaking engagements, research, or "consultation" you can do a whole lot better than making a comfortable living. Imagine the effects if the medical-legal climate dictated that every depressed person had to be offered twice-weekly psychotherapy as an alternative to medication. The financial effects would be catastrophic for all of the major players in the depression industry. The interests of the psychiatric profession, the pharmaceutical companies, and Health Maintenance Organizations are so intertwined that it is hard to begin to get an objective view of the questions surrounding depression.

It should come as no surprise that the clearest current look at the issue of depression comes from the hard science researchers. In the late 1990's several striking findings began to emerge from their laboratories.

Perhaps the most unexpected and important finding was that the brain continues to make new brain cells in some key areas all the way through the life span. This ran contrary to the commonly accepted belief that the number of our brain cells was fixed by early adulthood and that a gradual decline in these cells was about the best that could be hoped for. We now know that stem cells—the cells capable of transforming themselves into any other kind of cell—operate in the nervous system. And it is looking like the activities of these multipotential cells may be involved in depressive illness.

Two main areas that continue to produce new neurons in the brain have emerged. The olfactory bulb (which is involved with our sense of smell) and the hippocampus. The hippocampus has been the focus of much of the latest depression research. It is a part of the limbic system, an ancient area of the brain that is involved in the generation of emotions in humans and other mammals. Specifically, the hippocampus appears to be primarily involved in the formation of memories. How memory actually works remains quite mysterious. The idea that we can recall specific events from our past as a result of instantaneous electrochemical communications between living nerve cells seems almost far-fetched if one really thinks about it. The idea that forming new nerve cells would be involved does make some intuitive sense. The evolving data suggesting that we add new brain cells in the hippocampus every day raises the intriguing possibility that nerve cells that we make today are somehow connected to the memories that we make *of* today. Perhaps the common experience of having odors trigger powerful, specific memories is related to the fact that each of these brain areas has nerve cells and brain connections that were formed at the same time.

Scientists have also been surprised to discover a connection between the size of the hippocampus and depressive illness. One study suggests that the hippocampus may shrink by an average of 19% in depression. Other research has found that SSRI antidepressants and shock treatment, among other factors, restore the hippocampus to more normal volume. This increase in size of the hippocampus is now considered to be a possible mechanism by which these treatments promote recovery from depressive illness. This puzzling idea would have seemed beyond the realm of possibility even a decade ago. Modern psychiatry is in the very early stages of trying to make sense of these findings. How it will impact the treatment of depression in psychiatric practice is anybody's guess.

Psychiatrists have known for decades that there is a powerful connection between depression and memory. Anyone who has been around a lot of depressed people has become aware of an interesting phenomenon: memories change when one is depressed. Ask a person who is suffering from severe depression about their childhood and a depressing picture may emerge. They had no friends, they had no particular talents, their parents were mean, and nothing good ever happened to them. Ask the same question when they have recovered to a more normal mood and very different, more optimistic stories are recounted.

In some severe depressions a syndrome called *pseudodementia* is encountered. Basically, the memory functions become so impaired that it can be difficult to determine whether the person is actually suffering from Alzheimer's disease or some other dementing illness rather than major depression. A number of sophisticated neuropsychological tests have been developed to help make this determination. So the connection between depression and memory is a robust one. But psychiatry has not really considered the possibility that the memory problems could be anything but a simple result of the depressive process. The idea that *causation* could somehow be involved is new to us.

Depression involves a good deal more than sad feelings or even memory problems. When we are exposed to any incoming stimuli a predictable sequence of events occurs. The brain processes this raw sensory data through a primary and then a secondary association cortex. Once the information is in usable form it is sent directly down to the limbic system. The brain asks "What is out there? What is new? What have I seen like this before?" This involves comparing the new data with existing memories and stored symbols. Once evaluated, we then must decide what to do about it; the appropriate emotions, impulses, and responses are then generated. The most striking feature of many people who suffer from severe memory disorders is that they cannot activate themselves in response to the changes in their world. They may seem listless and incapable of motivation or they respond in ways that don't fit their surroundings.

As the link between depression and changes in the hippocampus has become clearer a search for factors that increase or decrease the growth of these critical cells has ensued. Even more interesting than the emerging list of positive and negative growth factors has been the new picture of brain functioning that has developed within just a matter of a few years. This new model of the brain may ultimately shed some light on the age-old question of what depression really is.

For the past couple of decades psychiatrists have been very concerned with events occurring at the synapse—the area where two nerve cells meet and communicate via the release of neurotransmitters. Antidepressants have been presumed to work by affecting the messages transmitted across these synapses. The introduction of SSRIs is believed to inhibit the reabsorbtion of serotonin by the cell that released it, extending its time at the synapses and therefore communication with the receiving cells. Or so the theory goes. But why the increase in serotonin should have an antidepressant effect has remained a mystery. The fact that an antidepressant medication used in Europe (Tianeptine) has exactly the *opposite* effect at the synapse, i.e. increases serotonin reuptake, but works equally well, has called into question our assumptions about how SSRI's actually exert their effects.

The new neuroscience has shifted attention from synapses to genes. Messages carried across synapses by neurotransmitters represent just one type of communication that neurons receive. They also receive direct hormonal signals through circulating chemicals like steroids and sex hormones. Even gases such as nitrous oxide are used by neurons to communicate with each other. The ultimate effect of these communications is eventually mediated by turning individual genes on and off.

Several surprising findings have come out of the mapping of the human genome. The actual number of our genes—approximately 35,000—is startlingly low compared to earlier estimates, until one considers the possible variations in arrangement. And the search for factors responsible for influencing genes that are responsible for developing new neurons in the hippocampus—and for fending off depression—has turned up some candidates that psychiatrists may have intuitively expected.

Shock treatment, antidepressant medications, and physical exercise appear to have this effect. And an enriched, stimulating environment promotes new neuronal growth in these key areas involving memory. This might translate into having a decent, safe place to live, some meaningful work, and loving relationships with other humans but there is much room for individual variation.

Novelty—experience that is new or unexpected—is another logical factor that has been shown to positively affect the growth of hippocampal neurons. Why would we spend a lot of our resources supporting the areas of the brain involved with making new memories if we weren't having any new experiences to remember? An intriguing outgrowth of this research is the possibility that *sameness* might ultimately prove to be the worst stressor of all for the human brain.

Mundane jobs, boring routines, and the absence of real struggles for survival may all contribute to depression's increasing place in our society. We cannot discount the possibility that the activities which seem to add diversity to our modern existence don't provide the sorts of stimulation that healthy brains thrive on. Perhaps the novelty of images dancing on electronic screens is enough to capture our attention but is insufficient to cause brain changes that depend on real life experiences.

The role of sleep in the generation of new neurons is an interesting story in itself. Research has suggested that in rats a gene called zif-268 is involved in the ongoing reorganization of the memory portion of our nervous system. This gene becomes activated during Rapid Eye Movement sleep—the sleep in which we dream. Activation only takes place, however, if the rat has been exposed to sufficiently powerful stimulation (e.g. mazes, toys, exploration, etc.) during the waking hours before sleep. The implication may be that we sleep differently—and do different work reconstructing our brains—if our days are filled with new and interesting experiences. Disturbed sleep or a stimulus-poor life might result in a decrease in new neurons.

Circulating hormones are known to affect the hippocampus. Premenstrual mood changes, depression following pregnancy, and depression around menopause may all be mediated by changes in estrogen levels. One researcher suggests that the hippocampus "almost pulsates" in response to estrogens. Testosterone has been implicated in the migration and hook up of undifferentiated neurons throughout the brain. Sex hormones, and sexual activity, are likely to be recognized as major factors in the emerging model of depression. And the glucocorticoid hormones—released by the adrenal glands in response to stress—may have the most far-reaching implications in terms of why we become depressed.

Scientists have determined that we humans share about 97 percent of our genes with chimpanzees—but that 3 percent difference is very important. Some of the difference is obvious in how our big human frontal lobes are constructed and wired. This enlargement of our frontal lobes is responsible for our ability to manipulate *symbols* to a far greater extent than all other mammals. We are unparalleled in our ability to construct a different reality in our minds, one that can be entirely separate from the objective external reality that all animals must interact with. The biggest problem with this talent is that we can also attach *emotions* to these private internal events.

When it comes to the sorts of emotions that we attach to our incessant thoughts, we are more similar to the chimpanzees than we care to admit. Our big symbol producing frontal lobes are basically hooked up to limbic—or emotional systems—that are not too evolved from other primates. As a result we are hard-wired to deal with the same issues and emotional responses as the other social primates. Who is superior in the troop to whom? Who will be an acceptable and willing mate? Take away these two basic issues: mating, and dominance to other humans in the social group and there would be nothing to put on television. We wouldn't know what to think about anymore. Some have suggested that there wouldn't be as much depression in humans either.

When we humans worry, what is it about? Our place in the hierarchy? What other humans thinks of us? How the boss will react if we don't land a deal or make our productivity goals? Are our neighbors superior to us because of their expensive possesions? Do the latest objects of our sexual desires have any inclination to copulate with us? How do we compare today to what we were like when we were at our best? Each of these sorts of mental events can trigger the release of glucocorticoid—the molecular carriers of the stress reaction, which directly impact the genes. No interaction with a synapse is necessary; they result in the inhibition of factors that would lead to continued neural growth in the hippocampus and, perhaps, keep depression at bay. But to what end?

An interesting current theory of depression is that it develops as a way to limit our strivings for dominance in the social hierarchy. Humans aren't generally comfortable with the idea that they are built to compete for status within the social troop, just like the apes, chimps, people that drive slowly in the left lane, and other lower primates. One need look no further than the modern equivalent of the Rorschach test, the american freeway, to see these competitive strivings in action.

People buy expensive cars aimed at making themselves look successful and important—in fact to establish a particular identity. Cut in front of another human's automobile and rage reactions akin to a gorilla tearing up shrubbery may result. Drivers compete furiously to get to their destination before their competitors, even though the time saved driving like a Nascar driver may only amount to a minute or less compared to traveling at a more moderate speed. Is there really something important that will be done with the extra minute? Or is this about competition?

If we examine our emotional reactions to the person who is trying to get down the highway faster than us, we may have to admit that some deep-seated and irrational feelings seem to be at work. These same competitive feelings lie behind our culture's preoccupation with accumulating other visible trappings of success. The latest fashions, the biggest homes, the fanciest restaurants all give expression to our desire to set ourselves apart from humans of lesser status. The "silverback male" in our culture has become the man with the most zeroes on his net-worth statement.

Further proof of our strivings for status is our society's preoccupation with sexuality. Beautiful young people are used to sell all types of products. Entire industries are devoted to helping people convince themselves that they are sexually attractive to other people. The fact that actual copulation with the fantasied partners almost never results does not deter us from our preoccupation; our brains simply compel us to attach importance to our sexual status within our groupings.

While these competitive tendencies and sexual preoccupations have a great deal of significance for our species when we are in our reproductive years, they may ultimately be a burden as we get older. Continue to live life as though it were a contest and the brain will be constantly exposed to the stress hormones that result from that world view. If enough stress hormones circulate for a long enough period of time depression becomes increasingly likely.

I f there is one thing that we can absolutely count on, it is that our current ideas about how human brains work will seem hopelessly primitive a hundred years from now. We will certainly know more about the causes of depression. Already we are finding out that some of the ways that we use to try to feel good for a while may cause us to be more depressed in the long run.

Drink too much alcohol and the hippocampus suffers. Depression can result. Opiates? More tablets of Percocet were dispensed than any prescription drug in America in 2000. There may be a lot of severe pain being treated these days, but one suspects that a little mood elevation is going on as well. Unlike SSRI's, which typically take two to eight weeks to relieve depression, opiate medications like Percocet provide the sort of immediate increase in good feelings that people really want from their antidepressant pills. Unfortunately, opiates have already been shown to decrease the birth of new neurons in the hippocampus. While providing good feelings today they may carry the cost of increased depression tomorrow. Research finding this to be true of cocaine and methamphetamines is probably just around the corner.

Of course we'll find out that the whole theory of the hippocampus in depression is too simplistic. Maybe it's not just the

fact that the hippocampus isn't growing it's new nerve cells in depression, it's where that energy goes instead. The amygdala is looking like the next candidate for the root cause of depression. A tiny almond shaped organ that encapsulates the hippocampus, the amygdala is involved with producing negative emotions like fear and hostility. It is also involved in "reward pathways." It's activity appears to increase in depression (and addictions) just as the hippocampus declines. A good example may be the stereotype of the powerful businessman who becomes increasingly argumentative and suspicious after retirement. This might ultimately reflect a shift to using more amygdala as demands on the hippocampus are reduced.

Mundane jobs, boring routines, and the absence of real struggles for survival may all prove to contribute to depression's increasing place in our society. We cannot discount the possibility that the activities that seem to add diversity to our modern existence don't provide the sort of stimulation that healthy brains thrive on.

We may never achieve our goal of truly understanding the brain-mind problem. Our idea that one specific area of the brain is involved in one particular action or emotion is hopelessly outdated. Everything seems to happen as a simultaneous network of activities in different brain areas, but our scientific approaches demand that we study one variable at a time. For now the best way to think about depression may be that it is analogous to a warning light glowing on the dashboard of our car: it tells us that there is something amiss under the hood but not what the problem is or what should be done about it.

Like a good mechanic, the modern psychiatrist's job is to figure out what is really wrong with the engine. We should wonder whether someone is depressed because of an unstimulating environment, a lack of satisfying relationships, boring routines, or insufficient physical exercise. The depression might reflect an excessive preoccupation with one's self-importance or could be the result of a toxic substance. In some instances a diet poor in the Omega III fatty acids found in fish oil could be causing depression. In others the symptoms may be signaling that it is time to reassess one's values and make some basic life changes. Our antidepressant medications are pretty good but it's a bit unreasonable to think that they would address *all* of these problems.

Any enlightened model of Major Depression will have to take these new research findings about nerve cell growth into account. It will have to contain sufficient power to explain why so many diverse treatments may be equally effective in reducing depressive symptoms. The fact that depression is usually self-limited and will eventually go away without treatment must also be considered. The amazing impact of beliefs and expectations that is seen in the placebo response must have a physical correlate but we still know little about the mechanism. The fact that the incidence of depression in our population is increasing suggests that depression is related to sociological variables that are also poorly understood. The new model cannot come soon enough.

As we become more sophisticated in our understanding of depression the psychiatric profession will be challenged to help our society grow in new directions. We may eventually be able to provide information about how to raise our children in a manner that makes them more resistant to depression. More stimulating environments, enhanced curiosity, better relationships with caregivers, and more exercise will undoubtedly help our kids to build brains that are less depression prone. The influence of circulating maternal hormones (reflecting the mother's emotional state) on the fetus' brain development is becoming another exciting area of research.

Learning more about the fuels and activities that keep brains healthy should trigger changes in how humans lead their lives. For depressed adults, future prescriptions might include travel, activities aimed at increasing exposure to novel experiences, and new challenges for the memory apparatus. Therapies aimed at improved relationships or at decreasing our eternal preoccupation with striving for status may become as respected as medications—especially if neuroscience provides the means to document that they evoke similar changes in brain functioning.

For now, psychiatrists will continue to prescribe antidepressant medications with little regard for the factors that may have led to the depressive illness. In the future, however, our task will be to develop multidimensional treatments that are specifically tailored to the needs of the individual. Specialized environments may be developed to carry out the assessments and varied therapies that a more complex understanding of depression will require. Perhaps, ultimately, psychiatrists will be concerned with helping people to live more *memorable* lives.

DR. KEVIN TURNQUIST is a board certified psychiatrist, employed full time for Hennepin County and State of Minnesota outpatient programs. A 1984 graduate of the New York Hospital/Cornell Medical Center, he has lectured widely and received the 1996 Exemplary Psychiatric Award from the National Alliance for the Mentally Ill.

Drugs vs. Talk Therapy

3,079 readers rate their care for depression and anxiety

Where people turn for help to combat depression and anxiety can make a critical difference in the type of care they receive and how completely they recover. That's an important finding of a new survey, one of the largest of its kind, of thousands of CONSUMER REPORTS subscribers who recently sought treatment for those conditions.

The survey results, plus our interviews with patients and experts, offer a compelling snapshot of how people found mental-health care and how they fared given the choices they made. Among our other findings:

- Talk therapy rivaled drug therapy in effectiveness. Respondents who said their therapy was "mostly talk" and lasted at least 13 sessions had better outcomes than those whose therapy was "mostly medication." Therapy delivered by psychologists and clinical social workers was perceived as effective as that given by psychiatrists.
- Drug therapy relieved symptoms faster than talk therapy, and the majority of people who described their therapy as "mostly medication" also had good outcomes. But it can take much trial and error to find the right medication. More than 50 percent of survey respondents who took antidepressants tried two or more drugs; 10 percent tried five or more.
- The rates of adverse drug side effects that our respondents experienced were much higher than those noted on the medications' package inserts. Forty percent said they experienced a loss of sexual interest or performance, and almost 20 percent said they gained weight.
- Health-plan restrictions, such as limits on therapy visits, and costs kept some people from getting the best treatment.
- Consumers who did their own research and monitored their own care reported better results.

In recent years, depression and anxiety have come out of the closet, thanks in part to TV and magazine advertising campaigns for prescription drugs that treat everything from depression to "premenstrual dysphoric disorder" and social anxiety ("Hello My Name Is Anxious"). In 2003 alone, $275 million in consumer advertising helped sell $12.4 billion worth of drugs to treat depression and anxiety in the U.S. Even the federal National Institutes of Health has led an advertising campaign on "real men, real depression."

CR Quick Take

With or without drugs, most people who sought care for depression or anxiety gained relief. A survey of thousands of CR subscribers who recently received treatment for those conditions found that:

- A combination of talk therapy and drugs often worked best. But "mostly talk" therapy was almost as effective if it lasted for 13 or more visits.
- "Mostly drug" therapy was also effective for many people. Drugs had a quicker impact on symptoms than talk therapy, but it often took trial and error to find a drug that worked without unacceptable side effects.
- Forty percent of people who took antidepressants complained of adverse sexual side effects.
- Care from primary-care doctors was effective for people with mild problems, but less so for people with severe ones.

Talk therapy has also gotten off the couch and revitalized its image. The head mobster on HBO's "The Sopranos" sees a therapist. And many states mandate that health plans include at least some coverage for mental-health treatment.

The increased number of treatment options for emotional disorders might improve the odds of recovery for the 9 percent of American adults who suffer from depression and the 11 percent who experience an anxiety disorder in a given year. Indeed, more than 80 percent of our survey respondents said they found treatment that helped.

While more than 4,000 readers answered our two-and-a-half-page questionnaire in 2003, this report focuses on the 3,079 who described themselves as depressed (39 percent), anxious (16 percent), or both (43 percent). The survey did not include people with symptoms who never sought care, and probably also excluded those too ill to complete the questionnaire.

Mushrooming treatment options have made it more problematic for consumers to ferret out the best approaches. Does everyone in emotional distress need prescription antidepressants? Can talk therapy be enough? Where do you start on the path to recovery?

Some of our results confirm those of smaller, placebo-controlled clinical trials. But other findings—such as the effectiveness of specific drugs and talk therapy, and the side effects of

Had Trouble Getting Care

WHO Gale Burstein, 40, Decatur, Ga.

WHAT HAPPENED Burstein, a pediatrician specializing in adolescent health, recognized she had the symptoms of postpartum depression. She says that shortly after the birth of her second child, three years ago, she urgently needed help. But when she called the 800 number on her health insurance plan card, she got a runaround and could not obtain authorization for treatment. Reluctantly, she had to reveal her need to a human resources staffer at her workplace, who informed her that her health plan had turned over mental-heath benefits to another company to administer—using an 800 number not listed on her card. Six months' treatment with Effexor, prescribed by a psychiatrist, brought her to the point where "finally, life was good."

antidepressants—capture information that clinical trials cannot and challenge some of their findings.

Therapist vs. Family Doctor

Break an arm, and you head for the emergency room. Nagging cough, you see an internist or family doctor. But where should a depressed person turn for help when, as our questionnaire put it, emotional problems make life "usually pretty tough" or when he or she can "barely manage to deal with things"? The answer is crucial to the type of treatment received and its success.

"People may not go to the doctor and say, 'Hey, I'm depressed.' Often they show up saying, 'I can't sleep, I have stomach problems, my head hurts, my back hurts," says Michael Schoenbaum, Ph.D., a RAND Corporation health economist whose work focuses on improving the treatment of depression.

If you're not sure what the problem is, a family doctor might be the logical first stop in seeking care, but perhaps not the only stop for those with severe symptoms. While treatment outcomes from primary-care doctors were nearly as good as from therapists for people who said they started out with less severe symptoms, treatment by mental-health specialists yielded significantly better results for people who started out in poor shape.

And indeed, in our study, people who saw only a primary-care physician tended to have milder symptoms, and most had six or fewer treatment visits.

"Mostly drugs" was the type of therapy described by almost half of those who saw only a primary-care physician and 38 percent of those who saw a psychiatrist. The "mostly drugs" group typically received a prescription antidepressant. The few doctor visits they had were probably largely devoted to monitoring how well the medicine was working and checking for side effects. Others who saw only a primary-care physician received a combination of advice and medication.

Experts we interviewed noted that many independent studies have documented the less effective mental-health treatment delivered by primary-care doctors. "Your primary-care doctor has a million things to do and not a lot of time to see you, and in general does not have much training in diagnosing and treating mental illness," Schoenbaum says.

Referral: Friend vs. Employer

"People are more likely to ask their friends and colleagues who knows a good mechanic than who knows a good psychotherapist," says Gregory Simon, M.D., a psychiatrist and mental-health researcher at Seattle's Group Health Cooperative. "If one can screw up the courage to ask, word-of-mouth recommendations are very good."

Our findings confirm that advice. Only 20 percent of respondents who saw a mental-health therapist got the name from a friend or family member. But that group had a better outcome than those who saw a therapist recommended by their employer or through an advertisement. People who were referred by their medical doctor or another mental-health professional also got good results.

Though psychologists and social workers can't themselves prescribe drugs, some have arrangements with psychiatrists who will prescribe and monitor drugs for their patients. Among our respondents, 66 percent of psychologists' and social workers' patients reported that they received drug treatment as an adjunct to talk therapy.

"Many insurers refuse to allow psychiatrists to do anything but prescribe drugs, except for the most severely ill patients," notes Bruce Schwartz, M.D., associate professor of clinical psychiatry at Albert Einstein College of Medicine, in New York City, and one of two consultants who helped us design our survey and interpret the results.

Regardless of how ill respondents were when going into therapy, their outcomes were virtually identical whether they saw a psychiatrist, psychologist, or social worker. "This shows that if you leave people to their own devices, they're going to come up with a therapist they like and who helps them," says William Sanderson, Ph.D., professor of psychology at Hofstra University, in Hempstead, N.Y., our other consultant.

Meds vs. Talk

Drug therapy has become a more prevalent mode of treatment for emotional problems in the last decade. When we surveyed our readers in 1994, only 40 percent of those who sought care for any type of mental-health problem received drugs compared with 68 percent in the current survey (and 80 percent of those with depression or anxiety)—a number that reflects the fast-growing sales of antidepressant drugs over the past decade.

Still, someone entering treatment today has the same basic choices they would have had a decade ago: talk therapy, drug therapy, or a combination. While our results suggest that all of these options can work for many cases of anxiety and depression, the combination of talk and drugs was the overall winner.

The reason could be that drug and talk therapies work at very different paces. Respondents who took drugs improved substantially within a few visits (see "Therapy: short- and long-term," below). Within six visits, those whose treatment consisted of mostly medication had improved as much as those who

Therapy: Short- and Long-Term Combination of Talk and Drugs Worked Best

Survey respondents who took antidepressant medication, either with or without talk therapy, improved more quickly than those who had mostly talk therapy. But the improvement from drug treatment leveled off, regardless of the number of visits at the time of our survey, whereas people who had more talk sessions did better than those who had only a few. Overall, adding talk therapy to treatment produced more improvement. We measured improvement by combining readers' own reports of satisfaction with their treatment with the degree of improvement in their emotional condition since the start of therapy, then converting the result to a 100-point scale.

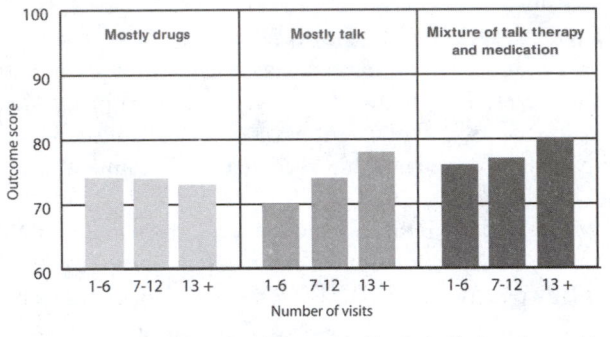

Based on 2,125 survey respondents who visited a mental-health professional for depression or anxiety.

had 13 or more visits. By contrast, respondents who elected mainly talk therapy improved more gradually. If they had just six visits or fewer, they fared worse than patients on medication. But if they stuck with their therapy for 13 or more visits, their outcome was better than those who relied mainly on medication. The most successful patients of all were those who received a balance of drug and talk therapies. They had the advantage of quick improvement with the drugs, followed by steady continuing improvement from the talk.

The number of talk therapy sessions received by people with a mental problem drastically declined over the last decade. In 1994, survey respondents averaged well over 20 visits with a mental-health professional, while in the current survey the average was 10 visits. Since our survey indicates that longer-term therapy is linked to more positive outcomes, that trend is troubling.

Striking the right balance between medications and "enough" talk therapy sessions can be tricky. Asking hard questions of the professional recommending treatment can help people understand their options. These questions should include: What's your understanding of this problem? What kind of treatments would you recommend and why? How long will it take to experience some relief of symptoms? How long will I need to stay on medication and/or continue with talk therapy to get the maximum benefit?

Drug vs. Drug

From 1999 through 2003, drugmakers spent more than $953 million promoting the major antidepressants directly to consumers. Much more is spent advertising to doctors. Antidepressants were the drug category most heavily advertised in medical journals in 2003. Escitalopram (Lexapro), a newer antidepressant, was the most heavily advertised drug of all, according to Medical Marketing & Media, a trade publication that tracks pharmaceutical ad sales.

Published clinical trials have not found meaningful differences in effectiveness for adults among the major antidepressants. When researcher Mark Zimmerman, M.D., director of outpatient psychiatry at Rhode Island Hospital, recently reviewed 24 trials, including 411 drug comparisons, he found that fewer than a dozen comparisons yielded significant differences.

The experiences of our respondents, however, did yield differences in both effectiveness and side-effect ratings for the six top-selling antidepressants (see "Readers rate antidepressants," on the next page), though no single "winner" emerged. Four of the six drugs—citalopram (Celexa), fluoxetine (Prozac), paroxetine (Paxil), and sertraline (Zoloft)—are known as SSRIs, or selective serotonin reuptake inhibitors. (Lexapro, now also a top-selling SSRI, was introduced in 2002, too late to show up in our survey.) SSRIs increase the brain's supply of available serotonin, a neurotransmitter that plays a central role in mood and alertness. Beginning with the 1987 introduction of Prozac, the first SSRI, this category of drugs has largely supplanted an older class of antidepressants, the tricyclics, which, though effective, caused much more severe side effects.

All of the SSRIs except Celexa have also received regulatory approval for treating some type of anxiety-related disorder. But there has been virtually no clinical testing of these medications on the combined depression and anxiety that is so often found in clinical practice and was common among our survey respondents.

There was a high frequency of anxiety disorders among respondents who took Paxil. That drug was prescribed most often to those who got their treatment from a medical doctor rather than a mental-health therapist. Perhaps not coincidentally, between 1999 and 2003, the year of our survey, Paxil was by far the antidepressant most heavily advertised to consumers, mainly to promote its use as a treatment for "social anxiety disorder."

Most INSURERS LIMIT the number of mental-health office visits they cover. Not so for other medical conditions.

"That Paxil was effective for the depressed and anxious patient was a great message to send out there," Zimmerman says. "The primary-care physician didn't have to be able to tell the difference." In our survey, a slightly smaller percentage of readers who took Paxil reported that it helped "a lot" compared with readers who took other SSRIs. This percentage was essentially the same among those who took Paxil for depression, or anxiety, or both.

Talk the Talk
Therapists and Therapies

Several types of health professionals offer talk therapy for depression, anxiety, and other mental-health problems. In our survey, respondents did equally well and were equally satisfied with the type of therapist they chose, though their likelihood of receiving drug therapy varied with the type of therapist.

Psychiatrists are medical doctors with specialized training in mental-health care; they can prescribe medications, and people who see other types of therapists may be referred to them for prescriptions. Of our survey respondents who went to psychiatrists, 38 percent received medication but little, if any, talk therapy, and 49 percent received a balance of both. Just 13 percent received mostly talk therapy.

Psychologists have a Ph.D. with a specialization in assessing and treating emotional disorders. Sixty-five percent of respondents who saw psychologists received mostly talk therapy, 32 percent received a balance of talk and drug therapy, and a mere 3 percent received mainly medication.

'Psychotherapist' is an unregulated term without legal meaning or licensure requirements. Check the education and credentials of any therapist using that title.

Social workers have a two-year master's degree (M.S.W.); they may also have professional certification or state licensure to provide psychotherapy. Their care patterns were similar to those of psychologists, with 74 percent of respondents receiving mostly talk therapy and 25 percent receiving a balance of talk and drug therapies.

Best Therapy Options

Of the dozens of types of talk therapies that have been used over the years, our consultants strongly recommend the two that have proven most consistently effective through repeated testing in clinical trials. Both types of therapies are designed to produce a meaningful improvement in symptoms, up to and including total remission, within 15 to 20 sessions. Both teach people to manage their moods—to think and behave their way to better mental health.

Cognitive behavioral therapy focuses on training patients to identify and consciously correct the distorted thought patterns associated with anxiety or depression. Anxious people tend to overestimate the likelihood of a catastrophe, while depressed people tend to react to setbacks or disappointments with extreme self-criticism and a feeling of hopelessness out of proportion to the situation.

The therapy typically involves specific "homework" assignments. For instance, a depressed person might be assigned to arrange an enjoyable social activity or become more assertive on the job. An anxious person who is afraid of public speaking will, with support and preparation, gradually and deliberately be exposed to the feared situation.

Interpersonal therapy, used primarily for depression, focuses more on the patient's relationship problems with others, such as spouses, children, or co-workers. It can be especially effective when depression results from a major life transition, such as the birth of a child, divorce, loss of a job, or bereavement. Therapy typically involves learning to change one's manner of dealing with family and friends, adapting to changed life circumstances, or building up one's social skills.

Managing Depression

WHO Claudia Meadows, 55, Shoreline, Wash.

WHAT'S HAPPENING To Meadows, managing her chronic major depression is "a full-time job." Because her husband's job provides membership in Seattle's Group Health Cooperative HMO, she has care from a well-coordinated team. "I can get useful therapy, face-to-face psychiatric appointments when I need them, medications at the walk-in pharmacy or by mail, online help, telephone nurse consultations, and my doctor returns phone calls within hours." With this support, Meadows has raised two sons, works part-time as a bus driver, and is developing a photo greeting card business.

may account for the fact that more of our readers found it effective. In our survey, respondents who took Effexor were likely to have started treatment with more severe symptoms, but even when we controlled for severity, respondents perceived Effexor to be quite effective. In August 2004 the Food and Drug Administration approved a second antidepressant drug in this category, duloxetine (Cymbalta).

Bupropion (Wellbutrin) is an older drug whose precise effect on the brain is not understood, although the drug has been clinically shown to work. Our respondents found it produced a lower level of side effects, but fewer found that it "helped a lot."

There was no clear favorite among the medications, and our findings confirm those of clinical studies that there is no single antidepressant that will work for everyone. "I tell my patients that there's probably one of these medications that's better for you than the others, but unfortunately we can't tell in advance which one it is," says Simon, the Seattle researcher and psychiatrist.

Our survey confirms that it often takes trial and error to find the right drug. Fifty-five percent of respondents who took med-

Two other drugs indicated for depression but not anxiety are different from the SSRIs. Venlafaxine (Effexor) is a dual-action drug that affects brain levels not only of serotonin but also of another neurotransmitter, norepinephrine. Effexor's dual action

Drug-Free Cure

WHO Robert MacNeill, 62, Hingham, Mass.

WHAT HAPPENED For four decades MacNeill experienced extreme fear, a pounding heart, and intense sweating and nausea when faced with the prospect of traveling for more than an hour's ride. He tried anti-anxiety drugs and a psychiatrist's treatment to quell his severe panic attacks, but found no relief. Finally the prospect of missing his son's wedding in Kansas impelled him to search for another treatment. He found it at Boston University's Center for Anxiety and Related Disorders. The cognitive-behavioral therapy involved deliberately inducing the symptoms of panic attacks and training himself not to fear them. After 11 weeks of intensive therapy, MacNeill passed his final behavioral "exam"—a plane trip to Kansas to visit his son. He now travels routinely. "I wish I had known this 40 years ago," he says.

ications had to try two or more, and nearly 10 percent had taken five or more, aiming to find a drug that helped and had acceptable side effects.

Since all of the drugs can be effective for some people, and there are many factors involved in choosing the one to start with, it's important to work with a health-care professional who understands you and all the drug options. Some experts recommend starting with whichever antidepressant is the cheapest. Lower-cost generics are available for bupropion, fluoxetine, and paroxetine. When starting a new medication it's important to have close follow-up with the doctor or therapist to make sure that it's working.

People who take an antidepressant should also be aware of the high risk of side effects, especially a loss of sexual interest or ability and weight gain. (Poor sexual functioning and weight gain can also be symptoms of depression itself.) The package inserts for antidepressants typically peg adverse sexual side effects as affecting 15 percent of patients or less, based on studies sponsored by drug companies. We found rates about three times that for the four SSRIs and Effexor, from a low of 41 percent for Prozac to a high of 53 percent for Paxil. Our findings are similar to those of the only published comparative study on this subject, headed by Anita Clayton, M.D., of the University of Virginia and reported in April 2002 in the Journal of Clinical Psychiatry. It found rates of adverse sexual side effects ranging from 36 to 43 percent for SSRIs and Effexor.

About 20 percent of people who took SSRIs or Effexor reported weight gain, and 15 to 21 percent noted that those drugs made them feel drowsy or disoriented. Wellbutrin, with its different chemical composition, had noticeably lower rates of side effects. Only 21 percent of the people taking it said they experienced sexual problems, 10 percent complained of sedation, and 12 percent experienced weight gain.

For many people, side effects were more than annoyances. Of the readers who said they stopped taking an antidepressant, 34 percent said they'd done so because the side effects were intolerable.

Readers Rate Antidepressants

The 1,664 survey respondents who took the antidepressants listed below told us whether the most recent one they took helped them "a lot" and whether they experienced common side effects. When the results were added up, some medications scored higher than others in the percentage of time they helped a lot and in the rate of side effects experienced.

Differences in methodology may account for the fact that our study found more differences among the drugs than clinical studies have. A key difference is that in the "real world" of our survey respondents, doctors match drugs to patients based on their symptoms and their likely response to side effects—and don't hesitate to switch if the first drug doesn't work. By contrast, clinical studies assign drugs randomly and usually don't allow switching. In the real world, unacceptable side effects often lead to a change in medication.

GENERIC (BRAND) ‡	% HELPED A LOT	% SIDE EFFECTS			APPROVED FOR:	PRICE PER MONTH ¤
		Drowsiness or disorientation	Decreased sexual interest or performance	Weight gain		
venlafaxine (Effexor)	76%	18%	51%	21%	Depression	$117 (brand)
fluoxetine (Prozac)	69	15	41	19	Depression, obsessive-compulsive disorder, bulimia, panic disorder	73 (generic) 113 (brand)
citalopram (Celexa)	68	17	45	18	Depression	80 (brand)
sertraline (Zoloft)	67	18	46	17	Depression, obsessive-compulsive disorder, panic disorder, post-traumatic stress disorder, premenstrual dysphoric disorder, social anxiety disorder	82 (brand)
paroxetine (Paxil)	59	21	53	22	Depression, general anxiety, social anxiety disorder, obsessive-compulsive disorder, panic disorder, post-traumatic stress disorder	72 (generic) 85 (brand)
bupropion (Wellbutrin)	57	10	21	12	Depression	68 (generic) 140 (brand)

‡ Some of these drugs are also available in extended-release versions, which may have approval for additional indications, including anxiety. ¤ Cost for a typical adult dose for one month of treatment, calculated from retail prescription price information provided by NDCHealth, a health-care information services company, July 2004.

Guide to the Ratings

Based on responses to our 2003 Annual Questionnaire; 1,664 readers reported on their most recent experience taking an antidepressant between January 2000 and April 2003. Drugs are listed in order of reader-reported effectiveness. Ratings results were similar when we controlled for severity and types of symptoms reported. Ratings for previously tried medications were typically lower. Since this type of study has no control group, it is not possible to calculate placebo effects or what the rates of recovery would be with no treatment. The results reflect the experiences of CONSUMER REPORTS subscribers and might not be representative of the U.S. population.

Safetywise

Antidepressants and Adolescent Suicide

The number of U.S. children taking antidepressants has more than doubled since the early 1990s. That's when the SSRI type of antidepressants (such as Celexa, Paxil, Prozac, and Zoloft) began to dominate the market. Yet only one SSRI, fluoxetine (Prozac), has been approved in the U.S. for treating pediatric depression. The U.S. Food and Drug Administration denied manufacturers' applications for approval to prescribe Celexa, Effexor, Paxil, or Zoloft for patients under 18 because studies showed they were not effective.

In the past year, new evidence has emerged suggesting a possible connection between starting antidepressant treatment and an increase in suicide risk.

- A never-published pooled analysis of all pediatric trials of paroxetine (Paxil) by the manufacturer Glaxo-SmithKline, which came to light during U.S. and British government studies in 2003, found that 3.4 percent of children aged 7 to 18 who took the medication during clinical trials showed an increase in suicidal behavior and thoughts—though none actually killed themselves—compared with just 1.2 percent of the children given a placebo pill.
- An analysis of records of 3 million British patients of all ages, published in July 2004 in the Journal of the American Medical Association, compared patients in their first nine days on an antidepressant with patients who had been taking antidepressants for three months or longer. The analysis showed there was 4 times the risk of suicidal behavior and 38 times the risk of actual suicide in the group taking antidepressants over the shorter period. There were no suicides among patients aged 10 to 19, but their increased risk of suicidal behavior was similar to that of the group as a whole.

Researchers aren't sure why antidepressants have this effect. One theory is that SSRIs quickly reverse the lethargy associated with depression but take several weeks to ease the depression itself, giving patients the energy to contemplate or carry through suicide attempts in the interim.

The FDA says to watch for signs of INCREASED SUICIDAL THINKING in children and adults who start taking antidepressants.

British authorities have told doctors not to prescribe paroxetine to children and adolescents. In March 2004, the FDA asked the makers of 10 major antidepressants, including all the SSRIs and buproprion (Wellbutrin), to warn doctors and patients to watch for increased suicidal tendencies in children and adults in their first weeks on the medicines or when the dose changes. The agency is now gathering more evidence on the issue.

Trial Results Concealed

The Paxil episode has exposed a potentially dangerous information gap in drug regulation: the ability of drug manufacturers to effectively conceal study results that find their products to be ineffective or potentially hazardous. The three Glaxo studies that when combined showed increased suicidal thinking in children who took Paxil were submitted to the FDA when the manufacturer sought approval for pediatric use. The only one of the three that showed that Paxil worked for depression was published in the Journal of the American Academy of Child and Adolescent Psychiatry. This report labeled suicidal thoughts as "emotional lability."

The two negative Paxil studies were never published in a journal. Meanwhile, doctors could and did prescribe Paxil for children—an estimated 2.1 million prescriptions in 2002. (Paxil's manufacturer, GlaxoSmith-Kline, has now posted all the studies on its Web site, at www.gsk.com.)

Treating Depressed Minors

Until more is known, experts advise parents of a depressed child to follow these guidelines:

- Treat depression promptly and aggressively because the condition itself is a major risk factor for suicide.
- Try intensive talk therapy first. Use antidepressant medication only as a last resort, if there's no improvement.
- When medication is necessary, children starting a drug should be watched very closely for signs of thoughts of self-harm. Symptoms include talking or writing about death, self-mutilation, abrupt withdrawal from family and friends, and giving away prized possessions. Other symptoms that warrant concern include increased anxiety, agitation or restlessness, insomnia, irritability, and hostility.
- Children who have been on antidepressants for more than a few months can safely continue if the medication is helping and they are not having suicidal thoughts or unacceptable side effects.
- Never discontinue an SSRI without consulting your doctor. Abrupt stopping can bring on discontinuation symptoms such as increased agitation or restlessness. Your doctor can provide a schedule for gradually tapering off the dose.

Insurance vs. Pay Your Way

Mental-health professionals use apocalyptic language in speaking of their financial arrangements with the managed-care companies that dominate their field. The major targets of their ire are low reimbursement rates and annual limits on the number of mental-health visits patients may make. "It's disgusting," Zimmerman says. "Insurance limits on mental-health treatment are the norm, rather than the exception. If you have difficult-to-control diabetes, you can have as many visits as you need. If you have difficult-to-control depression, you may be limited to 20 visits a year."

A study of mental-health benefits, published in the September-October 2003 issue of Health Affairs, found that though 98 percent of insured employees had some kind of mental-health coverage, 32 percent were allowed no more than 20 outpatient visits per year, and 22 percent had to pay a higher share of the costs for mental-health care than for other types of health care.

Even Medicare treats mental illness differently from other medical conditions, requiring patients to bear half the cost, rather than the usual 20 percent for other types of outpatient care.

In our study, most people did get better in the number of visits for which their coverage paid, but a significant minority ran into trouble. Of the 80 percent who secured treatment through their health plans, 23 percent said they had some type of problem with it. Problems included restrictions on the number of visits, long waits for appointments, hassles with red tape, or difficulty finding a doctor in the plan directory who was willing to accept new patients.

These frustrations, as well as privacy concerns, may lead some people to avoid using their health insurance to pay for mental-health care. Federal privacy laws make it illegal for mental-health professionals to disclose, without the patient's permission, "personal notes" containing the therapists' impressions. But health plans are allowed access to information about diagnosis, drugs prescribed, treatment plan, and prognosis. So a health plan or employer may be able to find out that a person is getting, say, Zoloft for depression, but not the therapist's opinion on the causes of depression.

That's thin protection for people concerned that having an antidepressant prescription on their record might result in insurance or employer discrimination. Whether from lack of coverage or fears about using it, 19 percent of our respondents said their health plan didn't pay for any of their mental-health treatment. As a result, many spent $500 or more out of pocket for therapy over the previous year. And of the 57 percent of respondents who said they had stopped their mental-health treatment, 14 percent said it was because they couldn't afford to continue.

Active vs. Passive

It requires some consumer savvy to get the best results from treatments for depression and anxiety, our research has found. Survey respondents who were most satisfied with their care and had the best outcomes were more likely to:

- Research their problem in advance of seeking help.
- Interview more than one professional.
- Ask therapists whether they had experience treating that problem.
- Bring a family member or friend to an office visit.
- Keep a written record of their treatment and emotional state.
- Apply what they were learning in treatment to their daily lives.
- That last step, which involves working hard at therapy and putting suggestions into action, was the best predictor of a good outcome.

Only 1 percent of respondents followed all of the steps listed above, and 18 percent followed none at all.

People with depression and anxiety might need to involve family or friends to help them get the best care and make the best use of it. Restrictive insurance policies, social stigma, and a feeling of "What's the use?" can all present barriers.

But if social and personal barriers are overcome and appropriate treatment is started, the experience of CR readers demonstrates that relief is available.

"My whole life has changed," says Robert MacNeill, speaking of his successful treatment for panic disorder. "It's like being reborn."

Body of Emotion

Sometimes physical health is just a state of mind. Your feelings help determine how well your immune system works, how fast you age, and much more

ALICE LESCH KELLY

C all it a clinical study for two: You and your sister attended a family reunion filled with sniffling cousins. Now you have a cold, but your sister's in perfect health. Why? You both eat well, exercise regularly, don't smoke, and it's not like your sister has superior genes.

Sorry to use the 's' word, but it could be stress. All those budgets and deadlines and seven-year itches you've been dealing with can depress your immune system. In fact, researchers have shown stress can take years off you—and not in the good way.

These scientists are now proving in the laboratory what traditional healers have instinctively known: That the mind and body are intricately linked, and when either is weak, the other suffers. In fact, your emotions are so strongly connected to your physical being that they can elicit tangible physical responses. One field in particular has made great strides in understanding the connections between our emotions, well-being, and immune-system function. It's called—take a breath—psychoneuroimmunology (also referred to as PNI).

PNI originated in the 1970s, a time when the Western medical establishment still believed the immune system worked autonomously, without much help from the heart or mind.

Then Robert Ader, Ph.D., and his colleagues in the department of psychiatry at the University of Rochester, New York, discovered the immune system could be psychologically conditioned to perform a certain way.

In a laboratory study, Ader fed rats saccharine while simultaneously giving them an immunosuppressive drug that caused an upset stomach. After just one pairing of the sweetener with the medication, the rodents learned to avoid the saccharine, because they associated it with stomach discomfort. And the more of the stomach-upsetting drug they received, the greater their avoidance of the saccharine.

The study was then repeated using only the saccharine, and, much to Ader's surprise, many of the rats died.

Then he figured it out: Even when the rats did not receive the drug, their bodies associated the saccharine with the suppression of immune function; in response, their immune systems actually became weaker. In other words, Ader had conditioned an immunosuppressive response—and the more saccharine the rats received, the more likely they were to die. The experiment led to a then-radical conclusion: The mind and the immune system are linked.

"There were lots of responses to our study—and some of them you can't print," Ader says today. "But our results showed you've got to deal with the whole adaptive system of the organism and not just a single element of the system."

Molecules of Emotion

Mind-body medicine took another big step forward in the lab of Candace Pert, Ph.D., a scientist at Johns Hopkins University. Pert made history when she discovered the receptors that allow the body to use natural and synthetic opiates. That led to the discovery of peptides—the short chains of amino acids that act as chemical messengers—and peptide receptors. Pert found that emotions trigger the release of peptides, which then travel to receptors throughout the body. She calls peptides the molecules of emotion. "A feeling sparked in your mind will translate as a peptide being released somewhere," says Pert, now a neuropharmacologist at Georgetown University School of Medicine. "Peptides regulate every aspect of your body, from whether you're going to digest your food properly to whether you're going to destroy a tumor cell."

Peptide receptors, which are in the organs, endocrine muscle, and other body tissues, store emotional information received from the peptides. Therefore, emotional memories can be stored not only in the brain, but also in many places in the body. That would explain, for example, why people have "gut feelings" or why memories and emotions sometimes pop up during massage or acupuncture—because emotional memories "live" in the body's tissues, Pert says.

The discovery of peptides and peptide receptors offered, for the first time, tangible evidence of the actual physical exchange between mind and body and the biochemical basis of emotion—and confirmed what Eastern healers have long known intuitively. Also, while peptides and their receptors are located throughout the body, they're concentrated in the places that correspond to the chakras, the seven areas around the spine where, according to Eastern medicine, energy is gathered and then distributed to organs and tissues. "It blew me away when I realized this," Pert says.

When your body is in balance, peptides and receptors are able to do their jobs correctly, but when the body is thrown out of balance by intense emotions, the system works less effectively. For example, nervousness might cause a peptide miscommunication that would result in too much water being held in the intestines, and thus, diarrhea—a direct physical result of an emotional state.

What does this mean for you? Fighting off and healing from disease requires a strong immune system and balanced emotions. It's never an either-or situation: The immune system works well when your system of peptides and receptors is in balance, and the peptide system is in balance when you are emotionally strong and healthy. Thus, when you're dealing with difficult emotions, both your peptide and immune systems may be compromised. That's why it's important to stay emotionally healthy—not an easy task in this stressful world.

Healing emotional stress can be complicated, but it's worthwhile because of the positive effect this can have on your immune system. Finding a way to let go of deep-seated anger, for example, can boost your immunity. "Anger and blaming others takes a lot of energy away from healing," Pert says. "One of the most powerful emotions that has to be expressed is forgiveness."

Mind-Body Connections

In the years since Ader and Pert made their discoveries, researchers have been busy learning more about how the nervous, immune, and endocrine systems work together. Several large-scale epidemiological studies have established that depressive feelings are associated with an increased incidence of death from all causes, says Neff Schneiderman, Ph.D., a professor of psychology at the University of Miami. Other investigations have shown that people who are prone to hostility and anger have an increased risk of developing heart disease.

Here are some of the most recently found links between emotional and physical health:

Chronic stress ages human cells. Scientists at the University of California, San Francisco, compared the mothers of healthy children with the mothers of chronically ill children. Their report, published last December in the Proceedings of the National Academy of Sciences, found the stress of caring for a sick child causes cellular changes. The stressed women's cells had shorter telomeres, which are bits of DNA found at the end of chromosomes. Telomeres shorten slightly each time a cell divides; as a result, they're much shorter in older people. The telomeres of the most stressed participants had cells that appeared about 10 years older than the women were chronologically; the cells also had lower levels of an enzyme that repairs damaged telomeres, and higher levels of free radicals, which can damage DNA.

Psychological tension may speed the onset of cancer. In a study at the Sidney Kimmel Comprehensive Cancer Center at Johns Hopkins University, mice were exposed to a psychologically stressful situation—the smell of fox urine—along with large amounts of ultraviolet light. The results, published in the December 2004 *Journal of the American Academy of Derma-*

tology, found that the mice developed skin cancers more than twice as fast as mice exposed to only the UV light. The researchers suggested humans could have a similar response.

Disturbing emotions can cause physical damage. Researchers at the University of California, Los Angeles, asked one group of college students to write about an upsetting experience that made them feel bad about themselves, while a second group of students wrote about neutral topics. The study, published in *Psychosomatic Medicine*, determined the first group secreted greater amounts of a marker of pro-inflammatory activity than the second group. The more shame and anxiety the participants felt, the more of this inflammatory marker their bodies produced.

Patient confidence boosts treatment results. In a recent study published in the journal *Prevention & Treatment,* Italian researchers administered pain medicine to two sets of people: those who knew they were receiving a potent treatment and those who received the treatment without their knowledge. The same medication ended up being more effective in the aware patients.

These are the kinds of findings Pert has in mind when she says emotions "run every system in our bodies." Stress, anxiety, depression, and other difficult feelings dampen the immune system. So what started as an odd experiment with rats and artificial sweetener has grown into a whole new way of looking at human health. Says Aden "The field has burgeoned beyond what anyone would have expected."

Emotions are double-edged swords. They allow us to fully experience our humanity, but they also impact our immune systems. That means we need a new definition of wellness. Because the mind and body are essentially one, relieving stress, letting go of anger, and finding productive ways to cope with the difficulties of life may be as important to our health as nutrition, exercise, and all the other steps we take to keep our bodies healthy.

How To Feel More Energy

Do you try to do too much too quickly? The results can be frustration, exhaustion, a compromised immune system, and not enough physical and emotional resources to face your next challenge.

"A hidden energy crisis threatens our world," says Judith Orloff, M.D., assistant clinical professor of psychiatry at the University of California, Los Angeles, and author of *Positive Energy.* "Society throws people into chronic physical, emotional, and spiritual depletion. Multitasking lets us manage a deluge of very real duties, but it also jeopardizes the now."

Likewise, rushing depletes energy. "We haven't been taught to guard positive energy, to see slowing down as a virtue," says Orloff, who suggests examining the pace of your life to determine whether it supplies energy or siphons it away.

Here are seven strategies from *Positive Energy* for cultivating just that:

1. Ask yourself: "Does my pace feel good?" and take a few long, deep breaths until you"re relaxed. After a minute or two, go ahead and ask the question. You know you're operating at just the right speed if your answer is yes.

2. Then, assess your need for speed. Start asking yourself: How does my pacing feel at work? At home? On vacation? With friends? Rely on intuition for answers.

3. If you're a multitasker, take 10 minutes to work at a nurturing pace. Use that time to do only one thing—answer e-mail, talk on the phone, read a report—and don't let your focus scatter. Do you feel more energetic? If so, savor that feeling and build on it. And don't sweat the time out. "Energy never lies," Orloff says. "If you work at your right rhythm, you will be more productive; trust me."

4. When time is crunched, plan mini-breaks to energize yourself. For just a minute, take a few deep breaths as you touch your intuitive center between your eyebrows (press lightly with two fingers). This heightens your focus and brings you back into balance.

5. Commit to at least one self-compassionate action a week. "Planning regular downtime nurtures positive energy," Orloff says. Schedule a nap, a movie, or time to sit still and listen to music.

6. Prioritize your to-do list. Recognize that not everything has to be tackled today. Do what is essential, and stop there.

7. Get completely absorbed in doing just one thing. Whether you are playing golf or filing papers, take a little time each day to fully inhabit your body.

See Less Stress

There's no way to avoid stressful situations. Does that mean we're destined to get stress-related illnesses? Not necessarily, says Carl A. Hammerschlag, M.D., a psychiatrist at University of Arizona Medical School, and author of *The Theft of the Spirit: A Journey to Spiritual Healing*.

Meditation, yoga, acupressure, guided imagery, and other relaxation techniques can reduce levels of stress hormones. A healthy diet, exercise, sufficient sleep, and spiritual faith can also help build resilience and keep stress in check. So can learning to focus on the positive.

"An event itself is not inherently stressful," Hammerschlag says. We create stress when we perceive stress, he explains: A traffic jam is only stressful if we think it is; we'll fare better if we see it as an opportunity to do breathing exercises instead of as a huge problem. It's definitely worth practicing this shift in P.O.V. "You can stimulate the immune system actively with hope and joy," he adds.

20 Weeks to Happiness

Can a course in Positive Psychology change your life?

RICHARD HANDLER

If Thomas Jefferson were a psychology graduate student to-day, he'd probably think of himself as a positive psychologist. It was Jefferson, after all, who began the Declaration of Independence with the statement that human beings aren't only created equal but "endowed by their Creator with certain unalienable Rights, [and] that among these are Life, Liberty and the pursuit of Happiness." Happiness was the word he chose, not pursuit of power or economic gain.

Jefferson didn't formally study happiness. He wanted each man to find his own. Judging by his writings, he wasn't always happy himself, especially if you define happiness as a smiley-faced succession of positive feelings. Nor was he a particularly religious man. He didn't think that a happy human life was a reward for obeying a Supreme Being or a set of rules laid down in a holy book. He was a lover of the Greek classics, a believer in progress, a deist, and a man of the Enlightenment. His faith lay in the notion that philosophic inquiry, reason, and study of the natural world could lead one to what Aristotle called "the good life." That was the bedrock of Jefferson's secular faith—a view that many positive psychologists share today.

That faith led Jefferson to a full and productive life, replete with the factors that today's positive psychologists say are crucial to the whole-grained, solid, muscular happiness they promote. Jefferson had many friends (recent demographic research finds that the happiest people have huge social networks). He didn't agonize about his faults, but rather exercised his creative talents as a writer, politician, and thinker (positive psychologists urge people to maximize strengths rather than correct weaknesses, and to turn their work into a moral calling). He was a man of complex identities: not only a lawyer and slaveowner, but a farmer, Southerner, architect of Monticello, letter-writer, father, gracious host, bon vivant, and lover of women and wine, of oysters and sonatas. Such complex identities, positive psychologists say, are a crucial ingredient in that elusive, nebulous, eternally-sought-after state we call happiness

Today, Positive Psychology, as popularized by former American Psychological Association president and bestselling author Martin Seligman, is taking folk wisdom and Greek philosophy, mixing them with solid contemporary research on joy, optimism, satisfaction, contentment, forgiveness, and gratitude, and popularizing the result as scientifically validated fact. The result, they hope, will be a new take on psychology, at once Victorian and scientific.

They're doing so in a country Jefferson wouldn't recognize. Even as Americans spend $76 billion a year on antidepressants and additional millions on talk therapy for depression; even as they overwork relentlessly in pursuit of the "good life" defined in material terms; even as they grope their way through crises in divorced and blended families stripped of the aunties and grandmothers who once stabilized extended families, positive psychologists are administering happiness questionnaires, writing happiness books, and giving radio interviews on how to be happy.

Much of what they say is as old-fashioned as Jefferson's viewpoint and cuts hard against the modern grain: their studies, for instance, suggest that within certain constraints, money doesn't buy happiness (Brazilians, according to demographic data, are almost as satisfied with their lives as Americans, despite having only 23 percent of the purchasing power). Positive psychologists say that most folks are as happy as they make up their minds to be. Like Victorian moralists, they argue that almost stoic moral and emotional practices—lowering your expectations, looking on the bright side, counting your blessings, volunteering, forgiving others, expressing gratitude—can make you much happier than going shopping or excavating childhood hurts in therapy.

This list may make some therapists cringe (and make positive psychologists sound like nuns), but its proponents include many of the most creative and influential psychological researchers alive in America today. Seligman, for instance, is the original elucidator of "learned helplessness." He's Fox Leadership Professor of Psychology at the University of Pennsylvania, and attracts grant money the way a magnet attracts iron filings.

George Vaillant of Harvard Medical School is the chief architect of a respected, 60-year longitudinal study of the lives of Harvard graduates and blue-collar Boston men. Social scientist Mikhail Csikszentmihalyi is a noted business professor at Claremont College and author of the bestseller *Flow*, the famous study of work satisfaction.

In the seven short years since Seligman convened Positive Psychology's first organizational summit in a resort in Mexico, the surge to popularize this new discipline—and challenge clinical psychology's 60-year preoccupation with mental pain and illness—has spilled far beyond academic backwaters. Positive psychologists have set up courses in at least 20 universities in North America, leavening syllabuses previously heavy on abnormal psychology and DSM criteria with courses discussing "signature strengths," learned optimism, faith, and contentment. While the National Institute of Mental Health gives millions of dollars each year to study schizophrenia, panic, depression, and other mental illnesses, the Templeton, Mellon, Annenberg, and Pew foundations are now funding research into the happiness-producing potential of civic engagement, gratitude lists, forgiveness, hope, and altruism.

Last January, *Time* magazine devoted 40 pages to "The Science of Happiness," and similar cover stories have appeared in *O: The Oprah Magazine, Psychology Today, Scientific American*, and *Tricycle: The Buddhist Review*. Books on the subject range from Seligman's 2002 bestseller *Authentic Happiness: Using the New Positive Psychology to Realize Your Potential for Lasting Fulfillment* to British economist Sir Richard Layard's *Happiness: Lessons from a New Science* to Richard Nettle's *Happiness: The Science Behind Your Smile* and the Dalai Lama's *The Art of Happiness*. Google "science of happiness" and you'll get close to 70,000 hits.

Seligman and his colleagues are trying to forge a new cultural role for psychology. This isn't psychology as practiced for the past half-century plus—as a diagnostic system for the many ways human beings go horribly wrong, dedicated to changing pathological misery into ordinary unhappiness, one damaged client at a time. Nor is it psychology as a research profession so focused on administering shocks to rats or measuring eye-blink rates that it forgets about overarching questions of life satisfaction, social contribution, effectiveness, and connection. And despite their emphasis on nebulous concepts like joy, compassion, virtue, character, and what goes right in life, positive psychologists vigorously differentiate themselves from their forerunners like Carl Rogers and Abraham Maslow in the Human Potential Movement, dismissing that earlier work as short on hard-boiled research and long on therapeutic intuition and quests for radical, almost effortless, personal transformation. Theirs is a new vision of psychology as a muscular, morally prescriptive, socially influential, positively focused, and thoroughly researched discipline. It's psychology as a way of life.

Beyond Helplessness

The Positive Psychology movement is a sunny place for people whose lives have been lived at least partly in shadow. And it's impossible to fully understand it without understanding the less-than-rosy early life of its leading popularizer, Martin Seligman.

Seligman has called himself "a dyed-in-the-wool pessimist." His five home-schooled children have called him a grouch. His parents were civil servants who wanted to see him get into a good college, and so they saved from their modest salaries and, when he was 13, took him out of the local public school and enrolled him in a private military academy full of rich kids. There Seligman felt isolated and rejected. He calls the experience the "first crisis of my life," and adapted by becoming something of an amateur psychiatrist, like Luci, for pretty girls who wouldn't otherwise have looked at him.

One morning while he was still in military school and spending the night at a friend's house, he felt something was terribly wrong and ran home in a panic. There he watched his father, who'd recently been acting strangely and prone to weeping, being carried out in a stretcher, immobile. Three more strokes followed. His father, once a vital man who hoped to run for public office, was left permanently paralyzed, alternating between bouts of euphoria and sadness, as Seligman writes in his 1990 book, *Learned Optimism*. "This was my introduction to the suffering that helplessness engenders. Seeing my father in this state, as I did again and again until his death years later, set the direction of my quest. His desperation fueled my vigor."

For the next two decades, Seligman committed himself to the study of helplessness, while making double-sure that he wasn't helpless himself. A high achiever, he graduated from Princeton and went on to graduate studies in psychology at the University of Pennsylvania. In 1964, when he was 21, he watched a group of lab dogs in their electrified wire cages there, acting as despairing as his own dad. They were slumped with their heads on their paws, whimpering, and doing nothing to avoid the shocks being administered to them. In a previous experiment, they'd been unable to escape being shocked. Now, even though the experimental parameters had changed and they could leap to safety on the other side of the cage, they didn't. They simply endured.

Seligman concluded that the dogs were no longer learning sets of discrete behaviors through reward and punishment, as the Skinnerian behaviorism of the time maintained they would. They'd come to an overarching conclusion: that "nothing they did mattered," which perpetuated its own reality even when circumstances changed. Seligman's observation was heretical—animals weren't supposed to adopt abstract, generalized attitudes like helplessness.

Fascinated, Seligman (in loose concert with Aaron Beck, the father of cognitive psychology, the rationalist Albert Ellis, and others) began studying the effect of helplessness. Such thinking styles, they hypothesized, generated depressed moods. They then dissected the thinking styles of pessimists and noted that they globalized their failures like the dogs had ("I'm no good with people" or "Nothing I do makes any difference") and minimized their successes ("I was just lucky"). Not surprisingly, the pessimists' moods measured consistently low. In the face of adversity, they often gave up. Optimists, by contrast, were consistently cheerier and more effective. They drew global conclusions about their successes ("I'm an excellent athlete") and considered their failures and disappointments to be momentary flukes that weren't their responsibility ("She must have been in a bad mood"). The optimists had huge advantages. They got depressed at half the rate of pessimistic people. Even though they were less realistic, their thoughts helped them create their own sunnier universes: their good moods helped them get along better with others, and they performed better on tests of creativity, efficacy, and intelligence.

Seligman figured that if depressed people had somehow learned to be helpless, they could also unlearn it, but as he moved from animal research into clinical psychology, he didn't just want to undo negative thinking, he wanted to foster good feelings. He had a hunch that people who consistently celebrated and exercised their strengths would be buffered against inevitable bad times when they struck. This had worked for Seligman himself: he'd learned to focus on his strengths, becoming a prolific researcher and a popular writer. He also successfully used cognitive therapy techniques on himself, learning to dispute "negative self-talk" and to marshal reality-based data that supported looking on the bright side. People, he contended, could argue themselves out of their black moods if they took action. They just had to stick to it, dispute their knee-jerk negative globalizations and catastrophizing, engage in "positive self-talk," and do their homework in journals and exercise books.

Seligman's career progressed and his grants and awards piled up throughout the 1970s and 1980s, but he was after bigger fish. He didn't want to simply bump unhappy people a few steps up the misery scale. He wanted to expand human happiness, and he wanted to do it in a much larger theater. Having morphed from researcher to clinical psychologist, he now morphed again—to social scientist and small-pond politician.

Seligman didn't like the direction his own profession was taking. For more than two decades (as private insurance reimbursements for treating DSM -defined disorders and NIMH grants for the study of mental illnesses mushroomed) he'd watched clinical psychologists who weren't interested in research-based psychology come to dominate the American Psychological Association (APA). Many of these clinicians, Seligman thought, accentuated the negative and used treatments that weren't proving effective. He liked active, evidence-based, cognitive and behavioral therapies, not those that encouraged clients to talk about their pain. He believed that many therapists were promoting a therapeutic ethos preoccupied with childhood woundedness, consumeristic entitlement, passivity, and self-centeredness. That approach, he thought, unrealistically raised expectations and set people up for disappointment and social

isolation, which, in turn, contributed to the skyrocketing rates of depression.

In 1997, after campaigning vigorously, he was voted president of the APA by the widest margin in the association's history. As a researcher in an association now numerically dominated by clinicians, he was an unusual choice. His theme for his three-year term was an equally unusual choice: he'd push for a change in the focus of psychology, he announced, away from the study of some of the worst things in life to the study of what makes life worth living.

For years, Seligman had been assembling contacts and shaping his vision. On New Year's Day 1998, at a resort in Akumal, Mexico, he got together with fellow researcher Czikszentmihalyi and Ray Fowler, then the Executive Director of the APA, to brainstorm a taxonomy for a new field of Positive Psychology. They decided their new field would have three main pillars: the study of positive emotion, positive character, and positive institutions. They'd also recruit psychology's best and brightest to do longitudinal, demographic, and outcome studies—all unimpeachably rigorous and scientific—of everything from civic engagement to forgiveness.

Within a year, the Templeton Foundation (which specializes in the interface of science and religion) had approached Seligman to fund more research. In 1999, Seligman began to teach a Positive Psychology class at the University of Pennsylvania, assigning homework that included performing altruistic acts, writing autobiographies that showcased strengths, and making gratitude lists. The movement was on its way.

Growth of a Movement

In the seven years since the founding of Positive Psychology in Akumal, its adherents have done their best to lay claim to a large, sprawling, and only partially mapped field of inquiry, which they've framed as the study of happiness. The twists and turns of Seligman's exploration have been distilled into a simple and elegant theory of the three features that constitute happiness: the pleasant life, the good life, and the meaningful life.

He defines the "pleasant life" as characterized by fleeting positive moods and immediate experiences of comfort and pleasure. At its best, the pleasant life can be defined as the Epicureans did: the simple satisfaction of a mind and body at peace. It can be amplified by learning to savor good moments and to lighten up habitual patterns of thought. But in Seligman's scheme, the "pleasant life" is the least important aspect of happiness, because it depends heavily on an inherited positive temperament and on good fortune: luck and genes. Simply enjoying the pleasant life doesn't build character or resilience. It's perilously close to shallow hedonism, and when pursued too hard, it leads to a grasping "hedonic treadmill."

Seligman, who loves to work himself, is much more enthusiastic about the next tier of the pyramid: "the good life"—what Thomas Jefferson meant by happiness. This part of happiness is anchored in building a full life that goes well. It comes from exercising our talents and virtues—what Seligman calls our "signature strengths"—and it depends heavily on the ability to lose oneself in the earned pleasures of sustained effort, absorbing work, conversation, accomplishment, contemplation, or what Csikszentmihalyi calls "flow." To many people's surprise, studies in which people record their mood states in daily diaries have revealed that most people feel happy far more often at work than at home.

The third aspect of Seligman's happiness is the "meaningful life," defined as the dedication of one's life to something larger than yourself—something beyond family and personal or intellectual achievement. Although Seligman rarely uses these words, the meaningful life includes altruism and love. His definition harkens back to the Victorian moralists and to Enlightenment figures like Jefferson, who once said "Happiness is the aim of life, but virtue is the foundation of happiness." Meaningfulness is encouraged, Seligman says, by "positive institutions" that support the virtues—thriving schools, churches, community groups, and democracies—and is weakened by the splintered, consumeristic society that surrounds us. In a secular society barraged by advertising celebrating the individualistic and consumer-driven life, this approach to happiness is a tough sell.

Positive Psychology's massive public relations successes may have encouraged millions to take a fresh look at their attitudes and to think, at least fleetingly, about what really brings them satisfaction. But what happens when the movement moves from the realm of ideas to the realm of experience, and people try to carry out the snappy exhortations they read in a *Time* magazine article? Can descriptive research be made prescriptive? Can Positive Psychology materially change the lives of ordinary people?

Practicing Positive Psychology

In the fall of 2004, I had a chance to find out when I joined a Telecourse called "Authentic Happiness Coaching," presided over by Seligman from his office in Philadelphia. Every Thursday at 1:00 p.m. for 20 weeks, I sat at the telephone in my home in Toronto, Canada, linked not only to Seligman in Philadelphia, but to 190 fellow students. We came together to listen to lectures by Positive Psychology's leading lights, and to absorb research. We were also expected to try out practices distilled from grandma's wisdom and the sayings of the ancient Greeks and 19th-century moralists, all scientifically researched and packaged for a new secular century.

Some might consider me a hard case for this kind of stuff. For starters, there's my occupation: I'm neither a coach nor a therapist, but a producer for the Canadian Broadcasting System. As a journalist, I've tried through the years to hone my natural skills in critical thinking, which makes me wary. On top of that, my disposition is reflective, rueful, at times downright melancholy. I'm a former New Yorker descended from Jewish immigrants and refugees who fled Europe and the Holocaust. I grew up, like Woody Allen and many other Jews, with thoughts of historic catastrophe and personal dis-

content, each feeding the other. My family is a case study in how to live with a long list of cognitive distortions, from assuming the worst will happen to thinking it should, because either they deserved it or other people thought they did. Personally, when it came to rah-rah notions like "thinking positive," I remained decidedly ambivalent; I'd try them, and then curse myself for failing.

Four years ago, my doctors discovered a large, dangerous, benign brain tumor in my cerebellum. I survived three difficult brain surgeries (the last one should have killed me, said one doctor). I still work part-time, walk with a cane, and suffer from physical imbalance and fatigue. At times, it was hard to put a positive spin on all that, although knowing others who'd succumbed, I felt downright lucky. So I bucked myself up through four months in the hospital and a long recuperation. I'm rightly proud of my staying power and my sheer doggedness, which helped me during the many low points and reversals. Perhaps my pride in triumphing over odds—including my own temperament—explains why I'm a secret fan of self-help literature.

All told, I was delighted to take the Telecourse, thinking it might do me some good; but, yes, I did drag the rest of my character into the enterprise, too. Seligman—he had us call him "Marty"—has the silky baritone of an accomplished lecturer and was a delight to behold by telephone. Early on, he told us a story that he's told and retold in many interviews, about the experience that led him to come up with his version of Positive Psychology. In 1998, he was in the garden with his daughter Nikki, who was throwing weeds into the air and fooling around while Seligman was toiling away. Getting exasperated, he yelled at her for not taking her gardening more seriously. Nikki, who was only 5 at the time, looked straight at him and told him that, on her fifth birthday, she'd decided not be a whiner. She said it was the hardest thing that she'd ever done. "If I can stop whining, Daddy, you can stop being a grouch." This encounter, Seligman told us, forced him to further examine questions like: Why, after 30 years of inner work, was he still a grouch? Why have psychologists ignored positive emotion and well-being? How can we flourish as human beings?

The meat of the Telecourse was the weekly lecture, which deftly packaged Seligman's findings, collected from 30 years of research (by him and others). He ended the lectures with a homework assignment, which we'd discuss in our weekly "pods" or telephone tutorials, comprised of about 15 students. Our pod leaders assigned us different partners with whom to talk about our experiences of doing the exercises. A couple of weeks into the course, Marty gave us an exercise he called the Three Blessings. At the end of every day, we were to write down three good things that had happened to us, and why we found them beneficial. It seemed like a feel-good cliché—like "Count your blessings," the advice of grandmas everywhere.

I did the assignment like a good little student. And I was a bit dumfounded by what happened. For years, I'd kept diaries filled with ruminations—to blow off steam and to practice writing. They bored me when I wrote them, and only succeeded in tying me in knots. They read something like a transcript of the obsessions of Woody Allen's unfunny younger brother, stripped of any redeeming humor. Over the years, writing these morbid documents only made me feel worse.

Then, some years ago, I was assigned to criss-cross Canada producing documentaries on the environment. Before I left, I thought, if I were killed in a plane crash, I didn't want anybody to find my journals—they weren't what I wanted to be remembered by. So I gathered them up, piles and piles of them, and tossed them out in the garbage. Even now, I imagine my notebooks depressing the trash that surrounds them in some landfill north of Toronto.

But Marty's assignment of diligently writing down three daily blessings asked me to pay attention to the good stuff, not the sores. As the Buddhists say, scratch the good dog, not the bad one. In years of writing drivel, I'd never done that before. It'd never even occurred to me to write out of a sense of pleasure.

I loved it.

I soon found that I had far more than three blessings to write about: conversations with friends and good, simple things, like walks and yoga sessions and exercise. By eleven or noon, I'd find myself stopping to check for what had gone well already. And lots of little things had! I began to mark little events in my mind, so I could include them in my notebook later that night. Reviewing my notebook, I discovered I often wrote about what I ate and drank (though I often experience great difficulty eating and drinking because of my surgeries). I relished small victories. It was simple stuff, but it worked in making me feel good.

Positive Psychology research, meanwhile, reassured me that writing my gratitude list wouldn't turn me into a softie, incapable of dealing with life's glancing blows. Strange as it seemed, being grateful might even better equip me. In a 2003 two-month experimental comparison conducted by psychologists Robert Emmons of the University of California at Davis and Michael McCullough of the University of Miami, volunteer subjects who kept gratitude journals on a weekly basis exercised more regularly, reported fewer physical symptoms, felt better about their lives, and were more optimistic about the upcoming week than subjects who recorded neutral life events or hassles, as I'd done for years.

Over time, cultivating gratitude helped me experience everyday events as gifts—part of the basic bounty of life. "For the grateful man," a Turkish proverb says. "the gnats make music." I kept the assignment up long past the due date, but eventually I stopped. Why, I don't know. Was I addicted to negativity? Lazy? Didn't know what was good for me?

The second most important exercise for me was the one that followed: we had to express gratitude to another human being. We were to pick a person important to us whom we'd never thanked, and then write him or her a letter describing what we valued in the relationship, and how it affected our lives. Marty told us that this was one of the most powerful exercises. It would make us happier, and make those who got the letters happier, too.

I picked a dear friend of mine, an 82-year-old Anglican priest I'd known for more than 25 years, who now lives in a retirement home. I love this man. When I was in my mid-thirties, I used to visit him in the country, where he had a rural parish. We had serious talks about God and philosophy. He loved to cook and garden, and had a grand appreciation for the natural world. I loved his eye for the wonders of creation, a gift from his God. But he isn't an overly pious man. He also shares my absurdist sense of humor. I'm his Jewish media friend, very different from the old ladies who used to lavish attention on him and bring him pot roast dinners. He isn't a father figure to me because he's hardly stern and has never given me personal advice. Jung has a better term for what he is to me: a warm, embracing "male mother."

So I sat down and wrote a letter detailing what he means to me. Then, following Marty's instruction, I called him up and told him I wanted to read him something . I arrived at his retirement home, cane in hand. Entering his small apartment, I embraced him, sat down in his new La-Z-Boy chair, and read him my gratitude letter. He smiled, looking a little puzzled. Then he folded the letter up and told me, "I'm not the sort who gets depressed, but if I ever do, I'll take this out and read it."

Struggling for Happiness

During our telephone lecture a few days later, Marty called on some students to describe their gratitude visits. All their stories seemed much better than mine. Their visits were life affirming, full of positive emotion. One fellow had given a letter to his wife as a birthday present. Another had taken the train to another city to read a letter to an old friend, who welcomed it as if it were a gift from God. I felt a little cheated. My visit was so matter of fact, so incidental—a hiccup in a long friendship, followed by a spot of tea.

Another exercise Marty had us do was to "design a good day." Since I wasn't working much at the time, I seemed always to be designing a nice day (as my wife kept telling me). So I began writing out lists of what I was going to do to have a good day, only to discover that I was just writing the simple chores that I'd do anyway. My messages to myself (about exercise and yoga and reading this book or that) created much amusement in my house. Lists are supposed to be for what you think you'll forget. My life was already an endless self-improvement exercise, without the benefit of great good health. But this assignment gave my leisure the dignity of a homework assignment.

There was much more, of course, to our curriculum in happiness. We took pen-and-pencil tests to identify our "signature strengths" (like perseverance, critical thinking, love of learning, social intelligence, spirituality, bravery, and zest). We were encouraged to try using them to turn a mundane task into one with "flow." We were sent out to savor routine events, like a meal or a walk in the park. We were even taught how to lower our expectations when we went shopping. Guest lecturer Barry Schwartz of Swarthmore College, the author of *The Paradox of Choice*, talked to us about the research showing that all the choice in our wealthy, consumer-driven world, could make you dither yourself into a state of unhappiness. For the first time in human history, huge numbers of people may become mental from all the choice in front of them. (Have you seen how many colors of beige there are?) All the choice can make people anxious about making mistakes—not getting the perfect "one." Schwartz sent us out shopping with this simple message: lower your expectations, and settle on something "good enough." This he calls "satisfysing," shorthand for not driving yourself crazy.

I went searching for a pair of winter boots way too late in the season. There was choice, but not many boots left. After trying different footware, I settled on a pair in a size that usually doesn't fit (it was shorter but wider), but that's all there was. When I got home, I completely panicked thinking I'd made a mistake. I worried that, because I bought the boots at a small store, I couldn't get my money back. So I went to other stores and tried on other pairs, just to see if I'd made the right choice. All in all, I spent more time looking for these $150 boots than I did buying the biggest investment in my life, my house. Schwartz was right: choice can make you plain neurotic, especially if you're neurotic to begin with.

I never told people this story: everybody in my pod was just too sane or on their best Positive Psychology behavior. Or perhaps they were more accomplished shoppers than I was, and didn't have my traces of OCD. This was more the stuff of Seinfeld than Authentic Happiness. I don't think that George was somebody Marty would approve of.

Listening to the Inner Cynic

But Seinfeld may have a point that Positive Psychology should consider. This show—famously devoted to "nothing"—is so popular precisely because it speaks to something elemental in ourselves. However much we may aspire to be solid citizens and publicly embody the classic virtues, the makers of Seinfeld captured our secret: we're filled with internal quirks, psychic peccadilloes, and unaccountable likes and dislikes, including many "negative" traits and predilections. Altogether, they're what make us distinctive, identifiable to ourselves as ourselves. Imagine Jerry Seinfeld without his characteristic sense of irony, or George or Elaine without their whining, which certainly wouldn't rank high on the Positive Psychology Scale of Approval.

At my worst moments in the course, I feared that positive psychologists were in danger of sandblasting the rough edges of individual personality and character to produce a shiny idealization of virtue. I wasn't at all sure that they appreciate how much the search for the "positive" can interfere with the natural rhythms of life; how necessary it is to include all the ups and downs, all the bumps and fissures that make us complete human beings.

During the course, I learned some truly valuable lessons about appreciation, gratitude, optimism, and the often underestimated role of conscious will and perseverance in the pursuit of happiness. And yet, as the weeks went by, I became gradually

more aware that something about this experience just wasn't going deep enough; no new, positive roots were being planted. Was it simply the curmudgeon within me, my long-standing "bah-humbug" that kept me from getting with the program? Perhaps. But as our class continued marching relentlessly toward positiveness, I became aware of my own growing sense of difference. In short, I felt lonely.

I felt it when others raved about their epiphanies following the gratitude exercise. By contrast, all I could come up with was a pleasant, but low-key, anticlimax. I couldn't even bring myself to tell my boot-buying story! And I felt this same sense of loneliness during an exercise called "One Door Closes and Another Opens." Here, people talked about seemingly dreadful things that'd worked out well. One person didn't get the job he wanted, but got a better job instead. Another was fired, which prompted her to go into business for herself, forcing her to finally do what she always wanted to do, while making more money. I dared not say what I wanted to say: that even to the present day, behind some of the doors I've closed lay the lingering stench of regret.

So, instead of revelling in a connection with 200 souls in exploring the true meaning of life, I often found myself retreating into my own solitary consciousness. I knew what was required of me as a good student: that I be upbeat and cooperative in our discussion groups between classes—our pods. But it seemed that the conversations lacked openness and candor, and had little spontaneity. Our happiness lessons and tasks dominated the agenda; ordinary human vulnerability and undue attention to tragedy, failure, disappointment, and loss weren't permitted, except as asides. Once I talked about "the inevitability of suffering," and ended up feeling like a jerk. Nice, positive people don't think, much less talk, about such things. Or if they do, they have to "move on" quickly. Negative emotion is only acceptable if it's in the past.

After the stilted atmosphere of the discussion groups, however, I was always a little surprised to discover that whenever a homework assignment gave me an opportunity to talk one-on-one with my fellow pod members, they were bright, alive, and interesting, and I felt a real, authentic connection. But however simpatico I might feel, even with the most sympathetic partner, there was one topic I never brought up: how much shame I found myself feeling as the course dragged on.

What was I ashamed of? How could a course on Positive Psychology shame a smart, cynical person like me? I was ashamed of my loneliness, sure (though I knew the course wasn't therapy). But I was also ashamed that I didn't seem to "get it." As the course, and the brutal Canadian winter unfolded, I often felt in the pods that I was a small, nasty person who knew he'd best keep all of his doubts and inadequacies well hidden. I simply couldn't be as positive as Seligman or his instructors wanted me to be. And like the George character on Seinfeld, I felt ridiculous. But, unfortunately, I didn't have Jerry and the gang to kvetch to over lunch.

To be sure, Seligman wisely includes community—and the devotion to a cause larger than the lonely, isolated self—as one of the keys to a "meaningful life." Yet the actual experience of the course seemed to ignore the deep human hunger for real community. If our culture's infatuation with the "maximal self," as Seligman describes our inbred individualism, is one of the major causes of unhappiness in our time, then surely a course in Positive Psychology ought to make genuine human connection a central element, at least in the small community of the pods. But the structure of the course and its implicit pressure to "be positive," whatever the cost, undermined the experience of this critical source of human satisfaction. True, we only had 20 weeks. And true, our last homework assignment was to go out and join an organization. But it was as if we were being told, "Okay, folks, commit to something larger than ourselves. But you're on your own, from here on in." I know Seligman was trying to condense a lifetime's work into a few short weeks, but just because you're a great lecturer doesn't mean the message gets embedded in people's lives: that's what the real work of human culture is about.

Oddly enough, while we were never supposed to give in to negativity and depression, they both shadowed the whole course; they were the unacknowledged elephants lurking in the corner. It sometimes felt that the strategies of Positive Psychology—shopping trips, savoring tips, play days, counting blessings, and gratitude exercises—were being used as amulets to ward off life's inevitable miseries. If you suffered from these miseries, Seligman eventually advised that you see a REAL therapist, quickly. But if you weren't "clinically depressed," the full range of human mood seemed to be something to be engineered out of your soul. He told us to dispute our bad moods in the theater of our minds, like the lawyerly cognitive therapists we should all learn to be—as if negativity were just a kind of superstitious taboo. In the end, I thought, Positive Psychology shares with that very unscientific cousin, positive thinking, this one thing: if you don't have the right optimistic temperament, you need to regularly apply heavy doses of intentionality and embrace the positive with an iron will. In this, there's an odd parallel between Freud and the positive psychologists: repression, said Freud, is at the heart of civilization. And it's at the heart of Positive Psychology.

Seligman himself spoke about depression during almost every session, and admitted freely to being temperamentally pessimistic, though he never called himself a depressive, recovering or not. But when he did point out his negative quirks, it was as if to remind us (and himself, perhaps) that they'd been resolutely banished to his past life. My pod leader admitted to being a reformed hysteric—a catastrophist who'd learned to soothe herself when little details of her life went awry. It had required work for her to get past these feelings, but it wasn't that hard to do: you just had to use a few cue words and internal exercises. As with Seligman's depressive tendencies, it felt as though she was telling us to throw our negative feelings into the dirty laundry basket.

The point of these admissions by Seligman and others was to renounce "the dark side" as castoffs from an old personality—primitive throwbacks to an earlier, less evolved self we in the class should learning to transcend. To improve ourselves in this way, we should all be vigorously programming ourselves by do-

ing the exercises and tests, "disputing ourselves" out of our negativity when it showed its atavistic head.

Seligman says he's interested in restoring old-time character to its rightful place—a worthy goal for our self-indulgent time. But does that mean that we must return to the rigid Victorian rule that you keep all your darkness under wraps; let the world see your Dr. Jeykll and keep your Mr. Hyde to yourself? One of the great advances made by the much maligned therapeutic culture is that it actually allows people to look compassionately at their own pain and gives them the vocabulary to describe it. Therapy helps them eliminate the necessity of suffering in silent shame. For all the powerful insights of Positive Psychology, it won't advance the cause of human happiness if it too enthusiastically endorses the antiquated ethic of the stiff upper lip.

Certainly Seligman and his colleagues can claim credit for turning the fuzzy, mushy concept of happiness—always before the exclusive purview of poets and philosophers—into a truly objective, empirically backed science. They've systemically defined particular habits of thought, will, intention, and feeling that are correlated with the good life. And these pioneers have even gone further; for that we should be thankful. They're constructing from this new science a set of principles, a practical discipline, a program of concrete procedures and exercises whereby those of us not naturally blessed with the gift of happiness can learn how to acquire it. Is this the culmination of America's revolutionary promise—the pursuit of happiness—or what?

But a basic question still nags at me. Whatever science might discover about the constitution of happiness and optimism, is it possible for science to teach us how to get them? Can you teach human beings the proper principles of living by displaying your evidence and drawing from it a series of rules that people can learn in 20 weeks? Is it really possible to devise a system, a curriculum of happiness that we can really weave into the fabric of our daily lives? Can this system become as much a part of our neural makeup as, say, the ability to read or ride a bicycle? No doubt we can all learn better habits of mind that'll relieve suffering and reduce our tendency to fly toward misery rather than away from it—after all, that's the basis of cognitive therapy. But learning how to be happy, wise, and virtuous still seems far too difficult and elusive a quest to be fulfilled by taking a didactic course, no matter how scientific its pedigree.

Seligman has undoubtedly done the field of psychology an enormous service by demonstrating that, for any science purporting to understand human nature, the study of what makes people happy, optimistic, and wise is just as important as the study of what makes them anxious, depressed, and crazy. If this work did no more than remind a therapy-soaked population that grandma's old values—gratitude, forgiveness, generosity, selflessness, dedication to something larger than oneself—have never been surpassed as the map to a life well lived, it would be worthwhile. Reminding us what's valuable in our lost traditions is no small thing. And yet, I still am left wondering if the spark that fires the flame of happiness, the will to try for the optimistic life, must come from something deeper, more mysterious, less definable than anything science can devise. After all, the question of what makes for a happy, meaningful, worthwhile life has preoccupied philosophers, mystics, and masters of ancient wisdom traditions since the beginning of human history. Will we finally be able to resolve this primeval riddle with a neat, scientifically based set of cognitive procedures and prescriptions? Allow me this last bit of negativity—I have my doubts.

RICHARD HANDLER is a radio producer with the Canadian Broadcasting Corporation in Toronto, Canada. Contact: rhandler@sympatico.ca.

Glossary

This glossary of psychology terms is included to provide you with a convenient and ready reference as you encounter general terms in your study of psychology and personal growth and behavior that are unfamiliar or require a review. It is not intended to be comprehensive, but taken together with the many definitions included in the articles themselves, it should prove to be quite useful.

abnormal behavior Behavior that contributes to maladaptiveness, is considered deviant by the culture, or that leads to personal psychological distress.

absolute threshold The minimum amount of physical energy required to produce a sensation.

accommodation Process in cognitive development; involves altering or reorganizing the mental picture to make room for a new experience or idea.

acculturation The process of becoming part of a new cultural environment.

acetylcholine A neurotransmitter involved in memory.

achievement drive The need to attain self-esteem, success, or status. Society's expectations strongly influence the achievement motive.

achievement style The way people behave in achievement situations; achievement styles include the direct, instrumental, and relational styles.

acquired immune deficiency syndrome (AIDS) A fatal disease of the immune system.

acquisition In conditioning, forming associations in first learning a task.

actor-observer bias Tendency to attribute the behavior of other people to internal causes and our own behavior to external causes.

acupuncture Oriental practice involving the insertion of needles into the body to control pain.

adaptation The process of responding to changes in the environment by altering responses to keep a person's behavior appropriate to environmental demands.

adjustment How we react to stress; some change that we make in response to the demands placed upon us.

adrenal glands Endocrine glands involved in stress and energy regulation.

adrenaline A hormone produced by the adrenal glands that is involved in physiological arousal; adrenaline is also called epinephrine.

aggression Behavior intended to harm a member of the same or another species.

agoraphobia Anxiety disorder in which an individual is excessively afraid of places or situations from which it would be difficult or embarrassing to escape.

alarm reaction The first stage of Hans Selye's general adaptation syndrome. The alarm reaction is the immediate response to stress; adrenaline is released and digestion slows. The alarm reaction prepares the body for an emergency.

all-or-none law The principle that states that a neuron only fires when a stimulus is above a certain minimum strength (threshold), and when it fires, it does so at full strength.

alogia Individuals with schizophrenia that show a reduction in speech.

alpha Brain-wave activity that indicates that a person is relaxed and resting quietly; 8–12 Hz.

altered state of consciousness (ASC) A state of consciousness in which there is a redirection of attention, a change in the aspects of the world that occupy a person's thoughts, and a change in the stimuli to which a person responds.

ambivalent attachment Type of infant-parent attachment in which the infant seeks contact but resists once the contact is made.

amphetamine A strong stimulant; increases arousal of the central nervous system.

amygdala A part of the limbic system involved in fear, aggression, and other social behaviors.

anal stage Psychosexual stage during which, according to Sigmund Freud, the child experiences the first restrictions on his or her impulses.

anorexia nervosa Eating disorder in which an individual becomes severely underweight because of self-imposed restrictions on eating.

antidepressants Drugs used to elevate the mood of depressed individuals, presumably by increasing the availability of the neurotransmitters norepinephrine and/or serotonin.

antisocial personality disorder Personality disorder in which individuals who engage in antisocial behavior experience no guilt or anxiety about their actions; sometimes called sociopathy or psychopathy.

anxiety disorder Fairly long-lasting disruption of a person's ability to deal with stress; often accompanied by feelings of fear and apprehension.

applied psychology The area of psychology that is most immediately concerned with helping to solve practical problems; includes clinical and counseling psychology as well as industrial, environmental, and legal psychology.

aptitude test Any test designed to predict what a person with the proper training can accomplish in the future.

archetypes In Carl Jung's personality theory, unconscious universal ideas shared by all humans.

arousal theory Theory that focuses on the energy (arousal) aspect of motivation; it states that we are motivated to initiate behaviors that help to regulate overall arousal level.

asocial phase Phase in attachment development in which the neonate does not distinguish people from objects.

assertiveness training Training that helps individuals stand up for their rights while not denying rights of other people.

assimilation Process in cognitive development; occurs when something new is taken into the child's mental picture.

attachment Process in which the individual shows behaviors that promote proximity with a specific object or person.

attention Process of focusing on particular stimuli in the environment.

attention deficit disorder Hyperactivity; inability to concentrate.

attitude Learned disposition that actively guides us toward specific behaviors; attitudes consist of feelings, beliefs, and behavioral tendencies.

attribution The cognitive process of determining the motives of someone's behavior, and whether they are internal or external.

autism A personality disorder in which a child does not respond socially to people.

autonomic nervous system The part of the peripheral nervous system that carries messages from the central nervous system to the endocrine glands, the smooth muscles controlling the heart, and the primarily involuntary muscles controlling internal processes; includes the sympathetic and parasympathetic nervous systems.

aversion therapy A counterconditioning therapy in which unwanted responses are paired with unpleasant consequences.

avoidance conditioning Learning situation in which a subject avoids a stimulus by learning to respond appropriately before the stimulus begins.

avolition Individuals with schizophrenia who lack motivation to follow through on an activity.

backward conditioning A procedure in classical conditioning in which the US is presented and terminated before the termination of the CS; very ineffective procedure.

basal ganglia An area of the forebrain that is important to smooth muscle movement and actions. This area works in conjunction with the midbrain to help us avoid moving in choppy, fragmented ways.

behavior Anything you do or think, including various bodily reactions. Behavior includes physical and mental responses.

behavior genetics How genes influence behavior.

behavior modification Another term for behavior therapy; the modification of behavior through psychological techniques; often the application of conditioning principles to alter behavior.

behaviorism The school of thought founded by John Watson; it studied only observable behavior.

belongingness and love needs Third level of motives in Maslow's hierarchy; includes love and affection, friends, and social contact.

biological motives Motives that have a definite physiological basis and are biologically necessary for individual or species survival.

biological response system Systems of the body that are important in behavioral responding; includes the senses, muscles, endocrine system, and the nervous system.

biological therapy Treatment of behavior problems through biological techniques; major biological therapies include drug therapy, psychosurgery, and electroconvulsive therapy.

bipolar disorder Mood disorder characterized by extreme mood swings from sad depression to joyful mania; sometimes called manic depression.

blinding technique In an experiment, a control for bias in which the assignment of a subject to the experimental or control group is unknown to the subject or experimenter or both (a double-blind experiment).

body dysmorphic disorder Somatoform disorder characterized by a preoccupation with an imaginary defect in the physical appearance of a physically healthy person.

body language Communication through position and movement of the body.

bottom-up processing The psychoanalytic process of understanding communication by listening to words, then interpreting phrases, and finally understanding ideas.

brief psychodynamic therapy A therapy developed for individuals with strong egos to resolve a core conflict.

bulimia nervosa Eating disorder in which an individual eats large amounts of calorie-rich food in a short time and then purges the food by vomiting or using laxatives.

California Psychological Inventory (CPI) An objective personality test used to study normal populations.

Cannon-Bard theory of emotion Theory of emotion that states that the emotional feeling and the physiological arousal occur at the same time.

cardinal traits In Gordon Allport's personality theory, the traits of an individual that are so dominant that they are expressed in everything the person does; few people possess cardinal traits.

catatonic schizophrenia A type of schizophrenia that is characterized by periods of complete immobility and the apparent absence of will to move or speak.

causal attribution Process of determining whether a person's behavior is due to internal or external motives.

central nervous system The part of the human nervous system that interprets and stores messages from the sense organs, decides what behavior to exhibit, and sends appropriate messages to the muscles and glands; includes the brain and spinal cord.

central tendency In statistics, measures of central tendency give a number that represents the entire group or sample.

central traits In Gordon Allport's personality theory, the traits of an individual that form the core of the personality; they are developed through experience.

cerebellum The part of the hindbrain that is involved in balance and muscle coordination.

cerebral cortex The outermost layer of the cerebrum of the brain where higher mental functions occur. The cerebral cortex is divided into sections, or lobes, which control various activities.

cerebrum (cerebral hemisphere) Largest part of the forebrain involved in cognitive functions; the cerebrum consists of two hemispheres connected by the corpus callosum.

chromosome Bodies in the cell nucleus that contain the genes.

chunking Process of combining stimuli in order to increase memory capacity.

classical conditioning The form of learning in which a stimulus is associated with another stimulus that causes a particular response. Sometimes called Pavlovian conditioning or respondent conditioning.

clinical psychology Subfield in which psychologists assess psychological problems and treat people with behavior problems using psychological techniques (called psychotherapy).

cognition Mental processes, such as perception, attention, memory, language, thinking, and problem solving; cognition involves the acquisition, storage, retrieval, and utilization of knowledge.

cognitive behavior therapy A form of behavior therapy that identifies self-defeating attitudes and thoughts in a subject, and then helps the subject to replace these with positive, supportive thoughts.

cognitive development Changes over time in mental processes such as thinking, memory, language, and problem solving.

cognitive dissonance Leon Festinger's theory of attitude change that states that, when people hold two psychologically inconsistent ideas, they experience tension that forces them to reconcile the conflicting ideas.

cognitive expectancy The condition in which an individual learns that certain behaviors lead to particular goals; cognitive expectancy motivates the individual to exhibit goal-directed behaviors.

cognitive learning Type of learning that theorizes that the learner utilizes cognitive structures in memory to make decisions about behaviors.

cognitive psychology The area of psychology that includes the study of mental activities involved in perception, memory, language, thought, and problem solving.

cognitive restructuring The modification of the client's thoughts and perceptions that are contributing to his or her maladjustments.

cognitive therapy Therapy developed by Aaron Beck in which an individual's negative, self-defeating thoughts are restructured in a positive way.

cognitive-motivational-relational theory of emotion A theory of emotion proposed by Richard Lazarus that includes cognitive appraisal, motivational goals, and relationships between an individual and the environment.

collective unconscious Carl Jung's representation of the thoughts shared by all humans.

collectivistic cultures Cultures in which the greatest emphasis is on the loyalty of each individual to the group.

comparative psychology Subfield in which experimental psychologists study and compare the behavior of different species of animals.

compulsions Rituals performed excessively such as checking doors or washing hands to reduce anxiety.

concept formation (concept learning) The development of the ability to respond to common features of categories of objects or events.

concrete operations period Stage in cognitive development, from 7 to 11 years, in which the child's ability to solve problems with reasoning greatly increases.

conditioned response (CR) The response or behavior that occurs when the conditioned stimulus is presented (after the CS has been associated with the US).

conditioned stimulus (CS) An originally neutral stimulus that is associated with an unconditioned stimulus and takes on the latter's capability of eliciting a particular reaction.

Glossary

conditioned taste aversion (CTA) An aversion to particular tastes associated with stomach distress; usually considered a unique form of classical conditioning because of the extremely long interstimulus intervals involved.

conditioning A term applied to two types of learning (classical and operant). Conditioning refers to the scientific aspect of the type of learning.

conflict Situation that occurs when we experience incompatible demands or desires; the outcome when one individual or group perceives that another individual or group has caused or will cause harm.

conformity Type of social influence in which an individual changes his or her behavior to fit social norms or expectations.

connectionism Recent approach to problem solving; the development of neural connections allows us to think and solve problems.

conscientiousness The dimension in the five-factor personality theory that includes traits such as practical, cautious, serious, reliable, careful, and ambitious; also called dependability.

conscious Being aware of experiencing sensations, thoughts, and feelings at any given point in time.

conscious mind In Sigmund Freud's psychoanalytic theory of personality, the part of personality that we are aware of in everyday life.

consciousness The processing of information at various levels of awareness; state in which a person is aware of sensations, thoughts, and feelings.

consensus In causal attribution, the extent to which other people react as the subject does in a particular situation.

conservation The ability to recognize that something stays the same even if it takes on a different form; Piaget tested conservation of mass, number, length, and volume.

consistency In causal attribution, the extent to which the subject always behaves in the same way in a situation.

consolidation The biological neural process of making memories permanent; possibly short-term memory is electrically coded and long-term memory is chemically coded.

contingency model A theory that specific types of situations need particular types of leaders.

continuum of preparedness Martin Seligman's proposal that animals are biologically prepared to learn certain responses more readily than they are prepared to learn others.

control group Subjects in an experiment who do not receive the independent variable; the control group determines the effectiveness of the independent variable.

conventional morality Level II in Lawrence Kohlberg's theory, in which moral reasoning is based on conformity and social standards.

conversion disorder Somatoform disorder in which a person displays obvious disturbance in the nervous system without a physical basis for the problem.

correlation Statistical technique to determine the degree of relationship that exists between two variables.

counterconditioning A behavior therapy in which an unwanted response is replaced by conditioning a new response that is incompatible with it.

creativity A process of coming up with new or unusual responses to familiar circumstances.

critical period hypothesis Period of time during development in which particular learning or experiences normally occur; if learning does not occur, the individual has a difficult time learning it later.

culture-bound The idea that a test's usefulness is limited to the culture in which it was written and utilized.

cumulative response curve Graphed curve that results when responses for a subject are added to one another over time; if subjects respond once every 5 minutes, they will have a cumulative response curve value of 12 after an hour.

curiosity motive Motive that causes the individual to seek out a certain amount of novelty.

cyclothymia disorder A moderately severe problem with numerous periods of hypomanic episodes and depressive symptoms.

death instinct (also called Thanatos) Freud's term for an instinct that is destructive to the individual or species; aggression is a major expression of death instinct.

decay Theory of forgetting in which sensory impressions leave memory traces that fade away with time.

defense mechanisms Psychological techniques to help protect ourselves from stress and anxiety, to resolve conflicts, and to preserve our self-esteem.

delayed conditioning A procedure in classical conditioning in which the presentation of the CS precedes the onset of the US and the termination of the CS is delayed until the US is presented; most effective procedure.

delusion The holding of obviously false beliefs; for example, imagining someone is trying to kill you.

dendrites The branch-like structures of neurons that extend from the cell body (soma). The dendrites are the receivers of neural impulses (electrical and chemical signals) from the axons of other neurons. Although there are some areas of the body that contain dendrites that can act like axon terminals, releasing neurotransmitters in response to impulses and local voltage changes, most dendrites are the receiving branches of the neuron.

dependent variable In psychology, the behavior or response that is measured; it is dependent on the independent variable.

depersonalization disorder Dissociative disorder in which the individual escapes from his or her own personality by believing that he or she does not exist or that his or her environment is not real.

depolarization Any change in which the internal electrical charge becomes more positive.

depression A temporary emotional state that normal individuals experience or a persistent state that may be considered a psychological disorder. Characterized by sadness and low self-esteem.

descriptive statistics Techniques that help summarize large amounts of data information.

developmental psychology Study of physical and mental growth and behavioral changes in individuals from conception to death.

Diagnostic and Statistical Manual of Mental Disorders (DSM) Published by the American Psychiatric Association in 1952, and revised in 1968, 1980, 1987, and 1994, this manual was provided to develop a set of diagnoses of abnormal behavior patterns.

diffusion of responsibility Finding that groups tend to inhibit helping behavior; responsibility is shared equally by members of the group so that no one individual feels a strong commitment.

disorganized schizophrenia A type of schizophrenia that is characterized by a severe personality disintegration; the individual often displays bizarre behavior.

displacement Defense mechanism by which the individual directs his or her aggression or hostility toward a person or object other than the one it should be directed toward; in Freud's dream theory, the process of reassigning emotional feelings from one object to another one.

dissociative disorder Psychological disorder that involves a disturbance in the memory, consciousness, or identity of an individual; types include multiple personality disorder, depersonalization disorder, psychogenic amnesia, and psychogenic fugue.

dissociative fugue Individuals who have lost their memory, relocated to a new geographical area, and started a new life as someone else.

dissociative identity disorder (multiple personality disorder) Dissociative disorder in which several personalities are present in the same individual.

distinctiveness In causal attribution, the extent to which the subject reacts the same way in other situations.

Down syndrome Form of mental retardation caused by having three number 21 chromosomes (trisomy 21).

dream analysis Psychoanalytic technique in which a patient's dreams are reviewed and analyzed to discover true feelings.

drive Motivational concept used to describe the internal forces that push an organism toward a goal; sometimes identified as psychological arousal arising from a physiological need.

dyssomnia Sleep disorder in which the chief symptom is a disturbance in the amount and quality of sleep; they include insomnia and hypersomnia.

dysthymic disorder Mood disorder in which the person suffers moderate depression much of the time for at least two years.

ego Sigmund Freud's term for an individual's sense of reality.

egocentric Seeing the world only from your perspective.

eidetic imagery Photographic memory; ability to recall great detail accurately after briefly viewing something.

Electra complex The Freudian idea that the young girl feels inferior to boys because she lacks a penis.

electroconvulsive therapy (ECT) A type of biological therapy in which electricity is applied to the brain in order to relieve severe depression.

emotion A response to a stimulus that involves physiological arousal, subjective feeling, cognitive interpretation, and overt behavior.

empiricism The view that behavior is learned through experience.

encoding The process of putting information into the memory system.

encounter group As in a sensitivity training group, a therapy where people become aware of themselves in meeting others.

endorphins Several neuropeptides that function as neurotransmitters. The opiate-like endorphins are involved in pain, reinforcement, and memory.

engram The physical memory trace or neural circuit that holds memory; also called memory trace.

episodic memory Highest memory system; includes information about personal experiences.

Eros Sigmund Freud's term for an instinct that helps the individual or species survive; also called life instinct.

esteem needs Fourth level of motives in Abraham Maslow's hierarchy; includes high evaluation of oneself, self-respect, self-esteem, and respect of others.

eustress Stress that results from pleasant and satisfying experiences; earning a high grade or achieving success produces eustress.

excitement phase First phase in the human sexual response cycle; the beginning of sexual arousal.

experimental group Subjects in an experiment who receive the independent variable.

experimental psychology Subfield in which psychologists research the fundamental causes of behavior. Many experimental psychologists conduct experiments in basic research.

experimenter bias Source of potential error in an experiment from the action or expectancy of the experimenter; might influence the experimental results in ways that mask the true outcome.

external locus of control In Julian Rotter's personality theory, the perception that reinforcement is independent of a person's behavior.

extraversion The dimension in the five-factor personality theory that includes traits such as sociability, talkativeness, boldness, fun-lovingness, adventurousness, and assertiveness; also called surgency. The personality concept of Carl Jung in which the personal energy of the individual is directed externally.

factor analysis A statistical procedure used to determine the relationship among variables.

false memories Memories believed to be real, but the events never occurred.

fast mapping A process by which children can utilize a word after a single exposure.

fetal alcohol syndrome (FAS) Condition in which defects in the newborn child are caused by the mother's excessive alcohol intake.

five-factor model of personality tracts A trait theory of personality that includes the factors of extraversion, agreeableness, conscientiousness, emotional stability, and openness.

fixed action pattern (FAP) Unlearned, inherited, stereotyped behaviors that are shown by all members of a species; term used in ethology.

fixed interval (FI) schedule Schedule of reinforcement where the subject receives reinforcement for a correct response given after a specified time interval.

fixed ratio (FR) schedule Schedule of reinforcement in which the subject is reinforced after a certain number of responses.

flashbulb memory Memory of an event that is so important that significant details are vividly remembered for life.

forgetting In memory, not being able to retrieve the original learning. The part of the original learning that cannot be retrieved is said to be forgotton.

formal operations period Period in cognitive development; at 11 years, the adolescent begins abstract thinking and reasoning. This period continues throughout the rest of life.

free association Psychoanalytic technique in which the patient says everything that comes to mind.

free recall A verbal learning procedure in which the order of presentation of the stimuli is varied and the subject can learn the items in any order.

frequency theory of hearing Theory of hearing that states that the frequency of vibrations at the basilar membrane determines the frequency of firing of neurons carrying impulses to the brain.

frustration A cause of stress that results from the blocking of a person's goal-oriented behavior.

frustration-drive theory of aggression Theory of aggression that states that it is caused by frustration.

functionalism School of thought that studied the functional value of consciousness and behavior.

fundamental attribution error Attribution bias in which people overestimate the role of internal disposition and underestimate the role of external situation.

gate-control theory of pain Theory of pain that proposes that there is a gate that allows pain impulses to travel from the spinal cord to the brain.

gender-identity disorder (GID) Incongruence between assigned sex and gender identity.

gender-identity/role Term that incorporates gender identity (the private perception of one's sex) and gender role (the public expression of one's gender identity).

gene The basic unit of heredity; the gene is composed of deoxyribonucleic acid (DNA).

general adaptation syndrome (GAS) Hans Selye's theory of how the body responds to stress over time. GAS includes alarm reaction, resistance, and exhaustion.

generalized anxiety disorder Anxiety disorder in which the individual lives in a state of constant severe tension, continuous fear, and apprehension.

genetics The study of heredity; genetics is the science of discovering how traits are passed along generations.

genotype The complete set of genes inherited by an individual from his or her parents.

Gestalt therapy Insight therapy designed to help people become more aware of themselves in the here and now and to take responsibility for their own actions.

grandiose delusion Distortion of reality; one's belief that he or she is extremely important or powerful.

group therapy Treatment of several patients at the same time.

groupthink When group members are so committed to, and optimistic about, the group that they feel it is invulnerable; they become so concerned with maintaining consensus that criticism is muted.

Glossary

GSR (galvanic skin response) A measure of autonomic nervous system activity; a slight electric current is passed over the skin, and the more nervous a subject is, the easier the current will flow.

hallucinations A sensory impression reported when no external stimulus exists to justify the report; often hallucinations are a symptom of mental illness.

hallucinogens Psychedelic drugs that result in hallucinations at high doses, and other effects on behavior and perception in mild doses.

halo effect The finding that once we form a general impression of someone, we tend to interpret additional information about the person in a consistent manner.

Hawthorne effect The finding that behavior can be influenced just by participation in a research study.

health psychology Field of psychology that studies psychological influences on people's health, including how they stay healthy, why they become ill, and how their behavior relates to their state of health.

heuristic Problem-solving strategy; a person tests solutions most likely to be correct.

hierarchy of needs Abraham Maslow's list of motives in humans, arranged from the biological to the uniquely human.

hippocampus Brain structure in the limbic system that is important in learning and memory.

homeostasis The state of equilibrium that maintains a balance in the internal body environment.

hormones Chemicals produced by the endocrine glands that regulate activity of certain bodily processes.

humanistic psychology Psychological school of thought that believes that people are unique beings who cannot be broken down into parts.

hyperphagia Disorder in which the individual continues to eat until he or she is obese; can be caused by damage to ventromedial hypothalamus.

hypersomnia Sleep disorder in which an individual falls asleep at inappropriate times; narcolepsy is a form of hypersomnia.

hypnosis Altered state of consciousness characterized by heightened suggestibility.

hypochondriasis Somatoform disorder in which the individual is obsessed with fears of having a serious medical disease.

hypothalamus Part of the brain's limbic system; involved in motivational behaviors, including eating, drinking, and sex.

hypothesis In the scientific method, an educated guess or prediction about future observable events.

iconic memory Visual information that is encoded into the sensory memory store.

id Sigmund Freud's representation of the basic instinctual drives; the id always seeks pleasure.

identification The process in which children adopt the attitudes, values, and behaviors of their parents.

identity diffusion In Marcia's adolescent identity theory, the status of individuals who have failed to make a commitment to values and roles.

illusion An incorrect perception that occurs when sensation is distorted.

imitation The copying of another's behavior; learned through the process of observation.

impression formation Developing an evaluation of another person from your perceptions; first, or initial, impressions are often very important.

imprinting A form of early learning in which birds follow a moving stimulus (often the mother); may be similar to attachment in mammals.

independent variable The condition in an experiment that is controlled and manipulated by the experimenter; it is a stimulus that will cause a response.

indiscriminate attachment phase Stage of attachment in which babies prefer humans to nonhumans, but do not discriminate among individual people.

individuation Carl Jung's concept of the process leading to the unification of all parts of the personality.

inferential statistics Techniques that help researchers make generalizations about a finding based on a limited number of subjects.

inferiority complex Adler's personality concept that states that because children are dependent on adults and cannot meet the standards set for themselves they feel inferior.

inhibition Restraint of an impulse, desire, activity, or drive.

insight A sudden grasping of the means necessary to achieve a goal; important in the Gestalt approach to problem solving.

insight therapy Therapy based on the assumption that behavior is abnormal because people do not adequately understand the motivation causing their behavior.

instinct Highly stereotyped behavior common to all members of a species that often appears in virtually complete form in the absence of any obvious opportunities to learn it.

instrumental conditioning Operant conditioning.

intelligence Capacity to learn and behave adaptively.

intelligence quotient (IQ) An index of a person's performance on an intelligence test relative to others in the culture; ratio of a person's mental age to chronological age.

interference Theory of forgetting in which information that was learned before (proactive interference) or after (retroactive interference) causes the learner to be unable to remember the material of interest.

internal locus of control In Rotter's personality theory, the perception that reinforcement is contingent upon behavior.

interstimulus interval Time interval between two stimuli; in classical conditioning, it is the elapsed time between the CS and the US.

intrinsic motivation Motivation inside the individual; we do something because we receive satisfaction from it.

introspection Method in which a subject gives a self report of his or her immediate experience.

introversion The personality concept of Carl Jung in which the personal energy of the individual is directed inward; characterized by introspection, seriousness, inhibition, and restraint.

James-Lange theory of emotion Theory of emotion that states that the physiological arousal and behavior come before the subjective experience of an emotion.

kinesthesis The sense of bodily movement.

labeling of arousal Experiments suggest that an individual experiencing physical arousal that cannot be explained will interpret those feelings in terms of the situation she or he is in and will use environmental and contextual cues.

language acquisition device (LAD) Hypothesized biological structure that accounts for the relative ease of acquiring language, according to Noam Chomsky.

latent dream content In Sigmund Freud's dream theory, the true thoughts in the unconsciousness; the true meaning of the dream.

latent learning Learning that occurs when an individual acquires knowledge of something but does not show it until motivated to do so.

law of effect Edward Thorndike's law that if a response produces satisfaction it will be repeated; reinforcement.

learned helplessness Condition in which a person learns that his or her behavior has no effect on his or her environment; when an individual gives up and stops trying.

learned social motives Social motives that are learned; include achievement and affiliation.

learning The relatively permanent change in behavior or behavioral ability of an individual that occurs as a result of experience.

learning styles The preferences students have for learning; theories of learning styles include personality differences, styles of information processing, and instructional preferences.

life instinct (also called Eros) Sigmund Freud's term for an instinct that helps the individual or species survive; sex is the major expression of life instinct.

life structure In Daniel Levinson's theory of adult personality development, the underlying pattern of an individual's life at any particular time; seasonal cycles include preadulthood, early adulthood, middle adulthood, and late adulthood.

linguistic relativity hypothesis Proposal that the perception of reality differs according to the language of the observer.

locus of control Julian Rotter's theory in which a person's beliefs about reinforcement are classified as internal or external.

long-term memory The permanent memory where rehearsed information is stored.

love An emotion characterized by knowing, liking, and becoming intimate with someone.

low-ball procedure The compliance technique of presenting an attractive proposal to someone and then switching it to a more unattractive proposal.

magic number 7 The finding that most people can remember about seven items of information for a short time (in short-term memory).

magnetic resonance imaging (MRI) A method of studying brain activity using magnetic field imaging.

major depressive disorder Severe mood disorder in which a person experiences one or more major depressive episodes; sometimes referred to simply as depression.

maladjustment Condition that occurs when a person utilizes inappropriate abilities to respond to demands placed upon him or her.

manic depressive reaction A form of mental illness marked by alternations of extreme phases of elation (manic phase) and depression.

manifest dream content In Sigmund Freud's dream theory, what is remembered about a dream upon waking; a disguised representation of the unconscious wishes.

maturation The genetically controlled process of growth that results in orderly changes in behavior.

mean The arithmetic average, in which the sum of scores is divided by the number of scores.

median The middle score in a group of scores that are arranged from lowest to highest.

meditation The practice of some form of relaxed concentration while ignoring other sensory stimuli.

memory The process of storing information so that it can be retrieved and used later.

memory attributes The critical features of an event that are used when the experience is encoded or retrieved.

mental age The age level on which a person is capable of performing; used in determining intelligence.

mental set Condition in which a person's thinking becomes so standardized that he or she approaches new problems in fixed ways.

microexpressions Facial expressions that last a fraction of a second. Since microexpressions do not last long, they go undetected in our everyday lives. Microexpressions are a type of nonverbal communication.

Minnesota Multiphasic Personality Inventory (MMPI-2) An objective personality test that was originally devised to identify personality disorders.

mnemonic technique Method of improving memory by combining and relating chunks of information.

modeling A process of learning by imitation in a therapeutic situation.

mood disorder Psychological disorder in which a person experiences a severe disruption in mood or emotional balance.

moral development Development of individuals as they adopt their society's standards of right and wrong; development of awareness of ethical behavior.

motivated forgetting (repression) Theory that suggests that people want to forget unpleasant events.

motivation The forces that initiate and direct behavior, and the variables that determine the intensity and persistence of the behavior.

motivator needs In Frederick Herzberg's theory, the factors that lead to job satisfaction; they include responsibility, the nature of the work, advancement, and recognition.

motive Anything that arouses the individual and directs his or her behavior toward some goal. Three categories of motives include biological, stimulus, and learned social.

Müller-Lyer illusion A well-known illusion, in which two horizontal lines have end lines either going in or out; the line with the end lines going in appears longer.

multiple approach-avoidance conflict Conflict that occurs when an individual has two or more goals, both of which have positive and negative aspects.

multiple attachment phase Later attachment stage in which the baby begins to form attachments to people other than the primary caretaker.

multiple intelligences Howard Gardner's theory that there exists several different kinds of intelligence.

Myers-Briggs Type Indicator (MBTI) Objective personality test based on Carl Jung's type theory.

narcotic analgesics Drugs that have an effect on the body similar to morphine; these relieve pain and suppress coughing.

naturalistic observation Research method in which behavior of people or animals in their normal environment is accurately recorded.

Necker cube A visual illusion. The Necker cube is a drawing of a cube designed so that it is difficult to determine which side is toward you.

negative reinforcement Removing something unpleasant to increase the probability that the preceding behavior will be repeated.

NEO Personality Inventory (NEO-PI) An objective personality test developed by Paul Costa Jr. and Robert McCrae to measure the five major factors in personality; consists of 181 questions.

neodissociation theory Idea that consciousness can be split into several streams of thought that are partially independent of each other.

neuron A specialized cell that functions to conduct messages throughout the body.

neurosis A Freudian term that was used to describe abnormal behavior caused by anxiety; it has been eliminated from *DSM-IV*.

neutral stimulus A stimulus that does not cause the response of interest; the individual may show some response to the stimulus but not the associated behavior.

norm A sample of scores representative of a population.

normal curve When scores of a large number of random cases are plotted on a graph, they often fall into a bell-shaped curve; as many cases on the curve are above the mean as below it.

observational learning In social learning theory, learning by observing someone else behave; people observe and imitate in learning socialization.

obsessions Fears that involve the inability to control impulses.

obsessive compulsive disorder Anxiety disorder in which the individual has repetitive thoughts (obsessions) that lead to constant urges (compulsions) to engage in meaningless rituals.

object permanence The ability to realize that objects continue to exist even if we can no longer see them.

Oedipus complex The Freudian idea that the young boy has sexual feelings for his mother and is jealous of his father and must identify with his father to resolve the conflict.

olfaction The smell sense.

Glossary

openness The dimension in the five-factor personality theory that includes traits such as imagination, creativity, perception, knowledge, artistic ability, curiosity, and analytical ability; also called intellect.

operant conditioning Form of learning in which behavior followed by reinforcement (satisfaction) increases in frequency.

opponent-process theory Theory that when one emotion is experienced, the other is suppressed.

optimum level of arousal Motivation theory that states that the individual will seek a level of arousal that is comfortable.

organic mental disorders Psychological disorders that involve physical damage to the nervous system; can be caused by disease or by an accident.

organizational psychology Area of industrial psychology that focuses on worker attitudes and motivation; derived primarily from personality and social psychology.

orgasm The climax of intense sexual excitement; release from building sexual tension, usually accompanied by ejaculation in men.

paired-associate learning A verbal learning procedure in which the subject is presented with a series of pairs of items to be remembered.

panic disorder Anxiety disorder characterized by the occurrence of specific periods of intense fear.

paranoid schizophrenia A type of schizophrenia in which the individual often has delusions of grandeur and persecution, thinking that someone is out to get him or her.

partial reinforcement Any schedule of reinforcement in which reinforcement follows only some of the correct responses.

partial reinforcement effect The finding that partial reinforcement produces a response that takes longer to extinguish than continuous reinforcement.

pattern recognition Memory process in which information attended to is compared with information already permanently stored in memory.

Pavlovian conditioning A bond or association between a neutral stimulus and a response; this type of learning is called classical conditioning.

perception The active process in which the sensory information that is carried through the nervous system to the brain is organized and interpreted; the interpretation of sensation.

persecutory delusion A delusion in which the individual has a distortion of reality; the belief that other people are out to get him or her.

person perception The process of using the information we gather in forming impressions of people to make evaluations of others.

personal unconscious Carl Jung's representation of the individual's repressed thoughts and memories.

personality disorder Psychological disorder in which there are problems in the basic personality structure of the individual.

phantom-limb pain Phenomenon in which people who have lost an arm or leg feel pain in the missing limb.

phobias Acute excessive fears of specific situations or objects that have no convincing basis in reality.

physiological needs First level of motives in Abraham Maslow's hierarchy; includes the biological needs of hunger, thirst, sex, exercise, and rest.

placebo An inert or inactive substance given to control subjects to test for bias effects.

plateau phase Second phase in the human sexual response cycle, during which the physiological arousal becomes more intense.

pleasure principle In Freudian theory, the idea that the instinctual drives of the id unconsciously and impulsively seek immediate pleasure.

positive reinforcement Presenting a subject something pleasant to increase the probability that the preceding behavior will be repeated.

Positron Emission Tomography (PET) Similar to the MRI, this method enables psychologists and doctors to study the brain (or any other living tissue) without surgery. PET uses radioactive glucose (instead of a strong magnetic field) to help study activity and locate structures in the body.

postconventional morality Level III in Lawrence Kohlberg's theory, in which moral reasoning is based on personal standards and beliefs; highest level of moral thinking.

posttraumatic stress disorder (PTSD) Condition that can occur when a person experiences a severely distressing event; characterized by constant memories of the event, avoidance of anything associated with it, and general arousal.

Prägnanz (law of) Gestalt psychology law that states that people have a tendency to group stimuli according to rules, and that people do this whenever possible.

preconscious mind In Sigmund Freud's psychoanalytic theory of personality, the part of personality that contains information that we have learned but that we are not thinking about at the present time.

preconventional morality Level I of Lawrence Kohlberg's theory, in which moral reasoning is largely due to the expectation of rewards and punishments.

prejudice An unjustified fixed, usually negative, way of thinking about a person or object.

Premack principle Principle that states that, of any two responses, the one that is more likely to occur can be used to reinforce the response that is less likely to occur.

preoperational thought period Period in cognitive development; from two to seven years, the period during which the child learns to represent the environment with objects and symbols.

primary appraisal Activity of determining whether a new stimulus event is positive, neutral, or negative; first step in appraisal of stress.

primary narcissism A Freudian term that refers to the oral phase before the ego has developed; the individual constantly seeks pleasure.

primary reinforcement Reinforcement that is effective without having been associated with other reinforcers; sometimes called unconditioned reinforcement.

probability (p) In inferential statistics, the likelihood that the difference between the experimental and control groups is due to the independent variable.

procedural memory The most basic type of long-term memory; involves the formation of associations between stimuli and responses.

projection Defense mechanism in which a person attributes his or her unacceptable characteristics or motives to others rather than himself or herself.

projective personality test A personality test that presents ambiguous stimuli to which subjects are expected to respond with projections of their own personality.

proximity Closeness in time and space. In perception, it is the Gestalt perceptual principle in which stimuli next to one another are included together.

psyche According to Carl Jung, the thoughts and feelings (conscious and unconscious) of an individual.

psychoactive drug A drug that produces changes in behavior and cognition through modification of conscious awareness.

psychoanalysis The school of thought founded by Sigmund Freud that stressed unconscious motivation. In therapy, a patient's unconscious motivation is intensively explored in order to bring repressed conflicts up to consciousness; psychoanalysis usually takes a long time to accomplish.

psychobiology (also called biological psychology or physiological psychology) The subfield of experimental psychology concerned with the influence of heredity and the biological response systems on behavior.

psychogenic amnesia A dissociative disorder in which an individual loses his or her sense of identity.

psychogenic fugue A dissociative disorder in which an individual loses his or her sense of identity and goes to a new geographic location, forgetting all of the unpleasant emotions connected with the old life.

psychographics A technique used in consumer psychology to identify the attitudes of buyers and their preferences for particular products.

psycholinguistics The psychological study of how people convert the sounds of a language into meaningful symbols that can be used to communicate with others.

psychological dependence Situation in which a person craves a drug even though it is not biologically needed by the body.

psychological disorder A diagnosis of abnormal behavior; syndrome of abnormal adjustment, classified in *DSM*.

psychological types Carl Jung's term for different personality profiles; Jung combined two attitudes and four functions to produce eight psychological types.

psychopharmacology Study of effects of psychoactive drugs on behavior.

psychophysics An area of psychology in which researchers compare the physical energy of a stimulus with the sensation reported.

psychosexual stages Sigmund Freud's theoretical stages in personality development.

psychosomatic disorders A variety of body reactions that are closely related to psychological events.

psychotherapy Treatment of behavioral disorders through psychological techniques; major psychotherapies include insight therapy, behavior therapy, and group therapy.

psychotic disorders The more severe categories of abnormal behavior.

puberty Sexual maturation; the time at which the individual is able to perform sexually and to reproduce.

quantitative trait loci (QTLs) Genes that collectively contribute to a trait for high intelligence.

rational-emotive therapy A cognitive behavior modification technique in which a person is taught to identify irrational, self-defeating beliefs and then to overcome them.

reaction formation Defense mechanism in which a person masks an unconsciously distressing or unacceptable trait by assuming an opposite attitude or behavior pattern.

reality principle In Freudian theory, the idea that the drives of the ego try to find socially acceptable ways to gratify the id.

reciprocal determinism The concept proposed by Albert Bandura that the behavior, the individual, and the situation interact and influence each other.

reciprocal inhibition Concept of Joseph Wolpe that states that it is possible to break the bond between anxiety provoking stimuli and responses manifesting anxiety by facing those stimuli in a state antagonistic to anxiety.

reflex An automatic movement that occurs in direct response to a stimulus.

regression Defense mechanism in which a person retreats to an earlier, more immature form of behavior.

reinforcement Any event that increases the probability that the behavior that precedes it will be repeated; also called a reinforcer; similar to a reward.

reinforcement therapy A behavior therapy in which reinforcement is used to modify behavior. Techniques in reinforcement therapy include shaping, extinction, and token economy.

REM Sleep There are two main categories of sleep, Non-Rapid Eye Movement Sleep (NREM; which contains stages 1–4; basically everything except REM), and Rapid Eye Movement Sleep (REM). REM sleep is a sleep period during which your brain is very active, and your eyes move in a sharp, back-and-forth motion as opposed to a slower, more rolling fashion that occurs in other stages of sleep. People often believe mistakenly that humans only dream during REM sleep, although humans also dream during slow wave sleep (stages 3 and 4). However it is true that the majority of our dreaming occurs during REM sleep.

repression Defense mechanism in which painful memories and unacceptable thoughts and motives are conveniently forgotten so that they will not have to be dealt with.

residual schizophrenia Type of schizophrenia in which the individual currently does not have symptoms but has had a schizophrenic episode in the past.

resistance Psychoanalytic term used when a patient avoids a painful area of conflict.

resolution phase The last phase in the human sexual response cycle; the time after orgasm when the body gradually returns to the unaroused state.

Restricted Environmental Stimulation Technique (REST) Research technique in which environmental stimuli available to an individual are reduced drastically; formerly called sensory deprivation.

retrograde amnesia Forgetting information recently learned because of a disruptive stimulus such as an electric shock.

reversible figure In perception, a situation in which the figure and ground seem to reverse themselves; an illusion in which objects alternate as the main figure.

Rorschach Inkblot Test A projective personality test in which subjects are asked to discuss what they see in cards containing blots of ink.

safety needs Second level of motives in Abraham Maslow's hierarchy; includes security, stability, dependency, protection, freedom from fear and anxiety, and the need for structure and order.

Schachter-Singer theory of emotion Theory of emotion that states that we interpret our arousal according to our environment and label our emotions accordingly.

scheme A unit of knowledge that the person possesses; used in Jean Piaget's cognitive development theory.

schizophrenia Severe psychotic disorder that is characterized by disruptions in thinking, perception, and emotion.

scientific method An attitude and procedure that scientists use to conduct research. The steps include stating the problem, forming the hypothesis, collecting the information, evaluating the information, and drawing conclusions.

secondary appraisal In appraisal of stress, this is the evaluation that an individual's abilities and resources are sufficient to meet the demands of a stressful event.

secondary reinforcement Reinforcement that is effective only after it has been associated with a primary reinforcer; also called conditioned reinforcement.

secondary traits In Gordon Allport's personality theory, the less important situation-specific traits that help round out personality; they include attitudes, skills, and behavior patterns.

secure attachment Type of infant-parent attachment in which the infant actively seeks contact with the parent.

self-actualization A humanistic term describing the state in which all of an individual's capacities are developed fully. Fifth and highest level of motives in Abraham Maslow's hierarchy, this level, the realization of one's potential, is rarely reached.

self-efficacy An individual's sense of self-worth and success in adjusting to the world.

self-esteem A measurement of how people view themselves. People who view themselves favorably have good self-esteem whereas people who view themselves negatively have poor self-esteem. Self-esteem affects a person's behavior dramatically.

self-evaluation maintenance model (SEM) Tesser's theory of how we maintain a positive self-image despite the success of others close to us.

self-handicapping strategy A strategy that people use to prepare for failure; people behave in ways that produce obstacles to success so that when they do fail they can place the blame on the obstacle.

self-serving bias An attribution bias in which an individual attributes success to his or her own behavior and failure to external environmental causes.

Glossary

semantic memory Type of long-term memory that can use cognitive activities, such as everyday knowledge.

sensation The passive process in which stimuli are received by sense receptors and transformed into neural impulses that can be carried through the nervous system; first stage in becoming aware of environment.

sensitivity training group (T-group) Therapy group that has the goal of making participants more aware of themselves and their ideas.

sensorimotor period Period in cognitive development; the first two years, during which the infant learns to coordinate sensory experiences with motor activities.

sensory adaptation Tendency of the sense organs to adjust to continuous stimulation by reducing their functioning; a stimulus that once caused sensation and no longer does.

sensory deprivation Situation in which normal environmental sensory stimuli available to an individual are reduced drastically; also called REST (Restricted Environmental Stimulation Technique).

serial learning A verbal learning procedure in which the stimuli are always presented in the same order, and the subject has to learn them in the order in which they are presented.

sex roles The set of behaviors and attitudes that are determined to be appropriate for one sex or the other in a society.

shaping In operant conditioning, the gradual process of reinforcing behaviors that get closer to some final desired behavior. Shaping is also called successive approximation.

short-term memory Part of the memory system in which information is only stored for roughly 30 seconds. Information can be maintained longer with the use of such techniques as rehearsal. To retain the information for extended periods of time, it must be consolidated into long-term memory where it can then be retrieved. The capacity of short-term memory is also limited. Most people can only store roughly 7 chunks of information plus or minus 2. This is why phone numbers only have seven digits.

signal detection theory Research approach in which the subject's behavior in detecting a threshold is treated as a form of decision making.

similarity Gestalt principle in which similar stimuli are perceived as a unit.

simple phobia Excessive irrational fear that does not fall into other specific categories, such as fear of dogs, insects, snakes, or closed-in places.

simultaneous conditioning A procedure in classical conditioning in which the CS and US are presented at exactly the same time.

Sixteen Personality Factor Questionnaire (16PF) Raymond Cattell's personality test to measure source traits.

Skinner box B. F. Skinner's animal cage with a lever that triggers reinforcement for a subject.

sleep terror disorder (pavor nocturnus) Nonrapid eye-movement (NREM) sleep disorder in which the person (usually a child) wakes up screaming and terrified, but cannot recall why.

sleepwalking (somnambulism) NREM sleep disorder in which the person walks in his or her sleep.

social cognition The process of understanding other people and ourselves by forming and utilizing information about the social world.

social cognitive theory Albert Bandura's approach to personality that proposes that individuals use observation, imitation, and cognition to develop personality.

social comparison Theory proposed by Leon Festinger that we tend to compare our behavior to others to ensure that we are conforming.

social exchange theory Theory of interpersonal relationships that states that people evaluate the costs and rewards of their relationships and act accordingly.

social facilitation Phenomenon in which the presence of others increases dominant behavior patterns in an individual; Richard Zajonc's theory states that the presence of others enhances the emission of the dominant response of the individual.

social influence Influence designed to change the attitudes or behavior of other people; includes conformity, compliance, and obedience.

social learning theory An approach to social psychology that emphasizes observation and modeling; it states that reinforcement is involved in motivation rather than in learning, and proposes that aggression is a form of learned behavior.

social phobia Excessive irrational fear and embarrassment when interacting with other people. Social phobias may include fear of assertive behavior, fear of making mistakes, or fear of public speaking.

social psychology The study of how an individual's behavior, thoughts, and feelings are influenced by other people.

sociobiology Study of the genetic basis of social behavior.

sociocultural Emphasizes the importance of culture, gender, and ethnicity in how we think, feel, and act.

somatic nervous system The part of the peripheral nervous system that carries messages from the sense organs and relays information that directs the voluntary movements of the skeletal muscles.

somatization disorder Somatoform disorder in which a person has medical complaints without physical cause.

somatoform disorders Psychological disorders characterized by physical symptoms for which there are no obvious physical causes.

specific attachment phase Stage at about six months of age, in which the baby becomes attached to a specific person.

split-brain research Popular name for Roger Sperry's research on the syndrome of hemisphere deconnection; research on individuals with the corpus callosum severed. Normal functioning breaks down in split-brain subjects when different information is presented to each hemisphere.

SQ5R A technique to improve learning and memory. Components include survey, question, read, record, recite, review, and reflect.

stage of exhaustion Third stage in Hans Selye's general adaptation syndrome. As the body continues to resist stress, it depletes its energy resources and the person becomes exhausted.

stage of resistance Second stage in Hans Selye's general adaptation syndrome. When stress is prolonged, the body builds some resistance to the effects of stress.

standardization The process of obtaining a representative sample of scores in the population so that a particular score can be interpreted correctly.

Stanford-Binet Intelligence Scale An intelligence test first revised by Lewis Terman at Stanford University in 1916; still a popular test used today.

state-dependent learning Situation in which what is learned in one state can only be remembered when the person is in that state of mind.

statistically significant In inferential statistics, a finding that the independent variable did influence greatly the outcome of the experimental and control group.

stereotype An exaggerated and rigid mental image of a particular class of persons or objects.

stimulus A unit of the environment that causes a response in an individual; a physical or chemical agent acting on an appropriate sense receptor.

stimulus discrimination Responding to relevant stimuli.

stimulus generalization Responding to stimuli similar to the stimulus that had caused the response.

stimulus motives Motivating factors that are internal and unlearned, but do not appear to have a physiological basis; stimulus motives cause an individual to seek out sensory stimulation through interaction with the environment.

stimulus trace The perceptual persistence of a stimulus after it is no longer present.

strange-situation procedure A measure of attachment developed by Mary Ainsworth that consists of eight phases during which the infant is increasingly stressed.

stress Anything that produces demands on us to adjust and threatens our well-being.

Strong Interest Inventory An objective personality test that compares people's personalities to groups that achieve success in certain occupations.

structuralism First school of thought in psychology; it studied conscious experience to discover the structure of the mind.

subject bias Source of potential error in an experiment from the action or expectancy of a subject; a subject might influence the experimental results in ways that mask the true outcome.

subjective organization Long-term memory procedures in which the individual provides a personal method of organizing information to be memorized.

sublimation Defense mechanism; a person redirects his or her socially undesirable urges into socially acceptable behavior.

successive approximation Shaping; in operant conditioning, the gradual process of reinforcing behaviors that get closer to some final desired behavior.

superego Sigmund Freud's representation of conscience.

surface traits In Raymond Cattell's personality theory, the observable characteristics of a person's behavior and personality.

symbolization In Sigmund Freud's dream theory, the process of converting the latent content of a dream into manifest symbols.

systematic desensitization Application of counterconditioning, in which the individual overcomes anxiety by learning to relax in the presence of stimuli that had once made him or her unbearably nervous.

task-oriented coping Adjustment responses in which the person evaluates a stressful situation objectively and then formulates a plan with which to solve the problem.

test of significance An inferential statistical technique used to determine whether the difference in scores between the experimental and control groups is really due to the effects of the independent variable or to random chance. If the probability of an outcome is extremely low, we say that outcome is significant.

Thanatos Sigmund Freud's term for a destructive instinct such as aggression; also called death instinct.

Thematic Apperception Test (TAT) Projective personality test in which subjects are shown pictures of people in everyday settings; subjects must make up a story about the people portrayed.

theory of social impact Latané's theory of social behavior; it states that each member of a group shares the responsibility equally.

Theory X Douglas McGregor's theory that states that the worker dislikes work and must be forced to do it.

Theory Y Douglas McGregor's theory that states that work is natural and can be a source of satisfaction, and, when it is, the worker can be highly committed and motivated.

therapy In psychology, the treatment of behavior problems; two major types of therapy include psychotherapy and biological therapy.

time and motion studies In engineering psychology, studies that analyze the time it takes to perform an action and the movements that go into the action.

tip-of-the-tongue phenomenon A phenomenon in which the closer a person comes to recalling something, the more accurately he or she can remember details, such as the number of syllables or letters.

token economy A behavior therapy in which desired behaviors are reinforced immediately with tokens that can be exchanged at a later time for desired rewards, such as food or recreational privileges.

trace conditioning A procedure in classical conditioning in which the CS is a discrete event that is presented and terminated before the US is presented.

trait A distinctive and stable attribute in people.

trait anxiety Anxiety that is long-lasting; a relatively stable personality characteristic.

transference Psychoanalytic term used when a patient projects his feelings onto the therapist.

transsexualism A condition in which a person feels trapped in the body of the wrong sex.

trial and error learning Trying various behaviors in a situation until the solution is found.

triangular theory of love Robert Sternberg's theory that states that love consists of intimacy, passion, and decision/commitment.

triarchic theory of intelligence Robert Sternberg's theory of intelligence that states that it consists of three parts: componential, experiential, and contextual subtheories.

Type-A behavior A personality pattern of behavior that can lead to stress and heart disease.

unconditional positive regard Part of Carl Rogers's personality theory; occurs when we accept someone regardless of what he or she does or says.

unconditioned response (UR) An automatic reaction elicited by a stimulus.

unconditioned stimulus (US) Any stimulus that elicits an automatic or reflexive reaction in an individual; it does not have to be learned in the present situation.

unconscious mind In Sigmund Freud's psychoanalytic theory of personality, the part of personality that is unavailable to us; Freud suggests that instincts and unpleasant memories are stored in the unconscious mind.

undifferentiated schizophrenia Type of schizophrenia that does not fit into any particular category, or fits into more than one category.

variable interval (VI) schedule Schedule of reinforcement in which the subject is reinforced for the first response given after a certain time interval, with the interval being different for each trial.

variable ratio (VR) schedule Schedule of reinforcement in which the subject is given reinforcement after a varying number of responses; the number of responses required for reinforcement is different for every trial.

vestibular sense Sense that helps us keep our balance.

vulnerability-stress model Theory of schizophrenia that states that some people have a biological tendency to develop schizophrenia if they are stressed enough by their environment.

Weber's Law Ernst Weber's law that states that the difference threshold depends on the ratio of the intensity of one stimulus to another rather than on an absolute difference.

Wechsler Adult Intelligence Scale (WAIS) An intelligence test for adults, first published by David Wechsler in 1955; it contains verbal and performance subscales.

Wechsler Intelligence Scale for Children (WISC-III) Similar to the Wechsler Adult Intelligence Scale, except that it is designed for children ages 6 through 16, and helps diagnose certain childhood disorders such as dyslexia and other learning disabilities.

Wechsler Preschool and Primary Scale of Intelligence (WPPSI-R) Designed for children between the ages of 4 and 7; helps diagnose childhood disorders, such as dyslexia and other learning disabilities.

withdrawal Unpleasant physical reactions that a drug dependent user experiences when he or she stops taking the drug.

within-subject experiment An experimental design in which each subject is given all treatments, including the control condition; subjects serve in both experimental and control groups.

working memory The memory store, with a capacity of about 7 items and enduring for up to 30 seconds, that handles current information.

Yerkes-Dodson Law Popular idea that performance is best when arousal is at a medium level.

Sources for the Glossary: *The majority of terms in this glossary are from* Psychology: A ConnecText, *4th Edition, Terry F. Pettijohn. ©1999 Dushkin/ McGraw-Hill, Guilford, CT 06437. The remaining terms were developed by the* Annual Editions *staff, 2001.*

Index

Tianepine, 154
trait, invisible/visible divide, 95
treatment, sex differences when
    determining, 43, 46–47
tricyclic antidepressants, 153

U

U.S. military, mental health efforts and,
    144–145

V

ventromedial prefrontal cortex, 98
Vichrow, Rudolf, 135
vulnerability, male, sex and, 129

W

weight gain, adult, and resulting risks, 83
Weschler, David, 97

Whitehall studies, 135, 136
Wilkinson, Richard, 137
women: brains of, 43–47
World Wide Web, 139

Z

Zeitgeist, 98

Test Your Knowledge Form

We encourage you to photocopy and use this page as a tool to assess how the articles in *Annual Editions* expand on the information in your textbook. By reflecting on the articles you will gain enhanced text information. You can also access this useful form on a product's book support Web site at *http://www.mhcls.com/online/*.

NAME: DATE:

_____

TITLE AND NUMBER OF ARTICLE:

_____

BRIEFLY STATE THE MAIN IDEA OF THIS ARTICLE:

_____

LIST THREE IMPORTANT FACTS THAT THE AUTHOR USES TO SUPPORT THE MAIN IDEA:

_____

WHAT INFORMATION OR IDEAS DISCUSSED IN THIS ARTICLE ARE ALSO DISCUSSED IN YOUR TEXTBOOK OR OTHER READINGS THAT YOU HAVE DONE? LIST THE TEXTBOOK CHAPTERS AND PAGE NUMBERS:

_____

LIST ANY EXAMPLES OF BIAS OR FAULTY REASONING THAT YOU FOUND IN THE ARTICLE:

_____

LIST ANY NEW TERMS/CONCEPTS THAT WERE DISCUSSED IN THE ARTICLE, AND WRITE A SHORT DEFINITION:

We Want Your Advice

ANNUAL EDITIONS revisions depend on two major opinion sources: one is our Advisory Board, listed in the front of this volume, which works with us in scanning the thousands of articles published in the public press each year; the other is you—the person actually using the book. Please help us and the users of the next edition by completing the prepaid article rating form on this page and returning it to us. Thank you for your help!

ANNUAL EDITIONS: Personal Growth and Behavior 07/08

ARTICLE RATING FORM

Here is an opportunity for you to have direct input into the next revision of this volume.
We would like you to rate each of the articles listed below, using the following scale:

1. **Excellent: should definitely be retained**
2. **Above average: should probably be retained**
3. **Below average: should probably be deleted**
4. **Poor: should definitely be deleted**

Your ratings will play a vital part in the next revision.
Please mail this prepaid form to us as soon as possible.
Thanks for your help!

RATING	ARTICLE	RATING	ARTICLE
_____	1. Carl Roger's Life and Work: An Assessment on the 100th Anniversary of His Birth	_____	21. Staving Off Middle-Age Spread Requires Portion Control and Plenty of Exercise
_____	2. Freud in Our Midst	_____	22. Lost & Found
_____	3. Skepticism of Caricatures: B.F. Skinner Turns 100	_____	23. Good Life, Good Death
_____	4. Psychology of Safety: The "Big Five" and You: How Personality Traits Can Affect Behavior	_____	24. Mirror, Mirror: Seeing Yourself As Others See You
_____	5. Nature Versus Nurture: How Is Child Psychopathology Developed?	_____	25. Feeling Smart: The Science of Emotional Intelligence
_____	6. Empirical Science for the Spotless Mind	_____	26. What's Your Emotional IQ?
_____	7. Nature vs. Nurture: Two Brothers With Schizophrenia	_____	27. Us vs. Them
_____	8. Genetic Influence on Human Psychological Traits	_____	28. Relationships, Human Behavior, and Psychological Science
_____	9. The Amazing Brain: Is Neuroscience the Key to What Makes Us Human?	_____	29. Budding Friendships Fill Out the Family Tree
_____	10. His Brain, Her Brain	_____	30. Nurturing Empathy
_____	11. Cultural Psychology: Studying the Exotic Other	_____	31. Contagious Behavior
_____	12. Ambition: Why Some People Are Most Likely to Succeed	_____	32. The Emperor's New Woes
_____	13. How to Keep Those New Year's Resolutions	_____	33. 50th Anniversary: Brown v. Board of Education
_____	14. Stand and Deliver	_____	34. Sick of Poverty
_____	15. The Biology of Aging	_____	35. Work-life: Organizations in Denial
_____	16. Childhood Is for Children	_____	36. Life-Saving Communication
_____	17. The Importance of Resilience	_____	37. Soldier Support
_____	18. Kaleidoscope of Parenting Cultures	_____	38. Brain Imaging Struggles for Psychiatric Respect
_____	19. What American Schools Can Learn from Hogwarts School of Witchcraft and Wizardry	_____	39. Are We Becoming a Nation of Depressives?
_____	20. The Divided Self	_____	40. Drugs vs. Talk Therapy
		_____	41. Body of Emotion
		_____	42. 20 Weeks to Happiness

(Continued on next page)

BUSINESS REPLY MAIL
FIRST CLASS MAIL PERMIT NO. 551 DUBUQUE IA

POSTAGE WILL BE PAID BY ADDRESEE

McGraw-Hill Contemporary Learning Series
2460 KERPER BLVD
DUBUQUE, IA 52001-9902

ABOUT YOU

Name _____   Date _____

Are you a teacher? ☐   A student? ☐
Your school's name _____

Department _____

Address _____   City _____   State _____   Zip _____

School telephone # _____

YOUR COMMENTS ARE IMPORTANT TO US!

Please fill in the following information:
For which course did you use this book?
_____

Did you use a text with this ANNUAL EDITION? ☐ yes ☐ no
What was the title of the text?
_____

What are your general reactions to the *Annual Editions* concept?
_____

Have you read any pertinent articles recently that you think should be included in the next edition? Explain.
_____

Are there any articles that you feel should be replaced in the next edition? Why?
_____

Are there any World Wide Web sites that you feel should be included in the next edition? Please annotate.
_____

May we contact you for editorial input? ☐ yes ☐ no
May we quote your comments? ☐ yes ☐ no